DEMOCRATIC
IDEALS
AND REALITY

陆权论

（经典文库　汉英对照）

[英] 哈尔福德·约翰·麦金德⊙著

余　杰⊙译

台海出版社

图书在版编目(CIP)数据

陆权论：汉英对照 /（英）哈尔福德·约翰·麦金
德著；余杰译 . —— 北京：台海出版社，2017.2
　ISBN 978-7-5168-1273-0

　Ⅰ.①陆… Ⅱ.①哈… ②余… Ⅲ.①世界史－研究
－汉、英 Ⅳ.① K107

中国版本图书馆CIP数据核字(2017)第030703号

陆权论：汉英对照

著　　者：（英）哈尔福德·约翰·麦金德	译　　者：余　杰	
责任编辑：刘　峰	装帧设计：同人书业 文化传媒·书装设计	
版式设计：同人书业 文化传媒·书装设计	责任印制：蔡　旭	

出版发行：台海出版社

地　　址：北京市东城区景山东街 20 号　　　邮政编码：100009

电　　话：010 - 64041652（发行，邮购）

传　　真：010 - 84045799（总编室）

网　　址：www.taimeng.org.cn/thcbs/default.htm

E－mail：thcbs@126.com

经　　销：全国各地新华书店

印　　刷：北京市燕鑫印刷有限公司

本书如有破损、缺页、装订错误，请与本社联系调换

开　　本：787mm×1092mm　　　　1/16

字　　数：358 千字　　　　　　　印　　张：15.5

版　　次：2017年5月第1版　　　　印　　次：2017年5月第1次印刷

书　　号：ISBN 978-7-5168-1273-0

定　　价：32.80 元

PREFACE

This book, whatever its value, is the outcome of more than the merely feverous thought of War time; the ideas upon which it is based were published in outline a good dozen years ago. In 1904, in a paper on "The Geographical Pivot of History," read before the Royal Geographical Society, I sketched the World-Island and the Heartland; and in 1905 I wrote in the National Review on the subject of "Man-power as a Measure of National and Imperial Strength," an article which I believe first gave vogue to the term Man-power. In that term is implicit not only the idea of fighting strength but also that of productivity, rather than wealth, as the focus of economic reasoning. If I now venture to write on these themes at somewhat greater length, it is because I feel that the War has established, and not shaken, my former points of view.

H. J. M,
1st February, 1919.

序

无论本书有没有什么价值，它都并非只是我在战争时期那种狂热思想的诱使下写就的；因为早在十几年前，我就已经概括地发表过构成本书基础的许多观点了。1904年，我在皇家地理学会[1]宣读了一篇题为《历史的地理学枢要》的论文，其中简要地说明了"世界岛"和"中心地带"这两个概念；而在1905年，我又为《国家评论》杂志[2]写了一篇题为《衡量国家和帝国优势的人力》的文章——我相信，正是我的这篇文章，才使得"人力"一词开始流行于世。这个术语当中，不仅蕴含着战斗力的思想，而且蕴含着生产力而非财富乃是经济论证之核心的思想。如今，本人之所以大胆地、更加详尽地来阐述这些思想，原因就在于我认为，我之前的观点业已为此次大战所巩固，而非为此次大战所动摇。

H·J·麦金德
1919年2月1日

---

[1] Royal Geographical Society：皇家地理学会。英国成立于1830年的一个科学机构，拥有世界上规模最大的地理学档案。

[2] National Review：《国家评论》。英国一种杂志，创刊于1883年，1950年改为《国家和英国评论》，1960年停刊。

目录 Contents

Napoleon / 拿破仑

Bismarck / 俾斯麦

The strategical mentality of Prussia / 普鲁士的战略精神

　"Kultur" and strategy / "德国文化"[1]和战略

The German war map / 德国的战争地图

Strategical thought in Economics / 经济学里的战略思想

But Democracy thinks ethically / 但民主从道德方面来考虑问题

　"No annexations, no indemnities" / "不吞并，不索赔"

Refuses to think strategically unless compelled to do so for defense / 除非是为了防御而被迫这样做，否则就不愿从战略角度来思考问题

Must fail unless it reckons with both geographical and economic Reality / 倘若不重视地理与经济现实，那么民主必败无疑

III THE SEAMAN'S POINT OF VIEW

The Unity of the Ocean, the first geographical Reality / 从地理学角度来看海洋的整体性

The consequences not yet fully accepted / 其诸多重要性却尚未得到世人的完全公认

Therefore necessary to take a historical view / 因此有必要从一种历史学的观点来加以看待

Contending river-powers in Egypt / 埃及河流两岸各个相互争战的强国

The Nile "closed" by land-power / 尼罗河被陆上力量"封锁"了

Contending sea-powers in the Mediterranean / 地中海地区相互争战的海上强国

The Mediterranean "closed" by land-power / 地中海被陆上力量"封锁"了

The Latin Peninsula as a sea-base / 拉丁半岛是一个海上基地

The encompassing of the World-Promontory by sea-power from the Latin peninsular base / 海上力量通过拉丁半岛这个基地包围了"世界海角"

Division within the Latin European Peninsula / 拉丁欧洲半岛内部的分裂

Hence the opportunity for sea-power from the lesser but insular sea-base of Britain / 因此，海上力量便有了机会，能够从面积虽然较小、却以海岛为海上基地的不列颠发展起来

Of sea-bases in general / 关于通常的海上基地

Of sea-power in the Great War / 关于第一次世界大战中的海上力量

---

[1] Kultur: 本义指"文化，文明"，后演变成贬义，暗指含有沙文主义、军国主义等内涵的"德国文化"，也可用于指纳粹分子统治下的社会组织。

History of the relations of East and West Europe / 东、西欧之间的关系史

Their fundamental opposition / 它们之间的根本性对抗

Their essential difference / 它们之间的主要分歧

German and Slav in East Europe / 位于东欧的日耳曼人和斯拉夫人

Trafalgar seemed to split the stream of history into two for a century / 特拉法尔加[1]海战似乎将一个世纪的历史长河分为了两支

Britain and the Not-Europe / 不列颠与"不是欧洲"

But East Europe is really within the Heartland, and there were no two streams / 但实际上东欧位于"中心地带"内部，历史长河也并未分成两支

British and French policy agreed in the Nineteenth Century / 英、法两国的政策在19世纪保持着一致

The Great War caused by German attempt to control East Europe and the Heartland / 德国人企图控制东欧和"中心地带"，从而引发了第一次世界大战

The Economic Reality of organized man-power — the Going Concern / 有组织的人力这一经济现实——即"进行中的事业"

Political Economy and National Economy / 政治经济与国民经济

The great Economic change of 1878 / 1878年的经济巨变

The German policy was to stimulate growth of man-power and then use it to occupy the Heartland / 德国的政策是刺激人力增长，然后利用人力来占领"中心地带"

But Laissez-fairs also a policy of Empire / 但自由经济[2]也是帝国的一种政策

Clash of the two policies / 这两种政策的冲突

Inevitable from the fact that they were two Going Concerns / 它们是两种"进行中的事业"，这一事实使得冲突无法避免。

VI THE FREEDOM OF NATIONS

We have won the War, but were nearly defeated / 尽管我们已经赢得此次大战，但差点儿失败了

---

[1] Trafalgar：特拉法尔加。西班牙位于直布罗陀海峡西端的一个城市。1805年，英国海军在此海域与法、西联合舰队作战并大获全胜，从而巩固了英国海洋霸主的地位。

[2] Laissez-faire：(经济上的)放任政策，不干涉主义。源自法语，19世纪早期和中期变成了自由市场经济学的同义词。自由放任主义反对政府干涉经济，并且反对政府征收除足以维持和平、治安和财产权以外的其他税赋。

Had Germany won, if only on land, you should have had to reckon with a Heartland Empire / 若是德国获胜，就算只是在陆地上获胜，我们可能也得严肃认真地去对付一个"中心地带"的帝国了

The Heartland the persistent Geographical threat to World liberty / "中心地带"在地理上对世界自由构成了持久威胁

How came Germany to make the mistake of offensive on West front / 德国怎样犯下了在西线发动攻势的错误

Hamburg and the man-power policy / 汉堡及其人力政策

We must now divide up East Europe and the Heartland / 我们如今必须把东欧和"中心地带"分割开来

It must be a division into three not two State-systems / 东欧必定会分成3种国家体制，而非两种国家体制

The peoples of the Middle Tier / 处于"中间层"国家中的各个民族

Feasibility of League of Nations, if this done / 实现这一点之后，国际联盟才有可行性

But there must be no predominant partner / 但是，其中决不能有"占据支配地位的伙伴"[1]

Yet you will have to reckon with Going Concerns / 不过，我们仍须去应对各个"进行中的事业"

A reasonable equality of power needed among a considerable number of members of your League / 在你们的国际联盟中，多数会员国应当保持合理的势力均衡

Of certain strategical positions of World importance / 具有全球重要性的某些战略要地

The Going Concerns in the future, and the unequal growth of Nations / 未来"进行中的事业"，以及各国的不均衡发展

The ideal is the Independent Nation of balanced economic development / 理想的情况是经济发展均衡的"独立国家"

Tragedies of the Going Concern / "进行中的事业"的悲剧

The policy of truly free nations which makes for Peace / 走向和平与真正自由的国际联盟的政策

VII   THE FREEDOM OF MEN

Whether men and women will be more free in such free Nations / 在这样一种自由的国际联盟内，人民是否会变得更加自由

---

[1] predominant partner：优先合伙人，占有支配地位的伙伴。多用于喻指英格兰在英国国内的重要地位。作者此处显然是指国际联盟中各个成员国应当平等。

The need of basing organization within the Nation on localities / 在国内以地区为基础建立起组织的必要性

The alternative organization is based on nation−wide classes and interests / 另一种组织是以全国范围的阶级和利益集团为基础而建立起来的

This leads inevitably to international war of classes / 这必然会导致阶级间的国际战争

Therefore the ideal is balanced provinces within balanced nations / 因此理想的情况便是，在势力均衡的国家当中，各个地区的势力也保持均衡

Such organization gives greatest opportunity to greatest number of men / 这种组织能够让最多的人获得最大的机会

Cause of Nationality movement / 民族运动的起因

Opposed to undue centralization / 反对过度集权化

Fraternal nations must be balanced economically, and formed of fraternal provinces / 友好国家间的经济实力必须保持均衡，并由友好地区所组成

Fraternity, if it is to last, depends on controlling the development of Going Concern / 友好关系若想持久，必须掌控各个"进行中的事业"的发展

I PERSPECTIVE

Our memories are still full of the vivid detail of an all—absorbing warfare; there is, as it were, a screen between us and the things which happened earlier even in our own lives. But the time has at last come to take larger views, and we must begin to think of our long War as of a single great event, a cataract in the stream of history. The last four years have been momentous, because they have been the outcome of one century and the prelude to another. Tension between the nations had slowly accumulated, and, in the language of diplomacy, there has now been a d é tente. The temptation of the moment is to believe that unceasing peace will ensue merely because tired men are determined that there shall be no more war. But international tension will

第一章　远景

我们如今依然清楚地记得这场吞噬一切的战争的种种具体细节；而就算是我们以前生活中发生的一些事情，如今回想起来，也会像与我们隔了一层纱窗那样模糊。但是，高瞻远瞩的时刻终于到来了，所以我们必须开始把这场漫长的战争看成是一桩孤立的重大事件，看成是历史长河当中的一道急流。过去的4年极其重要，因为这段时间既是一个世纪的结束，也是另一个世纪的发端。在这4年间，各国关系已经日趋紧张，而用外交辞令来说，此种紧张局势如今却已经有所缓和了。目前我们很容易认为，仅凭疲惫了

第一次世界大战

accumulate again, though slowly at first; there was a generation of peace after Waterloo. Who among the diplomats round the Congress table at Vienna in 1814 foresaw that Prussia would become a menace to the world? Is it possible for us so to grade the stream bed of future history as that there shall be no more cataracts? That, and no smaller, is the task before us if we would have posterity think less meanly of our wisdom than we think of that of the diplomats of Vienna.

The great wars of history — we have had a world–war about every hundred years for the last four centimes — are the outcome, direct or indirect, of the unequal growth of nations, and that unequal growth is not wholly due to the greater genius and energy of some nations as

的人们不想再战的决心，永久的和平就会随之而来。不过，尽管刚开始的时候可能会很缓慢，但国际关系却还是会再次日趋紧张起来的；比如说，滑铁卢之战后，就曾有过一个世代的和平。1814年围坐在维也纳议会桌旁进行谈判的那些外交家们当中，又有哪一个曾经预见到普鲁士会变成世界的一大威胁呢？我们有没有可能，把未来的历史这条长河的河床弄得平缓一点儿，使得其中不会再出现更多的急流呢？倘若不想要我们的后代像我们自己鄙视当年维也纳那些外交家们的智慧一样来鄙视我们的智慧，那么，这就是我们必须面对的一项相当重大的任务。

历史上的各次大战——在过去的4个世纪里，每隔大约100年便会发生一场世界大战——都是各国发展不均衡的直接结果或间接结果，而此种不均衡发展，又并非全是因

滑铁卢之战

滑铁卢之战

Compared with others; in large measure it is the result of the uneven distribution of fertility and strategical opportunity upon the face of our globe. In other words, there is in nature no such thing as equality of opportunity for the nations. Unless I wholly misread the facts of geography, I would go further, and say that the grouping of lands and seas, and of fertility and natural pathways, is such as to lend itself to the growth of empires, and in the end of a single World Empire. If we are to realize our ideal of a League of Nations which shall prevent war in the future, we must recognize these geographical realities and take steps to counter their influence. Last century, under the spell of the Darwinian theory, men came to think that those forms of organization should survive which adapted themselves best to their natural environment. Today we realize, as we emerge from our fiery trial, that human victory consists in our rising superior to such mere fatalism.

为某些民族比其他民族具有更多的天才和更大的能力；在很大程度上，这是我们地球表面上肥沃程度和战略机遇分配不均的结果。换言之就是，自然界中根本就没有各民族机会均等这样的事情。除非我是把地理事实全都弄错了，否则我还要更进一步说，海洋与陆地组合起来，肥沃程度与天然通道组合起来，本身就会影响到各个帝国的发展，并且最终有助于一个单一的世界帝国发展起来。我们倘要实现自己的理想，成立一个可以在未来阻止战争的国际联盟，那么便必须承认这些地理现实，并且逐步消除掉它们的影响。上一个世纪，人类在达尔文主义的魅惑之下开始认为，只有那些最能适应其自然环境的生命形式才应当生存下来。而如今，因为刚刚经历了一场严峻的考验，所以我们认识到，只有逐步超越这种纯粹的宿命论，人类才能获得胜利。

国际联盟

Civilization is based on the organization of society so that we may render service to one another, and the higher the civilization the more minute tends to be the division of labor and the more complex the organization. A great and advanced society has, in consequence, a powerful momentum; without destroying the society itself you cannot suddenly check or divert its course. Thus it happens that years beforehand detached observers are able to predict a coming clash of societies which are following convergent paths in their development. The historian commonly prefaces his narrative of war with an account of the blindness of men who refused to see the writing on the wall, but the fact is, that, like every other going concern, a national society can be shaped to a desired career while it is young, but when it is old its character is fixed and it is incapable of any great change in its mode of existence. Today all the nations of the world are about to start afresh; is it within the reach of human forethought so to set their courses as that,

文明建立在社会组织的基础之上，从而使得我们可以为彼此提供服务，并且文明程度越高，社会分工就越细，社会组织也就越复杂。所以，一个伟大、进步的社会，便会具有强大的动力；除非彻底摧毁这个社会本身，否则便是无法迅速阻止或者扭转其进程的。因此，那些独立的观察者在数年之前就能预见到，一些沿着渐趋会合的道路发展下去的不同社会，最终都会爆发出冲突。历史学家在论述战争之前，通常都会先对那些不肯审视不祥之兆的人的盲目加以批评，但事实是，与其他所有"进行中的事业"一样，一个民族社会在其初期还能够塑造成一种理想的事业，可待它发展成熟之后，因其特征已经固定下来，故其存在形式也就不可能再做什么重大的改变了。如今，世界各国都正在准备着从头再来；那么，人类能不能做到未雨绸缪，制定好各国的发展道路，使得尽管有着地理上的

notwithstanding geographical temptation, they shall not clash in the days of our grandchildren?

In our anxiety to repudiate the ideas historically associated with the Balance of Power, is there not perhaps some danger that we should allow merely juridical conceptions to rule our thoughts in regard to the League of Nations? It is our ideal that justice should be done between nations, whether they be great or small, precisely as it is our ideal that there should be justice between men, whatever the difference of their positions in society. To maintain justice as between individual men the power of the State is invoked, and we now recognize, after the failure of international law to avert the Great War, that there must be some power or, as the lawyers say, some sanction for the maintenance of justice as between nation and nation. But the power which is necessary for the rule of law among citizens passes easily into tyranny. Can we establish such a world power as shall suffice to keep the law between great and small States, and yet shall not grow into a world tyranny? There are two roads to such a tyranny, the one the conquest of all other nations by one nation, the other the perversion of the very international power itself which may be set up to coerce the lawless nation. In our great replanning of human society we must recognize that the skill and opportunity of the robber are prior facts to the Law of Robbery. In other words, we must envisage our vast problem as business men dealing with realities of growth and opportunity, and not merely as lawyers defining rights and remedies.

My endeavor, in the following pages, will be to measure the relative significance of the great features of our globe as tested by the events of history, including the history of the last four years, and then to consider how we may best adjust our ideals of freedom to these lasting realities of our Earthly Home. But first we must recognize certain tendencies of human nature as exhibited in all forms of political organization.

诸多考验,但到了我们儿孙那一代的时候,各国也不至于再发生什么冲突呢?

在我们急于否定历史上各种与"势力均衡"相关的观念之时,假如允许用纯粹的法律概念来支配我们关于国际联盟的各种思想,会不会有危险呢?无论大小,各个国家都应当得到公平对待,这是我们的理想;它与我们的另一个理想——即不论人们的社会地位有着什么样的差异,都应当公平对待——也是完全一致的。要像维持个人之间的公平正义那样维持好国家之间的公平正义,就得动用国家力量;而因为国际法没能避免这次世界大战,所以如今我们已经认识到,必须存在某种权力,或者像律师们所说的那样,必须具有某种惩处手段,才能维护好国家之间的公平正义。但是,在公民中实施法治所必须的那种权力,却很容易演变成一种专制。我们能不能确立起这样一种全球性的权力,使之既足以让大小各国依法相处,又不至于发展成为一种全球性的暴政呢?形成此种暴政有两条途径,一是由一个国家征服其他国家,二是这种国际性的权力本身堕落了——而原本却很可能是为了强制约束不法国家,才确立下这种国际性权力的。在对人类社会进行大规模的重新规划之时,我们必须认识到,世间是先有了窃盗之术和盗贼行窃之机,然后才有了《盗窃法》的。换言之就是,我们必须像商人应对企业的发展和机遇等现实情况那样来正视我们的重大问题,而不能只是像律师那样,只是说明有哪些权利、应该采取什么样的补救办法就行了。

在接下来的篇幅中,我首先会对地球的各种伟大特征在经历了诸多历史事件(包括过去4年来的历史)考验之后的相对重要性进行衡量,然后再去研究如何才能让我们的自由理想最好地适应地球家园上这些永恒的现实。不过,我们首先还是必须认识到人类本性在所有政治组织形式中表现出来的某些倾向性。

II SOCIAL MOMENTUM

" To him that hath shall be given"

In the year 1789 the lucid French People, in its brain-town of Paris, saw visions, generous visions — Liberty, Equality, Fraternity. But presently French Idealism lost its hold on Reality, and drifted into the grip of Fate, in the person of Napoleon. With his military efficiency Napoleon restored order, but in doing so organized a French Power the very law of whose being was a denial of Liberty. The story of the great French Revolution and Empire has influenced all subsequent political thought; it has seemed a tragedy in the old Greek sense of a disaster predestined in the very character of Revolutionary Idealism.

When, therefore, in 1848, the peoples of Europe were again in a vision-seeing mood, their idealism was of a more complex nature. The principle of Nationality was added to that of Liberty, in the hope that liberty might be secured against the overreaching organizer by the independent spirit of nations. Unfortunately, in that year of revolutions, the good ship Idealism again dragged her anchor, and by and by was swept away by Fate, in the person of Bismarck. With his Prussian efficiency Bismarck perverted the new ideal of German Nationality, just

第二章　社会的动力

"已经拥有者，上天当给予更多"[1]

在1789这一年，一些理性的法国人在人才荟萃的巴黎看到了许多幻景，看到了许多美好的幻景——自由、平等、友爱。但是，法国人的理想主义很快便掌控不了现实，落到了以拿破仑为化身的命运之神的手中，任其摆布了。凭借着自己的军事效率，拿破仑恢复了法国国内的秩序；但在这样做的过程中，他也建立起了一个法兰西强国——这种强国的存在法则，正是对自由的一种否定。法国大革命和法兰西帝国的历史，影响到了后来所有的政治思想；而这段历史，也像是一出古希腊的悲剧，因为革命理想主义的特征，早就注定了它必定会是一场灾难。

因此到1848年，当欧洲各国人民再次以为看到了一幅美好的幻景之时，他们的理想主义心态就更加复杂了。在自由的原则之上，他们还添加了民族原则，寄望各民族的独立精神可以对抗那些野心太大的组织者，从而确保自由。不幸的是，在那一年的革命中，理想主义这艘好船又流了锚，逐渐被化身为俾斯麦的命运之神冲走了。凭借自己普鲁士式的效率，俾斯麦曲解了日耳曼民族的新理想，就像拿破仑歪曲了法兰西民族关

---

[1] To him that hath shall be given：已经拥有者，上天当给予更多。引自《圣经·马太福音》：For whosoever hath, to him shall be given, and he shall have more abundance; but whosoever hath not, from him shall be taken away even that he hath，即"富有者上天当多加给予，令他有余；贫穷者原本所有的，也当夺走。"后来，这句话演变成为经济学中所谓的"马太效应"（即贫者愈贫、富者愈富的现象）。

1789年法国大革命（1789年～1799年）爆发之年。此次资产阶级革命推翻了法国的君主统治。

　　拿破仑和法国大革命。指1848年的欧洲革命。此次革命首先从意大利西西里发起，然后差不多席卷了整个欧洲，是欧洲平民反对贵族的一场革命。

as Napoleon had perverted the simpler French ideals of Liberty and Equality. The tragedy of National Idealism, which we have just seen consummated, was not, however, predestined in the disorder of Liberty, but in the materialism, commonly known as Kultur, of the organizer. The French tragedy was the simple tragedy of the breakdown of Idealism; but the German tragedy has, in truth, been the tragedy of the substituted Realism.

In 1917 the Democratic Nations of the whole Earth thought they had seen a great harbor light when the Russian Czardom fell and the American Republic came into the War. For the time being, at any rate, the Russian Revolution has gone the common revolutionary way, but we still put our hope in Universal Democracy. To the eighteenth-century ideal of Liberty, and the nineteenth-century ideal of Nationality, we have added our twentieth-century ideal of the League of Nations.

俾斯麦

If a third tragedy were to ensue, it would be on a vast scale for democratic ideals are today the working creed of the greater part of humanity. The Germans, with their Real-Politik, their politics of reality — something other than merely practical politics — regard that disaster as being sooner or later inevitable. The War Lord and the Prussian military caste may have been fighting for the mere maintenance of their power, but large and intelligent sections of German society have acted under the persuasion of a political philosophy which was none the less sincerely held because we believed it to be wrong. In this War German anticipations have proved wrong in many regards,

于自由和平等的那些更单纯的理想一样。但是，我们如今刚刚看到业已臻于极致的民族理想主义这出悲剧，却并不是自由的毫无秩序所预先注定的，而是因组织者的实利主义所预先注定的；这种实利主义，就是人们通常所知的"德国文化"。法兰西的悲剧，不过是理想主义坍塌的单纯悲剧罢了；可德意志的悲剧，实际上却是因为用实利主义取代了理想主义而导致的悲剧。

1917年，沙皇俄国垮台、美利坚合众国参战之后，全球的民主国家都以为它们看到了一盏伟大的领路明灯。虽说在目前看来，俄国革命无论如何走的仍是一条常见的革命道路，可我们依然把希望寄托在"普世民主"之上。所以，在18世纪的自由理想和19世纪的民族理想之上，我们又加入了自己属于20世纪的那种国际联盟的理想。倘若第三次悲剧必定会发生，那么这次悲剧就会是规模空前的，因为民主理想如今已成了大多数人孜孜以求的信条。德国人崇尚现实政治[1]，即崇尚现实的政治——并非仅仅是一种实用政治——因此他们认为，灾难或迟或早都是必然会发生的。该国的军阀和普鲁士军人阶层或许只是为了维护其权力而战，但德国社会中的大多数有识之士，却是在一种政治哲学

[1] Real-Politik：现实政治（主张）。由普鲁士宰相奥托·冯·俾斯麦提出的一种政治理论。现实政治主义认为，当政者应当以国家利益为从事内政外交的最高考量，而不该受当政者的感情、道德伦理观、理想甚至是意识形态所左右。人们普遍认为，普鲁士在这一思想的指导下完成了德意志统一战争，并随后称霸欧陆；此外，这一思想也导致了各国穷兵黩武，从而加速了第一次世界大战的爆发。

1917年俄国二月革命

but that has been because we have made them so by a few wise principles of government, and by strenuous effort, notwithstanding our mistakes in policy. Our hardest test has yet to come. What degree of International Reconstruction is necessary if the world is long to remain a safe place for democracies? And in regard to the internal structure of those democracies, what conditions must be satisfied if we are to succeed in harnessing to the heavy plow of Social Reconstruction the ideals which have inspired heroism in this War? There can be no more momentous questions. Shall we succeed in soberly marrying our new Idealism to Reality?

※　　　　※　　　　※　　　　※　　　　※　　　　※　　　　※　　　　※　　　　※

Idealists are the salt of the Earth; without them to move us, society would soon stagnate and civilization fade. Idealism has, however, been associated with two very different phases of

的诱导之下行动的；我们认为，这种政治哲学的错误并不会削弱他们对它的真诚信仰。在这场大战中，许多方面都已经证明了德意志的估计是错误的；但那都是因为我们制定了一些明智的行政准则、做出了不懈的努力，才令他们做出了错误的估计，尽管我们在政策方面也出现了诸多失误。我们最艰巨的考验还在后头。如果想让世界长治久安，想让世界安全容纳下各个民主国家，那我们必须进行一种什么程度的国际重建呢？至于民主国家的内部结构，假如我们想让在这次战争中曾经激发出了英雄主义的那些理想成功地推动社会重建这一艰巨的任务，又必须满足哪些条件呢？其他方面的问题，不可能比这些问题意义更为重大了。我们是否应当冷静地把这种新的理想主义与现实结合起来呢？

※　　　　※　　　　※　　　　※　　　　※　　　　※　　　　※　　　　※　　　　※

理想主义者是整个世界的中坚分子；若是没有他们来激励我们，整个社会很快就会变得死气沉沉，而文明也会失去活力。然而，理想主义却一直与两种截然不同的特征性

北美大陆会议通过《独立宣言》

temper. The older idealisms, such as Buddhism, Stoicism, and Mediaeval Christianity, were based on self-denial; the Franciscan Friars vowed themselves to Chastity, Poverty, and Service. But modern democratic idealism, the idealism of the American and French Revolutions, is based on self-realization. Its aim is that every human being shall live a full and self-respecting life. According to the preamble of the American Declaration of Independence, all men are created equal and endowed with the rights of liberty and the pursuit of happiness.

These two tendencies of idealism have corresponded historically with two developments of reality. In older times the power of nature over man was still great. Hard reality put limits to his ambitions. In other words, the world as a whole was poor, and resignation was the only general

阶段相关联着。古时的理想主义，比如佛教、斯多亚学派[1]和中世纪的基督教，都是以克己节制为基础的；圣方济各会[2]的修士，都立誓贞洁、安贫并且服务众生。而现代的民主理想主义，即美国革命和法国革命中的理想主义，却是以实现自我为基础的。这种理想主义的目标，就是人人都能过上一种丰足而有自尊的生活。美国《独立宣言》的前言中称，人人生而平等，生而拥有自由与追求幸福的权利。

在历史上，理想主义的这两种倾向与现实的两种发展态势相对应。在古时，大自然加于人类身上的力量依然很强大。严酷的现实制约了人类的种种雄心壮志。换言之，因为整个世界都贫穷得很，所以清心寡欲就是人们通往幸福的唯一的康庄大道。的确，少

---

[1] Stoicism：斯多亚学派。大约公元前308年，古希腊哲学家们在雅典一个画廊里创立了一个学派，因画廊在希腊文中叫斯多亚（stoa），故称该学派为斯多亚学派。晚期斯多亚学派着重发展了宿命论和禁欲主义的伦理学，故Stoicism一词也逐渐成为了"禁欲主义"的代名词。

[2] Franciscan：（基督教）圣方济各会。天主教的托钵修会之一，亦称法兰西斯派。拉丁文名Ordo Fratrum Minorum，意为"小兄弟会"。其修士身着灰色会服，故又称灰衣修士。

road to happiness. The few could, no doubt, obtain some scope in life, but only at the cost of the serfdom of the many. Even the so-called Democracy of Athens and the Platonic Utopia were based on domestic and industrial slavery. But the modern world is rich. In no small measure man now controls the forces of nature, and whole classes, formerly resigned to their fate, have become imbued with the idea that with a fairer division of wealth there should be a nearer approach to equality of opportunity.

This modern reality of human control over nature, apart from which democratic ideals would be futile, is not wholly due to the advance of scientific knowledge and invention. The greater control which man now wields is conditional, and not absolute like the control of nature over man by famine and pestilence. Human riches and comparative security are based today on the division and coordination of labor, and on the constant repair of the complicated plant which has replaced the simple tools of primitive society. In other words, the output of modern

数人可能活得有所余裕，但那不过是用奴役众人的代价换来的。就算是所谓的"雅典的民主"和"柏拉图的乌托邦"，也都是建立在国内奴隶制度和产业奴隶制度的基础之上的。但是，现代世界却富裕得很。如今人类已经极大地掌控住了种种大自然之力，而以前任凭命运摆布的所有阶层，心中也都已经深深地拥有了如下这种观念：假如财富分配得更加公平一点，那么他们得到平等的可能性就更大。

现代人类掌控自然的这种现实，并非完全是因为科学知识的进步和发明创造而导致的；没有这种现实的话，种种民主之理想便会徒劳无功。人类如今能够行使更大的掌控力，这一点是相对的，并不像大自然用饥荒和瘟疫来掌控人类那样绝对。如今人类的富裕和相对安全的状况，是以劳动分工和相互协作为基础的，是以对那些已经替代原始社会简单工具的复杂设备不断地进行维护为基础的。换言之就是，现代财富的创造，是以

"雅典的民主"

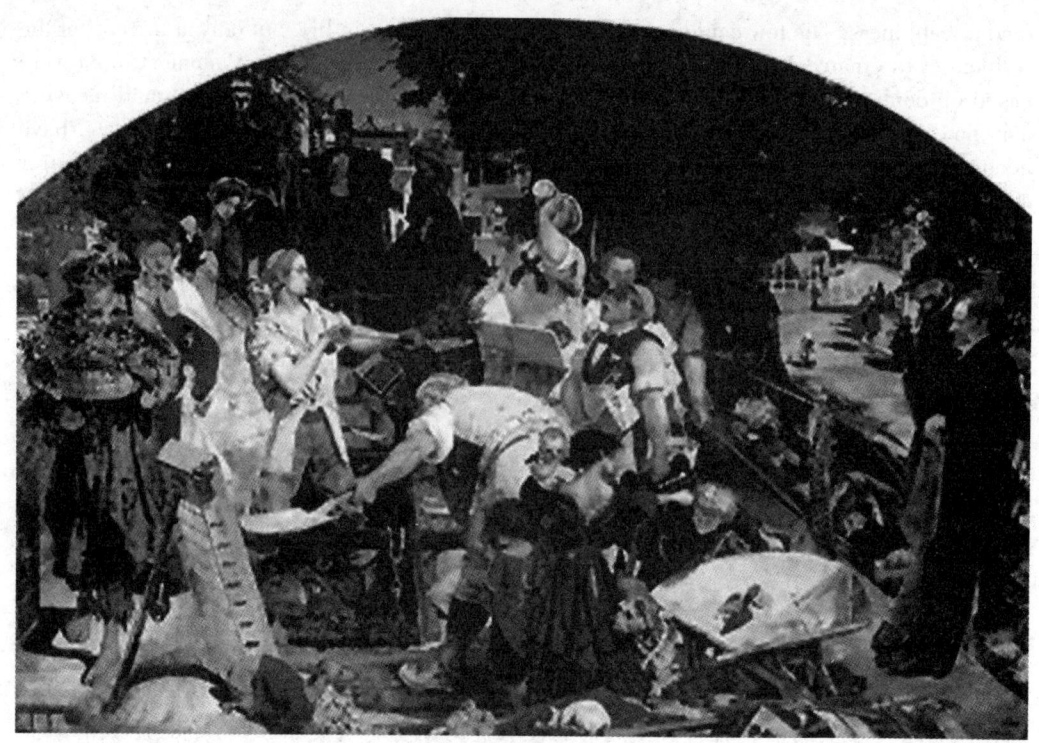

柏拉图的乌托邦

wealth is conditional on the maintenance of our social organization and capital. Society is a "going concern," and no small part of our well-being may be compared with the intangible "goodwill" of a business. The owner of a business depends on the habits of his customers no less than on the regular running of the machinery in his factory; both must be kept in repair, and when in repair they have the value of the "going concern"; but should the business stop, they have merely a break-up value — the machinery becomes so much scrap metal, and the goodwill is reduced to the book debts.

Society reposes on the fact that man is a creature of habit. By interlocking the various habits of many men, society obtains a structure which may be compared with that of a running machine. Mrs. Bouncer was able to form a simple society for the occupation of a room, because Box slept by night and Cox by day, but her society was dislocated when one of her lodgers took

我们对社会组织和资本的维护情况为条件的。社会是一种"进行中的事业",而我们的幸福,可能绝大部分都可与那种无形的企业"商誉"相比拟。企业主对于顾客消费习惯的依赖程度,并不亚于他对工厂内机器正常运行的依赖;因为二者都必须加以经常维护才行,而在维护好了之后,二者便都具有了"进行中的事业"的价值;但是,倘若企业停产,二者便都只具有支离破碎的价值了——机器设备会变成一堆废铜烂铁,而商誉则会沦落成账面债务。

社会倚赖于人类是一种习惯性动物这一现实。通过把许多人各种各样的习惯相互结合起来,社会便形成了一种结构;这种结构,可与运行中的机器设备的结构相比拟。比如说,庞瑟太太能够让房客租用的一个房间形成一个简单的社会,因为包克斯晚上睡觉,考克斯则是白天睡觉;但是,假如两个房客中的一个去度假了,暂时性地改变了起

a holiday, and for the nonce changed his habit. Let any one try to realize what would happen to himself if all those on whom he depends — the postmen, railwaymen, butchers, bakers, printers, and very many others — were suddenly to vary their settled routines; he will then begin to appreciate in how great a degree the power of modern man over nature is due to the fact that society is a "going concern," or, in the language of the engineer, has momentum. Stop the running long enough to throw men's habits out of gear with one another, and society would quickly run down to the simple reality of control by nature. Vast numbers would die in consequence.

Productive power, in short, is a far more important element of reality in relation to modern civilization than is accumulated wealth. The total visible wealth of a civilized country, notwithstanding the antiquity of some of its treasures, is generally estimated as equal to the output of not more than seven or eight years. The significance of this statement does not lie in its precise accuracy, but in the rapid growth of its practical meaning for modern men, owing to their dependence on a machinery of production, mechanical and social, which in the past four or five generations has become increasingly delicate and complicated. For every advance in the application of science there has been a corresponding change in social organization. It was by no mere coincidence that Adam Smith was discussing the division of labor when James Watt was inventing the steam-

瓦特

居习惯，那么庞瑟太太的这个社会就被打乱了。大家不妨都来设想一下，要是我们所依赖的那些人——比如邮递员、铁路工人、屠夫、面包师、印刷工人，以及其他许许多多的人——突如其来地改变了他们一贯的例行工作，我们自己会怎样呢？这样一来，我们就会开始领悟到，现代人类具有掌控自然的力量，在很大程度上是因为社会是一种"进行中的事业"这个事实，或者用工程师的话来说，是因为社会具有动力。倘若将社会这台运转着的机器停下来，让人们的习惯相互脱了节，那么整个社会很快便会沦落到受大自然摆布的简单现实里去。结果，就将有大批的人活不下去。

亚当·斯密

简单而言，生产力是一个涉及现代文明、且比财富积累重要得多的现实因素。人们通常估计，一个文明国家全部的有形财富，差不多跟该国不超过七八年的生产总值相等，尽管其中有些财富是从久远的古时流传下来的。这种说法的重要性，并不在于它很精确，而在于它对现代人类的实际意义正在急剧增加，因为人类依赖于机械的和社会的生产机器，而在过去四五个世代里，这种生产机器已经变得日益精巧和复杂了。应用科学每前进一步，社会组织方面都会出现一次相应的变革。瓦特发明蒸汽机的时候，亚当·斯密正在讨论劳动分工，这种现象并非纯属巧

engine. Nor, in our own time, is it by blind coincidence that beside the invention of the internal combustion engine — the key to the motor-car, submarine, and aeroplane — must be placed an unparalleled extension of the credit system. Lubrication of metal machinery depends on the habits of living men. The assumption of some scientific enthusiasts that the study of the humane arts has ceased to be important will not bear examination; the management of men, high and low, is more difficult and more important under the conditions of modern reality than it ever was.

We describe the managers of the social machine as Organizers, but under that general term are commonly included two distinct categories. In the first place, we have Administrators, who are not strictly organizers at all — begetters, that is to say, of new organs in an organism. It is the function of the administrator to keep the running social machine in repair and to see to its lubrication. When men die, or for reasons of ill-health or old age retire, it is his duty to fill the vacant places with men suitably trained beforehand. A foreman of works is essentially an administrator. A Judge administers the Law, except in so far as in fact, though not in theory, he may make it. In the work of the administrator, pure and simple, there is no idea of progress. Given a certain organization, efficiency is his ideal — perfect smoothness of working. His characteristic disease is called "Red Tape". A complicated society, well administered, tends in fact to a Chinese stagnation by the very strength of its momentum. The goodwill of a long-established and well-managed business may often be sold for a large sum in the market. Perhaps the most striking illustration of social momentum is to be seen in the immobility of markets themselves. Every seller wishes to go where buyers are in the habit of congregating in order that he may be sure of a purchaser for his wares. On the other hand, every buyer goes, if he can, to the place where sellers are wont to assemble in order that he may buy cheaply as the result of their competition. The authorities have often tried in vain to decentralize the markets of London.

合。在我们所处的这个时代，除了内燃机的发明——这是汽车、潜水艇和飞机出现的关键——信贷制度也必须得到前所未有的发展，这也并非是一种盲目的巧合。金属机器的滑润，取决于人们的习惯。一些热衷于科学的人想当然地认为，研究人文艺术已经不再重要，这种观点是经不起细究的；因为在当代这种现实情况下，管理属于不同社会阶层的人比以往任何时候都更加困难、也更加重要了。

我们把社会机器的管理者称为组织者，但这个笼统的术语通常还蕴含着两种不同的类别。首先，我们有行政人员；严格说来，他们根本就不属于组织者——更确切地说，他们是导致某一组织里出现新的机构的人。行政人员的作用，在于让运转着的社会机器保持良好的状况，并确保这台社会机器的润滑作用正常。倘有人员辞世，或者因身体不好、年老而退休，行政人员的职责便是用事先经过恰当培训的人员来填补这些空缺职位。工厂里的工长，从本质上来说就是一个行政人员。法官是实施法律的人，不过除此之外，法官在事实上而非理论上还可以制定法律。在行政人员那种纯粹而简单的工作中，可以说是全然没有进步思想的。假如让他去管理某个组织，那么效率便是他的理想——即他希望工作起来毫无阻碍。他的典型弊病，就是所谓的"官僚习气"。一个复杂的社会就算治理得井井有条，事实上往往也会因为社会动力所固有的力量而形成一种中国式的闭关锁国状态。一家开业已久、经营良好的企业，其信誉在市场上往往可以卖个好价钱。或许，社会动力最显著的一个例证，便是市场本身的固定性。每个卖家都愿意到买家喜欢聚集的地方去，以确保有人买他的东西。而从另一方面来说，如果做得到，每个买家也都会去卖家惯常聚集的地方，以便利用卖家之间的相互竞争来买到便宜

In order to appreciate the other type of organizer, the Creator of social mechanism, let us again consider for a moment the common course of Revolutions. A Voltaire criticises the running concern known as French Government; a Rousseau paints the ideal of a happier society; the authors of the great Encyclopédie prove that the material bases for such a society exist. Presently the new ideas take possession of some well-meaning enthusiasts — inexperienced,

however, in the difficult art of changing the habits of average mankind. They seize an opportunity for altering the structure of French society. Incidentally, but unfortunately, they slow down its running. Stoppage of work, actual breakage of the implements of production and government, removal of practiced administrators, and substitution of misfitting amateurs combine to reduce the rate of production of the necessaries of life, with the result that prices rise, and confidence and credit fall. The Revolutionary leaders are, no doubt, willing enough to be poor for a time in order to realize their ideals, but the hungry millions rise up around them. To gain time the millions are led to suspect that the shortage is due to some interference of the deposed powers, and the Terror inevitably follows. At last men become fatalists, and, abandoning ideals, seek some organizer who shall restore efficiency. The necessity is reinforced by the fact that foreign enemies are

伏尔泰

的东西。伦敦当局总想疏散该市的各个市场，可每次都是徒劳无功，正是这个原因。

为了理解另一种形式的组织者，即社会机构的创造者，我们不妨再来研究一下各种革命的共同进程。有位伏尔泰，曾经批评过法国政府这个"进行中的事业"；有位卢梭，曾经描绘出了关于一种更幸福的社会的理想；而《大百科全书》的作者们，则证明这样一种社会的物质基础是存在的。很快，这些新思想便迷住了一些善意的热心人——不过，对于改变普通人的习惯这一艰巨的任务，他们却毫无经验可谈。他们抓住了一个改变法国社会结构的机会。意外却又可惜的是，他们放缓了法国社会的运行速度。罢工、生产工具和管理方面真正的四分五裂、把有经验的行政人员解职、让不称职的门外

卢梭

汉来代替，这些因素结合在一起，既降低了生活必须品的生产效率，从而使得物价高涨，也导致了社会信心和信用的下降。毋庸置疑，革命领袖们是非常乐意贫苦一个时期，以便实现他们的理想的；可千千万万饥肠辘辘的民众，却会起而将他们包围。为了争取时间，革命领袖们便诱导这些民众，让他们疑心物资短缺是因被废政权实施某种阻挠而导致的，于是恐怖统治就必定会随之而来。最终，人们便会变成宿命论者，并且抛

invading the national territory, and that less production and relaxed discipline have reduced the defensive power of the State. But the organizer needed for the task of reconstruction is no mere administrator; he must be able to design and make, and not merely to repair and lubricate social machinery. So Carnot, who "organizes victory", and Napoleon with his Code Civil, win eternal fame by creative effort.

The possibility of organization in the constructive sense depends on discipline. Running society is constituted by the myriad interlocking of the different habits of many men; if the running social structure is to be altered, even in some relatively small respect, a great number of men and women must simultaneously change various of their habits in complementary ways. It was impossible to introduce Daylight Saving except by an edict of Government, for any partial adherence to the change of hour would have thrown society into confusion. The achievement

弃理想，再去寻求一个能够恢复效率的组织者。外敌正在入侵国家领土，生产减少和纪律松弛业已削弱了国家的抵抗实力，它们都会强化这种必然性。但是，需要担负起重建任务的组织者并非只是一个行政人员；他必须能够设计和制造社会机器，而不能只是维修和滑润社会机器。这样，"组织胜利"的卡诺，以及拿破仑和他那部《民法典》便通过创造性的努力而赢得了不朽的声名。

在建设性的意义方面来看，组织的可能性取决于纪律。运行中的社会，是由许多人的不同习惯环环相扣地结合起来构成的；如果要改变这种运行的社会结构，就算是在某个相对较小的方面对其加以改变，许多人也必须采用互补的方式，同时改变各自不同的习惯才行。除非政府颁布法令，否则便不可能引入夏令时，因为如果只有一部分人遵守这种时

拿破仑和他那部《民典法》

of Daylight Saving was, therefore, dependent on social discipline, which is thus seen to consist not in the habits of men but in the power of simultaneous and correlated change of those habits. In an ordered State the sense of discipline becomes innate, and the police are but rarely called upon to enforce it. In other words, social discipline, or the alteration of habit at will or command, itself becomes a habit. Military discipline, in so far as it consists of single acts at the word of command, is of a simpler order, but the professional soldier knows well the difference between habitual discipline and even the most intelligent fighting by quick-trained men.

In times of disorder the interlocking of productive habits breaks down step by step, and society as a whole becomes progressively poor, though robbers of one kind or another may for a while enrich themselves. Even more serious, however, is the failure of the habit of discipline, for that implies the loss of the power of recuperation. Consider to what a pass Russia was brought by a year of cumulative revolutions; her condition was like that terrible state of paralysis when the mind still sees and directs, but the nerves fail to elicit any response from the muscles. A nation does not die when so smitten, but the whole mechanism of its society must be reconstituted, and that quickly, if the men and women who survive its impoverishment are not to forget the habits and lose the aptitudes on which their civilization depends. History shows no remedy but force upon which to found a fresh nucleus of discipline in such circumstances; but the organizer who rests upon force tends inevitably to treat the recovery of mere efficiency as his end.

卡诺（Lazare Nicolas Marguerite Carnot, 1753～1823），法国大革命时期共和军的军事家之一。他整顿了当时的法国军队，采取了新的战术，改善了军需供应，对筑城学也有贡献，故被誉为法军"胜利的组织者"。后来他身居高位，在拿破仑一世手下任职。

间上的变化，那么整个社会就会陷入混乱之中。因此，成功推行夏令时取决于社会纪律；从而可以看出，纪律并非存在于人们的习惯当中，而是存在于同时且相互关联地改变那些习惯的权力当中。在一个秩序井然的国家，人们会自然而然地拥有纪律感，几乎不需要警察来强制执行这种纪律。换言之就是，社会纪律，或者说随意抑或奉命改变习惯的行为，本身就会变成一种习惯。从它含有按照命令简单地行动这个方面来看，军规只是一种维持较为简单之秩序的纪律；不过，职业军人却很清楚，习惯性地遵规守纪，与只经过短期训练的士兵最有水平的战斗之间，还是具有差别的。

在社会动荡时期，各种生产习惯之间的相互关联会逐步脱节，尽管这种抑或那种盗贼可能会暂时地发上一笔财，但整个社会却会逐渐贫困下去。然而更严重的是，遵规守纪的习惯将会沦丧，因为这就意味着整个社会失去了复原的实力。想想一年来接连不断的革命已将俄罗斯带入了一种何种危险的境地吧；该国的状况，就像是陷入了那种可怕的瘫痪之症，虽然脑子还能看、还能用，可神经却无法从肌得到任何反应了。虽说一个国家受到此种重创后并不会灭亡，可该国社会的整体结构却必须重新构建，而且要快，才能让所有经历了艰难困苦之后存活下来的人不至于忘掉自己的习惯，不至于失去

Idealism does not flourish under his rule. It was because history speaks plainly in this regard, that so many of the idealists of the last two generations have been internationalist; the military recovery of discipline is commonly achieved either by conquest from another national base or incidentally to a successful national resistance to foreign invasion.

The great organizer is the great realist. Not that he lacks imagination — very far from that; but his imagination turns to "ways and means", and not to elusive ends. His is the mind of Martha and not of Mary. If he be a Captain of Industry the counters of his thought are labor and capital; if he be a General of Armies they are units and supplies. His organizing is aimed at intermediate ends — money if he be an industrial, and victory if he be a soldier. But money and victory are merely the keys to ulterior ends, and those ulterior ends remain elusive for him throughout. He dies still making money, or, if he be a victorious soldier, weeps like Alexander because there are no more worlds to conquer. His one care is that the business or the army which he has organized shall be efficiently administered; he is hard on his administrators. Above all, he values the habit of discipline; his machine must answer promptly to the lever.

The organizer inevitably comes to look upon men as his tools. His is the inverse of the mind of the idealist, for he would move men in brigades and must therefore have regard to material limitations, whereas the idealist appeals to the soul in each of us, and souls are winged and can soar. It does not follow that the organizer is careless of the well-being of the society

其文明所依赖的那些本领。历史表明，在这种情况下，补救办法只有一个，那就是以武力为基础，建立起一种全新的制度核心来；不过，倚赖武力的组织者，往往必定会把恢复效率当成自己的最终目标。在这种组织者的统治下，理想主义不会蓬勃发展起来。正是因为历史在这个方面已经有了明白无误的呈现，所以过去两代理想主义者当中那么多的人才同时也是国际主义者；通常来说，要么是通过被别国征服，要么是通过偶然地击退了入侵之外敌，才能做到用军事手段恢复规章制度。

一个伟大的组织者，同时也是一个伟大的现实主义者。他并不是没有想象力——完全不是这样的；只不过，他的想象力转向了"手段和方法"，而不是转向了某些难以言说的目标。他所具有的，是马大而非马利亚的头脑。倘若他是一位产业资本家，那他心中的筹码就是劳动力和资本；倘若他是一位统率部队的将军，那他的筹码便是作战单位和给养。他进行组织，旨在达到某个中间目标——若是产业资本家，这个中间目标就是金钱；若是军人，这个中间目标就是取得胜利。但是，金钱和胜利都只是通向未来目标的钥匙罢了，而对于组织者来说，这些未来的目标自始至终都是难以言说的。若是产业资本家，那么他到死都会去赚钱；或者，若是一名所向披靡的军人，那么他就会像亚历山大大帝[1]那样，因为再也没有世界可让他去征服而悲叹。他的关注点之一便是，自己组建起来的企业或者军队应当得到有效的管理；所以，他对手下行政人员的要求会非常严厉。最重要的是，他很重视遵规守纪的习惯；只要一动手，他的机器就必须立即做出反应。

因此，组织者必定会把人们看成自己的工具。他的头脑与理想主义者的头脑正好相反，因为他调动的是大批人马，所以必须考虑物质条件的制约；但理想主义者却会感染我们每个人的心灵——心灵可是长了翅膀，能够翱翔天际的。我们由此并不能得出结

---

[1] Alexander：亚历山大大帝（公元前356~323），古马其顿国王（公元前336~323在位），曾率军征服了希腊和波斯，建立起大帝国，故史称亚历山大大帝（Alexander the Great）。他自以为全世界有人居住的地方都已属于他，再也没有可以让他去征服的地方了。

　　马大和马利亚，《圣经》中的两个女性人物，是一对姐妹。由于年长，家计均由马大承担。耶稣到了她家后，马大忙里忙外尽力招待，但马利亚却只是听耶稣讲道。马大忙不过来，便向耶稣抱怨妹妹不帮忙，谁知却受到了耶稣的批评。参见《圣经·新约全书·路加福音》第10章第38节至第42节。此处作者显然是喻指组织者关注世俗、讲求实际，不是理想主义者。

beneath him; on the contrary, he regards that society as so much man-power to be maintained in efficient condition. This is true whether he be militarist or capitalist, provided that he be far-sighted. In the sphere of politics the organizer views men as existing for the State — for the "Leviathan" of the Stuart philosopher Hobbes. But the Democratic Idealist barely tolerates the State as a necessary evil, for it limits freedom.

In the established Democracies of the West, the ideals of Freedom have been transmuted into the prejudices of the average citizen, and it is on these "habits of thought" that the security of our freedom depends, rather than on the passing ecstasies of idealism. For a thousand years such prejudices took root under the insular protection of Britain; they are the outcome of continuous experiment, and must be treated at least with respect, unless we are prepared to think of our forefathers as fools. One of these prejudices is that it is unwise to take an Expert as Minister of State. In the present time of War, when freedom even in a democracy must yield to efficiency, there are those who would have us say that the experts whom we have for the time being installed in some of the high offices should be succeeded henceforth by experts, and that our prejudice is antiquated. None the less even in war time Britain has returned to a Civilian Minister for War! The fact is, of course, that the inefficiencies of the normally working British Constitution are merely the obverse of the truth that democracy is incompatible with the organization necessary for war against autocracies. When the present Chilian Minister first came to England he was entertained by some members of the House of Commons. Referring to the Mother

霍布斯

论，说组织者对于所管社会的福利漠不关心；相反，他将社会看成是许许多多必须维持高效状态的人力。不管是军事家还是资本家，只要具有远大的目光，组织者都会这样认为的。在政治领域，组织者觉得人类是为国家而存在的——就是为霍布斯这位支持斯图亚特王室的哲学家所说的那种"庞然大物"而存在的。然而，民主的理想主义者却认为，国家是一种无可避免的祸害，因为国家限制了自由，所以他们几乎无法忍受国家的存在。

在西方业已根基深扎的民主国家中，自由的理想已经变成了普通公民的种种成见，而确保我们的自由，依赖的却正是这些"观念上的习惯"，而不是那种短暂的理想主义狂热情绪。一千年来，在与世隔绝的不列颠岛的保护之下，这些成见已经在英国深深地扎下了根；它们都是持续试验的产物，因此，除非我们成心将自己的祖先看成傻瓜，否则它们就应该得到起码的尊重。这些成见当中，有一种就是认为让专业人士来担当国务大臣之职并不明智。在目前的战争状态下，即便是在民主国家当中，自由也必须服从于效率；可有些人却希望让我们说，我们暂时地置于一些高位上的专业人士的职务，此后也应该由专业人士来继任，并且希望我们指出自己的成见已经过时了。虽说如此，但即便是在战争时期，英国却仍然重新采用了文官担任陆军大臣的做法！的确，事实就是，正常实施中的《英国宪法》效率不高，不过是对应着这样一条真理罢了：民主与对抗专

　　霍布斯描述的"庞然大物"源自《圣经》故事，原指海中一种巨大的、象征着邪恶的怪兽。17世纪英国的霍布斯（T. Hobbes, 1588～1679）以此为名写了一本论述国家组织的著作（书名多音译为《利维坦》），故此后leviathan一词又用于指组织机构庞大的极权主义（国家或政府）。

of Parliaments, as seen from the far Pacific, and to the chronic grumbling in regard to Parliamentary government which he found on his arrival in London, he exclaimed, "You forget that one of the chief functions of Parliaments is to prevent things being done!"

The thought of the organizer is essentially strategical, whereas that of the true democrat is ethical. The organizer is thinking how to use men; but the democrat is thinking of the rights of men, which rights are so many rocks in the way of the organizer. Undoubtedly the organizer must be a master, for, given the waywardness of human nature and the inveteracy of habit, he would make little progress otherwise. But he is a bad supreme master, because of his "ways and means" mind.

The Nemesis of democratic idealism, if it break from the bonds of reality, is the supreme rule of the organizer and of blind efficiency. The organizer begins innocently enough; his executive mind revolts from the disorder, and above all from the indiscipline around him. Soldierly efficiency undoubtedly saved Revolutionary France. But such is the impetus of the going concern, that it sweeps forward even its own creator. To improve the efficiency of his man-power he must in the end seek to control all its activities — working and thinking, no less than fighting. He is in supreme command, and inefficiency is pain to him. Therefore Napoleon added to his Grand Army and his Code Civil, also his Concordat with the Papacy, whereby the priest was to become his servant. He might have enjoyed lasting peace after the Treaty of Amiens, but must needs continue to prepare war. Finally he was impelled to his Moscow, just as a great money maker will overreach himself and end in bankruptcy.

制政体的战争所必须的那种组织并不相容。现任智利公使第一次来到英格兰时，是几位下院议员招待的。在谈到远东太平洋地区各国对"议会之母"[1]的看法，以及他抵达伦敦后听到人们老是在抱怨议会制政体的时候，他大声说道："你们忘了吧，议会的主要功能之一就是让事情干不成！"

从本质上来说，组织者的思想是战略性的，而真正的民主主义者的思维却是道德性的。组织者考虑的是如何用人，民主主义者考虑的却是人的权利；可人的权利，又是组织者前进道路上为数众多的绊脚石。毋庸置疑，组织者必定是一位统治者；因为人性刚愎自任、习惯根深蒂固，如果不是这样，组织者便不会有什么作为。不过，因为他具有"手段和方法"式的思维，所以组织者又会是一个糟糕的最高统治者。

如果摆脱了现实的束缚，民主理想主义的报应[2]，便会是组织者与盲目的效率共同统治一切。组织者刚开始组织的时候会单纯得很；他的行政思维，会让他讨厌无秩序的状态，并且尤其反感身边那些无组织无纪律的行为。毫无疑问，是军人式的效率挽救了法国革命。但是，这种"进行中的事业"的动力是如此的强劲，以至于将它自身的创造者也一齐席卷前去了。为了提高手下人力的效率，组织者最终必定会想法去控制人力的所有活动——像控制战斗一样去控制人力的工作和思想。组织者具有至高无上的指挥权，令其苦恼的就是效率低下。因此，拿破仑才会在手下大军和《民法典》之外，又加上了他与罗马教皇之间的政教协约，从而使得神职人员也变成了他的仆役。《亚眠和约》[3]签订之后，拿破仑本来是可以享受持久之和平的，可他却非得继续备战。最终，他

---

[1] Mother of Parliaments：议会之母。英国是议会制的创始者，故被称为"议会之母"。

[2] Nemesis：涅墨西斯。古希腊神话中的复仇女神，性格冷酷无情。此处意译为"报应"。

[3] Treaty of Amiens：《亚眠和约》。1802年法、英两国在法国北部亚眠所签订的休战和约。但和约签订之后双方并未全面遵守，从而导致了第三次反法联盟成立。

拿破仑在巴黎圣母院的加冕典礼。

Bismarck was the Napoleon of the Prussians, their man of blood and iron, yet he differed from his French prototype in certain regards which, for our present purpose, are worth attention. His end was unlike the end of Napoleon. There was no banishment to Elba after a Moscow, no imprisonment in St. Helena after a Waterloo. True that, after thirty years at the helm, the old pilot was dropped in 1890 by a new captain with a mind to piracy, but it was because of his caution and not because of vaulting ambition. Both Napoleon and Bismarck had supreme minds of the "ways and means" order, but there was something more in Bismarck. He was not merely the great business man, which is Emerson's description of Napoleon. No statesman ever adjusted war to policy with a nicer judgment than Bismarck. He fought three short and

不得不在莫斯科遭受惨败，就像是一个很会赚钱的人弄巧成拙，最终沦落到破产那样。

　　虽说俾斯麦是普鲁士人心目中的拿破仑，是普鲁士铁血男子汉的典范，但在某些方面，他与法国的拿破仑还是有所不同；从我们当前的研究目的来看，这种差异是值得我们去加以注意的。俾斯麦的结局，与拿破仑的结局并不一样。他并没有在莫斯科大败之后被流放到厄尔巴岛[1]去，也没有在滑铁卢之战后被囚禁在圣海伦那岛[2]上。确实，在掌了30年的舵之后，俾斯麦这个老领航员也在1890年被一个想要从事海盗行径的新船长抛弃了；不过，这是由于他太过谨慎，而不是由于他野心太大所致。虽说拿破仑和俾斯麦这两人都有着超常的"手段和方法"式的头脑，不过俾斯麦还有别的长处。他不像爱

[1] Elba：厄尔巴岛。意大利的一个岛屿，位于意大利半岛和科西嘉岛之间的第勒尼安海上，是拿破仑第一次被流放（1814年5月～1815年2月）的地点。
　　[2] St. Helena：圣海伦娜岛。南大西洋中的一个英属岛屿。1815年至1821年，拿破仑在滑铁卢大败之后，被放逐并囚禁于该岛之上。

俾斯麦

爱默生（Ralph Waldo Emerson，
1803～1882）。美国作家、哲学家和超越主义的
中心人物，其诗歌、散文和论文——如《自然》
（Nature，1836）——被认为是美国思想与文学
发展史上的里程碑。

successful campaigns, and made three treaties of peace, from each of which ensued a harvest of advantage to Prussia. Yet what different treaties they were! After the War of 1864 against Denmark, Bismarck took Schleswig and Holstein, with the idea, beyond question, of a Kiel Canal. After the War of 1866 against Austria he refused to take Bohemia, and thereby so offended his King that they were not fully reconciled until after the victories of 1870. There can be no doubt that in this clemency Bismarck foresaw a time when Prussia might need the alliance of Austria. In 1871, after Sedan and the Siege of Paris, Bismarck yielded to the pressure of the military party, and took Lorraine as well as Alsace.

The great Chancellor had, in truth, what the Prussian, as a rule, lacks, an insight into the minds of other nations than his own. His

默生所描述的拿破仑那样，只是一个伟大的生意人。还没有哪一位政治家比俾斯麦具有更好的判断力，更知道如何让战争去适应政策呢。他打了三场时间短暂却大获全胜的战役，缔结了三份和约，并且每一次都给普鲁士带来了莫大的利益。不过，这3份和约却是多么的大不相同啊！1864年普（鲁士）、丹（麦）之战后，俾斯麦攫取了史莱茨威格和霍斯坦两地，而他的目的，无疑就是想得到基尔运河[1]。1866年普、奥之战后，他不肯占领波希米亚[2]，并因此而得罪了普鲁士国王，直到1870年节节取胜之后，两人的关系才完全和好如初。俾斯麦之所以有此仁慈之举，无疑在于他预见到了将来会有一个时期，普鲁士可能需要和奥地利结盟。直到1871年色当战役[3]和围攻巴黎之后，俾斯麦才屈从于军方的压力，占领了洛林和阿尔萨斯。

事实上，这位伟大的首相具有其他普鲁

[1] Kiel Canal：基尔运河。基尔是德国北部的一个城市，于1242年被特许建立，1284年加入自由日耳曼城市商人联盟，1773年并入丹麦，1866年被普鲁士占领。

[2] Bohemia：波希米亚。欧洲历史上的一个地区和王国，在如今的捷克斯洛伐克西部。

[3] Sedan：色当。法国东北部城市，是普法战争中拿破仑三世最终被击败和投降（1870年9月2日）的地方。

色当战役后，法国皇帝拿破仑三世会见德国首相俾斯麦，正式签署投降书

methods were psychological by preference. Once he had achieved German unity under Prussia, he waged no more wars. Yet he accomplished great things — for a time he ruled Europe — and his method was no mere exploitation of military prestige. At the Berlin Congress of 1878 he secured the occupation of the provinces of Bosnia and Herzegovina for Austria, and thereby deepened the rivalry of Austria and Russia in the Balkan Peninsula. At the same Berlin Congress he privately incited France to occupy Tunis, and when France presently effected that occupation, Italy, as he foresaw, was sharply wounded. The Dual Alliance with Austria followed in 1879, and the Triple Alliance with Austria and Italy in 1881. It was as though he had sent his sheep-dog round his flock to drive his sheep to him. By subtleties of the same order he antagonized France and Britain, and also Britain and Russia. So, too, did he deal in his domestic policy. In 1886 he ceased from struggling with the Vatican, and brought over the Catholic party to his support, thereby neutralizing the socialist tendency in the industrial but Catholic Province of the Rhineland, and the particularist tendency in the Catholic kingdom of Bavaria in the south.

The true parallel is to be drawn not between Napoleon and Bismarck, but between Napoleon and the entire Prussian ruling caste. The end of that caste, which we are now witnessing, is like the end of Napoleon; the blindly organizing man goes to his Moscow, and the blindly organizing State to its Armageddon. Kultur is the name given to that philosophy and education which imbued a whole race with the "ways and means" mind. The French are an artistic, and therefore an idealistic people; Napoleon prostituted their idealism with the glory of

士人通常并不具备的一种远见卓识，能够洞察到别国而并非仅仅是本国的民心。他最喜欢的方法便是心理战。一旦将德意志诸邦统一到了普鲁士之下，他便没有再发动任何战争了。不过，他还是干了许多大事——他曾一度统治了整个欧洲；而他的方法，也并非纯属利用普鲁士的军事优势。在1878年的柏林大会[1]上，他确保奥地利占领了波斯尼亚和黑塞哥维那两个省份，从而加剧了奥、俄两国在巴尔干半岛上的敌对。在同一次柏林大会上，他私下怂恿法国去占领突尼斯，而当法国不久真的占领了突尼斯之后，意大利果真受到了极大的伤害，完全与他所预计的那样。随后，便是1879年与奥地利订立的两国同盟，以及1881年与奥地利和意大利订立的三国同盟了。这种方法，就好像是他派了一条牧羊犬围住了他放牧的羊群，并把羊儿都赶向他那样。通过同样巧妙的手段，他不但让法、英反目，还使得英、俄成了仇人。在处理内政时，他也是这样做的。1886年，他不再与梵蒂冈争斗，又拉拢天主教党徒支持自己，由此压制住了以产业为主却又信奉天主教的莱因省内的社会主义倾向，还消除了南方信奉天主教的巴伐利亚王国内出现的独立主义倾向。

真正的比较，其实不应在拿破仑和俾斯麦这两人之间进行，而应当在拿破仑和普鲁士的整个统治阶层之间来进行。我们如今正在见证的这个统治阶层的结局，将会与拿破仑的结局相似：盲目地进行组织的拿破仑，走向了他的莫斯科大败；而盲目地进行组织的普鲁士，则走向了它的末日之战[2]。"德国文化"这个术语，指的就是让整个民族都激发出"手段和方法"式思维的那种哲学和教育。法兰西人是一个崇尚艺术、并因而也

[1] Berlin Congress：柏林大会。1878年欧洲列强与奥斯曼帝国在柏林举行的一次会议，主要议题是重建巴尔干半岛的秩序，系由俾斯麦代表德国倡议召开的，会上签署了《柏林条约》。

[2] Armageddon：大规模战争，大决战。源于《圣经·新约》，本指世界末日的善恶大决战。

处理内政的俾斯麦。

哲学家费希特。他关于世界道德规律以及社会道德本性的思想，对黑格尔产生了重要的影响。

his genius. Bismarck, on the other hand, was the child of materialistic Kultur, but, greater than the average of his race, he could reckon also with spiritual forces.

Kultur had its origin not in the victories of Frederick the Great, but in the defeat of Jena. The rule of Frederick in the eighteenth century was a personal rule like that of Napoleon, whereas the Prussia of the nineteenth century, behind whatever other pretense, was governed by an oligarchy of intellectual "Experts" — staff officers, bureaucrats, professors. Frederick, sole organizer, raised only administrators, with the result that when he died he left Prussia a mere mechanism, to be broken on the field of Jena.

In the very winter of Jena the philosopher Fichte came to lecture in Berlin, while it was still in the occupation of the French.[1] There was no University in the Prussian capital of those days, and the lectures were delivered not to young students, but to the maturest brains of the country in the fever of a great crisis. Fichte taught the philosophy of Patriotism at a time when the German Universities were devoted to the abstract worship of

[1] See The Evolution of Prussia, by Marriott and Grant Robertson. Clarendon Press, 1915.

崇尚理想主义的民族；可拿破仑却用自己天才的荣耀，出卖了法兰西人的理想主义。另一方面，俾斯麦却是崇尚实利主义的"德国文化"的产物；不过，因为他比本民族中的普通民众更加伟大，所以他也能够重视精神的力量。

"德国文化"的源头，并不是腓特烈大帝[1]所打的场场胜仗，而是耶拿之战中遭受的惨败。腓特烈大帝在18世纪的统治与拿破仑的统治一样，都属于一种个人专政；而19世纪的普鲁士，无论其表面伪装成什么样子，背后实际上都是由少数高智商的"专业人士"——即参谋人员、官吏和教授——所组成的寡头政府统治着。腓特烈大帝是一个独断专行的组织者，他只是擢升行政人员，结果他死后，只是给普鲁士留下了一种注定要在耶拿战场上被打破的体制罢了。

就在耶拿之战的那个冬天，哲学家费希特到柏林讲学，当时柏林仍处在法军的占领之下［作者注：参见玛丽奥特·罗伯逊和葛兰特·罗伯逊的《普鲁士发展史》（The Evolution of Prussia）一书，牛津大学出版部印刷所，1915］。那个时候，作为普鲁士首都的柏林还没有大学，费希特也并非是给青年学生们讲学，而是为该国那些最深思熟虑的头脑人物讲学；当时，这些头脑人物都因国家陷入了重大危机当中而深感

[1] Frederick the Great：腓特烈大帝（1712～1786）。普鲁士国王，1740～1786在位，亦即腓特烈二世（Frederick II）。

— 29 —

耶拿之战。耶拿，德国中部城市，位于莱比锡西南。1806年拿破仑一世在此大败普鲁士军队。

knowledge and art. In the next few years, between 1806 and 1813, was established that close connection between the army, the bureaucracy, and the schools, or, in other words, between the needs of government and the aims of education, which constituted the essence and perverse strength of the Prussian system. Universal military service was correlated with universal compulsory schooling, inaugurated in Prussia two generations before the English Education Act of 1870; the University of Berlin, with a brilliant professoriate, was established as sister to the Great General Staff. Thus knowledge in Prussia was no longer pursued mainly for its own sake, but as a means to an end, and that end was the success of a State which had experienced bitter disaster. It was a Camp–State, moreover, in the midst of a plain, without the natural bulwarks of a Spain, a France, or a Britain. The end determines the means, and since the Prussian end was military strength, based of necessity on stark discipline, the means were inevitably materialistic. Judged from the standpoint of Berlin, it was a wonderful thing to have impressed Kultur, or Strategical mentality, on the educated class of a whole people, but from the standpoint of civilization at large it was a fatal momentum to have given to a nation — fatal, that is to say, in the long run, either to civilization or that nation.

We have had for a byword in these times the German war map. It may be questioned, however, whether most people in Britain and America have fully realized the part played by the map in German education during the past three generations. Maps are the essential apparatus of Kultur, and every educated German is a geographer in a sense that is true of very few Englishmen or Americans. He has been taught to see in maps not merely the conventional boundaries established by scraps of paper, but permanent physical opportunities — "ways and means" in the literal sense of the words. His Real–Politik lives in his mind upon a mental

不安。费希特传授的是爱国主义哲学，而那时德意志各大学院所热衷的却是对知识和艺术的抽象崇拜。接下来的数年中，即从1806年到1813年，该国的军队、官僚机构和院校之间确立起了一种密切的联系，或者换言之，就是在政府的需求和教育的目标之间确立起了密切的联系，从而构成了普鲁士政治制度的根本，使得普鲁士具有了反常的实力。在1870年英国实施《教育法案》之前的两个世代，普鲁士早就推行全民兵役制度和全面义务教育制度了；柏林大学拥有一帮才华横溢的教授，它是作为该国总参谋部的姊妹机构而设立的。因此在普鲁士，人们已经不再主要是为了知识去追求知识，而是将追求知识当成了一种达到目标的手段；这个目标，就是要使曾经遭受过巨大苦难的国家获得胜利。此外，普鲁士也是一个处在平原之中的"兵营国家"，不具有像西班牙、法国或英国那样的天然壁垒。目标决定手段；既然普鲁士的目标是拥有那种必须以绝对纪律为基础的军事实力，那么他们所采取的就必然是实利主义的手段。从柏林的立场来看，倘若能够把"德国文化"或者说"战略心理"灌输给整个民族中的知识阶层，自然是一件再好不过的事了；但从整个文明的角度来看，这种做法却是给整个民族注入了一种致命的动力——也就是说，从长远来看，这种做法要么会毁掉文明，要么就会毁灭这个民族。

这些年来，我们一直都在拿德国的军事地图做笑柄。然而值得怀疑的是，英、美两国中的绝大多数人，是否已经充分了解到过去3个世代里地图在德国教育中所起的作用呢？地图是"德国文化"的基本工具，因此从某种意义上来说，每一个受过教育的德国人都是地理学家；而在英国人或美国人当中，这种情况却是极其罕见的。德国人受到的教育一直都是，看地图时不能光看几张纸上画出来的那些普通界线，还要看到那种永久

map. The serious teaching of geography in German High Schools and Universities dates from the very beginning of Kultur. It was organized in the generation after Jena, mainly by the labors of four men — Alexander von Humboldt, Berghaus, Carl Bitter, and Stieler — who were attached to the new University of Berlin and to the since famous map-house of Perthes of Gotha. To this day, notwithstanding all that has been done by two or three exceptional map-houses in this country, if you want a good map, conveying accurately and yet graphically the fundamental contrasts, you must have resort as often as not to one of German origin. The reason is that in Germany there are many cartographers who are scholarly geographers and not merely surveyors or draftsmen. They can exist, because there is a wide public educated to appreciate and pay for intelligently drawn maps.[1]

In this country we value the moral side of education, and it is perhaps intuitively that we have neglected materialistic geography. Before the War not a few teachers, within my knowledge, objected to geography as a subject of education, on the ground that it tended to promote Imperialism, just as they objected to physical drill because it tended to militarism. We may laugh at such excesses of political caution, as men of former centuries scoffed at the anchorites who secreted themselves from the world, but the protest in each case was against an excess in the opposite direction.

Berlin-Bagdad, Berlin-Herat, Berlin-Pekin — not heard as mere words, but visualized on the mental relief map — involve for most Anglo-Saxons a new mode of thought, lately and

[1] In my Address to the Geographical Section of the British Association at Ipswich in 1895 will be found an account of the rise of the German schools of geography.

性的、实实在在的机会——真的是一种不折不扣的"手段和方法"式的教育。德国人的现实政治思想，存在于其心中的一张精神地图之上。德国的高中和大学都很严肃地教授地理；这种做法，甚至可以追溯到"德国文化"刚刚发端的时候。此种教育方式，是耶拿战役之后的那一代人系统地建立起来的，并且主要得益于四个人的努力——即亚历山大·冯·洪堡、伯格豪斯、卡尔·李特尔和史蒂勒；他们都隶属于新成立的柏林大学，以及自此声名远播、位于哥达的佩尔特斯地图出版社。时至今日，尽管我国有那么两、三家优秀的地图出版社也做了不少努力，但如果想要找一张好地图，想要找那种描绘精确而又轮廓分明地把最重要的对比之处表达出来的好地图，屡屡还得去找一张德国的原图才行。原因就在于，德国有许多的制图大师，这些人同时也都是学问渊博的地理学家，而不仅仅是测量员或者绘图员。他们之所以能够存在，是因为该国有一大批受过教育的民众，能够欣赏并愿意出钱购买绘制精妙的地图［作者注：在1895年我于伊普斯威奇对英国科学协会地理组所做的演讲中，可以看到德国各地理学派的兴起情况。］

在我国，虽说我们重视的是教育的道德教化作用，但忽视实用地理学的做法，却可能是直觉使然。据我所知，此次大战前，许多教师都反对把地理作为教学科目之一，理由便是地理容易助长帝国主义，就像他们因为体操容易助长军国主义而反对把体操作为教学科目那样。我们可能会嘲笑这种政治上的过分谨慎，就像数个世纪之前的人嘲笑那些让自己与世隔绝的隐士那样；不过，上述每种情形中的反对意见，针对的都是另一方的过分之处。

柏林-巴格达、柏林-赫拉特[1]，柏林-北京——这些都并非只是说来让人听听就罢

[1] Herat：赫拉特。阿富汗西北部的一座历史名城，赫拉特省的首府。

亚历山大·冯·洪保（1769～1859）。德国科学家和博物学家，近代地理学的主要创建者，也是世界首个大学地理系（即柏林大学地理系）的首任系主任。

卡尔·李特尔（1779～1859）。德国地理学家，近代地理学的创立者之一，曾任法兰克福大学历史学教授，1820年任柏林大学首任地理学教授。

海因里希·伯格豪斯（Heinrich Berghaus，1797～1884）。德国地理学家。

阿道夫·史蒂勒（Adolf Stieler，1775～1836）。德国地图测绘制作大师，大部分生涯都工作于哥达（Gotha）的贾斯特-佩尔特斯（Justus Perthes）地理研究所，以制作精良的《便携式地图集》（Handatlas）而著称。

imperfectly introduced among us by the rough maps of the newspapers. But your Prussian, and his father, and his grandfather have debated such concepts all their lives, pencil in hand. In arranging the detailed terms of peace, our statesmen will, no doubt, have the advice of excellent geographical experts, but the German representatives will have behind them not merely a few experts but a great geographically instructed public, long familiar with every important aspect of the questions which will arise, and quick to give a farsighted support to their leaders. This may easily become a decisive advantage, especially should our people pass into a magnanimous frame of mind. It would be a curious thing if the successes of Talleyrand and Metter-nich, in the secret diplomacy of 1814, were repeated by the spokesmen of the defeated States of our own time under the conditions imposed upon diplomacy by popular government! [1]

The map habit of thought is no less pregnant in the sphere of economics than it is in that of strategy. True that Laissez-faire had little use for it, but the "most favored nation" clause which Germany imposed on defeated France in the Treaty of Frankfurt had quite a different meaning for the strategical German mind to that which was attached to it by honest Cobdenites.

---

[1] It is true that there is a "horse-sense" of geography among those of us who have traveled. It is true, also, that we keep atlases in our offices and libraries, to be consulted as we would consult a dictionary for the spelling of a word. But correct spelling does not always imply literary power! A trained sense of geographical perspective is essential to the mode of thought here in question.

的几个词，而是可以在心中的地形图上想象出来的地方；对于大多数盎格鲁－撒克逊人[1]来说，它们都涉及一种新的思维模式，而这种思维模式，是不久之前才通过报纸上的草图零零碎碎地介绍给我们的。但普鲁士人和他们的父辈、祖辈们却是终生都手握铅笔，讨论着这些概念呢。在就和约的具体条款进行谈判时，无疑也有优秀的地理专家为我们的政治家们提供建议，可德国代表的身后，却不单单只是几个专家，而是还有一大批具有地理知识的民众；对于各种可能出现的问题中每一个重要的方面，他们早就已经烂熟于胸，故而能够迅速为其领导者提供颇具远见的支持。这种情况，可能很容易演变成一种关键性的优势；倘若我国人民在心态上也变得宽宏大量的话，就尤其如此了。假如在我们这个时代，在民选政府给外交政策强加了种种限制条件的形势之下，那些战败国的代言人还能像1814年的秘密外交中塔列朗和梅特涅那样大获成功，那可真是一桩咄咄怪事了！〔作者注：的确，我们当中那些曾经出门游历过的人会具有地理方面的某些常识。而我们将地图放在办公室和图书馆里以备查阅，就像在字典里查找单词如何拼写那样，这也是事实。不过，一个人能够正确拼写，却并不意味着他一定具有文学才能！对于此处我们所讨论的那种思维方式来说，具备训练有素的地理视角才是必不可少的。〕

这种运用地图的思维习惯在经济领域内的重要意义，并不亚于它在战略领域内的意义。诚然，这种思维方式对自由放任式经济几乎毫无用处；但是，《法兰克福条约》[2]中德国强加于法国这个战败国的"最惠国"条款，在具有战略头脑的德国人看来，却与

---

[1] Anglo-Saxon：盎格鲁－撒克逊人。指公元5至6世纪入侵不列颠的古代北欧日耳曼诸部族，包括盎格鲁人、撒克逊人和朱特人。现多指英国血统（或国籍）的人，尤指血统是盎格鲁－撒克逊族的英国人。

[2] Treaty of Frankfurt：《法兰克福条约》。1871年5月法兰西共和国与德意志帝国为结束普、法战争而在法兰克福河畔签订的一个和约，当时俾斯麦为德意志帝国代表之一。

科布登（Richard Cobden，1804～1865），英国政治家。他被称为"自由贸易的使徒"（Apostle of Free Trade），是英国自由贸易政策的主要推动者。他领导一群商人成立了反谷物法联盟，并且最终成功地促使国会在1846年废除了《谷物法》（规定谷物价格和供应的法律）。

塔列朗　　　　　　　　　　　　　　　　　　梅特涅

塔列朗（Charles Maurice de Talleyrand-Périgord，1754～1838）和梅特涅（Klemens Wenzel von Metternich，1773～1859）。塔列朗亲王是法国资产阶级革命时期的著名外交家，为法国资产阶级革命的巩固做出了极大贡献。从18世纪末到19世纪30年代，他曾连续在6届法国政府中担任外交部长、外交大臣甚至总理。梅特涅是19世纪奥地利的著名政治家、外交家，历任奥地利帝国外交大臣和首相。此处的"秘密外交"指的是1814年维也纳会议（拿破仑战败后，英、俄、普、奥等列强重新瓜分欧洲政治地图的一次会议）上，各列强国进行私下商谈、其他小国无权说话的情况。由于法国是战败国，一开始4个战胜国打算不让法国参与他们的内部交涉，但塔列朗很巧妙地将自己插了进去。此次会议在梅特涅的强势指导之下，定下了欧洲各国的"协调"方针，为日后"四国同盟"的建立打下了基础。

The German bureaucrat built upon it a whole structure of preferences for German trade. Of what use to Britain under her northern skies was the most favored nation clause when Germany granted a concession to Italy in the matter of import duties on olive-oil? Would there not also be railway trucks to be returned to Italy which might as well return loaded with German exports? The whole system of most voluminous and intricate commercial treaties between Germany and her neighbors was based on a minute study of commercial routes and of the lie of productive areas. The German official was thinking in the concrete detail of "living", while his British counterpart was absorbed in the negative principle of "letting live".

　　　　※　　　　※　　　　※　　　　※　　　　※　　　　※　　　　※　　　　※　　　　※

Kaiser Wilhelm told us that this War was a struggle between two views of the world. "View" is characteristic of the organizer; he sees things from above. Kipling agreed with the Kaiser, but in the language of simple men below, when he declared that there is human feeling and German feeling. The organizer, as organizer, is inevitably inhuman, or rather unhuman. No doubt both Kaiser and poet exaggerated in order to emphasize opposing tendencies; even a democracy must have organizers, just as there must be some remnant of kindliness even among the students of Kultur. The real question is as to which shall have the last word in the State — the idealists or the organizers. Internationalists are in futile revolt against all organization when they would have war of the proletariat on the bourgeoisie.

Democracy refuses to think strategically unless and until compelled to do so for purposes of defense. That, of course, does not prevent democracy from declaring war for an ideal, as was seen during the French Revolution. One of the inconsistencies of our pacifists today is that they

在实诚的科布登主义者眼中的意义有着天渊之别。德国的官吏阶层在此基础上，建立起了一整套有利于德国贸易的制度。当该国在橄榄油进口关税的问题上对意大利做出让步之后，对于英国北方的各个地区来说，这一最惠国条款又有什么用呢？会不会出现与其让铁路货车空着返回意大利，还不如让它们装满了德国的出口商品再返回意大利呢？德国与各个邻国之间的贸易条约为数众多且错综复杂，构成了一个完整的体系；它们都是在对各条商路和产区位置进行了缜密研究的基础之上制订出来的。德国的官吏阶层所考虑的，是关乎"生存"的实实在在的细节；而英国的官吏阶层所热衷的，却是"让别人生存"这种消极的原则。

※　　　　※　　　　※　　　　※　　　　※　　　　※　　　　※　　　　※　　　　※

德皇威廉告诉我们说，这场大战是世界上两种观点之间的斗争。"观点"正是组织者的典型特征；他是从上往下看问题的。虽说基普林赞同德皇的意见，但当他说到有"人类的感情"和"德国人的感情"这两种感情时，用的却是下层普通百姓的话语。组织者之所以成为组织者，必定是不近人情的，或者更准确一点来说，必定是没有人性的。毫无疑问，德皇和基普林这位诗人都言过其实了，他们的目的都是为了强调两种对立的倾向，因为就算是一个民主国家，也必定具有组织者；这一点，跟即便是"德国文化"培养出来的学生身上也必定存有某种仁慈之心，道理是一样的。真正的问题在于，一国之中究竟是理想主义者还是组织者具有最终的决定权。当国际主义者想要发动无产阶级对资产阶级的战争时，他们其实就是在对一切组织做着无益的反抗。

除非是为了防御，否则民主国家是不愿从战略上来考虑问题的，并且它们一直要到不得不进行防御的时候才会这样做。自然，这并不会阻碍到民主国家为了某种就像人

基普林（Rudyard Kipling, 1865～1936）。英国作家，其作品主要反映英国殖民扩张政策。1907年获诺贝尔文学奖。

so often urge intervention in the affairs of other nations. In the Middle Ages vast unorganized crowds set out to march against the infidel and perished recklessly by the way. It was not from lack of warning that the Western democracies were unprepared for the present War. At the same moment, early in this century, to cite only the case of Great Britain, three honored voices were appealing to our sovereign people and were not heard: Lord Rosebery called for efficiency, Mr. Chamberlain for economic defense, and Lord Roberts for military training. Democracy implies rule by consent of the average citizen, who does not view things from the hill-tops, for he must be at his work in the fertile plains. There is no good in railing at the characteristics of popular government, for they are its qualities and no mere defects. President Wilson admits them when he says we must make the world a safe place henceforth for democracies. They were

们在法国大革命中见到的理想而发动战争。如今我们的和平主义者言行不一致的一个方面，就是他们经常要求我们去干涉别国的事务。在中世纪，大批毫无组织的民众曾经成群结队地出发去对抗异教徒，却都稀里糊涂地死在了半路上。西方民主国家之所以对眼前的这场战争毫无准备，并不是由于它们事先没有得到警示。其实早在本世纪初，只要一提到大不列颠，就总会有三位可敬的人向我国那些至高无上的人民发出呼吁，可他们的呼声却总是无人理睬：罗斯伯里勋爵曾经呼吁提高效率，张伯伦先生曾经呼吁注意经济防御，罗伯茨勋爵曾经呼吁加强军事训练。民主意味着必经普通公民同意才能统治国家，但由于必须在肥沃的平原上劳作，所以普通公民并不是从山顶居高临下地看待事物的。指责民选政府的这些特点并无益处，因为这些特征不仅是民选政府的缺点，也是民选政府的优点。当威尔逊总统说，我们必须让世界从今往后变成民主国家的安身之所

罗斯伯里勋爵（Archibald
Philip Primrose，1847～1929）。
英国自由党政治家，曾任英国首相
（1894年～1895年在任）。

张伯伦。此处指老张伯伦（Joseph
Chamberlain，1836～1914）。英国著
名的企业家、政治家、演说家，也是著
名的激进帝国主义者，曾任英国对外贸
易大臣、殖民大臣。他是签订慕尼黑协
定、时任英国首相的张伯伦之父。

罗伯茨勋爵（Frederick
Roberts，1832～1914）。
英国政治家和军事家，曾
任英军总司令。

no less admitted in the British House of Commons when responsible Ministers took pride in the fact that, save in respect of the defensive force of the Navy, we were not prepared for the War.

The democrat thinks in principles, be they — according to his idiosyncrasy — ideals, prejudices, or economic laws. The organizer, on the other hand, plans construction, and, like an architect, must consider the ground for his foundations and the materials with which he will build. It must be concrete and detailed consideration, for bricks may be most suitable for his walls, but stone for his lintels, and timber and slate for his roof. If it be a State which he is erecting — not, be it noted, a nation which is growing — he must carefully consider the territory which it is desirable to occupy and the social structures — not economic laws — which are to his hand as the result of history. So he opposes his strategy to the ethics of the democrat.

Fierce moralists allow no extenuation for sin however persistent the temptation, and great

时，他就是承认了这些特征。而当那些负有责任的重臣还在因为我们海军的防御力量对这次战争做好了准备（其他方面却毫无准备）的事实而沾沾自喜的时候，英国下议院实际上也同样认可了这些特征。

民主主义者是按照原则来考虑问题的，而不论这些原则究竟是理想、成见还是经济法则——这些方面，都取决于民主主义者的个人癖好。另一方面，组织者则会对建设做出规划，并且会像一名建筑师那样，必须考虑地基以及自己所需的建筑材料。这种考虑必须具体而周到，因为砖头可能最适合于砌墙，石头可能最适合于砌门楣，而木料和板瓦则可能最适合于盖屋顶。如果他建立的是一个国家——应当注意，这里不是指一个正在成长中的国家——那么，他就必须仔细考虑可以占有哪些领土，考虑历史遗留给他的社会结构而非经济法则这个问题。这样，他就会让自己的战略思想与民主主义者的道德准则形成对立。

undoubtedly must be the reward in heaven for the slum-dweller who "keeps straight". But practical reformers give much of their thought to the Housing problem! Of late our political moralists have been very fierce. They preached the narrow way of "no annexations, no indemnities". In other words, they refused to reckon with the realities of geography and economics. Had we but faith as a grain of mustard seed in average human nature, could we not remove the mountains!

Practical sense, however, warns us that it would be wise to seize the present opportunity, when for once the democratic nations are efficiently armed, to make the world a safe place for democracies when going about their ordinary business. In other words, we must see to the housing problem of our coming League of Nations. We must reckon presciently with the realities of space and time, and not be content merely to lay down on paper good principles of conduct. The good may not always appear the same even to those who are now Allies, and will pretty surely appear not good, for a time at least, to our present enemies.

"No annexations, no indemnities" was no doubt a rallying cry not meant by its authors to support existing tyrannies. But it is surely legitimate to remark that there is a wide difference between the attitude of the lawyer with his presumptions unless there be proof

约瑟夫二世（1741～1790）。奥地利哈布斯堡-洛林王朝的神圣罗马帝国皇帝。他在国内推行了一系列激进的改革，却忽略了帝国内部矛盾的复杂性，故其改革措施遭到了强烈的反对。

狂热的道学家不容许有罪不罚，而不管诱人犯罪的因素有多么持久，并且还认为那些虽然住在贫民窟里却"循规蹈矩"的人，死后在天堂里必定会得到极大的好报。可是，务实的改革者们却还在住房问题上大费心思!近来，我国的政治道学家们也狂热得很。他们不遗余力地宣扬，要走"不吞并，不索赔"这条正道。换言之就是，他们根本不愿认真地去思考地理上的现实和经济上的现实。如果我们对普通人的本性只有"一粒芥种"式的那种信仰[1]，又怎能移走座座大山呢!

然而，务实观念提醒我们，当各个民主国家为了在正常运作时让世界变成一个安全之所而难得一次有效地把自己武装起来的时候，我们最好还是抓住眼前的这个机会。也就是说，我们必须确保未来的国际联盟。我们必须预先考虑空间与时间两种现实，而不能只满足于在纸面上制定出好的行动原则。就算是对此时的协约国来说，这些行动原则也可能并非总是同样良好的，而对我们目前的敌人来说，这些原则显然至少也会在一段

---

[1] a grain of mustard seed：一粒芥种。语出《圣经·路加福音》：And the Lord said, If ye had faith as a grain of mustard seed …（主说，你们若有信心像一粒芥种……）。后多用于指"大有发展前途的微小事物"。

to the contrary, and that of the business man untied by formulae. The one does things, and the other, at best, allows them to be done.

In the past, democracy has looked with suspicion on the activities even of popular governments, and therein has shown a wise self-knowledge. It used to be thought, and sooner or later will be thought again, that the main function of the State in free countries is to prevent tyrannous things from being done whether by offenders at home or invaders from abroad. Average citizenship is not a likely base for daring innovations. Adventurers, sole or corporate, must therefore be left to blaze the way to progress. In military and bureaucratic States it is otherwise; Napoleon could be a pioneer, as might have been Joseph II. if his conservative subjects had not successfully revolted against him. In Prussia all progress has been State-engineered, but then progress there has meant merely increase of efficiency.[1]

To save democracy, however, in its recent jeopardy we suspended the very safeguards of democracy, and allowed our governments to organize us not merely for defense but for offense. Had the War been short, this would have been a mere parenthesis in history. But it has been long, and social structures have wasted in part, and in part have been diverted to new uses, so that habits and vested interests have dissolved, and all society is as clay in our hands, if only we have the cunning to mold it while it is still yielding. But the art of the clay-molder, as of the worker in hot metal, lies not merely in knowing what he would make, but also in allowing for the properties of the material in which he is working. He must not only have artistic aims, but also technical knowledge; his human initiative must reckon with reality; he must cultivate his "ways

[1] Twelve years ago I met a Prussian Staff Officer who told me that be spent his life trying to save half an hour on mobilisation.

时期内显得不那么好。

毫无疑问，"不吞并，不索赔"是个激动人心的口号，而提出此种口号的人也并非是在支持现存的暴政。不过，说律师们那种除非有反证否则就必须坚持推定的态度与商人打破常规的态度之间有着天渊之别，这种说法却是完全合情合理的。有些人是办实事的，而另一些人充其量也不过是容许他们办这些实事罢了。

在过去，就算是对民选政府的做法，民主也是存着怀疑之心来看待的，从而表现出了一种审慎的自觉意识。人们以前经常认为，并且将来迟早还会同样认为，自由国家中国家机构的主要作用，就是防止出现暴政，无论这种暴政究竟是国内违法乱纪之人所导致的，还是国外入侵者所导致的。普通的老百姓，不太可能成为大胆革新的基础。因此开辟进步道路的重任，就只能由单个的或者一群冒险家来完成了。由军人和官僚体系掌控的国家，情况却并不一样；拿破仑可能是一个先驱，而约瑟夫二世本来也可以这样，要是他手下那些保守的国民没有起来反抗他并且成功了的话。在普鲁士，所有的进步措施都是由国家设计的；但另一方面，该国的进步措施不过都是为了提高效率罢了。［作者注：12年之前，我曾遇到过普鲁士军队里的一位参谋，他告诉我说，他终生都在致力于节省半个小时的动员时间。］

然而，为了在近来的危难处境中拯救民主，我们却已经废止了那些本是保卫民主的安全措施，允许政府不仅可以为了防御、也可以为了进攻而把我们组织起来。倘若战争为时甚短，那么这不过是历史上的一个小插曲罢了。但是，此次战争旷日持久，社会结构中的一部分已经浪费掉了，还有一部分则被转做了新的用途；因此习惯和既得利益集

and means" mind, while he tries to retain his ideals of form.

As the artist endeavors to his dying day to learn ever more about the medium in which he works — and not merely more in a scientific sense, but in a practical "tactile" way, gaining, as we say, greater command over his material — so has it been with the knowledge of humanity at large in regard to the Realities of the round world on which we must practice the intricate art of living together. It is not merely that we have amassed vast encyclopedias of fact, but that, as we live through each new epoch, we see all the past and all the present with new eyes and from new standpoints. It is obvious that these four years of war have wrought a change in human outlook the like of which was not effected in all the previous life of those of us who have gray hairs. Yet, when we look back with our present knowledge, is it not clear that the currents of thought now running so tumultuously were already setting in gently some twenty years ago? In the last years of last century and the first of this, the organizers at Berlin and the minorities in London and Paris had already discerned the new drift of the straws.[1]

I propose trying to depict some of the Realities, geographical and economic, in their twentieth-century perspective. The facts will most of them be old and familiar. But, in the language of the Mediaeval schoolmen, there is a great difference between Vera causa and Causa causans — mere academic learning and the realization which impels to action.

---

[1] Mr. Chamberlain resigned from the Cabinet in order to free himself as a leader in September, 1903, and Lord Roberts resigned from Commander-in-Chief with a similar idea in January, 1904.

团已经分解开来,而只要我们有能耐在它还松软的时候去塑造它,那么整个社会就将变成我们手中的一团陶泥。但是,泥塑工人的技艺与热金属铸模工人的技术一样,不仅必须知道自己要制造什么样的产品,还须考虑到自己所用材料的性能。他既须带有艺术目的,还得掌握技术知识;他在发挥人的主动性时,还必须考虑到现实情况;他在试图保持形式上的种种理想时,还须培养自己那种"手段和方法"式的思维。

艺术家到死都在努力学习与材料相关的更多知识——并且,不只是更多地从科学的角度,而是用一种务实的、"感触的"方式来学习——从而像我们所称的那样,更好地掌握和运用艺术材料,而整个人类获得关于这个圆形世界现实情况的知识的过程,也是这样;在这个世界上,我们必须不断练习共同生活这门复杂的艺术才行。这一过程,并非仅仅是我们积累了一大堆关于事实的百科全书,而是随着经历每一个新的时代,我们都会用新的眼光、从新的角度来看待过去发生的一切与现在的一切。很显然,这4年的战争已经为人类的前景带来了改变,而像我们这种已生华发的人在过去的一生当中,都没有发生过这样的改变。然而,当带着我们目前的知识去回顾过往的时候,如今涌动得这般喧嚣的那些思想潮流,大约20年前其实就已经平缓发端了,这一点难道不是很明显的吗?在上个世纪的最后几年和本世纪的头几年里,柏林的组织者以及伦敦和巴黎的少数人,事实上早已看出这种新的苗头了。[作者注:1903年9月,为了不再担任领导人,张伯伦先生辞退了内阁职务;1904年1月,罗伯茨勋爵也出于同样的考虑而辞去了总司令一职。]

在下文中,笔者打算从20世纪的远景角度,来描述一下若干的地理现状和经济现状。其中,绝大多数都是些年代久远、且人们都已熟知的事实。不过,用中世纪经院哲学家的话来说,在真正原因与直接原因——即纯粹的学问与迫使人采取行动的认识——之间,还是有着天渊之别的。

III   THE SEAMAN'S POINT OF VIEW

"And God said, Let the waters be gathered together in one place"

The physical facts of geography have remained substantially the same during the fifty or sixty centuries of recorded human history. Forests have been cut down, marshes have been drained, and deserts may have broadened, but the outlines of land and water, and the lie of mountains and rivers have not altered except in detail. The influence of geographical conditions upon human activities has depended, however, not merely on the realities as we now know them to be and to have been, but in even greater degree on what men imagined in regard to them. The ocean has been one throughout history, but for effective human purposes there were two oceans, Western and Eastern, until the Cape of Good Hope was rounded only four hundred years ago. So did it happen that Admiral Mahan in the closing years of last century could still base a new message in regard to sea-power on a text from the first chapter of Genesis. The ocean was one ocean all the time, but the practical meaning of that great reality was not' wholly understood until a few years ago — perhaps it is only now being grasped in its entirety.

Each century has had its own geographical perspective. Men still living, though past the

第三章　海洋民族的观点

"上帝曰：让世间之水，汇聚一处。"[1]

在人类有史以来的五、六千年间，地理方面的现实情况基本上都保持着一致。虽说森林被砍伐、沼泽被排干、沙漠的范围也可能扩大了，但除了局部之处，海洋与陆地的轮廓、山川河流的位置并没有改变。然而，地理环境对人类活动的影响，并非仅仅依赖于我们如今所知的、目前和过去的现实，甚至还在更大程度上依赖于人们如何去设想这些现实。在整个历史上，海洋始终都是一个整体，可人类却出于实用目的而把它分成了两个部分，即东大洋和西大洋，直到区区400年前人类绕航好望角之后才不再如此。这样，海军上将马汉[2]才会在上个世纪的最后几年中，仍根据《创世纪》[3]第一章中的文句，提出自己关于海权的新论点。虽说海洋一直以来就是一个整体，但直到几年之前，人们才全面理解这个伟大现实的实际意义——或许只是到了如今，人们才理解了这个现实的全部意义呢。

每一个世纪，都有着各自的地理学远景。如今仍然在世但过了服兵役年龄的人，

---

[1] 语出《圣经·创世纪》。原文为：And God said, Let the waters under the heaven be gathered together unto one place …

[2] Mahan：马汉（Alfred Thayer Mahan，1840~1914）。美国著名的海军上将和地缘战略学家，也是"海权论"的提出者。

[3] Genesis：《创世纪》。基督教《圣经》中的首卷，讲述神创造世间万物的经过。

军事理论家马汉（Alfred Thayer Mahan, 1840～1914）。美国著名的海军上将和地缘战略学家，也是"海权论"的提出者。

史沫兹将军（Jan Christiaan Smuts, 1870～1950）。前英属南非军事领导人和政治家，曾任南非战争中布尔军队的司令（1899～1902年）和南非联邦总理（1919～1924及1939～1948年在任）。

age of military service, were taught from a map of the world on which nearly all the interior of Africa was a blank; yet last year General Smuts could address the Royal Geographical Society on the German ambition to control the world from the now explored vantage-ground of Central Africa. The geographical perspective of the twentieth century differs, however, from that of all the previous centuries in more than mere extension. In outline our geographical knowledge is now complete. We have lately attained to the North Pole, and have found that it is in the midst of a deep sea, and to the South Pole, and have found it upon a high plateau. With those final discoveries the book of the pioneers has been closed. No considerable fertile new land, no important mountain-range, and no first-class river can any more be the reward of adventure. Moreover, the

上学时学到的世界地图上，非洲大陆内部差不多还是空白一片；可到了去年，史沫兹将军却能在皇家地理学会进行讲演，论述德国人想要利用如今已经勘探清楚的中非地区、并且利用那儿的有利地位来控制世界的野心了。然而，20世纪的地理远景与以前各个世纪地理远景的差异，却并非仅仅只是范围上有所不同。总体来说，我们的地理知识如今几近完整了。近来，人们成功地到达了北极，发现该地为一处深海所环绕着；人们也成功地抵达了南极，并且发现该地位于一处高原之上。有了这些结论性的发现之后，先驱们的使命就算是告一段落了。不会有再有诸多肥沃的新大陆，不会再有重要的山脉和主要的河流，还需经过探险才能发现了。此外，世界地图刚一粗略地制成，所有陆地便都标定了界限，从政治上被瓜分掉了。无论我们考虑的是地球表面事物之间在自然上、经济上、军事上还是政治上的相互

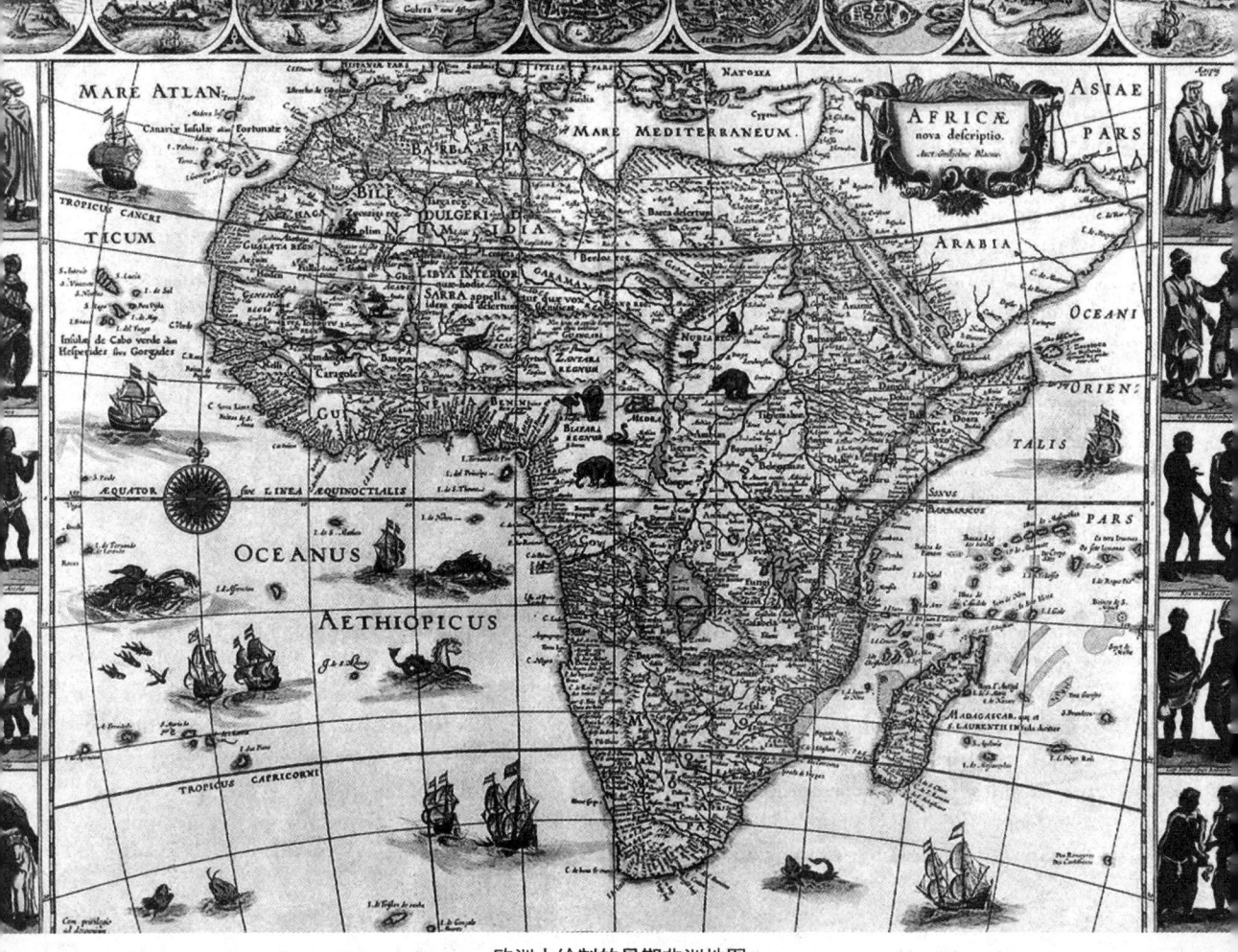

欧洲人绘制的早期非洲地图

map of the world had hardly been sketched before claims to the political ownership of all the dry land had been pegged out. Whether we think of the physical, economic, military, or political interconnection of things on the surface of the globe, we are row for the first time presented with a closed system. The known does not fade any longer through the half–known into the unknown; there is no longer elasticity of political expansion in lands beyond the pale. Every shock, every disaster or superfluity, is now felt even to the antipodes, and may indeed return from the antipodes, as the air waves from the eruption of the volcano Krakatoa in the year 1883 were propelled in rings over the globe until they converged to a point in the opposite hemisphere, and

关联，如今首次呈现在我们面前的，都是一个封闭的体系了。人类已知的事实不会再衰退为一知半解，进而变成未知的事实；而对于界外土地[1]，人们也不可能再灵活地进行政治扩张了。每一次地震、每一场灾难或者每一次生产过剩，即便是发生在地球的另一边，地球这一面的人们如今也可以感知得到，而且事实上它们也有可能从地球的那一边反转回来，就像1883年喀拉喀托火山[2]爆发后，喷出的气浪呈环状在地球上推进，直到

---

[1] Beyond the Pale：界外之地。The Pale原指12世纪后才并入英国的爱尔兰东部地区，后来 beyond the Pale多用于指"越轨（之事），越界"。

[2] Krakatoa：喀拉喀托。印度尼西亚的一座活火山，其1883年的喷发是人类历史上最大的火山喷发之一，导致大约5万人死亡。

thence diverged again to meet once more over Krakatoa, the seat of their origin. Every deed of humanity will henceforth be echoed and reechoed in like manner round the world. That, in the ultimate analysis, is why every considerable State was bound to be drawn into the recent War, if it lasted, as it did last, long enough.

To this day, however, our view of the geographical realities is colored for practical purposes by our preconceptions from the past. In other words, human society is still related to the facts of geography not as they are, but in no small measure as they have been approached in the course of history. It is only with an effort that we can yet realize them in the true, the complete, and therefore detached, perspective of the twentieth century. This War has taught us rapidly, but there are still vast numbers of our citizens who look out on to a vivid Western foreground, but only to a very dim Eastern background. In order therefore to appreciate where we now stand, it will be worth while to consider shortly the stages by which we have arrived. Let us begin with the succeeding phases of the seaman's outlook.

※　　　　※　　　　※　　　　※　　　　※　　　　※　　　　※　　　　※　　　　※

Imagine a vast tawny desert, raised a few hundred feet above the sea level. Imagine a valley with precipitous rocky slopes trenched into this desert plateau, and the floor of the valley carpeted with a strip of black soil, through the midst of which winds northward for five hundred miles a silvery navigable river. That river is the Nile flowing from where the granite rocks of Assouan break its navigability at the first cataract to where its waters divide at the head of the Delta. From desert edge to desert edge across the valley is a crow-fly distance of some ten or twenty miles. Stand on one of the brinks with the desert behind you; the rocky descent falls from your feet to the strip of plain below, and away over the floods of the summertime, or the green of the growing winter-time, or the golden harvests of the spring, you are faced by the opposing wall

在地球另一面的某个地方汇集起来，然后再次扩散，并再次在其发源地喀拉喀托火山之上汇集起来那样。自此以后，人类的所有行为，都会通过相同的方式在全世界产生反响并且一再回荡。归根结底，倘若这次战争持续得足够长久——事实也的确如此——那么每个大国必定都会卷入其中，原因就在这里。

然而时至今日，我们对地理现实的观点，仍然因为带有来自过去的那种先入之见，所以为了实利目的而被歪曲了。换言之就是，人类社会和地理现实的关系，并非基于如今的地理事实，而是在对待此种关系时，我们很大程度上依然沿用了历史上的做法。只有通过努力，我们才能用一种正确、全面、因而也是客观的、20世纪的视角来认识这些地理现实。此次战争让我们很快得到了教训，可我们的公民当中却仍然有许多人，虽说清清楚楚地面对着西方国家的前景，但对东方国家的背景却只有一种极其模糊的印象。因此，为了理解目前的处境，简单研究一下我们业已经历过的各个阶段，就是一件很有意义的事情。我们不妨先从研究海洋民族的观点所经历的不同阶段开始。

※　　　　※　　　　※　　　　※　　　　※　　　　※　　　　※　　　　※　　　　※

设想一下，有一处褐色大漠，海拔数百英尺。再设想一下，有一处峡谷，两岸崖壁峭立，切入了这片大漠高原；谷底则是黑土成带，有一条银白如练、可以通航的长河蜿蜒其中，绵延500英里，滔滔向北。这条大河就是尼罗河，它从阿斯旺一路奔涌而下，直到尼罗河三角洲顶部，然后分流入海；阿斯旺的花岗岩形成了第一道大瀑布，阻断了航路。沙漠两边，横跨峡谷的直线距离大约是10到20英里。站在峭壁一侧，身后便是沙漠；峭壁从脚边一路下落，直达下面的那片平原——放眼望去，或是夏季肆虐的洪

古代埃及人生活

of rock rising to the other desert. The recesses in those rock fronts were carved long ago into cavernous temples and tombs, and the salients into mighty effigies of kings and gods. Egypt, in this long sunken belt, was anciently civilized because all the essential physical advantages were here combined for men to work upon. On the one hand were a rich soil, abundant water, and a powerful sunshine; hence fertility for the support of a population in affluence. On the other hand was a smooth waterway within half a dozen miles or less of every field in the country. There was also motive power for shipping, since the river-current carried vessels northward, and the Etesian winds — known on the ocean as the trade winds — brought them southward again. Fertility and a line of communications — manpower and facilities for its organization; there are

水，或是入冬时的一片碧绿，或是春季时金黄的庄稼，而眼前又有直抵对面沙漠的一堵峭壁。崖壁之上有许多的凹处，很久以前人们就将其凿成了一座座石窟寺庙和墓穴，而那些凸出来的地方则刻成了历代帝王和诸多神祇的雕像，座座都威风凛凛。处在这片狭长下凹地带上的埃及，远古时期就已开化，原因就是此处汇聚了一切基本的物质便利条件，可供人们利用。一方面，这里土地肥沃、水量丰富、日照强烈，因此富饶得很，足以让民众生活丰足。另一方面，该国的每一处土地，距那条通畅无阻的水道都不过5、6英里远，甚至更近。该国也有从事航运的动力，因为尼罗河河水会带着船只向北航行，而地中海季风——即海运中所称的贸易风——又会将船只吹向南行。富饶，再加上一条交通运输线——它们都提供了人力以及该国组织上的便利条件；这样，就具有了形成一

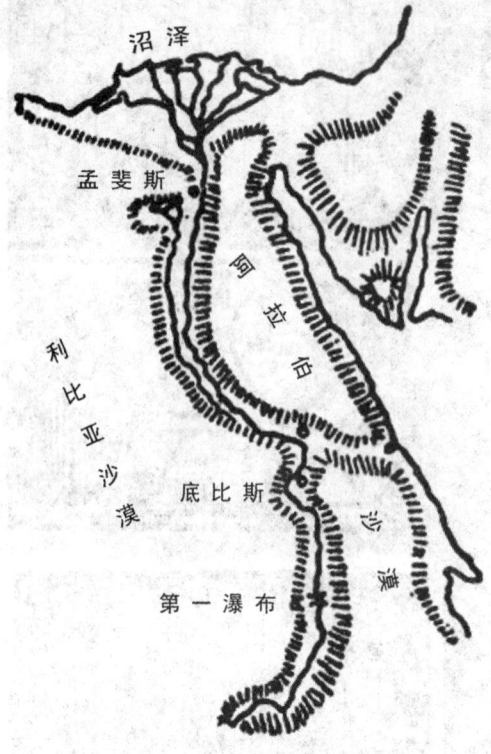

图1　一个孤立的河流世界

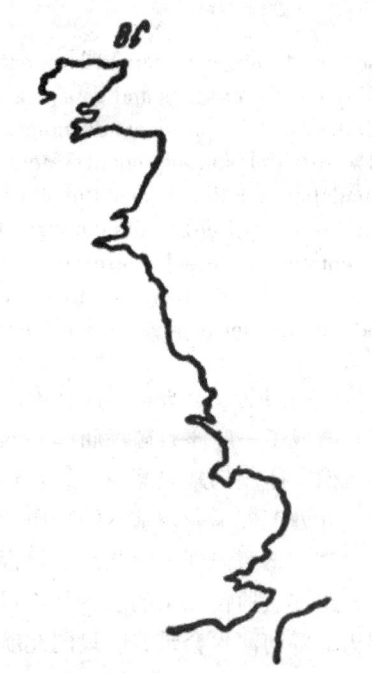

图2　用与前述河运图相同的比例尺绘制而成的英国沿海航运图

the essential ingredients for a kingdom.

We are asked to picture the early condition of Egypt as that of a valley held by a chain of tribes, who fought with one another in fleets of great war-canoes, just as later tribes have fought on the river Congo in our own time. Some one of these tribes, having defeated its neighbors, gained possession of a longer section of the valley, a more extensive material basis for its man-power, and on that basis organized further conquests. At last the whole length of the valley was brought under a single rule, and the kings of all Egypt established their palace at Thebes. Northward and southward, by boat on the Nile, traveled their administrators — their messengers and their magistrates. Eastward and westward lay the strong defense of the deserts, and at the northern limit, against the sea pirates, a belt of marsh round the shore of the Delta.[1]

[1] See The Dawn of History, by Professor J. L. Myres.

个王国所必不可少的那些要素了。

　　我们需要这样来描述埃及的早期环境才行：一连串的部落相继占据着尼罗河河谷，相互用大型战船组成舰队进行征战，就像如今我们所处的这个时代，仍有许多后起部族在刚果河上相互征战那样。当这些部落中的某一个打败了其邻近部落，占有了尼罗河河谷中较长的区域，并因而使其人力有了更广泛的物质基础之后，这个部落便会在此种基础之上开始发动进一步的征战。最终，整个河谷地区便被归入了一个君主的统治之下，而埃及历代国王也都把皇宫建在了底比斯。在尼罗河上乘坐船只南来北往的，都是历朝历代的行政人员——即各朝的使节和官吏。其东面和西面，都是沙漠所构成的强大屏障，而在北方边界，尼罗河三角洲沿岸的一条沼泽带又可以抵御海盗的袭扰。［作者注：请参阅 J·L·梅尔斯教授所著的《历史之黎明》一书。］

Now carry your mind to the "Great Sea", the Mediterranean. You have there essentially the same physical ingredients as in Egypt but on a larger scale, and you have based upon them not a mere kingdom but the Roman Empire. From the Phoenician coast for two thousand miles westward lies the broad water way to its mouth at Gibraltar, and on either hand are fertile shorelands with winter rains and harvest sunshine. But there is a distinction to be made between the dwellers along the Nile banks and those along the Mediterranean shores. The conditions of human activity are relatively uniform in all parts of Egypt; each of the constituent tribes would have its farmers and its boatmen. But the races round the Mediterranean became specialized; some were content to till their fields and navigate their rivers at home, but others gave most of their energy to seamanship and foreign commerce. Side by side, for instance, dwelt the home-staying, corn-growing Egyptians and the adventurous Phoenicians. A longer and more sustained effort of organization was therefore needed to weld all the kingdoms of the Mediterranean into a single political unit.

Modern research has made it plain that the leading seafaring race of antiquity came at all times from that square of water between Europe and Asia which is known alternatively as the Aegean Sea and the Archipelago, the "Chief Sea" of the Greeks. Sailors from this sea would appear to have taught the Phoenicians their trade in days when as yet Greek was not spoken in the "Isles of the Gentiles". It is of deepest interest for our present purpose to note that the center of civilization in the pre-Greek world of the Aegean, according both to the indications of mythology and the recent excavations, was in the Island of Crete. Was that the first base of sea-power? From that home did the seamen fare who, sailing northward, saw the coast of the rising

现在，我们不妨把心思放到地中海这个"伟大之海"上来。这里具有本质上与埃及相似的物质要素，不过此处这些要素具有更大的规模，因此以这些要素为基础而建立起来的，并非仅仅是一个王国，而是整个罗马帝国。从腓尼基[1]沿海往西2000英里，绵亘着一条辽阔浩淼的水路，直达直布罗陀海口，并且两岸沃土千里，冬季雨水丰沛，收获时节日照充足。不过，尼罗河沿岸居民和地中海两岸居民之间，还是有所不同的。在埃及各地，适于人类活动的条件相对都比较统一；组成王国的每一个部落当中，都会有各自的农民和船夫。但是，居住在地中海沿岸的各个民族却是术业有专攻；有些人满足于在家种地，或者从事国内河运业，而其他人却把大部分精力都投入了掌握航海技术和进行国际贸易方面。打个比方，这就像是居家务农、种植谷物的埃及人与喜欢冒险的腓尼基人比邻而居了。因此，要把地中海沿岸的各个王国紧密联合起来形成一个统一的政治单位，就需要付出更长久、更持之以恒的努力去组织才行。

现代研究业已表明，那个从事航海的最主要的古代民族，一直都是来自欧亚大陆之间的那片方形水域——这片水域或称爱琴海和爱琴列岛，是希腊人的"主海"。来自这片海域的水手，似乎在这些"异教徒群岛"上还没有说希腊语的时候，就把他们的买卖交给了腓尼基人。根据神话所示和近代发掘的结果，在希腊诞生之前，爱琴海地区的文明中心位于克里特岛上；注意到这一点，与我们眼下的目标有着深切的利害关系。那里是不是有史以来的第一个海权基地呢？从这处故土而来的那些海员，是不是遇到过一些向北航行的人，那些人因为看到太阳在自己右边升起、在自己左边落下，便把他们右边

---

[1] Phoenecian：腓尼基人（的）。腓尼基是古代地中海东岸地区一系列小城邦的总称，其地域大概位于黎凡特海岸中部的狭长地带。

腓尼基商船

sun to their right hand, and of the setting sun to their left hand, and named the one Asia and the other Europe? Was it from Crete that the sea-folk settled round the other shores of the Aegean "sea-chamber", forming to this day a coastal veneer of Greek population in front of peoples of other race a few miles inland? There are so many islands in the Archipelago that the name has become, like the Delta of Egypt, one of the common descriptive terms of geography. But Crete is the largest and most fruitful of them. Have we here a first instance of the importance of the larger base for sea-power? The man-power of the sea must be nourished by land-fertility somewhere, and other things being equal — such as security of the home and energy of the people — that power will control the sea which is based on the greater resources.

The next phase of Aegean development teaches apparently the same lesson. Horse-riding tribes of Hellenic speech came down from the north into the peninsula which now forms the

的陆地叫做亚细亚，而把左边的大陆叫做欧罗巴呢？一些航海者在爱琴海这个"海室"四周的其他海岸定居下来，形成了一个沿海的希腊人外圈，处在内陆方向数英里之外的其他民族前面，并且直到如今；这些航海者们是不是来自克里特岛呢？爱琴列岛中的岛屿数不胜数，使得"列岛"这个名称也与埃及的"三角洲"一样，已然变成地理学上的一个常用术语了。不过，克里特岛是其中最大的一个，也是其中成就最为斐然的一个岛屿。那么，我们在此是不是有了一个一流的例子，能够说明较大的基地对于海权而言极其重要呢？海上的人力，必定要由陆上某个地方的富饶资源来加以供养，因此，倘若其他方面——比如本土的安全和民众的精神状况——不相上下，那么具有更多资源做后盾的那种人力，便能掌控海洋。

爱琴海地区的下一个发展阶段，显然也给了我们相同的教训。那些说希腊语的游牧部落从北部南下，进入了如今形成希腊本土的希腊半岛并定居下来，从而把这个半岛上

mainland of Greece, and settled, Hellenizing the early inhabitants. These Hellenes advanced into the terminal limb of the peninsula, the Peloponnese, slenderly attached to the continent by the isthmus of Corinth. Thence, organizing sea-power on their relatively considerable peninsular base, one of the Hellenic tribes, the Dorians, conquered Crete, a smaller though completely insular base.

Some centuries passed, during which the Greeks sailed round the southern headlands of the Peloponnese into the Ionian Sea, and colonized along the shores of that sea also. So the peninsula came to be a citadel in the midst of the Greek sea-world. Along the outer shores of the twin waters, Aegean and Ionian, the Greek colonists were but a fringe exposed to attack from behind. Only in the central peninsula were they relatively, although as the sequel shows not absolutely, safe.

To the eastern, outer shore of the Aegean the Persians came down from the interior against the Greek cities by the sea, and the Athenian fleet carried aid from the peninsular citadel to the

的早期居民都希腊化了。这些希腊人挺进到了半岛最南端的伯罗奔尼撒，那里有一条细长的科林斯地峡与大陆相连。自此以后，属于希腊部落之一的多里安人通过以其相对较大的半岛为基地而建立起来的海上力量征服了克里特岛；克里特岛虽说面积相对较小，却是一个完完全全的海岛基地。

几个世纪过去了，期间希腊人航海绕过伯罗奔尼撒南部诸岬角进入了爱奥尼亚海，还沿着爱奥尼亚海海岸进行了拓殖。所以，伯罗奔尼撒这个半岛就成了地处希腊海洋世界中的一个大本营。在爱琴海和爱奥尼亚海这两处姊妹海域的外侧沿岸，希腊殖民者只占领了边缘地带，很容易受到来自背后的攻击。只有在半岛中心地带，他们才相对比较安全；可后来的事实表明，即便是在半岛中心地带，他们也并不是绝对安全的。

在东边，波斯人在爱琴海外侧海岸从内陆南下，进攻沿海的希腊城市，而雅典的舰队便从这个半岛大本营出发，越洋过海，前去支援那些受到威胁的亲族，从而使得海

伯罗奔尼撒战争

希波战争之萨拉米斯海战

threatened kinsfolk over the water, and issue was joined between sea–power and land–power. A Persian sea–raid was defeated at Marathon, and the Persians then resorted to the obvious strategy of baffled land–power; under King Xerxes they marched round, throwing a bridge of boats over the Dardanelles, and entered the peninsula from the north, with the idea of destroying the nest whence the wasps emerged which stung them and flew elusively away. The Persian effort failed, and it was reserved for the half–Greek, half–barbaric Macedonians, established in the root of the Greek Peninsula itself, to end the first cycle of sea–power by conquering to south of them the Greek sea–base, and then marching into Asia, and through Syria into Egypt, and on the way destroying Tyre of the Phoenicians. Thus they made a "closed sea" of the Eastern Mediterranean by depriving both the Greeks and the Phoenicians of their bases. That done, the

权和陆权之间爆发了纷争。他们在马拉松挫败了波斯人发动的一次海上袭击，于是波斯人便退了一步，采取受到了挫折的陆上力量所要采取的那种明显战略；在薛西斯[1]国王的率领下，他们迂回进军，在达达尼尔海峡上用船只架起浮桥，从北方攻入了伯罗奔尼撒半岛，想要捣毁这个马蜂窝——因为从这个蜂窝里冒出来的马蜂，蜇了他们就跑，根本逮不住。波斯人的这次进击失败了，直到后来半希腊化、半属野蛮民族、且其祖先原本就生活在希腊半岛上的马其顿人崛起，才结束了海上力量的首个周期；马其顿人攻克了位于他们南边的那个希腊海上基地，然后又进军亚细亚，经由叙利亚进入了埃及，还在途中摧毁了腓尼基人的提尔港[2]。这样一来，他们便通过夺取希腊人和腓尼基人的基地，把东地中海变成了自己的一个"内海"。完成这些事情之后，马其顿国王亚历山大大帝便可以一身轻松地进军上亚细亚了。虽然我们可以说船只具有机动性、舰队也便于

[1] Xerxes：薛西斯（Xerxes I，公元前486年～公元前465年）。波斯国王，又称"薛西斯大帝"。他曾于公元前480年率军在温泉关大败希腊军队，并洗劫了雅典，之后接连遭受惨败，退回波斯后又遭刺杀身亡。

[2] Tyre：提尔港。古代腓尼基人的首都，现属黎巴嫩。亚历山大大帝曾于公元前332年包围并占攻了此处。

Macedonian King Alexander could advance light-heartedly into Upper Asia. We may talk of the mobility of ships and of the long arm of the fleet, but, after all, sea-power is fundamentally a matter of appropriate bases, productive and secure. Greek sea-power passed through the same phases as Egyptian river-power. The end of both was the same; without the protection of a navy commerce moved securely over a water way because all the shores were held by one and the same land-power.

※　　　※　　　※　　　※　　　※　　　※　　　※　　　※　　　※

远征，但从根本上来说，海上力量归根结底还是取决于有没有一个物产丰富、安全稳固而又合适的基地。希腊海权所经历的阶段，与埃及的河权所经历的阶段并没有什么两样。二者的结局也是相同的；在没有海军保护的情况下，贸易之所以还能够安全地经由水路来进行，原因即在于水道沿岸全都是由同一个陆上强国占据着。

※　　　※　　　※　　　※　　　※　　　※　　　※　　　※　　　※

　　图3　希腊诸海，包括爱琴海和爱奥尼亚海。图中表明了克里特岛和希腊半岛这两个海上基地，以及薛西斯迂回包抄海上强国雅典的进军路线。

Now we go to the Western Mediterranean. Rome there began as a fortified town on a hill, at the foot of which was a bridge and a river–wharf. This hill–bridge–port–town was the citadel and market of a small nation of farmers, who tilled Latium, the "broad land" or plain, between the Apennines and the sea. "Father" Tiber was for shipping purposes merely a creek, navigable for the small sea–craft of those days, which entered thus from the coast a few miles into the midst of the plain, but that was enough to give Rome the advantage over her rivals, the towns crowning the Alban and Etruscan hills of the neighborhood. Rome had the bridge and the inmost port just as had London.

Based on the productivity of Latium, the Romans issued from the Tiber to traffic round the shores of the Western Mediterranean. Soon they came into competition with the Carthaginians, who were based on the fertility of the Mejerdeh valley in the opposite promontory of Africa. The First Punic or Phoenician War ensued, and the Romans victoriously held the sea. They then proceeded to widen their base by annexing all the peninsular part of Italy as far as the Rubicon River.

In the Second Punic War, the Carthaginian general, Hannibal, endeavored to outflank the Roman sea–power by marching round it, as Xerxes and Alexander had done in regard to the sea–powers opposed to them. He carried his army over the western narrows from Africa into Spain, and then advanced through Southern Gaul into Italy, He was defeated, and Rome annexed the Mediterranean coasts of Gaul and Spain. By taking Carthage itself in the

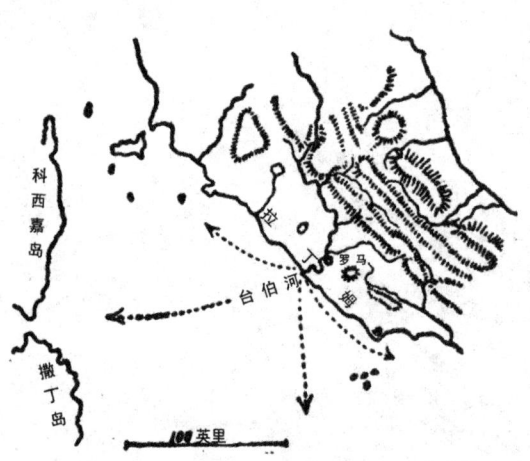

图4 拉丁姆：一处富饶的海上基地

现在，我们再来看一看西地中海。那里的罗马，起初只是一个筑有防御工事的山上城邦，山脚有着一座桥和一个沿河码头。这个"一山一桥一港"的城邦，是一个由农民所组成的小国的大本营和市场；而那些农民耕作的，则是地处亚平宁山脉和大海之间的拉丁姆这一"开阔地带"或者平原。就航运目的而言，台伯河这条"父亲河"不过是条小溪，只能航行当时的那种小型海船罢了——它们从沿海溯河而上，航行数英里便到了拉丁姆平原的中心地带；不过，就算那样，也足以让罗马具有了敌国所不具备的优势，胜过了附近地区阿尔班山和埃特鲁斯坎山上的其他城邦。罗马跟伦敦一样，既有桥，又拥有最深的港口。

以拉丁姆平原的丰富物产为基础，罗马人从台伯河出发，开始绕着西地中海沿岸进行贸易。不久之后，他们便开始与迦太基人展开争战，而后者所依赖的，是位于地中海对面非洲之角上的那个富庶的迈杰尔德河谷。接下来便爆发了第一次布匿战争，或称腓尼基战争，结果是罗马人获胜并控制了海洋。然后，他们便进而吞并了意大利在半岛上远至卢比孔河的那一部分领土，从而扩大了自己的基地。

在第二次布匿战争中，迦太基主将汉尼拔试图像过去薛西斯和亚历山大大帝对付那些敌对的海上强国一样，通过绕道进军来迂回包抄罗马这个海上强国。他率军越过西面的直布罗陀海峡，从非洲进入西班牙，然后穿过高卢南部地区，攻进了意大利。他被打败了，于是罗马又吞并了高卢和西班牙的地中海沿岸地区。在第三次布匿战争中，罗马

布匿战争

Third Punic War, she made a "closed sea" of the Western Mediterranean, for all the shores were held by one and the same land-power.

There remained the task of uniting the controls of the Western and Eastern basins of the Mediterranean, connected by the Sicilian Strait and the Strait of Messina. The Roman legions passed over into Macedonia and thence into Asia, but the distinction between Latin West and Greek East remained, as was evident when civil war came to be waged between the Roman Governors of the West and the East, Caesar and Antony. At the sea fight of Actium, one of the decisive battles of the world's history, the Western fleet of Caesar destroyed the Eastern fleet of Antony. Thenceforth for five centuries the entire Mediterranean was a "closed sea"; and we think in consequence of the Roman Empire as chiefly a land-power. No fleet was needed, save a few police vessels, to maintain as complete a command of the arterial sea-way of the Mediterranean as ever the Kings of Egypt exercised over their Nile-way. Once more land-

通过攻取迦太基本土，使得西地中海变成了它的一个"内海"，因为西地中海的所有沿岸，都被同一个陆上强国占领了。

罗马尚待完成的任务，就是把由西西里海峡和墨西拿海峡相连的地中海东、西两大海域统一控制起来。罗马军团越洋过海，攻入了马其顿，并从那里攻进了亚细亚，但说拉丁语的西部和说希腊语的东部之间那种差别却依然存在，因为东、西罗马的两位总督，即恺撒和安东尼之间开始爆发内战时，这种差别是非常明显的。亚克兴海战是世界历史上具有关键意义的战役之一；在此战中，恺撒率领的西罗马舰队摧毁了安东尼所率的东罗马舰队。自此以后，在长达5个世纪的时间里，整个地中海都成了罗马帝国的一个"内海"；也正是因为如此，我们才认为罗马帝国主要是一个陆上强国。除了少量的警用船只，罗马帝国根本不需要舰队，就能像埃及历代国王曾经控制尼罗河水道那样，

亚克兴海战：亚克兴，亦译阿克提姆。希腊西部的一处海角和古镇。公元前31年恺撒在此大败安东尼和埃及海军，为恺撒成为罗马帝国统治者打下了基础。

图5 两次旨在迂回包围海上强国的著名进军；同时也是把地中海"封锁"起来的一大胜利。

power terminated a cycle of competition upon the water by depriving sea-power of its bases. True that there had been the culminating sea battle of Actium, and that Caesar's fleet had won the reward of all finally successful fleets, the command over all the sea. But that command was not afterwards maintained upon the sea, but upon the land by holding the coasts.

※   ※   ※   ※   ※   ※   ※   ※   ※   ※

When Rome had completed the organization of her power round the Mediterranean, there followed a long transitional epoch, during which the oceanic development of Western civilization was gradually preparing. The transition began with the Roman road system, constructed for the greater mobility of the marching legions.

After the close of the Punic Wars four Latin-speaking provinces encircled the Western Mediterranean — Italy, Southern Gaul, Eastern and Southern Spain, and Carthaginian Africa. The outer boundary of the African province was protected by the Sahara Desert, and Italy had in rear the Adriatic moat, but in Gaul and Spain Rome found herself the uncomfortable neighbor of independent Celtic tribes. Thus the familiar dilemma of Empire presented itself; to advance and end the menace, or to entrench and shut it out, but leave it in being. A still virile

彻底地掌控住地中海这条海上动脉。通过夺取海上强国的基地，陆上强国便又一次结束了这一轮的水上争霸。亚克兴之战这样的终极海战的确发生过，而恺撒所率的舰队也的确像所有获得最后胜利的舰队一样，攫取了整个海洋的控制权。但是，这种控制权接下来并不是在海上得以保持的，而是通过占领沿海地区，在陆地上维持下来的。

※   ※   ※   ※   ※   ※   ※   ※   ※   ※

罗马完成其环地中海力量的组织工作之后，接下来就经历了一段长久的过渡时期，期间西方文明正逐步做好了向海洋扩张的准备工作。这种过渡，是从罗马的道路系统开始的，而罗马建立此种道路系统，本来是为了让罗马军团的进军具有更大的机动性。

3次布匿战争结束之后，便有4个说拉丁语的行省环绕着西地中海了——即意大利，南高卢，东、南西班牙以及迦太基属非洲。非洲行省的南界，有撒哈拉沙漠加以守护，而意大利后方也有亚得里亚海这道护城河；但在高卢，与西班牙、罗马人相邻的，却是一些令人不舒服的、独立不羁的凯尔特部族。所以，便出现了帝国熟悉的那种进退维谷

古代欧洲凯尔特人。凯尔特人是印欧民族的一支，最初分布在中欧，在前罗马帝国时期遍及欧洲西部、不列颠群岛和加拉提亚东南部。现尤指不列颠人或高卢人。

people chose the former course, and the frontier and the roads were carried through to the ocean along a thousand miles of frontage between Cape St. Vincent and the mouths of the Rhine. As a consequence the Latin portion of the Empire came to be based on two features of Physical Geography: on the one hand was the Latin Sea — the Western Mediterranean; and on the other hand was the Latin Peninsula, between the Mediterranean and the ocean.[1]

Julius Caesar penetrated to the Bay of Biscay, and built a fleet wherewith he defeated the fleet of the Veneti of Brittany. Then, because the Celts of Britain were giving help to their Gallic kinsmen, he crossed the Channel and smote them in their island base. A hundred years later the Romans conquered all the lower and more fruitful portion of Britain, and so eliminated the risk of the rise of a sea-power off the Gallic coast. In this way the Channel also became a "closed sea," controlled by land-power.

After four centuries the land-power of Rome waned, and the seas on either side of the Latin Peninsula then soon ceased to be "closed". The Norsemen raided over the North Sea from their fiords, and through the Channel, and through the Straits of Gibraltar, even into the recesses of the Mediterranean, enveloping with their sea-power the whole great peninsula. They seized forward bases in the islands of Britain and Sicily, and even nibbled at the mainland edges in Normandy and Southern Italy.

---

[1] I do not know whether these names, Latin Sea and Latin Peninsula, have been used beforehand. It seems to me that they serve to crystallize important generalizations, and I propose using them henceforth.

的局面；是挺身而出、消除此种威胁呢，还是广修战壕、把凯尔特部落拒之于外，并任由它存在下去呢？由于这个仍属年富力强的民族选择了前者，所以帝国的国境和道路便在圣文森特角和莱茵河河口之间绵延1000英里，直达大海了。这样一来，罗马帝国说拉丁语的那一部分领土，便开始依赖于自然地理学上的两个特征了：一个是拉丁海——即西地中海；另一个则是介于地中海和大西洋之间的拉丁半岛。〔作者注：我并不清楚前人是否用过"拉丁海"和"拉丁半岛"这两个名称。但在我看来，这两个名称将那些重要的一般性情况具体化了，因此我准备自此处起便继续沿用这两个名称。〕

裘力斯·恺撒率军深入到了比斯开湾，组建了一支舰队，并且凭借这支舰队，击败了布列塔尼[1]的威尼蒂人[2]的舰队。接下来，由于不列颠的凯尔特人向他们的高卢同族伸出了援手，所以恺撒便横渡英吉利海峡，在凯尔特人所据的不列颠这个海岛基地上将其击溃了。100年后，罗马人征服了不列颠岛南部和所有较为富庶的地区，从而消除了在高卢沿海之外兴起一个海上强国的危险。这样一来，英吉利海峡也变成了一个被陆上强国控制了的"内海"。

4个世纪之后，罗马这个陆上强国衰落下去，于是拉丁半岛两侧的海洋很快就不再"封闭"了。古挪威人从斯堪的纳维亚的诸峡湾出发，来到北海上四处劫掠，并且越过了英吉利海峡和直布罗陀海峡，甚至还攻入地中海地区各个港湾，从而将整个广袤的半岛全都置于其海上力量的包围之中了。他们还在不列颠群岛和西西里群岛上夺取了诸多的前沿基地，甚至还在诺曼底和意大利南部地区开始蚕食欧洲大陆的边缘。

---

[1] Brittany：布列塔尼。历史上的一个地区，原为法国西北部一省，位于英吉利海峡和比斯开湾之间的半岛上。公元500年，被盎格鲁－撒克逊人驱逐出家园的布立吞人定居于此。1532年该地区正式并入法国。

[2] Veneti：威尼蒂人。古代凯尔特部族之一，主要居住在高卢，即如今法国的布列塔尼地区。

图6　拉丁海，表明了3次布匿战争之后的罗马领土。

伊 斯 兰 教 教 徒

图7　拉丁半岛，被现代属于拉丁语系的各个国家占据着。

At the same time the Saracen camel-men came down from Arabia and took Carthage, Egypt, and Syria from the Empire — the provinces, that is to say, south of the Mediterranean. Then they launched their fleets on the water, and seized part of Sicily and part of Spain for overseas bases. Thus the Mediterranean ceased to be the arterial way of an Empire, and became the frontier moat dividing Christendom from Islam. But the greater sea-power of the Saracens enabled them to hold Spain, though north of the water, just as at an earlier time the greater sea-power of Rome had enabled her to hold Carthage, though south of the water.

For a thousand years Latin Christendom was thus imprisoned in the Latin Peninsula and its appendant island of Britain. Fifteen hundred miles

与此同时，骑着骆驼的撒拉逊游牧部落也由阿拉伯半岛南下，从帝国手中攫取了迦太基、埃及和叙利亚——也就是罗马帝国位于地中海南面的那几个行省。然后，他们又率领舰队，攻取了西西里岛的一部分和西班牙的部分地区，将其作为他们的海外基地。这样一来，地中海便不再是一个帝国的动脉干线，而变成划分基督教国家和伊斯兰教国家的边界鸿沟了。不过，虽说西班牙位于地中海以北，但撒拉逊人还是有着更强大的海上力量，所以能够占据西班牙；以前尽管迦太基位于地中海之南，但罗马帝国也拥有较为强大的海上力量，因此能够将其占领，这两种情况是一样的。

拉丁地区的基督教国家，就这样被禁锢在拉丁半岛及其附属的不列颠岛上，长达1000年之久。从古人所称的"神圣海角"[1]向东北方向而去，绵亘着直线距离长达1500

---

　　[1] Sacred Promontory：神圣海角。本是古希腊和罗马人用于指那些伸进海洋、具有战略意义的海角的通称，尤其是指那些修建了海神庙的海角。此处可能是指葡萄牙南部的圣文森特角。亦拼作Sacred Cape或Holy Promontory。

northeastward, measured in a straight line, trends the oceanic coast from the Sacred Promontory of the ancients to the Straits at Copenhagen, and fifteen hundred miles eastward, measured in the same way, lies the sinuous Mediterranean coast from the Sacred Promontory to the Straits at Constantinople. A lesser peninsula advances towards the main peninsula at each strait, Scandinavia on the one hand, and Asia Minor on the other; and behind the land bars so formed are two land-girt basins, the Baltic and Black Seas. If Britain be considered as balancing Italy, the symmetry of the distal end of the main peninsula is such that you might lay a Latin Cross upon it with the head in Germany, the arms in Britain and Italy, the feet in Spain, and the center in France, thus typifying that ecclesiastical empire of the five nations which, though shifted northward, was the mediaeval heir of the Roman Caesars. Towards the East, however, where the Baltic and Black Seas first begin to define the peninsular character of Europe, the outline is less shapely, for the Balkan peninsula protrudes southward, only tapering finally into the historic little peninsula of Greece.

Is it not tempting to speculate on what might have happened had Rome not refused to conquer eastward of the Rhine? Who can say that a single mighty sea-power, wholly Latinized as far as the Black and Baltic Seas, would not have commanded the world from its peninsular base? But Classical Rome was primarily a Mediterranean and not a peninsular power, and the Rhine-Danube frontier must be regarded as demarking a penetration from the Mediterranean coast rather than as the incomplete achievement of a peninsular policy.

It was the "opening" again of the seas on either hand which first compacted Europe in the peninsular sense. Reaction had to be organized, or the pressures from north and south would

英里的大西洋海岸，直达哥本哈根海峡；而从"神圣海角"往东，则是直线距离也达1500英里且蜿蜒起伏的地中海海岸，直抵君士坦丁堡的诸道海峡。在每一处海峡，都有一个较小的半岛伸向半岛大陆，且一侧是斯堪的那维亚，另一侧是小亚细亚[1]；而由此形成的两处大陆屏障背后，则是两个被陆地环绕的海域，即波罗的海与黑海。倘若可以用不列颠岛来与意大利保持平衡，那么这个大半岛的末端便是对称的；我们可以将其比作一个拉丁式的十字架[2]，顶部是德国，两侧是不列颠岛和意大利，底端是西班牙，而中心点则是法国——它象征着由5个国家所组成的那个基督教帝国，尽管位置有点儿偏北，这个帝国却在中世纪继承了罗马帝国历代恺撒的衣钵。然而，从波罗的海与黑海开始让欧洲具有半岛特征的那些地方往东，轮廓却不那么匀称了，原因在于巴尔干半岛向南伸展，直到末端才逐渐缩成了一个小小的、具有历史意义的希腊半岛。

倘若罗马征服了莱茵河以东的地区，会出现一种什么样的情况，进行此种推测难道不是一件令人很感兴趣的事情吗？谁又能说，一个强大的、远至黑海和波罗的海地区全都拉丁化了的海上强国，不会从其半岛基地出发，从而掌控住整个世界呢？不过，传统的罗马帝国主要还是一个地中海强国而非一个半岛强国，所以我们必须将莱茵河——多瑙河这条边界，看成是划定该国从地中海沿岸向北渗透活动的一处界限，而不能将它看成是一种半岛政策并未完全实现所导致的结果。

又是两侧海洋的"打开"，使得欧洲首次具有了半岛的特征。信奉基督教的那些国

---

[1] Asia Minor: 小亚细亚。指亚洲西部位于黑海与地中海之间的一个半岛，总体上与如今土耳其的范围相当。

[2] Latin Cross: 拉丁式十字架。通常指直长横短的那种十字架，即较短的水平线在中点上方与较长的垂直线相交的那种十字架。

have obliterated Christendom. So Charlemagne erected an Empire astride of the Rhine, half Latin and half German by speech, but wholly Latin ecclesiastically. With this Empire as base the Crusades were afterwards undertaken. Seen in large perspective at this distance of time, and from the seaman's point of view, the Crusades, if successful, would have had for their main effect the

查理曼大帝（742～814）。法兰克王国加洛林王朝的国王（公元768年～814年在位），也是神圣罗马帝国的皇帝（公元800年～814年在位）。

"closing" once more of the Mediterranean Sea. The long series of these wars, extending over two centuries, took two courses. On the one hand, fleets were sent out from Venice and Genoa to Jaffa and Acre on the Syrian coast; on the other hand, armies marched through Hungary, along the famous "corridor" of the Morava and Maritza valleys, and through Constantinople and Asia Minor into Syria. The comparison is obvious between these campaigns of the Crusaders by land, from a German base round to the back of the Mediterranean Sea, and the similar campaign of Alexander from his Macedonian base. A good many parallels might, indeed, be drawn between the half–Greek Macedonians and the half–Latin Germans. No Greek of the full blood but looked upon a Macedonian as a sort of bastard! But his position in the broad root of the Greek peninsula enabled the Macedonian to conquer the Greek sea–base, as the position of the German in the broad root of the greater Latin Peninsula has always made him dangerous to the Latin Sea bases beyond the Rhine and the Alps.

The peoples of the Latin civilization were thus hardened by a winter of centuries, called

家必须进行反攻才行，否则，南、北双方的夹击便会将这些国家消灭。于是，查理曼大帝就横跨莱茵河，建立了一个帝国；虽然所用的语言一半是拉丁语、一半是日耳曼语，但帝国信奉的宗教，却完全是古罗马天主教。后来的十字军东征，便是以这个帝国为基地。从时间相距如此久远的全面视角来看，从海洋民族的观点来看，倘若十字军东征获得成功，那么其主要作用便会是再一次"封锁"地中海。长达两个世纪之久的历次十字军东征，有两条进军路线。一条是从威尼斯和热那亚派遣舰队，前往叙利亚沿海的雅法和阿卡；另一条是陆军经由匈牙利进军，沿着摩拉瓦河谷和马里乍河谷那条著名的"走廊"，通过君士坦丁堡和小亚细亚，进入叙利亚。十字军从一个日耳曼基地出发、绕道抵达地中海背后的这几次陆上进军，跟亚历山大大帝从他的马其顿基地出发所进行的那次类似的战役，形成了很明显的对照。实际上，在半希腊化的马其顿人和半拉丁化的日耳曼人之间，确实具有很多可以的类似之处。没有哪一个血统纯正的希腊人，会仅仅把马其顿人看成是杂种！不过，由于在希腊半岛上占据了广泛而根基深厚的位置，所以马其顿人能够征服希腊的海上基地；这种情况，正像日耳曼人在大拉丁半岛上占据了广泛而根基深厚的地位，因而总能对莱茵河和阿尔卑斯山地区之外拉丁海的海上基地构成威胁那样。

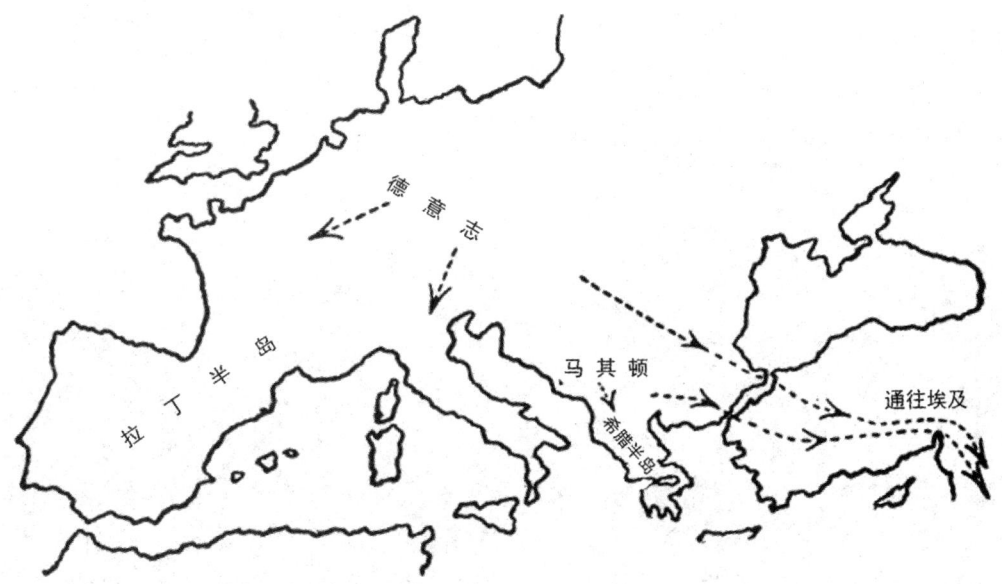

图8　位于拉丁半岛咽喉的德意志和位于希腊半岛咽喉的马其顿。

the Dark Ages, during which they were besieged in their homeland by the Mohammedans, and failed to break out by their Crusading sorties. Only in the fifteenth century did Time ripen for the great adventure on the ocean which was to make the world European. It is worth pausing for a moment to consider further the unique environment in which the Western strain of our human breed developed the enterprise and tenacity which have given it the lead in the modern world. Europe is but a small corner of the great island which also contains Asia and Africa, but the cradle land of the Europeans was only a half of Europe — the Latin Peninsula and the subsidiary peninsulas and islands clustered around it. Broad deserts lay to the south, which could be crossed only in some three months on camel back, so that that the black men were fended off from the white men. The trackless ocean lay to the west, and to the north the frozen ocean. To the northeast were interminable pine forests, and rivers flowing either to ice-choked mouths in the Arctic Sea or to inland waters, such as the Caspian Sea, detached from the ocean. Only to the southeast were there practicable oasis-routes leading to the outer world, but these were closed,

　　这样一来，属于拉丁文化的各个民族便经历了长达数个世纪的严冬、史称"黑暗时代"的考验；在此期间，他们全都被伊斯兰教徒围困在各自的本土内部，而数次十字军东征也没能突围。直到15世纪，进行大规模海洋探险的时机成熟之后，世界才变成了欧洲人的世界。在此，我们有必要暂时打住，来深入研究一下那种独特的环境——在此环境中，我们人类中的西方各民族培养出了积极进取和坚忍不拔的性格，使得西方人取得了现代世界的领导权。欧洲不过是还包括了亚、非两洲的这座大岛屿上一个小小的角落罢了，而欧洲人的发祥地却又只占了欧洲的一半——即拉丁半岛，以及聚在其周围的一些附属半岛和岛屿。它的南边，是一望无边的沙漠，只能骑着骆驼经过约3个月才能越过，从而将黑人与白人隔离开来。它的西面，是茫无边际的海洋，而北边又是冰封千里的北冰洋。在东北方向，有着无穷无尽的松林，其间的河流，要么是注入北冰洋内浮冰壅塞的河口，要么便是注入诸如与海隔绝的里海这种内陆水体。只有在东南面，才有可

十字军东征. 指11世纪至13世纪纪欧洲的基督教徒为了从穆斯林手中收复圣地而发动的军事远征。

拉斐尔壁画《查理曼加冕礼》，藏梵蒂冈博物馆。

more or less completely, from the seventh to the nineteenth century, by the Arabs and the Turks.

In any case, however, the European system of water ways was detached by the Isthmus of Suez from the Indian Ocean. Therefore from the seaman's point of view Europe was a quite definite conception, even though the landsman might think of it as merging with Asia. It was a world apart, but within that world was ample fertility, and in its water paths a natural provision for the intimacy of a family of nations. Water paths they were, with branchings and crossings, for the boatmen, not venturing out on to the high seas, still sailed between the coasts and the horizon, just as they threaded their way between the two banks of the rivers. In the relatively roadless days,

以通行的绿洲路线跟外界相通，可从7世纪到19世纪，这些路线却几乎被阿拉伯人和土耳其人完全封锁了。

然而不管怎么说，欧洲的水道体系，终是因苏伊士地峡而与印度洋隔断开来了。因此，从海洋民族的角度来看，欧洲就成了一个很具体的概念；即便陆地民族有可能认为欧、亚两洲联成了一体，海洋民族也会这样认为的。欧洲是一个独立的世界，但在这个世界内部，却有着丰富的资源，而它的水路交通中，也存在着一种能让各国结成一个亲密大家庭的自然条件。这种自然条件就是，各条水道支流密布且相互交汇，而那些不敢去冒海上狂风巨浪之险的船夫，则可以安然往来于沿海地区与内陆之间，就跟操舟往返

第一次十字军东征的四位首领：哥德弗鲁瓦公爵、雷蒙·德·圣吉尔伯爵、阿亲王博西穆德一世和他的侄子坦克雷德。

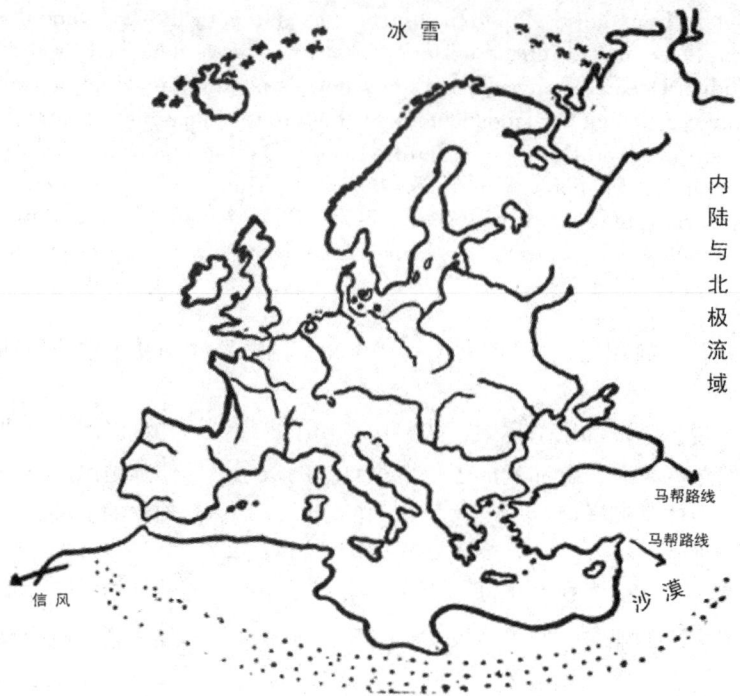

图9 海洋民族之欧洲的河流和沿海水道。整个欧洲的陆地面积，还不到地球表面积的2%。这里是中世纪基督教国家的囚牢，却是现代基督教国家的海上基地。

moreover, which followed on the decay of the Roman road system, the boatmen frequented many of the headwaters of the rivers, which we have now abandoned as no longer worth navigating.

There were two fortunate circumstances in regard to the mediaeval siege of Europe. On the one hand, the Infidels had not command of inexhaustible man-power, for they were based on arid and sub-arid deserts and steppes, and on comparatively small oasis-lands; on the other hand, the Latin Peninsula was not seriously threatened along its oceanic border, for the Norsemen, though fierce and cruel while they remained Pagan, were based on fiord-valleys even less extensive and less fruitful than the oases, and wherever they settled — in England, Normandy, Sicily, or Russia — their small numbers were soon absorbed into the older populations. Thus the whole defensive strength of Europe could be thrown against the southeastern danger. But as

于河流两岸之间没什么两样。此外，在罗马帝国的公路体系衰落之后道路相对较少的那个时代，船夫们也经常光顾许多河流的源头；如今是因为这些源头都已经不再具有航运价值，所以我们才将它们废弃掉了。

关于中世纪欧洲被围，其实还有两点是很幸运的。一方面是，异教徒并没有掌控那种取之不竭的人力资源，因为异教徒都是以干旱和半干旱的沙漠、草原以及相对较小的绿洲为基地。另一方面是，拉丁半岛沿海并没有受到严重的威胁，因为古挪威人虽然凶猛、残暴，却仍然属于异教徒，而他们所倚仗的基地，是范围比绿洲更加狭小、物产也没那么丰富的一些峡湾山谷，并且无论定居何处——无论是在英格兰、诺曼底、西西里，还是在俄罗斯——他们的人口数量都很少，所以很快就同化进了历史更为悠久的那

the European civilization gained momentum, there was energy to spare upon the ocean frontage; Venice and Austria sufficed for the later struggle against the Turks.

After the essays, without practical result, of the Norsemen to force their way through the northern ice of Greenland, the Portuguese undertook to find a sea-way to the Indies round the coast of Africa. They were inspired to the venture by the lead of Prince Henry "the Navigator" half Englishman and half Portuguese. At first sight it seems strange that pilots like Columbus, who had spent their lives on coasting voyages, often going from Venice to Britain, should so long have delayed an exploration southward as they issued from the Straits of Gibraltar. Still more strange does it appear that when at last they had set themselves to discover the outline of Africa, it took them two generations of almost annual voyaging before Da Gama led the way into the Indian Ocean. The cause of their difficulties was physical. For a thousand miles, from the latitude of the Canary Islands to that of Cape Verde, the African coast is a torrid desert, because the dry trade wind there blows off the land without ceasing. It might be a relatively easy matter to sail southward on that steady breeze, but how was the voyage back to be accomplished by ships which could not sail near the wind like a modern clipper, and yet dared neither sail out on to the broad ocean across the wind, nor yet tediously tack their way home off a coast with no supplies of fresh food and water, in a time when the plague of

诺登舍尔德（Adolf Erik Nordenskiold, 1832～1901）。瑞典地质学家、地理学家、矿物学家和探险家。1878年他率"维加号"和另一条船，经由巴伦支海和俄罗斯到达白令海峡，最后到达太平洋，一年后又到达了日本的横滨。1879年，他又率"维加号"首次通过大西洋和太平洋的北部，完成了环绕欧亚大陆的历史性航行，成为北冰洋东北航道的开拓者，并因此而受封为男爵。

些民族当中。这样一来，欧洲的防御力量便可以全部用于抵抗来自东南方向的威胁了。但是，随着欧洲文明获得了动力，欧洲便有了余力去开发海洋了；因此，只需有威尼斯和奥地利两个地方，欧洲就足以对付土耳其了。

古挪威人曾经多次试图强行穿越冰雪覆盖的格陵兰北部，却都是无果而终，后来葡萄牙人便开始寻找一条绕过非洲海岸通往印度群岛的海路。他们在半英国血统半葡萄牙血统、人称"航海者"的亨利王子这位领头人的激励之下，开始了探险。像哥伦布那样的航海家，虽说他们终生都在沿着海岸航行，且经常往返于威尼斯与不列颠岛之间，但驶出直布罗陀海峡之后，却都迟迟没有南下探险，这一点乍看起来似乎很奇怪。而看上去更为奇怪的是，等到他们终于下定决心去探索非洲的轮廓之后，虽说年年都进行了航海，却耗费了两个世代的时间，直到达·伽马才率先进入了印度洋。他们遇到的诸多困难，都属于物质上的原因。从加纳利群岛到佛得角，两地之间相距1000英里；由于干燥的信风无休无止地从内陆吹向海洋，所以两地之间的非洲海岸都是热带沙漠。虽说借着这种平稳的信风向南航行可能是件相对较易的事情，可那时的船只无法像现代快速帆船一样近风航行，它们既不敢冒着海风扬帆出海，又不敢沿着没有食物和淡水补给的海岸

达·伽马进入印度洋。

达·伽马（Vasco Da Gama，约1469年～1524年）。葡萄牙航海家，曾首先经由海路到达印度。

哥伦布船队

scurvy had not yet been mastered?

Once the Portuguese had found the ocean way into the Indian seas, they soon disposed of the opposition of the Arab dhows. Europe had taken its foes in rear; it had sailed round to the rear of the land, just as Xerxes, Alexander, Hannibal, and the Crusaders had marched round to the rear of the sea.

From that time until the opening of the Suez Canal in 1869, the seamen of Europe continued in ever-increasing number to round the Cape, and to sail northward on the Eastern Ocean as far as China and Japan. Only one ship, the Vega of the Swedish Baron Nordenskiold, has to this day made the passage round the north of Asia — with infinite risk, and in two years — and she happens not to have circumnavigated the Triple Continent, for she returned home through the Suez Canal. Nor was the overland journey to the Indies undertaken, except as an adventure, until last century. The trade to the Indies was conducted by coasting — no doubt in a bold way, from point to point — round the great southward promontory whose shores were European and African on the one side, and African and Asiatic on the other. From the point of view of the traffic to the Indies, the world was a vast cape, standing out southward from between Britain and Japan. This world-promontory was enveloped by sea-power, as had been the Greek and Latin promontories beforehand: all its coasts were open to ship-borne trade or to attack from the sea. The seamen naturally chose for the local bases of their trading or warfare small islands off the continental coast, such as Mombasa, Bombay, Singapore, and Hong-Kong, or small peninsulas, such as the Cape of Good Hope and Aden, since those positions offered shelter for their ships and security for their depots. When grown bolder and stronger they put their commercial cities, such as Calcutta and Shanghai, near the entry of great river ways into

长久地抢风[1]航行，因为那个时候坏血症还是一种不治之症；这样的船只，又要怎样才能返航呢？

葡萄牙人找出了通往印度海域的海道之后，很快便粉碎了阿拉伯单桅帆船的抵抗。欧洲已经击败了后方的敌人；欧洲人绕航到达了大陆背后，正如薛西斯、亚历山大、汉尼拔和十字军曾经绕道进军到地中海背后那样。

从那时起，直到1869年苏伊士运河通航，绕航好望角、在东大洋上向北航行并且远至中国和日本的欧洲水手络绎不绝，人数也越来越多。迄今为止还只有一条船，即瑞典诺登舍尔德男爵的那艘"维加"号，沿着亚洲北部航行过——这次航行历尽艰险，耗时两年；可这条船恰好并没有绕航亚、非、欧"三大洲"，因为它是经由苏伊士运河返航的。直到上个世纪，除了冒险活动，也没有人经由陆路到达过印度群岛。与印度群岛各国的贸易，都是通过沿海绕航南方那个巨大的海角来进行的——这无疑是一种点对点的冒险贸易方式——这个海角两侧，一边是欧洲和非洲的海岸，另一边则是非洲和亚洲的海岸。从通往印度群岛的交通贸易来看，整个世界就是一个巨大的海角，夹在不列颠和日本之间向南伸展着。这个"世界海角"为海上力量所包围，就像过去的希腊海角和拉丁海角一样：所有的沿海地区，既可以进行海上贸易，也可能遭到来自海上的攻击。自然，海洋民族会选取大陆沿海的各个小岛，比如蒙巴萨、孟买、新加坡、香港，或者像好望角和亚丁这样的小型半岛，把它们当成自己进行贸易或者发动战争的本土基地；因为那些地方既是他们的船只的避难所，又可以确保其补给场所的安全。海洋民族胆量渐

---

[1] tack：抢风（航行）。航海用语，指让船只逆风作Z字形航行。

productive and populous market-lands. The seamen of Europe, owing to their greater mobility, have thus had superiority for some four centuries over the landsmen of Africa and Asia.

The passing of the imminent danger to Christendom, because of the relative weakening of Islam, was, no doubt, one of the reasons for the break-up of Mediaeval Europe at the close of the Middle Ages; already in 1493 the Pope had to draw his famous line through the ocean, from Pole to Pole, in order to prevent Spanish and Portuguese seamen from quarreling. As a result of this break-up, there arose five competing oceanic powers — Portuguese, Spanish, French, Dutch, and English — in the place of the one power which would, no doubt, have been the ideal of the Crusaders.

Thus the outcome of a thousand years of transition, from the ancient to the modern conditions of sea-power, is such as to prompt a comparison between the Greek and Latin Peninsulas, each with its off-set island. Peninsular Greece and insular Crete anticipated in their relations the Latin Peninsula and the island of Britain. Under the Dorians the greater resources of the peninsular mainland were utilized for the conquest of Crete, but at a later time the rivalry of Sparta and Athens prevented a full exploitation of the peninsula as a sea-base. So in the case of the greater peninsula and greater island, Britain was conquered and held by Rome from the peninsular mainland; but when the Middle Ages were closing, several rival sea-bases occupied the Latin Peninsula, each of them

图10　世界海角

壮、实力日强之后，他们便把那些靠近大河大江入海口的商业城市，比如加尔各答和上海，变成了物产丰富、人口稠密的市场所在。由于具有了更大的机动性，欧洲的海洋民族便在大约4个世纪的时间内拥有了胜过非洲和亚洲陆地民族的优势。

基督教国家所面临的巨大危险，由于伊斯兰国家的实力相对衰弱下去而消除了，而这无疑也是中世纪的欧洲在中世纪末出现分裂的原因之一；还在1493年，教皇就已经被迫在大海上从南到北划出了那条有名的界线，来防止西班牙和葡萄牙两国的海洋民族发生纠纷。此种分裂的结果，无疑并不是出现了十字军所理想的一个大国，而是兴起了5个相互争雄的海上强国——即葡萄牙、西班牙、法国、荷兰和英国。

从古代海上强国的环境演变到现代海上强国的环境，这1000年间的变迁情况就是如此，使得我们必须将各有一个相应岛屿与之抗衡的希腊半岛和拉丁半岛来加以对比。希腊半岛和克里特岛之间的抗衡关系，形成时间要早于拉丁半岛和不列颠岛之间的抗衡关系。在多里安人的统治下，这个半岛大陆上的大部分资源都被用于去征服克里特岛，但后来斯巴达和雅典之间的争战，使得这个半岛并未被充分用作海上基地。拉丁半岛这个面积较大的半岛和不列颠这个较大岛屿的情况也是这样，不列颠岛被来自半岛大陆的罗马帝国攻克并占领了；不过，到了中世纪末期，数个相互争雄的海上基地占领了拉丁半岛，这些基地都像雅典和斯巴达曾经容易遭到马其顿入侵那样，都有可能遭到来自它们背后大陆上的攻击。在这些拉丁基地中，只有威尼斯这个基地正对着伊斯兰国家，而其

open to attack from the land behind, as Athens and Sparta had been open to the Macedonian invasion. Of these Latin sea-bases, one, Venice, fronted towards Islam, while the others contended with internecine feuds for the command of the ocean, so that in the end the lesser British insular base, faced by no united peninsular base, became the home of a power which enveloped and contained the greater peninsula.

Within Great Britain itself it is true that there was not effective unity until the eighteenth century, but the facts of physical geography have determined that there should always be a predominant English people in the south of the island, whether as foe or partner of the Scottish and Welsh peoples. From Norman days, until the growth of the modern industries upon the coal-fields, the English nation was almost uniquely simple in its structure. It is that which makes English history the epic story that it is until the histories of Scotland and Ireland come to confuse their currents with it. One fertile plain between the Mountains of the west and north and the Narrow Seas to the east and south, a people of farmers, a single king, a single parliament, a tidal river, a single great city for central market and port — those are the elements on which the England was built whose warning beacons blazed on the hilltops from Plymouth to Berwick-on-Tweed, in that night of Elizabeth's reign when the Spanish Armada had entered the Channel. On a smaller scale, Latium, the Tiber, the City, the Senate, and the People of Rome once presented a similar unity and a similar executive strength. The real base historically of British sea-power was our English plain — fertile and detached; coal and iron from round the borders of the plain have been added in later times. The white ensign of the Royal Navy is with some historic justice the flag of St. George, with a "difference" for the minor partners.

Every characteristic of sea-power may be studied in British history during the last three centuries, but the home-base, productive and secure, is the one thing essential to which all

他基地则为了争夺制海权而同室操戈、征战不休，于是，不列颠这个面积较小的海岛基地，由于无需去对抗一个团结的半岛基地而最终变成了一个强国的本土，包围并且遏制住了面积较大的拉丁半岛。

虽说大不列颠内部的确是直到18世纪才有效地团结起来的，但自然地理方面的实际情况，却决定了大不列颠内部总有一个地处不列颠岛南部且掌握着支配地位的英格兰民族，而不论它是苏格兰和威尔士这两个民族的仇敌还是伙伴。从诺曼时代[1]起，直到以煤田为基础的现代产业发展起来，英格兰这个民族的结构几乎一直都极其简单的。也正是这一点，使得英格兰的历史成为了英雄史诗般的历史，直到后来苏格兰和爱尔兰的历史潮流与之融合起来才不再如此。西部、北部的山脉和东面、南面的海峡之间，有着一片肥沃的平原、一个农耕民族，统一在一个国王的统治之下，有着一个国会，一条定时涨落的河，以及一座作为中心市场和港口的大城市——英格兰民族正是以这些要素为基础确立起来的，而在伊丽莎白女王统治之下，当西班牙无敌舰队入侵英吉利海峡的那个晚上，从普利茅斯到特威德河上的贝里克郡，无数座山顶都燃起了烽火。拉丁姆平原、台伯河、罗马城、元老院和罗马民族，也曾在较小的规模上呈现出了一种类似的统一，并且具有相似的执行力。从历史的角度来说，不列颠海上力量的真正基地，就是我们的英格兰平原——它沃土千里，且与世隔离；而在平原的边界地区，后来又开采出了煤矿

---

[1] Norman：诺曼人。指8～11世纪自北欧日德兰半岛和斯堪的纳维亚半岛等原住地，向欧洲大陆各国进行掠夺性和商业性远征的日耳曼人。在法国西北部建立公国的诺曼人接受了法语、基督教和法国的政治制度，并于1066年在英格兰建立诺曼底王朝，同时又在意大利南部建立起西西里王国。

英女王伊丽莎白一世

西班牙无敌舰队

图11　英格兰平原，一处富饶的海上基地。

things else have been added. We are told that we should thank God daily for our Channel, but as I looked out over the glorious harvest of this English plain in this critical year 1918, it seemed to me that our thanksgiving as a seafaring people should be no less for our fruitful soil. Insular Crete had to yield to the Dorians from the greater peninsula.

　　Four times in the past three centuries was it attempted to overthrow British sea-power from frontages on the peninsular coast opposite —— from Spain, from Holland, and twice from

和铁矿。皇家海军的白色军旗上是圣乔治[1]徽标，这既有着某种历史上的原因，也是为了跟它的那些次要伙伴们有所"区别"。

　　海上强国的每一个特点，都可以从过去3个世纪的英国历史中去加以探究，但有一个物产丰富、安然无恙的本土基地才是最根本的一个特点，而其他一切都是后加到这个特点之上的。有人说，我们应当每天都感谢上帝将英吉利海峡赐予了我们，但在1918这

---

　　[1] St. George：圣乔治。传说中的人物，据称他是罗马帝国时代生活在近东地区的一位基督徒，因为成功杀死了一条遗害当地人的毒龙而深受爱戴。圣乔治是英格兰文化的重要组成部分，他的标记是著名的圣乔治十字架，其特点是白底、红色正十字。下文中所称的"次要伙伴"指的是苏格兰和威尔士。

France. At last, after Trafalgar, British sea-power definitively enveloped the Latin Peninsula, having subsidiary bases at Gibraltar, Malta, and Heligoland. The continental coastline became the effective British boundary, notwithstanding the enemy privateers, and Britain could prepare war at her ease upon the sea. So she undertook the "Peninsular" campaigns in Spain, and landed armies in the Netherlands in aid of her military allies. She even anticipated Gallipoli by bringing away her armies from Walcheren and Corunna.

When the Napoleonic War was over, British sea-power encompassed, almost without competition, that great world-promontory which stands forward to the Cape of Good Hope from between Britain and Japan. British merchant ships on the sea were a part of the British Empire; British capital ventured abroad in foreign countries was a part of British resources,

关键性的一年，当我远眺英格兰平原上一片壮丽的丰收景象之时，在我看来，作为一个以航海为业的民族，我们对于这片富饶土地的感恩，似乎应当不亚于对英吉利海峡的感恩。毕竟，连克里特这个海岛基地也不得不屈服于从较大半岛来的多里安人。

在过去的4个世纪中，敌人曾经有4次企图从海峡对岸的半岛沿海地带来推翻不列颠这个海上强国——一次是从西班牙，一次是从荷兰，两次是从法国。最终，特拉法尔加海战之后，英国的海上力量绝对地包围了拉丁半岛，在直布罗陀、马耳他和赫尔戈兰都有了自己的附属基地。虽然还有敌对的私掠船出没，但整个欧洲大陆的海岸线变成了英国实际上的边界，于是英国便能够从容地在海洋上备战了。所以，英国便在西班牙发动了"半岛"战役[1]，并让陆军在尼德兰登陆，去支援自己的军事盟国。英国甚至还把军

---

[1] "Peninsular" campaigns："半岛"之战。此处的"半岛"指艾比利厄半岛，1808年～1814年英、西、葡在此和法军作战。

特拉法尔加海战

controlled from the city of London and available for the maintenance of power on and over the seas. It was a proud and lucrative position, and seemed so secure that the mid-Victorian folk thought it almost in the natural order of things that insular Britain should rule the seas. We were, perhaps, not quite a popular people in the rest of the world; our position behind a Channel seemed an unfair advantage. But warships cannot navigate the mountains, and since the French wars of the Plantagenets we have not sought to make permanent European conquests, so that, on the whole, we may hope that the verdict of foreign historians on our Britain of the nineteenth century may resemble that of the famous schoolboy who described his headmaster as "a beast, but a just beast".

Perhaps the most remarkable outcome of British sea-power was the position in the Indian Ocean during the generation before the War. The British "Raj" in India depended on support from the sea, yet on all the waters between the Cape of Good Hope, India, and Australia, there was habitually no British battle-ship or even first-class cruiser. In effect, the Indian Ocean was a "closed sea". Britain owned or "protected" most of the coast lines, and the remaining frontages were either on islands, as the Dutch East Indies, or on territories such as Portuguese Mozambique and German East Africa, which, although continental, were inaccessible under existing conditions by land-way from Europe. Save in the Persian Gulf, there could be no rival

队从瓦尔赫伦岛和科伦那调走，从而加速了加利波利[1]之战的爆发。

拿破仑战争[2]结束之后，英国的海上力量便几乎无人能敌，包围了位于英国与日本之间、直到好望角的这个巨大的"世界海角"。在海上航行的英国商船，是大英帝国的一部分；在海外各国所投入的英国资本，也是英国资源中的一部分，由伦敦城[3]加以掌控，可用于维持英国在海洋之上和海外的霸权。这种形势既令人骄傲，也带来了巨大的利益，因此生活在维多利亚王朝中期[4]的人便都认为不列颠这个岛国理应统治四海了。或许，我们在世界上的其他地方并不是广受欢迎的一个民族；因为我们有英吉利海峡庇护，这看上去似乎是一种并不公平的优势。但是，军舰并不能巡航于崇山峻岭之间，而且自金雀花王朝[5]对法国的那几场战争以来，我们也并没有想要去永远征服欧洲；因此总的来说，我们或许可以期望，外国史学家会像那个有名的男生描述他们校长那样，说我们19世纪的英国是"一头野兽，不过也是一头公正的野兽。"

或许，英国海上力量最引人注目的成果，便是第一次世界大战前一个世代里，该国在印度洋所取得的地位。英国对印度的那种"统治"，倚赖于来自海上的支援，但好望角、印度和澳大利亚之间的所有海域，平常却并没有英国战舰出没，甚至连一级巡洋舰

[1] Gallipoli：加利波利（半岛）。土耳其位于地中海海峡的一处要冲。此处指第一次世界大战中，1915年英军在该处登陆，企图打通达达尼尔海峡，结果被土军击败退出。

[2] Napoleonic War：拿破仑战争。指拿破仑执政时期（1799~1804）和法兰西第一帝国时期（1804~1815），法国资产阶级为了在欧洲建立政治和经济霸权，同英国争夺贸易和殖民地的领先地位，以及兼并新的领土而与奥、普、俄、英为核心的反法联盟进行的一系列战争。

[3] the city of London：伦敦城。伦敦郡中央的故城，是伦敦早年的核心，占地约1平方英里。此处指代的是英国的中央政府。

[4] mid-Victorian：维多利亚王朝中期的（人）。维多利亚王朝中期，指约1850年~1890年的英国，这一时期被称为英国"经济繁荣和宗教分裂的时期"。

[5] Plantagenet：金雀花王朝。指12世纪~14世纪曾经统治英国的封建王朝。王朝名称的由来，是因为亨利二世的父亲安茹伯爵杰弗里经常在帽子上饰以金雀花枝。亦称"安茹王朝"。

base for sea-power which combined security with the needful resources, and Britain made it a declared principle of her policy that no sea-base should be established on either the Persian or Turkish shores of the Persian Gulf. Superficially there is a striking similarity between the closed Mediterranean of the Romans, with the legions along the Rhine frontier, and the closed Indian Ocean, with the British Army on the Northwest Frontier of India. The difference lay in the fact that, whereas the closing of the Mediterranean depended on the Legions, the closing of the Indian Seas was maintained by the long arm of sea-power itself from the Home base.

※　　　※　　　※　　　※　　　※　　　※　　　※　　　※　　　※

In the foregoing rapid survey of the vicissitudes of sea-power, we have not stayed to consider that well-worn theme of the single mastery of the seas. Every one now realizes that owing to the continuity of the ocean and the mobility of ships, a decisive battle at sea has immediate and far-reaching results. Caesar beat Antony at Actium, and Caesar's orders were enforceable forthwith on every shore of the Mediterranean. Britain won her culminating victory at Trafalgar, and could deny all the ocean to the fleets of her enemies, could transport her armies to whatsoever coast she would and remove them again, could carry supplies home from foreign sources, and could exert pressure in negotiation on whatsoever offending State had a sea-front. Our concern here has been rather in regard to the bases of sea-power and the relation to these of land-power. In the long run, that is the fundamental question. There were fleets of war canoes on the Nile, and the Nile was closed to their contention by a single land-power controlling their fertile bases through all the length of Egypt. A Cretan insular base was conquered from a larger Greek peninsular base. Macedonian land-power closed the Eastern Mediterranean to the warships both of Greeks and Phoenicians by depriving them impartially of their bases. Hannibal struck overland at the peninsular base of Roman sea-power, and that

也没有。实际上，印度洋就是一个"内海"。英国占有或者说"保护"着海岸线上的大多数地区，而其余的前沿地带，要么是在诸如荷属东印度群岛这样的海岛上，要么就是在诸如葡属莫桑比克和德属东非那样的地方；这些地方虽然都属于大陆，但在现有条件下，从欧洲经由陆路都是无法到达的。除了在波斯湾内，世界上再也找不到别的既有安全保障、又有必要资源且足以争夺海上霸权的基地了，但在波斯湾两侧的波斯海岸和土耳其海岸上都不许建立海上基地，却是英国政策中一条公开确立下来的原则。从表面来看，罗马人封锁地中海并将罗马军团沿莱茵河边界分布，同英国封锁印度洋并将军队分布于印度西北边陲，这两种情形间有着显著的相似之处。它们之间的区别，即在于下述这样一种事实：封锁地中海倚赖的是罗马军团，而封锁印度诸海，却是依靠来自英国本土基地、且可以遥控印度诸海的海上力量本身来加以维持的。

※　　　※　　　※　　　※　　　※　　　※　　　※　　　※　　　※

在前面对海上强国的盛衰变迁进行快速审视的过程中，我们并没有停下来考虑一国独霸四海那个陈旧不堪的主题。如今大家都已经认识到，由于海洋是个相连的整体，舰船又具有机动性，所以一场决定性的海战既有当时的效果，也会具有长远的影响。恺撒在亚克兴打败了安东尼，所以地中海沿岸各处就必须执行恺撒的命令了。英国在特拉法尔加海战中赢得了最终的胜利，所以就能够不许敌人的舰队在海洋上航行，就能够把英国军队运送到任何海岸或者从任何海岸调离，就能够把源自外国的给养运回本国，就能够在谈判中对任何拥有海岸线、胆敢冒犯的国家施加压力了。更确切一点来说，此处我们所关注的，是海上强国的基地及其与陆上强国基地的关系这个方面。从长远来看，这才

base was saved by victory on land. Caesar won the mastery of the Mediterranean by victory on the water, and Rome then retained control of it by the defense of land frontiers. In the Middle Ages Latin Christendom defended itself on the sea from its peninsular base, but in modern times, because competing States grew up within that peninsula, and there were several bases of sea-power upon it, all open to attack from the land, the mastery of the seas passed to a power which was less broadly based, but on an island — fortunately a fertile and coal-bearing island. On sea-power, thus based, British adventurers have founded an overseas Empire of colonies, plantations, depots, and protectorates, and have established, by means of sea-borne armies, local land-powers in India and Egypt. So impressive have been the results of British sea-power that there has perhaps been a tendency to neglect the warnings of history and to regard sea-power in general as inevitably having, because of the unity of the ocean, the last word in the rivalry with land-power.

※　　　　※　　　　※　　　　※　　　　※　　　　※　　　　※　　　　※　　　　※

Never has sea-power played a greater part than in the recent War and in the events which led up to it. Those events began some twenty years ago with three great victories won by the British fleet without the firing of a gun. The first was at Manila, in the Pacific Ocean, when a German squadron threatened to intervene to protect a Spanish squadron, which was being defeated by an American squadron, and a British squadron stood by the Americans. Without unduly stressing that single incident, it may be taken as typical of the relations of the Powers during the war between Spain and America, which war gave to America detached possessions both in the Atlantic and Pacific, and led to her undertaking the construction of the Panama Canal, in order to gain the advantages of insularity for the mobilization of her warships. So was a first step taken towards the reconciliation of British and American hearts. Moreover the Monroe

是根本性的问题。尼罗河上曾经有着战舟组成的许多舰队，但由于埃及全境的肥沃基地都由一个陆上强国所掌控，因此各国之间的纷争也就此止歇了。克里特这个海岛基地，被希腊这个较大的半岛基地征服了。马其顿这个陆上强国，不分彼此地把希腊人和腓尼基人的基地统统都夺取了，从而使得后者的战船再也无法进入东地中海了。汉尼拔经由陆路进攻海上强国罗马的那个半岛基地，可这个基地却由于罗马在陆战中获胜而得以保存了下来。通过在海战中取得胜利，恺撒独霸了地中海；罗马继而凭借在陆上前沿进行防御而保持了对地中海的控制。在中世纪，拉丁地区的基督教国家是倚赖其半岛基地在海上进行防御的，但在现代，由于那个半岛内部各国崛起、彼此争雄，出现了数个海上强国的基地，并且它们都容易遭到陆上攻击，所以制海权便落入了一个强国手中；该国所据的基地并不广阔，而是位于海岛之上——幸运的是，那是个既富饶、又产煤的岛屿。以此种海上力量为基础，英国的冒险家们便建立起了一个由殖民地、种植园、补给站和保护国所组成的海外帝国，并且通过将部队海运至印度和埃及，在当地建立起了陆上力量。英国的海上力量取得了如此令人惊叹的成就，所以人们或许会形成一种忽视历史教训并且普遍认为由于海洋是个整体，故海陆争锋时海上强国必定具有最终发言权的倾向。

※　　　　※　　　　※　　　　※　　　　※　　　　※　　　　※　　　　※　　　　※

海上力量在最近这次世界大战以及导致这次战争的那些事件中，起到了前所未有的巨大作用。这些事件始于大约20年前，当时英国舰队不费一枪，便取得了3次大捷。第一次是在马尼拉附近的太平洋上，当时有支德国舰队威胁说要进行干涉，要保护一支快被美国舰队击溃了的西班牙分舰队，但英国分舰队却支持了美国人。倘若不去过分地强

美西战争

doctrine was upheld in regard to South America.

The second of these victories of the British fleet was when it held the ocean during the South African War, of such vital consequence to the maintenance of the British rule in India; and the third was when it kept the ring round the Russo–Japanese War, and incidentally kept the door open into China. In all three cases history would have been very different but for the intervention of the British fleet. None the less — and perhaps as a consequence — the growth of the German fleet under the successive Navy Laws, induced the withdrawal of the British battle squadrons from the Far East and from the Mediterranean, and cooperation in those seas with the Japanese and French sea–powers.

The Great War itself began in the old style, and it was not until 1917 that the new aspects of Reality became evident. In the very first days of the struggle the British fleet had

调这个孤立的事件，那我们就可以把它看作是美西战争时表现各个强国之间关系的一个典型；这次战争，既让美国在大西洋和太平洋都有了离岸领土，还促使该国开始开凿巴拿马运河，从而取得岛国的优势，使该国的战舰具有机动性。这样做，正是使英美关系趋于和解的第一步。此外，在南美问题上，英国也支持门罗主义[1]。

英国舰队的第二次胜利，便是在南非战争期间，当时英国舰队掌握了制海权，对英国维持它在印度的统治起到了至关重要的作用；第三次胜利，则是英国舰队控制住日俄战争的局势，并且偶然打开了中国的门户。在这3种情况下，倘若没有英国舰队的干预，历史走向可能就会大不相同了。尽管如此——或许也正是这种情况的结果——德国

---

[1] Monroe doctrine：门罗主义。指1823年美国总统门罗所提出的外交政策原则，主要包括三个方面的内容：（1）要求欧洲国家不在西半球殖民，这一原则不仅表示反对西欧国家对拉美的扩张，也反对俄国在北美西海岸的扩张；（2）要求欧洲不干预美洲独立国家的事务；（3）保证美国不干涉欧洲事务，包括欧洲现有的、在美洲各殖民地的事务。

already taken command of the ocean, enveloping, with the assistance of the French fleet, the whole peninsular theater of the war on land. The German troops in the German Colonies were isolated, German merchant shipping was driven off the seas, the British expeditionary force was transported across the Channel without the loss of a man or a horse, and British and French supplies from over the ocean were safely brought in. In a word, the territories of Britain and France were made one for the purpose of the war, and their joint boundary was advanced to within gunshot range of the German coast — no small offset for the temporary, though deeply regretted, loss of certain French departments. After the battle of the Marne the true war-map of Europe would have shown a Franco-British frontier following the Norwegian, Danish, German, Dutch, and Belgian coasts — at a distance of three miles in the case of the neutral

舰队还是在一系列的海军法案之下发展起来，从而迫使英国将战舰撤离了远东和地中海地区，并且使得英国在这两处海域开始与日、法两国的海上力量进行合作。

这次世界大战，本身是以一种古老的方式爆发的，因而直到1917年，现实的各个新的方面才变得明显起来。战争爆发之初，英国舰队便已取得了海洋的控制权，并在法国舰队的协助之下，包围了陆上战争在半岛上的整个战场。驻扎在各个殖民地的德国军队被孤立起来，德国商船无法再在海上航行，英国远征军没有损耗一兵一卒便渡过了英吉利海峡，而英、法两国的海上补给也确保安全了。一句话，因为这场战争，英、法两国的领土已经合二为一，而两国的共同边境，也已推进到了能够用大炮进击德国海岸线的

布尔战争（南非战争）中的布尔人战士。1899年至1902年间英国和南非两个国家之间爆发的一场战争。这两个南非国家是由荷兰移民建立的，因为这些荷兰移民被称为"布尔人"（即农民），故此战又称为"布尔战争"。

coasts — and then running as a sinuous line through Belgium and France to the Jura border of Switzerland. West of that boundary, whether by land or sea, the two Powers could make ready their defense against the enemy. Nine months later Italy dared to join the Allies, mainly because her ports were kept open by the Allied sea-power.

On the Eastern front also the old style of war held. Land-power was there divided into two contending forces, and the outer of the two, notwithstanding its incongruous Czardom, was allied with the sea-power of the Democratic West. In short, the disposition of forces repeated in a general way that of a century earlier, when British sea-power supported the Portuguese and Spaniards in 'the Peninsula", and was allied with the autocracies of the Eastern land-powers. Napoleon fought on two fronts, which in the terms of today we should describe as Western and Eastern.

In 1917, however, came a great change, due to the entry of the United States into the War, the fall of the Russian Czardom, and the subsequent collapse of the Russian fighting strength. The world-strategy of the contest was entirely altered. We have been fighting since, and can afford to say it without hurting any of our allies, to make the world a safe place for democracies. So much as regards Idealism. But it is equally important that we should bear in mind the new

地方了——这一点，差不多抵消了法国失陷了数省的损失，此种失陷虽说只是暂时的，却令人深感痛惜。马恩河战役之后，在欧洲真正的作战地图上可以看到，法、英前线沿着挪威、丹麦、德国、荷兰和比利时各国海岸——如果是中立国家的海岸，那么这条战线就是离岸3英里——然后弯弯曲曲地穿过比利时和法国，直到瑞士的侏罗边境。这条界线以西，无论是经由陆上还是经由海上，法、英这两个大国都可以做好准备，防御敌人的进攻。9个月后意大利之所以敢于加入协约国一方，主要原因就是在协约国海上力量的保护之下，该国的各个港口仍能通航。

在东线，战争也是以那种古老的方式进行的。在那里，陆上力量分成了两支相互敌对的部队，其中外围的那一支尽管属于与西方矛盾重重的沙皇俄国，但它还是跟民主的西方国家的海上力量结成了联盟。简而言之，这种作战力量的部署，总体上是上一个世纪那种力量部署方式的重复；当时英国的海上力量一面支持位于"半岛"上的葡萄牙人和西班牙人，一面又与一些东方陆上强国的专制政府结成了同盟。所以拿破仑是在两条战线上作战；用如今的话来说，我们应当称之为西线和东线。

马恩河。法国东北部的一条河流，是第一次世界大战和第二次世界大战的主要战场。

第一次世界大战中首批参战的美军士兵开赴欧洲.

face of Reality. We have been fighting lately, in the close of the War, a straight duel between land−power and sea−power, and sea−power has been laying siege to land−power. We have conquered, but had Germany conquered she would have established her sea−power on a wider base than any in history, and in fact on the widest possible base. The joint continent of Europe, Asia, and Africa, is now effectively, and not merely theoretically, an island. Now and again, lest we forget, let us call it the World−Island in what follows.

One reason why the seamen did not long ago rise to the generalization implied in the expression "World−Island", is that they could not make the round voyage of it. An ice−cap, two thousand miles across, floats on the Polar Sea, with one edge aground on the shoals off the north of Asia. For the common purposes of navigation, therefore, the continent is not an island. The seamen of the last four centuries have treated it as a vast promontory stretching southward

然而，1917年战局却发生了巨大的变化，原因是美利坚合众国参战、沙皇俄国崩溃以及随后俄国作战力量瓦解了。而此次战争的世界战略，也彻底改变了。自此以后，我们便是为了让世界成为民主国家的安全之所而战，并且，我们现在完全可以不得罪任何一个盟国地这样说了。关于理想主义，本书就说到这里吧。不过同样重要的是，我们应当牢牢记住现实的新面貌。直到最近战争即将结束之前，我们一直都在打一场彻底的、陆上力量对海上力量的决战，并且是海上力量围攻陆上力量。我们胜利了；不过，倘若德国得胜，该国就会在一个史无前例地广阔的基地上——并且，事实上可能是有史以来最为广阔的一处基地上——确立起其海上力量。欧、亚、非三洲共同组成的这个大陆，如今变成了一个实实在在的岛屿，而不仅仅是一个理论上的岛屿了。为了时时不让我们忘记这一点，在下文中我们不妨将其称作"世界岛"。

from a vague north, as a mountain peak may rise out of the clouds from hidden foundations. Even in the last century, since the opening of the Suez Canal, the eastward voyage has still been round a promontory, though with the point at Singapore instead of Cape Town.

This fact and its vastness have made men think of the Continent as though it differed from other islands in more than size. We speak of its parts as Europe, Asia, and Africa in precisely the same way that we speak of the parts of the ocean as Atlantic, Pacific, and Indian. In theory even the ancient Greeks regarded it as insular, yet they spoke of it as the "World". The school-children of today are taught of it as the "Old World", in contrast with a certain pair of peninsulas which together constitute the "New World". Seamen speak of it merely as "the Continent", the continuous land.

Let us consider for a moment the proportions and relations of this newly realized Great Island.[1] It is set as it were on the shoulder of the earth with reference to the North Pole. Measuring from Pole to Pole along the central meridian of Asia, we have first a thousand miles of ice-clad sea as far as the northern shore of Siberia, then five thousand miles of land to the southern point of India, and then seven thousand miles of sea to the Antarctic cap of ice-clad land. But measured along the meridian of the Bay of Bengal or of the Arabian Sea, Asia is only some three thousand five hundred miles across. From Paris to Vladivostok is six thousand miles, and from Paris to the Cape of Good Hope is a similar distance; but these measurements are on a globe twenty-six thousand miles round. Were it not for the ice impediment to its circumnavigation, practical seamen would long ago have spoken of the Great Island by some such name, for it is only a little more than one-fifth as large as their ocean.

---

[1] It would be misleading to attempt to represent the statements which follow in map form. They can only be appreciated on a globe. Therefore they are illustrated by diagrams; see Figs. 12 and 13.

海洋民族之所以没有在很早以前就领会到"世界岛"这个表达中所隐含的那种概括性的思想，原因之一就是他们不能做环球航行。北冰洋上漂浮着一座宽达2000英里的冰原，它的一侧与亚洲北部的浅滩相连。因此从普通的航海角度来看，这个大陆并不是一个岛屿。而过去4个世纪中的海洋民族，也都把它看成是一个巨大的、从捉摸不透的北方向南延伸的海角，就像一座从遮挡山脚的云海中突然冒出来的山峰一样。即便是在上个世纪，自苏伊士运河通航之后，人们向东航行的时候一直也要绕过一个海角才行；不过，绕航的这个海角是在新加坡，而不是在开普敦。

这个现实以及"世界岛"的广袤使得人们认为，这个大陆与其他岛屿的不同之处，并非仅仅是面积上的差异。我们把这个大陆的各个部分称为欧洲、亚洲和非洲，这跟我们把海洋的各个部分称为大西洋、太平洋和印度洋的做法是完全一样的。从理论上来看，即便是古代的希腊人也把它看成一个岛屿，只不过他们称之为"世界"罢了。教给如今小学生的说法是，它是"旧世界"，以有别于由另外两个半岛合二为一所组成的那个"新世界"。海洋民族却只是将其称为"大陆"，即一片连绵不断的陆地罢了。

我们不妨来研究一下最近才被人们意识到的这个"大岛"的大小及其内部关系吧。〔作者注：如果根据地图来表述下文，就会引起误解。下述说法只能在地球仪上去领会。因此，我们是用图表来对其加以说明的；参见图12和图13。〕从北极来看，这个"大岛"就像是坐在地球的肩膀之上。沿着亚洲的中央经线从北极量到南极，首先就是宽达1000英里的冰雪海域，直达西伯利亚北部海岸，然后就是绵亘5000英里的陆地，直到印度南端，接下来又是宽达7000英里的海洋，直到冰雪覆盖的南极大陆。不

The World-Island ends in points northeastward and southeastward. On a clear day you can see from the northeastern headland across Bering Strait to the beginning of the long pair of peninsulas, each measuring about one twenty-sixth of the globe, which we call the Americas. Superficially there is no doubt a certain resemblance of symmetry in the Old and New Worlds; each consists of two peninsulas, Africa and Euro-Asia in the one case, and North and South America in the other. But there is no real likeness between them. The northern and northeastern shores of Africa for nearly four thousand miles are so intimately related with the opposite shores of Europe and Asia that the Sahara constitutes a far more effective break in social continuity than does the Mediterranean. In the days of air navigation which, are coming, sea-power will use the water way of the Mediterranean and Red Seas only by the sufferance of land-power, for air-power is chiefly an arm of land-power, a new amphibious cavalry, when the contest with sea-power is in question.

But North and South America, slenderly connected at Panama, are for practical purposes insular rather than peninsular in regard to one another. South America lies not merely to south, but also in the main to east of North America; the two lands are in echelon, as soldiers would say, and thus the broad ocean encircles South America, except for a minute proportion of its outline. A like fact is true of North America with reference to Asia, for it stretches out into the ocean from Bering Strait so that, as may be seen upon a globe, the shortest way from Pekin to New York is across Bering Strait, a. circumstance which may some day have importance for the traveler by railway or air. The third of the new continents, Australia, lies a thousand miles from the southeastern point of Asia, and measures only one sixty-fifth of the surface of the globe.

Thus the three so-called new continents are in point of area merely satellites of the old continent. There is one ocean covering nine-twelfths of the globe; there is one continent —

过，倘若沿着孟加拉湾或者阿拉伯海的经线来测量的话，亚洲南北却只有大约3500英里。巴黎与符拉迪沃斯托克相距6000英里，而从巴黎到好望角之间的距离也差不多；不过这些数据，都是在一个周长达26000英里的球体上测量得到的结果。假如不是因为冰雪阻隔，使得人们无法环球航行的话，那些务实的海洋民族早就会用类似这样的名称来称呼这个"大岛"了，因为它的大小不过是海洋民族之海洋的1/5多一点儿罢了。

"世界岛"东北方向和东南方向末端，都是尖角。在天气晴朗的日子，你可以站在东北方向的岬角上，远眺白令海峡对岸，看到两个狭长的半岛的发端；每个半岛的长度都约占地球周长的1/26，我们称之为南美洲和北美洲。从表面上来看，"旧世界"与"新世界"无疑具有某种对称性上的相似点；它们都由两个半岛所组成，前者是非洲和欧亚大陆，后者则是南、北美洲。不过，它们之间其实并无真正的相似之处。非洲的北部海岸和东北海岸虽说绵亘约4000英里，却跟对面的欧、亚两洲海岸紧密相关，以至于撒哈拉沙漠割裂社会联系的效果，要远远超过了地中海。在即将到来的航空时代，海上强国只有在陆上强国的允许下，才能利用地中海和红海之间的那条水道；因为空军主要是陆上强国的一个兵种，而与海上强国争锋时，这个兵种便会变成一支新型的、能够协同作战的机动部队。

然而从实质上来看，在巴拿马这个狭长地峡相连的南、北美洲，却并非是半岛与半岛的关系，而是岛屿与岛屿的关系。南美洲并非仅仅是位于北美洲以南，还基本上位于北美洲以东；用军人的话来说，这两个大陆"列成了梯队"，所以除了其外围的一小部分地方，南美洲四周都环绕着广阔的海洋。从北美洲与亚洲的关系来看，情况也与此相似。由于北美洲从白令海峡向海洋延伸，因此从地球仪上可以看出，从北京到纽约

the World–Island — covering two–twelfths of the globe; and there are many smaller islands, whereof North America and South America are for effective purposes two, which together cover the remaining one–twelfth. The term "New World" implies, now that we can see the Realities and not merely historic appearances, a wrong perspective.

The truth, seen with a broad vision, is that in the great World–Promontory, extending southward to the Cape of Good Hope, and in the North American sea–base we have, on a vast scale, yet a third contrast of peninsula and island to be set beside the Greek peninsula and the island of Crete, and the Latin Peninsula and the British Island. But there is this vital difference, that the World–Promontory, when united by modern overland communications, is in fact the World–Island, possessed potentially of the advantages both of insularity and of incomparably great resources.

美国第28任总统威尔逊

Leading Americans have for some time appreciated the fact that their country is no longer a world apart, and President Wilson had brought his whole people round to that view when they consented to throw themselves into the War. But North America is no longer even a continent; in this twentieth century it is shrinking to be an island. Americans used to think of their three millions of square miles as the equivalent of all Europe; some day, they said, there would be a United States of Europe as sister to the United States of America. Now, though they may not all have realized it, they must no longer think of Europe apart from Asia and Africa. The Old World has become insular, or in other words a unit, incomparably the largest

的最短路线，便是越过白令海峡；这种情况，对于将来乘坐火车或者乘坐飞机的旅客来说，可能会具有重要的意义。第三处新大陆即是澳洲，它距亚洲的东南角达1000英里，而面积则只占地球表面积的1/65。

因此就面积来说，这3个所谓的新大陆，不过是旧大陆的3颗卫星罢了。一个大洋，覆盖了地球表面的9/12；而一个大陆——即"世界岛"，又占据了地球表面的2/12；还有许多较小的岛屿——南美洲和北美洲实际上就是其中的两个——它们合起来占据了地球表面剩下的那1/12。既然我们如今并非只能看到各种历史表象，而是能够看到种种现实情况了，那么"新世界"这个术语就隐含了一种错误的观点。

用一种远大的眼光来看，事实就是，在这个向南延伸至好望角的巨大的"世界海角"内，在北美洲这个海上基地内，我们除了希腊半岛和克里特岛、拉丁半岛和不列颠岛之间这两种对比关系，还需大规模地确定半岛与岛屿之间的第三种对照关系。不过，它与前两种关系之间有着下述这种至关重要的差异：这个"世界海角"被现代陆上交通联结成一体之后，实际上就成了"世界岛"，可能就会既具有岛屿的有利条件，又具有无比广大的资源优势。

美国的领导人认识到自己的国家不再是一个孤立的世界，已经有一段时间了，而威尔逊总统也已使全体美国人民改变了原有的观点，让他们认识到了这一事实，因而同意

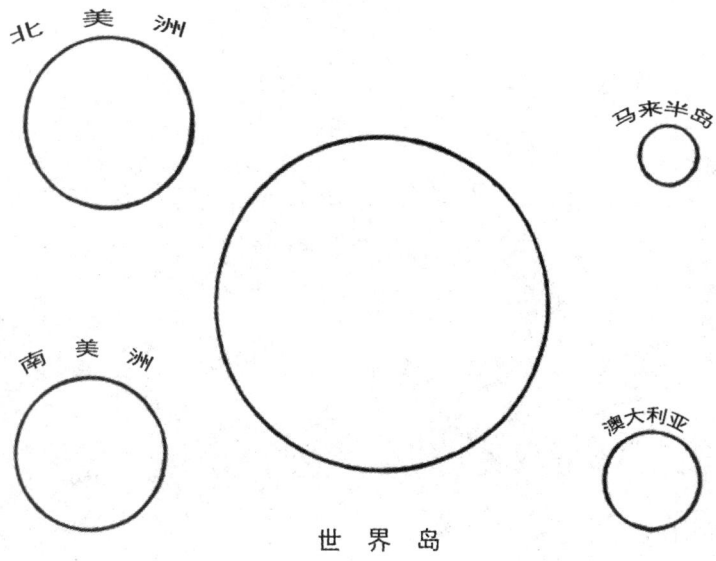

北 美 洲

马来半岛

南 美 洲

澳大利亚

世 界 岛

图12　图中的各个圆圈，代表了"世界岛"及其诸卫星岛屿的相对面积。

geographical unit on our globe.

There is a remarkable parallelism between the short history of America and the longer history of England; both countries have now passed through the same succession of Colonial, Continental, and Insular stages. The Angle and Saxon settlements along the east and south coast of Britain have often been regarded as anticipating the thirteen English Colonies along the east coast of North America; what has not always been remembered is that there was a continental stage in English history to be compared with that of Lincoln in America. The wars of Alfred the Great and William the Conqueror were in no small degree between contending parts of England, with the Norsemen intervening, and England was not effectively insular until the time of Elizabeth, because not until then was she free from the hostility of Scotland, and herself united, and therefore a unit, in her relations with the neighboring continent. America is today a unit, for the American people have fought out their internal differences, and it is insular, because events are compelling Americans to

参战了。但是，北美洲甚至也不再是一个大陆了；在如今这个20世纪，北美洲正在收缩并变成一个岛屿。美国人以前经常认为，他们那300万平方英里的国土与整个欧洲的面积相当；他们还说，将来终有一天会出现一个与美利坚合众国同类型的欧洲合众国。如今，虽说可能并非人人都认清了这一点，但他们已经决计不会再把欧洲和亚、非两洲分开来看了。"旧世界"已经变成了一个岛屿，或者换句话说，已经变成了一个单位，变成了我们这个地球上无与伦比的最大地理单位了。

在美国短暂的历史与英国更悠久的历史之间，具有一种显著的相似性；这两个国家迄今为止都经历了一系列相同的历史阶段，从殖民时期、大陆时期到岛屿时期。不列颠岛东部和南部沿海的盎格鲁和撒克逊人定居地，常常被人们认为是北美洲东部海岸13个英国殖民地的先声；而人们又总不记得，英国历史上也曾有过一段大陆时期，可与林肯治下的美国那段时期相媲美。阿尔弗雷德大帝和"征服者"威廉所发动的历次战争，在很大程度上还是英格兰各地区之间的内部斗争，只是有古挪威人横加干涉罢了，而英格

美国内战

realize that their so-called continent lies on the same globe as the Continent.

Picture upon the map of the world this War as it has been fought in the year 1918. It has been a war between Islanders and Continentals, there can be no doubt of that. It has been fought on the Continent, chiefly across the landward front of peninsular France; and ranged on the one side have been Britain, Canada, the United States, Brazil, Australia, New Zealand, and Japan — all insular. France and Italy are peninsular, but even with that advantage they would not have been in the War to the end had it not been for the support of the Islanders. India and China — so far as China has been in the War on the Manchurian front — may be regarded as advanced guards of British, American, and Japanese sea-power. Dutch Java is the only island of large population which is not in the Western Alliance, and even Java is not on the side of the Continentals. There can be no mistaking the significance of this unanimity of the Islanders. The collapse of Russia has cleared our view of the realities, as the Russian revolution purified the

兰也直到伊丽莎白女王统治时期才真正成为一个岛国，因为直到那时英格兰才摆脱苏格兰的敌视，也直到那时英格兰本身才统一起来并因而形成一个单位，并与相邻的欧洲大陆建立起关系来。如今的美国也是一个单位，因为美国人民已经通过战争解决了他们的内部纷争；如今的美国也变成了一个岛国，因为形势正在迫使美国人认识到，他们所称的这个"新大陆"，与原来的"旧大陆"一样，都处于同一个地球上。

我们不妨在世界地图上想象一下这次世界大战在1918年的战况。它是岛国与大陆国家之间进行的一场战争，这一点是毋庸置疑的。战争在欧洲大陆上进行，并且主要是横贯法国这个半岛国家的内陆前线；战争所针对的那一方，是英国、加拿大、美利坚合众国、巴西、澳大利亚、新西兰和日本——它们都是岛国。法国和意大利属于半岛国家，可就算具有此种优势，倘若没有岛国支援，两国也坚持不到大战结束。印度和中国——直到此时，中国一直都是在满洲前线作战——可以看作是英、美、日三国海上力量的前

ideals for which we have been fighting.

The facts appear in the same perspective if we consider the population of the globe. More than fourteen–sixteenths of all humanity live on the Great Continent, and nearly one–sixteenth more on the closely off–set Islands of Britain and Japan. Even today, after four centuries of emigration, only about one–sixteenth live in the lesser continents. Nor is time likely to change these proportions materially. If the middle–west of North America comes presently to support, let us say, another hundred million people, it is probable that the interior of Asia will at the same time carry two hundred millions more than now, and if the Tropical part of South America should feed a hundred millions more, then the Tropical parts of Africa and the Indies may not improbably support two hundred millions more. The Congo Forest alone, subdued to agriculture, would maintain some four hundred million souls if populated with the same density as Java, and the Javanese population is still growing. Have we any right, moreover, to assume that, given its climate and history, the interior of Asia would not nourish a population as virile as that of

卫。荷属爪哇是唯一一个人口众多且不属于西方协约国之列的岛屿；可即便是爪哇，也没有站在大陆国家这一边。各个岛国如此同心协力，这种做法无疑具有重要的意义。俄国的瓦解已经澄清了我们对于种种现实的看法，因为俄国革命净化了我们一直在为之战斗的那些理想。

假如我们考虑一下地球的总人口，事实情况看上去也是一样的。整个人类中的14/16都生活在那个"大大陆"上，只有大约1/16多一点的人生活不列颠和日本这两个差不多彼此平衡的岛屿上。即便是如今，在经历了4个世纪的移民之后，其他那几个较小的大陆上也仍然只生活着大约1/16的人类。而且时间再久，也不太可能使这些比例发生什么实质性的变化。比如说，倘若北美洲的中西部地区不久后可以多养活1亿人口，那么与此同时，亚洲内陆很可能就会比如今多养活2亿人口；而要是南美洲的热带地区能够多养活1亿人口的话，那么非洲的热带地区和印度群岛多养活2亿人口，也并非是一

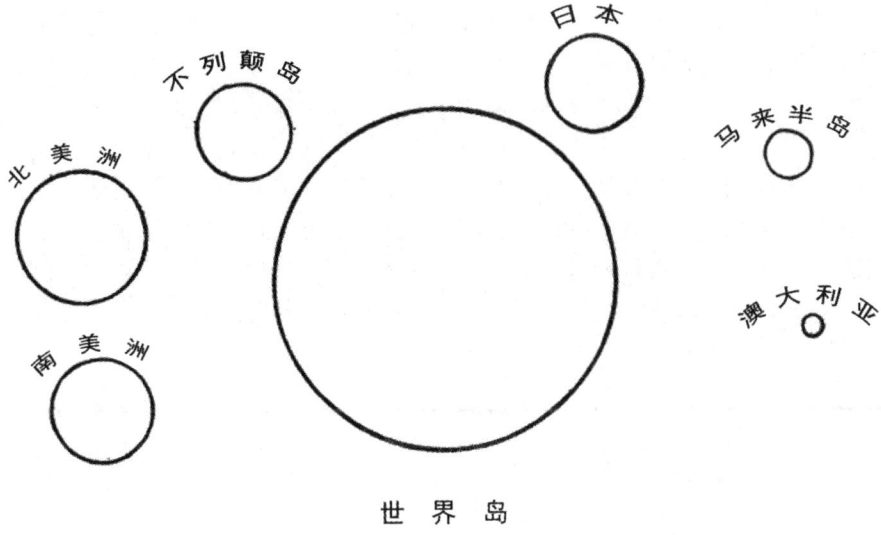

图13　图中的各个圆圈，代表了"世界岛"及其卫星岛屿的相对人口。

Europe, North America, or Japan?

What if the Great Continent, the whole World–Island or a large part of it, were at some future time to become a single and united base of sea–power? Would not the other insular bases be out–built as regards ships and outmanned as regards seamen? Their fleets would no doubt fight with all the heroism begotten of their histories, but the end would be fated. Even in the present War, insular America has had to come to the aid of insular Britain, not because the British fleet could not have held the seas for the time being, but lest such a building and manning base were to be assured to Germany at the Peace, or rather Truce, that Britain would inevitably be out–built and outmanned a few years later.

The surrender of the German fleet in the Firth of Forth is a dazzling event, but in all soberness, if we would take the long view, must we not still reckon with the possibility that a large part of the Great Continent might some day be united under a single sway, and that an invincible sea–power might be based upon it? May we not have headed off that danger in this War, and yet leave by our settlement the opening for a fresh attempt in the future? Ought we not to recognize that that is the great ultimate threat to the World's liberty so far as strategy is concerned, and to provide against it in our new political system?

Let us look at the matter from the Landsman's point of view.

件不可能做到的事情。单是刚果森林，倘若开垦出来进行耕作，倘若人口密度像爪哇那样，就可以养活大约4亿人口，而爪哇的人口，也还在不断地增加。何况，根据亚洲的气候和历史来看，我们又有什么权力说亚洲内陆不会养育出像欧洲、北美或者日本那样强壮的人口呢？

假如这个"大大陆"，即整个"世界岛"或者它的大部分地区，将来变成了海上强国一处单独而统一的基地，情况会怎么样呢？其他的那些岛屿基地，会不会建造不了那么多的船只、提供不了那么多的海员呢？它们的舰队，无疑会秉承其历史上的所有英雄主义来英勇作战的，不过它们的结局却早已命中注定了。即便是在目前的这次大战中，美利坚这个岛国也不得不去支援不列颠这个岛国，原因并非是英国舰队在目前无法控制住海洋，而是为了避免在和约上，或者更确切地说是在停战协议上，把这样一个既能造船、又有人力的基地交给德国；假如那样的话，数年之后英国在造船能力和人力数量上，就必定会被德国超过。

德国舰队在福思河口投降是一件辉煌无比的大事，但倘若我们带着长远的目光冷静下来，那么我们是不是仍然必须考虑到"大大陆"的大部分地区将来会不会统一于一种势力之下，考虑到以它为基地会建立起一个天下无敌的海上强国这种可能性呢？我们在这次世界大战中是不是并未消除掉这种危险，是不是仍然在停战协议中留下了空子，使得将来又有人会想要重新称霸世界呢？我们是不是应当认识到，从战略上来说那是对世界自由一种极大的终极威胁，从而在新的政治制度中制定出预防这种威胁的措施呢？

我们不妨再根据陆地民族的观点，来看一看这个问题。

无畏级战列舰

巨人级战列舰

猎户座号战列舰

君主号战列舰

IV THE LANDSMAN'S POINT OF VIEW

Four centuries ago the whole outlook of mankind was changed in a single generation by the voyages of the great pioneers, Columbus, Da Gama, and Magellan. The idea of the unity of the ocean, beforehand merely inferred from the likeness of the tides in the Atlantic and Indian waters, suddenly became a part of the mental equipment of practical men. A similar revolution is in progress in the present generation in the rapid realization of the unity of the Continent owing to modern methods of communication by land and air. The Islanders have been slow to understand what is happening. Britain went into the War for the defense of her neighbors, Belgium and France, seeing vaguely perhaps that she was herself threatened through their danger, but almost unanimous in her decision only because of a moral tie, her bond in regard

第四章　陆上民族的观点

四个世纪以前，哥伦布、达伽马和麦哲伦这三位伟大的先驱在一个世代的时间内，便通过他们的航行，改变了人类的整个眼界。海洋是个整体的这一观点，以前的人只是通过大西洋和印度洋海域相似的潮汐推断出来的，而到了此时，却突然变成实事求是者的一种必备知识了。在如今这一代，由于有了现代化的陆、空交通方式，因此在人们迅速认识到大陆也是一个整体的过程中，也正在发生着一场类似的革命。各个岛国对正在发生的这种情况，领悟得都很缓慢。英国是为了保卫比利时和法国这两个邻国才参与了此次大战，或许也是因为该国模模糊糊地意识到邻邦的危险也威胁到了该国自身，不过该国上下几乎一致决定参战的做法只是出于道义，只是因为英国与比利时缔结了条约。"路西塔尼亚号"惨案让美国深感震惊，而其最终参战，则是因为德国潜艇全面侵犯了中立国的权利。这两个同属盎格鲁–撒克逊血统的国家，一开始都没有看清这场战争

欧洲三大航海家——哥伦布

欧洲三大航海家——达·伽马

欧洲三大航海家——麦哲伦

to Belgium. America was shocked by the Lusitania tragedy, and was ultimately brought in because of the general infringement of the rights of neutrals by the German submarines. Neither of the Anglo–Saxon nations at first clearly saw the strategical meaning of the War. Theirs was an external view of the Continent, like that of the seamen who named the Guinea, Malabar, Coromandel, and Murman "Coasts". Neither in London nor in New York were International Politics commonly discussed in the way in which they are discussed in the cafes of Continental Europe. In order, therefore, to appreciate the Continental view we must remove our standpoint from without to within the great ring of the "Coasts".

Let us begin by "brigading" our data, for only so shall we be able to reason conveniently about the realities which the Continent presents for strategical thought. When you are thinking of large things you must think on broad lines; the colonel of a battalion thinks in companies, but the general of a division in brigades. For the purpose of forming our brigades, however, it will be necessary at the outset to go into some degree of geographical detail.

※　　※　　※　　※　　※　　※　　※　　※　　※

的战略意义。两国都只看到了欧洲大陆的表面现象，此种见识跟那个把几内亚、马拉巴尔、科罗曼德尔和穆曼都称作"海岸"的海员的见识并无两样。伦敦和纽约的人，都不像在欧洲大陆的人在咖啡馆里那样常常讨论国际政治问题。所以，为了充分理解欧洲大陆人的观点，我们必须将自己的立场从外部转移到"海岸"这个大圆圈之中来。

我们不妨首先把数据进行"编组"，因为只有这样做，我们才能方便地对这个大陆从战略思想方面所呈现出来的种种现实进行分析。在考虑大事的时候，我们必须根据广泛的原则来进行思考；指挥着一个营的校官，会以连队为单位来考虑问题，而指挥一个师的将官，则会以旅为单位来考虑问题。然而，为了将我们的数据进行编组，我们还是必须在开始时逐一讨论讨论地理上的具体情况。

※　　※　　※　　※　　※　　※　　※　　※　　※

"路西塔尼亚号"被德国潜艇击沉。英国的一艘远洋客轮，1915年被德国潜艇击沉于爱尔兰附近海域，1000多人丧生，其中包括128名美国人。

图14　图中所示为亚洲和欧洲的大部分地区，其中的河流不是流向冰雪覆盖的北方，便是流入并无出海口的咸水湖；本图还说明了非洲为何有长达4000英里的海岸线面对欧、亚两洲。（等面积投影）

The northern edge of Asia is the Inaccessible Coast, beset with ice except for a narrow water lane which opens here and there along the shore in the brief summer owing to the melting of the local ice formed in the winter between the grounded floes and the land. It so happens that three of the largest rivers in the world, the Lena, Yenisei, and Obi, stream northward through Siberia to this coast, and are therefore detached for practical purposes from the general system of the ocean and river navigations.[1] South of Siberia are other regions at least as large, drained into salt lakes having no outlet to the ocean; such are the basins of the Volga and Ural Rivers flowing to the Caspian Sea, and of the Oxus and Jaxartes to the Sea of Aral. Geographers usually

[1] This is true up to the present time, though, with the aid of modern ice-breakers, the efforts which are being made, especially by Tyneside enterprise, to open a direct route to the mouths of the Obi and Yenisei may perhaps result in the establishment of a sea-borne summer traffic to Western Siberia.

亚洲的北部边沿，就是"无法通航的海岸"，除了有一条窄窄的水道，整个海岸都被冰雪包围着；在短暂的夏季里，由于形成于冬季、在搁浅的浮冰与陆地之间冻起来的局部冰雪融化，这条水道便会沿着海岸此一处、彼一处地开封。碰巧，世界上最大的河流中有3条——即勒拿河、叶尼塞河和鄂毕河——都蜿蜒向北，流经西伯利亚并在这处海岸入海，因而同整个世界总的海、河航运体系实际上隔离开来了。［作者注：到目前为止情况还是这样，但在现代破冰船的协助下，人们（尤其是泰恩赛德[1]的企业）正在努力开辟一条直通鄂毕河与叶尼塞河两河河口的航线，并且可能会因此而确立一条夏季通往西西伯利亚的海运航线。］西伯利亚以南，是面积起码也跟西伯利亚差不多的一些其他地区，其中的河流都注入了没有入海口的咸水湖；比如属于伏尔加河流域和乌拉尔河流域的河流都注入里海，而属于阿姆河与锡尔河流域的河流则注入了

[1] Tyneside：泰恩赛德（地区）。指英国泰恩河沿岸，当时这一地区是造船、机器制造业和煤业中心之一。

describe these inward basins as "Continental". Taken together, the regions of Arctic and Continental drainage measure nearly a half of Asia and a quarter of Europe, and form a great continuous patch in the north and center of the continent. That whole patch, extending right across from the icy, flat shore of Siberia to the torrid, steep coasts of Baluchistan and Persia, has been inaccessible to navigation from the ocean. The opening of it by railways — for it was practically roadless beforehand — and by aeroplane routes in the near future, constitutes a revolution in the relations of men to the larger geographical realities of the world. Let us call this great region the Heartland of the Continent.

The north, center, and west of the Heartland are a plain, rising only a few hundred feet at most above sea level. In that greatest lowland on the globe are included Western Siberia,

咸海。地理学家通常把这些内陆流域称为"大陆流域"。北极地区和大陆水系加起来，几乎占到了亚洲的一半和欧洲的1/4，从而在这处大陆的北部和中部形成了延绵不断的一大片。从冰封、平坦的西伯利亚海岸一直延伸到了酷热而陡峭的俾路支斯坦[1]和波斯海岸的这一整片地区，一直都是无法通过海上航行到达的。通过铁路打通这片地区——因为以前这儿事实上根本就没有路——并且在不久的将来还通过开辟航空线路来把打通这个地区，将是改变人类与世界上这些更大的地理现实之关系的一次革命。我们不妨把这一广袤的区域叫做"大陆的中心地带"。

"中心地带"的北部、中部和西部都是一片平原，海拔最多不过几百英尺。地球上这个最大的低地，包括西西伯利亚、土耳其斯坦以及伏尔加河流域的欧洲部分，因为乌

[1] Baluchistan：俾路支斯坦。西南亚的一个地区，包括伊朗东南部和巴基斯坦西南部。现巴基斯坦有俾路支省。

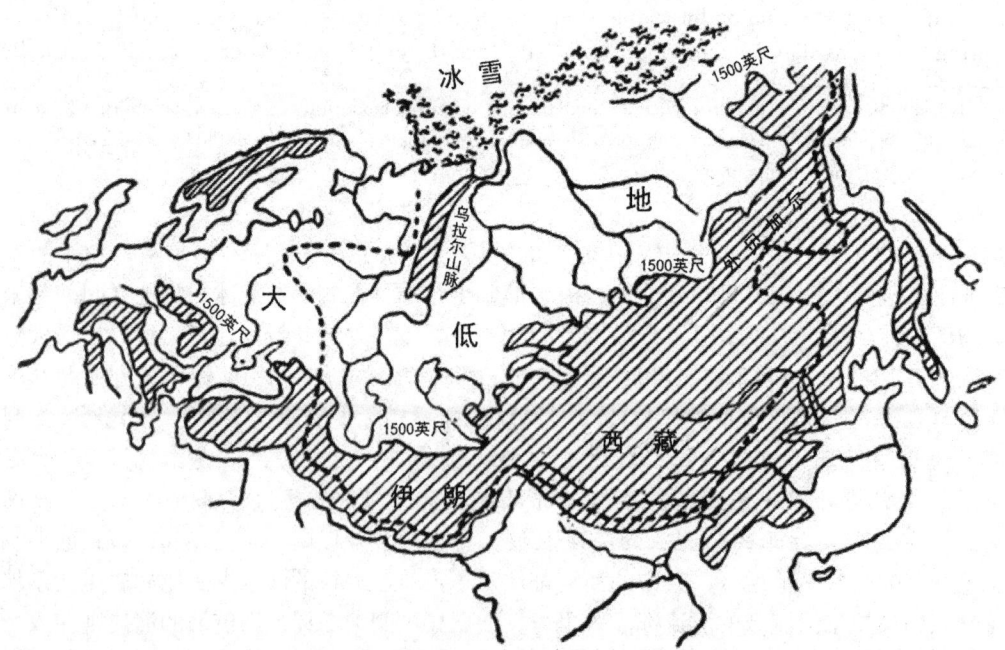

图15 从图中可以看出，"大低地"向西延伸进入欧洲，不再位于"中心地带"以内。此处所示"中心地带"的东部边界，包括了从地势高耸的高原上流入太平洋和印度洋的各条河流。

Turkestan, and the Volga basin of Europe, for the Ural Mountains, though a long range, are not of important height, and terminate some three hundred miles north of the Caspian, leaving a broad gateway from Siberia into Europe. Let us speak of this vast plain as the Great Lowland.

Southward the Great Lowland ends along the foot of a tableland, whose average elevation is about half a mile, with mountain ridges rising to a mile and a half. This tableland bears upon its broad back the three countries of Persia, Afghanistan, and Baluchistan; for convenience we may describe the whole of it as the Iranian Upland. The Heartland, in the sense of the region of Arctic and Continental drainage, includes most of the Great Lowland and most of the Iranian Upland; it extends therefore to the long, high, curving brink of the Persian Mountains, beyond which is the depression occupied by the Euphrates Valley and the Persian Gulf.

Now let us travel in imagination to the west of Africa. There, between the latitudes of the Canary and Cape Verde Islands, is a Desert Coast: it was the character of that coast, it will be remembered, which so long baffled the effort of the mediaeval sailors to make the southward voyage round Africa. With a breadth of a thousand miles the Sahara spreads thence across the north of Africa from the Atlantic Ocean to the Valley of the Nile. The Sahara is not everywhere an utter desert; there are many oases — trenched valleys with wells to the water percolating underground in their bottoms, or hilly tracts against which at times the clouds gather — but these are minute and scattered exceptions upon a barren and riverless area nearly as large as all Europe. The Sahara is the most unbroken natural boundary in the world; throughout History it has been a barrier between the White and the Black men.

Between the Sahara and the Heartland there is a broad gap which is occupied by Arabia. The two brinks of the Nile Valley are known as Libyan to the West and Arabian to the East; and away beyond the Lower Euphrates, at the foot of the Persian Mountains, is the district known

拉尔山脉虽然很长，海拔却并不高，并且止于里海以北约300英里，留下了一条从西伯利亚进入欧洲的广阔通道。我们不妨把这处巨大的平原叫做"大低地"。

这个"大低地"向南延伸到一处高原脚下便终止了，而高原的平均海拔约为半英里，上面的峰峦高达1.5英里。在这个广阔的高原上，有波斯、阿富汗和俾路支斯坦3个国家；为方便起见，我们可以把整个这片高原称为伊朗高原。从北极地区和大陆水系这个意义上来说，"中心地带"覆盖了"大低地"和伊朗高原的绝大部分地区；因此，"中心地带"一直延伸到了又长、又高、又蜿蜒的波斯山脉边缘，而这个边缘以外，便是幼发拉底河河谷和波斯湾所在的洼地了。

现在，让我们在想象中来神游一下非洲西部。西非加那利群岛和佛得角群岛之间，是一片沙漠海岸：我们还会记得，正是这个沙漠海岸的特点，才使得中世纪的水手们长久无法向南航行并绕过非洲。撒哈拉沙漠从此处开始绵亘1000英里，从大西洋直到尼罗河河谷，横贯整个非洲北部。撒哈拉沙漠也并非到处都是黄沙漫漫；其间还有许多绿洲——它们要么是下陷的山谷，谷底有泉，通着地下水，要么就是片片丘陵，时有云雨聚积——不过，它们的面积都很小，并且点缀分布，都是这片大小跟欧洲差不多、既荒芜又没有河流的沙漠上的例外情况。撒哈拉沙漠是世界上最完整的一处天然疆界；纵观整个历史，它一直都是横亘在白人与黑人之间的一道屏障。

撒哈拉沙漠和"中心地带"之间存在着一处宽阔的通道，由阿拉伯人占据着。尼罗河河谷的两侧，西面是利比亚，东面则是阿拉伯；而从此处到幼发拉底河下游，直抵波斯山脉脚下，就是那个被称作阿拉伯斯坦，或称阿拉伯人故乡的地区。因此，我们可

as Arabistan or the country of the Arabs. In complete harmony, therefore, with local usage, Arabia may be regarded as spreading for 800 miles from the Nile to beyond the Euphrates. From the foot of the Taurus Mountains, north of Aleppo, to the Gulf of Aden, it measures no less than 1800 miles. As to one-half, Arabia is desert, and as to the other half mainly dry steppes; although it lies in the same latitudes as the Sahara, it is more productive and carries a more considerable population of wandering Bedouin. Moreover, it has larger oases, and therefore larger cities. What, however, most distinguishes Arabia both from the Heartland and the Sahara is the fact that it is traversed by three great water ways in connection with the ocean — the Nile, the Red Sea, and the Euphrates and Persian Gulf. None of these three ways, however, affords naturally a complete passage across the arid belt. The Nile was navigable from the Mediterranean only to the first cataract, midway across the desert, though locks have now been constructed at Assouan which give access as far as the second cataract; and the navigation of the Euphrates ascends only to a point a hundred miles from the Mediterranean. Today it is true that the Suez Canal unites the Mediterranean to the Red Sea, but it was not only the isthmus which formerly impeded through traffic by this route; persistent north winds of the trade wind current blow down the northern end of the Red Sea, which is beset with rocks, and sailing ships do not willingly attempt the northward voyage to the Canal, which would therefore have been relatively useless but for steam navigation. The former Red Sea route to the Mediterranean was from Kosseir on the west coast over the desert to the Nile at Keneh, and then down the Nile; that was the way followed by the British Army when sent from India to Egypt more than a hundred years ago, at the time of the Napoleonic invasion of Egypt and Palestine.

It follows from the foregoing description that the Heartland, Arabia, and the Sahara together constitute a broad, curving belt inaccessible to seafaring people, except by the three

以认为阿拉伯地区是从尼罗河起延伸800英里、直达幼发拉底河以东，而这种观点同当地的习惯看法是完全一致的。从阿勒颇以北的托罗斯山脉脚下到亚丁湾，相距1800多英里。阿拉伯地区一半是沙漠，另一半主要是干旱的草原；尽管它与撒哈拉沙漠所处纬度相同，但此处物产却较为丰富，因此养活了数量众多的人口，主要是贝都因人这个游牧民族。此外，阿拉伯地区有许多面积更大的绿洲，因此也拥有规模较大的一些城市。然而，使得阿拉伯地区最有别于"中心地带"和撒哈拉沙漠的，还是下面这个事实：阿拉伯地区横亘着三条与海洋相通的大水道，即尼罗河、红海以及幼发拉底河与波斯湾。然而，这三条水道都没有天然地完全横贯整个干旱地带。从地中海出发，尼罗河只能通航到第一瀑布，这才跨过了撒哈拉沙漠的一半，但如今已经在阿斯旺建起了水闸，使得此河可以通航到第二瀑布了；而在幼发拉底河上，船只也只能逆行到距地中海尚有100英里的地方。如今，苏伊士运河的确已经连通了地中海和红海，但以前妨碍这条水路航运畅通的，也并非只有苏伊士地峡；因季风气流而形成的经常性北风，向南一直刮到了红海北端，那里礁石林立，帆船都不肯向北航行前往苏伊士运河，所以倘若没有汽轮航运，那么这条运河几乎就没有什么用处。以前经由红海到地中海的路线，是从红海西岸的库塞尔出发，横跨沙漠，到达基纳的尼罗河边，然后再顺尼罗河而下；100多年前拿破仑入侵埃及和巴勒斯坦时，从印度派往埃及的英军走的就是这条路线。

从前面这些描述即可看出，"中心地带"、阿拉伯半岛和撒哈拉沙漠这三处合起来形成了辽阔而呈弧形的一个地带；除了经由阿拉伯地区的那三条水道，航海民族是没法到达这一地带的。这一地带，完全贯穿了整个广袤的大陆，从北极地区直达大西洋沿岸。

拿破仑入侵埃及

Arabian water ways. This belt extends completely across the great continent from the Arctic to the Atlantic shores. In Arabia it touches the Indian Ocean, and, as a consequence, divides the remainder of the Continent into three separate regions whose rivers flow to the ice−free ocean. These regions are the Pacific and Indian slopes of Asia; the peninsulas and islands of Europe and the Mediterranean; and the great promontory of Africa south of the Sahara. The last−named differs from the other two regions in a very important respect. Its larger rivers, the Niger, Zambesi, and Congo, and also its smaller rivers, such as the Orange and Limpopo, flow across the tableland of the interior, and fall steeply over its edge to relatively short seaward reaches in the narrow coastal lowlands. The long upland courses of these rivers are navigable for several thousand miles, but are for practical purposes as completely detached from the ocean as the rivers of Siberia. The same, of course, is true of the Nile above the cataracts. We may, therefore, regard the interior of Africa south of the Sahara as a second Heartland. Let us speak of it as the

在阿拉伯半岛，它触伸到了印度洋，并因此又把整个大陆的其余部分分成了三个单独的区域，其间的河流都注入了不会封冻的海域。这三个区域，便是亚洲的环太平洋斜坡和印度斜坡，欧洲和地中海地区的半岛和岛屿，以及撒哈拉沙漠以南的非洲大海角。最后那个区域跟前面两个区域相比，在一个方面有着极其重大的差异。此区域中那些较大的河流，即尼日尔河、赞比西河与刚果河，以及一些较小的河流，诸如奥兰治河与林波波河，都是流经内陆高原并在高原边缘陡然下落，然后在狭窄的沿海低地上流经较短距离便入海了。这些河流漫长的高原河道都可通航，里程达数千英里，但实际上这些高原河道跟西伯利亚地区的河流一样，完全与海洋不相联通。自然，尼罗河各大瀑布以上河段的航运情况也是如此。所以，我们可以把撒哈拉沙漠以南的非洲内陆看成第二个"中心地带"。我们不妨称之为"南中心地带"，以对应并区别于欧、亚两洲所形成的"北中心地带"。

Southern Heartland, in contradistinction to the Northern Heartland of Asia and Europe.

Notwithstanding their very different latitudes the two Heartlands present other striking similarities. A great belt of forest, mainly of the evergreen type of the pines and firs, spreads from North Germany and the Baltic shore right across to Manchuria, connecting by a forest-ribbon, as it were, the forests of Europe with those of the Pacific Coast. South of this forest zone the Heartland lies open, with trees only along the river banks and upon the mountains. This vast, open ground is a luscious prairie along the southern border of the forest, and brilliant with bulb-flowers in the spring-time, but southward, as the aridity increases, the grass becomes coarser and more sparse. The whole grassland, rich and poor, is conveniently spoken of as the Steppes, although that name properly belongs only to the less fertile southern tracts which

尽管这两个"中心地带"所处的纬度位置截然不同,但它们却呈现出了其他一些显著的相似之处。从德国北部和波罗的海沿岸直到满洲里,延伸着一条巨大的森林带,主要是常绿的松、杉针叶林,仿佛是用一条森林缎带,将欧洲的森林和太平洋沿岸的森林连了起来。在这个森林区以南,"中心地带"变得开阔空旷起来,只是河岸和山脉上才有树木了。这片广袤而开阔的大地,就是森林区南沿一个水草甘美的大草原,春季繁花似锦,烂漫无垠;不过再往南去,随着干旱性渐增,草木也就变得越来越粗糙、越来越稀疏了。为了方便起见,我们将这一整片或肥沃、或贫瘠的草地统称为"大草原";但这个名称,原本只适合于称呼围绕着土耳其斯坦和蒙古那些零散沙漠的、也没有那么肥沃的南方地区。"大草原"十有

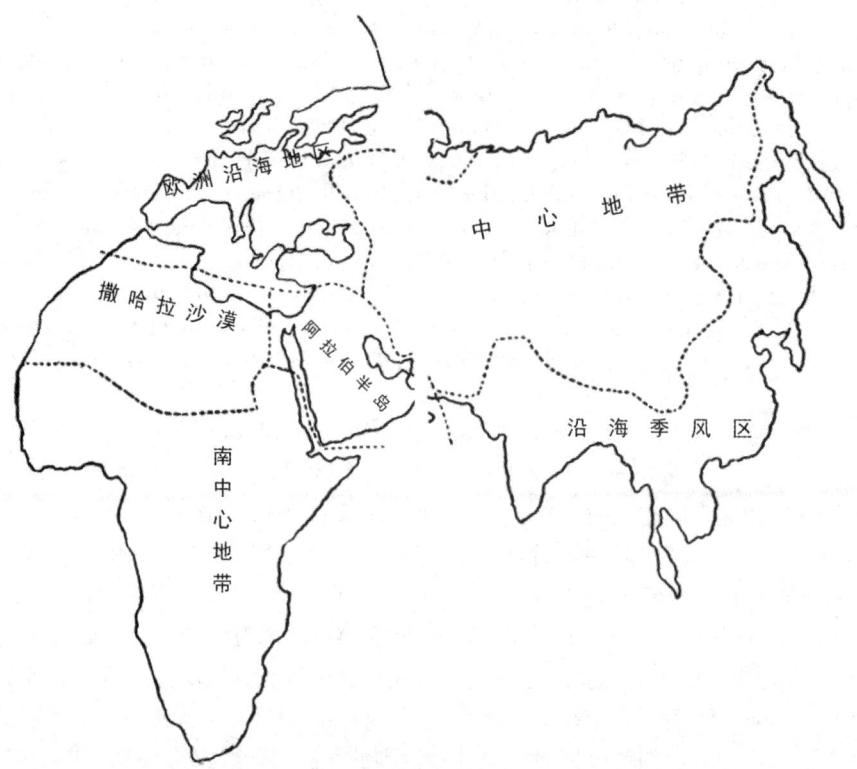

图16 世界岛",分成了六个自然区域。(等面积投影)。

surround the desert patches of Turkestan and Mongolia. The Steppes were probably the original habitat of the horse, and in their southern parts, of the two-humped camel.

The Southern Heartland also has its wide open grasslands, which in the Sudan gradually increase in fertility from the edge of the Sahara towards the tropical forest of the Guinea Coast and the Congo. The forests do not spread completely across to the Indian Ocean, but leave a belt of grassy upland which connects the grasslands of the Sudan with those of South Africa, and this immense, open ground, thus continuous from the Sudan to the Cape Veldt, is the home of the antelopes, zebras, and other large, hoofed game, which correspond to the wild horses and wild asses of the Northern Heartland. Though the zebra has not been successfully domesticated, and the South African natives had no usual beast of burden, yet the horse and the one-humped camel of Arabia were early introduced into the Sudan. In both Heartlands, therefore, although to a greater extent in the Northern than in the Southern, mobility by the aid of animals has been available to replace the riverwise and coastwise mobility of the ships of the Atlantic and Pacific coastlands.

The Northern Heartland adjoins Arabia, as we have seen, for many hundred miles where the Iranian Upland drops to the Euphrates Valley; the Southern Heartland, at its northeastern corner in Abyssinia and Somaliland, grasps, though with an interval of sea, the southern fertile angle of Arabia, known as Yemen. So the Steppes of Arabia, enframing its deserts, serve as a passage-land between the Northern and Southern Heartlands; and there is also the way by the banks of the Nile through Nubia. Thus it will be realized that the Northern Heartland, Arabia, and the Southern Heartland afford a broad, grassy way for horsemen and camel-men from Siberia through Persia, Arabia, and Egypt into the Sudan, and that but for the tsetse-fly and

八九是马类的原栖息地，而其南部地区则很可能是双峰驼的原栖息地（参见图18）。

"南中心地带"上，也有广袤而开阔的草原；这片草原在苏丹境内逐渐变得肥沃，从撒哈拉沙漠一直延伸到了位于几内亚海岸的热带森林和刚果森林。其间的森林并没有完全横贯大陆并直达印度洋，而是留下了一条高原草地带，把苏丹的草原和南非的草原连接起来了；因此从苏丹绵延至韦尔德角草原的这片广袤而空旷的土地，便成了羚羊、斑马以及其他大型有蹄动物的家园，与"北中心地带"这个野马、野驴的家园相呼应。虽说人们并未成功地驯服斑马，使得南非的土著没有常见的驮畜，不过阿拉伯半岛的马匹和单峰驼很早就已经引入了苏丹。因此，尽管在"北中心地带"使用驮畜的程度比在"南中心地带"更广泛，但这两个"中心地带"都有牲口来帮助人们进行迁徙，从而取代了大西洋和太平洋沿岸地区沿河或者沿海乘船迁徙的状况。

正如我们已经看到的那样，"北中心地带"与阿拉伯半岛毗连数百英里，伊朗高原则在此毗连之处下落到了幼发拉底河河谷；而"南中心地带"在位于阿比西尼亚[1]和索马里兰的东北角上，虽说隔着一片海域，却扼守住了阿拉伯半岛南部称为也门的那一角沃土。所以，沙漠四周的阿拉伯半岛大草原，就可以作为"南中心地带"和"北中心地带"之间的通道了；而且还有经由尼罗河两岸、穿过努比亚这另一条通道。这样一来，人们就会认识到，"北中心地带"、阿拉伯半岛和"南中心地带"为骑马、骑骆驼的民族提供了一条从西伯利亚经由波斯、阿拉伯半岛和埃及进入苏丹的宽广而多草的通道，并且要不是有采采蝇[2]和其他疫病的话，人们很可能早就骑着马和骆驼向南深入，差不

[1] Abyssinia：阿比西尼亚。非洲东部国家埃塞俄比亚的旧称。
[2] tsetse-fly：采采蝇。一种传播昏睡病的非洲蝇类，能够吸食人畜血液并导致人畜患上严重疾病。

other plagues men would probably have penetrated on horseback and camel–back southward almost to the Cape of Good Hope.

Outside Arabia, the Sahara, and the two Heartlands, there remain in the World–Island only two comparatively small regions, but those two regions are the most important on the globe. Around the Mediterranean, and in the European peninsulas and islands, there dwell four hundred million people, and in the southern and eastern coastlands of Asia, or, to use the historic expression, in the Indies, there dwell eight hundred million people. In these two regions, therefore, are three–quarters of the people of the world. From our present point of view the most pertinent

多直抵好望角了。

除了阿拉伯半岛、撒哈拉沙漠和两个"中心地带"，"世界岛"上便只剩下两个相对较小的区域了，不过它们却是地球上最重要的两个区域。在环地中海地区以及欧洲的各个半岛和岛屿上，居住着4亿人口；而在亚洲南部和东部沿海地区，或者沿用历史上的叫法，即在印度群岛上，又居住着8亿人口。所以，这两个区域内居住着世界上3/4的人口。从我们目前的观点来看，能够最中肯地说明这一伟大事实的说法，就是"大大陆"——即"世界岛"——4/5的人口，全都生活在面积总共只占"大大陆"1/5的这两

图17 南中心地带。＝河流上的瀑布，←阿拉伯人的入侵路线。

图18. //// 大草原

way of stating this great fact is to say that four-fifths of the population of the Great Continent, the World-Island, live in two regions which together measure only one-fifth of its area.

　　These two regions resemble one another in certain other very important respects. In the first place, their rivers are for the most part navigable continuously from the ocean. In the Indies we have this series of large rivers descending to the open sea; Indus, Ganges, Brahmaputra, Irrawady, Salwen, Menam, Mekong, Songho, Sikiang, Yangtse, Hoangho, Peiho, Liauho, Amur. Most of them are navigable from their mouths for some hundreds of miles; a British battleship once steamed up the Yangtse to Hankow, five hundred miles from the sea. There is not much space for such large rivers in peninsular Europe, but the Danube, Rhine, and Elbe carry a

个区域内。

　　这两个区域在其他一些极其重要的方面都有着相似之处。首先，这两个区域里的河流，大多数都可从海洋通航到内陆。在印度群岛，有许多这样的大河都是一路奔流、注入外海的；比如印度河、恒河、布拉马普特拉河[1]、伊洛瓦底江、萨尔温江[2]、湄南河、湄公河、红河、西江、长江、黄河、白河、辽河和阿穆尔河[3]。其中的大多数河流都可从河口逆流而上，通航数百英里；一艘英国战舰曾经沿着长江上航到了汉口，该地距海洋已达500英里了。在欧洲半岛，虽说没有容纳此种大河的空间，但多瑙河、莱茵河和易北河的航运却繁忙得很，并且直接与大海相通。莱茵河上游300英里处的曼海姆战前就已经是欧洲的主要港口之一了，其码头可以停靠长达100码、载重量达1000吨的驳船。至于其他方面，虽说欧洲的半岛性质具有约束性，使得其中的河流无法四通八

---

　　[1] Brahmaputra：布拉马普特拉河。亚洲河流之一，流经中国境内的一段称为雅鲁藏布江。

　　[2] Salwen：萨尔温江。亚洲河流之一，流经中国境内的一段称为怒江。亦拼作Salween。

　　[3] Amur：阿穆尔河。中俄界河，中国称黑龙江。注意，此处的河流名称中，原文中的Songho应指红河，Sikiang（西江）实应为珠江，Peiho（白河）实应为海河。

great traffic in direct connection with the ocean. Mannheim, three hundred miles up the Rhine, was one of the principal ports of Europe before the War; barges a hundred yards long and of a thousand tons burden lay beside its wharves. For the rest, the pen-insulation of Europe, which limits the development of rivers, itself offers even greater facilities for mobility by water.

The similarity of these two "Coastlands" is not limited to the navigability of their rivers. If we clear away from the more arid zone on the rainfall map of the World-Island the patches indicative of merely local rains, due to mountain groups, we perceive at once the preeminence of the coastlands in fertility, owing to their widespread rainfall on the plains as well as in the mountains. The Monsoon winds of the summer carry the moisture of the ocean from the southwest on to India and from the southeast on to China; the west winds from the Atlantic bring rain at all seasons upon Europe, and in the winter time upon the Mediterranean. Both coast-

达，但这一点本身就会让欧洲的水上交通具有更大的便利性。

这两个"沿海地区"的相似之处，并不仅仅在于两地河流的通航能力这个方面。假如我们在"世界岛"的雨量图上，把表示因为山脉群集而只有局部降雨的那些地区从较干旱地区中清除出去，那么我们马上就会认识到，由于沿海山区和平原降雨范围广泛，所以沿海地带也格外肥沃。盛夏的西南季风携带着海洋的水汽吹往印度，东南季风则吹往中国；而从大西洋吹来的西风，一年四季都会为欧洲带来降水，冬季还会给地中海地区带来降雨。所以，这两个沿海地区都耕地密布，并因此而养育了大量的人口。这样一来，欧洲和印度群岛便成了农民和船员的天地；而"北中心地带"、阿拉伯半岛和"南中心地带"的绝大部分土地却都并未开垦，航运船只也无法到达。但另一方面，这三个地方却天生适合于骑马、骑骆驼的民族带着他们的牛群羊群游牧迁徙。即便是在热带非洲那些既无马匹、也无骆驼的大草原上，当地人的财产主要也是牛和羊。当然，这些都属

鸦片战争时英国军舰炮轰清军的防御工事

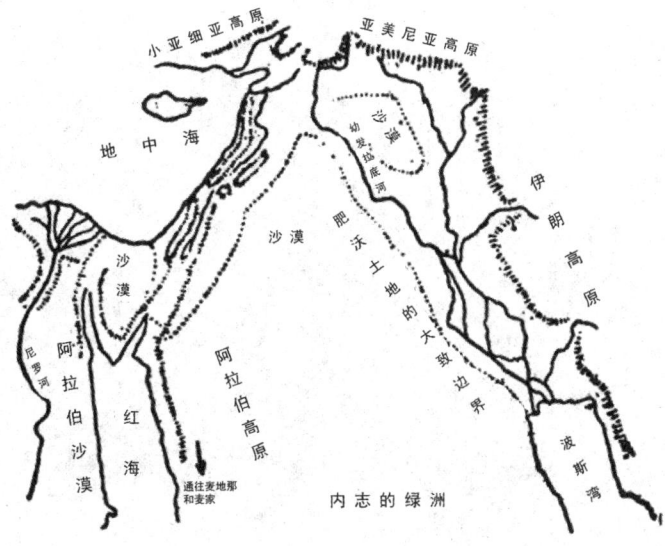

图19　北阿拉伯半岛

lands are therefore rich with tillage, and for that reason nourish their great populations. Thus Europe and the Indies are the regions of the ploughmen and shipmen; whereas the Northern Heartland, Arabia, and the Southern Heartland have for the most part been unplowed, and are inaccessible to sea-going ships. On the other hand, they are naturally adapted to the mobility of horsemen and camel-men, with their herds of cattle and flocks of sheep. Even on the savannahs of Tropical Africa, where horses and camels are absent, the wealth of the natives is chiefly of cattle and sheep. These are of course broad generalizations, with many local exceptions; they are none the less truly and sufficiently descriptive of immense geographical realities.[1]

　※　　　※　　　※　　　※　　　※　　　※　　　※　　　※　　　※

Let us now call History to our aid, for no practical idea, no idea which moves men to action, can be grasped statically; we must come to it with a momentum of thought either from our own

---

[1] Realities, that is to say, that have conditioned History, and have thus led to the present distribution of population and civilisation. These same realities have today begun to take on new aspects, owing to the higher organization of food production on the richer grasslands.

于宽泛而概括的情况，还有许多局部的例外情形；但尽管如此，这些情况还是真实而充分地描述了浩瀚的地理现实。［作者注：换言之，就是那些曾经制约过历史、并且因而导致目前人口和文化分布状况的现实情况。由于在一些较为富饶的草原上食品生产的组织化程度更高了，所以这些同样的地理现实如今已经开始呈现出新的面貌了。］

※　　　※　　　※　　　※　　　※　　　※　　　※　　　※　　　※

现在我们不妨转向历史，从历史中去寻求帮助；因为没有哪一种实用的观点、没有哪一种促人行动的思想，是可以在静态中领悟的。我们必须带着一种动态思维，要么从我们自身的经验当中，要么便是从整个民族的历史当中，去理解这种思想才是。东方的绿洲之所以在诗歌中被称颂为"世界花园"，原因只在于人们是从沙漠上到达这些绿洲的！

人类有记载的历史，始于围绕着阿拉伯半岛北部的那些大绿洲。我们确切了解的首次国际政治活动，与崛起于幼发拉底河、尼罗河两河下游冲积平原上的两个国家间的交

鸦片战争时英国军舰炮轰清军的防御工事

experience or from the history of the race. The oases of the East count in poetry as the Gardens of the World, only because they are approached over the desert!

Recorded History begins in the great oases round the north of Arabia. The first International Politics of which we have definite knowledge were concerned with the intercourse between two States which had grown up on the alluvial flats of the Lower Euphrates and Lower Nile; the maintenance of dykes to keep out the water, and of canals to distribute water, inevitably gives an impulse to social order and discipline. There was a certain difference in the two civilizations which may well have been the basis of interchange between them. In Egypt the rocky sides of the relatively narrow valley offered stone for building, and the papyrus reed afforded a material for writing; whereas building was of brick in the broad plain of Babylonia, and clay tablets bore the cuneiform inscriptions. The road between the two countries ran westward from the Euphrates across

往有关；为了防洪而维修堤坝、为了分流灌溉而维修沟渠，都必然会让人类拥有了确立社会秩序和规章制度的动力。那两个文明国家之间存在着某种差异，而这种差异很可能便是两国进行交流的基础。在埃及，相对较窄的尼罗河河谷两岸的岩壁提供了建筑所用的石材，莎草又为人们提供了书写材料；而在广阔的巴比伦平原上，人们则用砖建筑，并将楔形文字刻写在泥板上。两国之间的那条道路，是从幼发拉底河往西，横穿阿拉伯沙漠上的叙利亚一角，经过帕尔迈拉[1]诸泉，再到建立在绿洲之上的大马士革；这个绿洲，是从外黎巴嫩山脉和赫尔蒙山流下的阿巴纳河和法帕河这两条小河形成的。从大马士革出发，又有两条道路通往埃及；地势较低的那条路是沿着海岸前进，而地势较高的

[1] Palmyra：帕尔迈拉。叙利亚中部的一座古城，位于大马士革东北。据说是所罗门所建，它位于从埃及到波斯湾的贸易路线上，在罗马人的控制下兴盛起来。

the Syrian angle of the Arabian Desert, past the wells of Palmyra, to Damascus, which was built in the oasis formed by the streams Abana and Pharpar descending from Anti-Lebanon and Hermon. From Damascus there were alternative ways into Egypt; the lower by the coast, and the upper along the edge of the desert plateau east of the Jordan Valley. Aloof, on the rocky ridge of Judea, between these upper and lower ways, was the hill fortress of Jerusalem.

In a monkish map, contemporary with the Crusades, which still hangs in Hereford Cathedral, Jerusalem is marked as at the geometrical center, the navel, of the world, and on the floor of the Church of the Holy Sepulcher at Jerusalem they will show you to this day the precise spot which is the center. If our study of the geographical realities, as we now know them in their

那条路，则是沿着约旦河谷东面那个沙漠高原的边缘前进。在这两条路线之间，在朱迪亚[1]那多石的岭脊之上，便是耶路撒冷这个孤零零的山城要塞。

在一张十字军东征时期的僧侣所用的地图上——这张地图，至今仍然挂在赫里福德大教堂[2]里——耶路撒冷被标注为世界的几何中心，即"世界之脐"，而时至今日，在耶路撒冷的圣墓大教堂[3]，修士们还会在地板上为我们指出哪个地方正好是世界的中心。由于我们如今已经完全了解了各种地理现实，所以倘若对这些地理现实所进行的研究正在引领我们走向正确结论的话，那么中世纪的传教士们就错得并不是很离谱了。如果"世界岛"必然会成为人类在地球上生息繁衍的主要之地，如果作为从欧洲前往印度

[1] Judea：朱迪亚。古代巴勒斯坦南部的一个地区，包括如今以色列的南部以及约旦的西南部部分地区，曾是古罗马帝国叙利亚行省的一部分。亦译作"犹大"。

[2] Hereford Cathedral：赫里福德大教堂。位于英国赫里福德郡的一座大教堂，也是一处著名的观光景点，始建于1204年。

[3] the Church of the Holy Sepulcher：圣墓大教堂。位于耶路撒冷老城区，据说因耶稣复活前被安葬于此而得名。亦称复活堂。

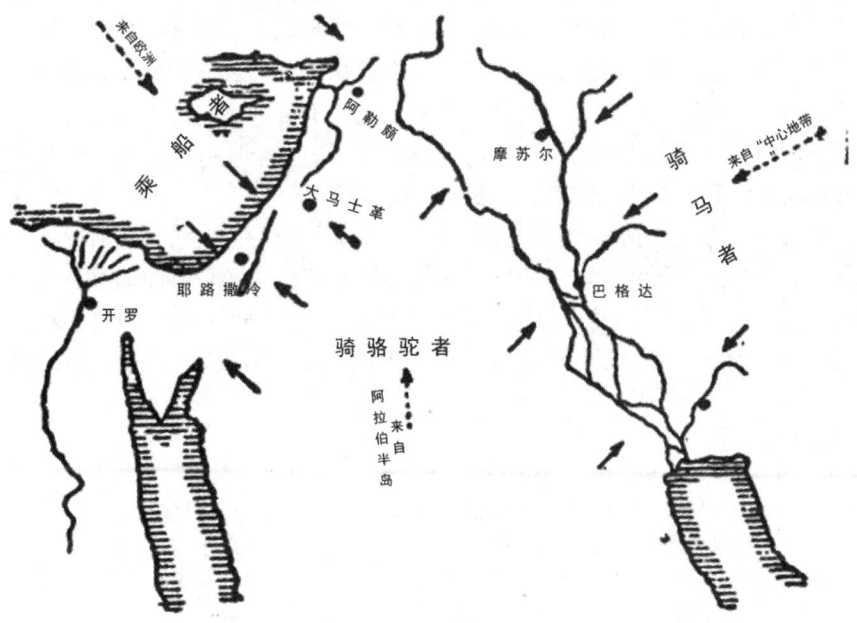

图20　已开垦土地上的流动征服者

completeness, is leading us to right conclusions, the mediaeval ecclesiastics were not far wrong. If the World–Island be inevitably the principal seat of humanity on this globe, and if Arabia, as the passage–land from Europe to the Indies and from the Northern to the Southern Heartland, be central in the World–Island, then the hill citadel of Jerusalem has a strategical position with reference to world–realities not differing essentially from its ideal position in the perspective of the Middle Ages, or its strategical position between ancient Babylon and Egypt. As the War has shown, the Suez Canal carries the rich traffic between the Indies and Europe to within striking distance of an army based on Palestine, and already the trunk railway is being built through the coastal plain by Jaffa, which will connect the Southern with the Northern Heartland. Who owns Damascus, moreover, will have flank access to the alternative route between the oceans down the Euphrates Valley. It cannot be wholly a coincidence that in the self–same region should be the starting point of History and the crossing point of the most vital of modern highways.

In the dawn of History we find the children of Shem, the Semites, conquering the cultivated margins of the Arabian deserts; there is no small similarity between the ring of their settlements round the sea of sand, and the settlements of the Greeks round the Aegean Sea. The invasion of the Promised Land from

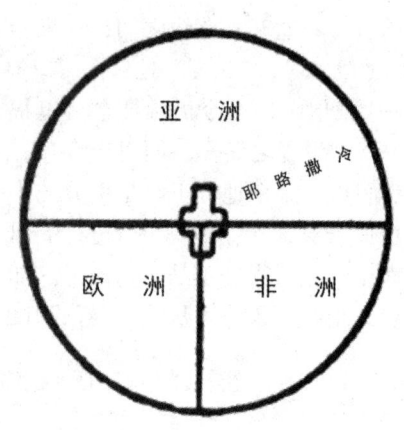

图21　中世纪的圆形地图

群岛、从"北中心地带"前往"南中心地带"通道的阿拉伯半岛处在"世界岛"中心位置，那么耶路撒冷这个山城要塞对于世界的现实情况就具有了战略上的重要性；这种战略地位，在本质上跟从中世纪的角度来看它所应处的理想位置，或者跟它在古巴比伦和古埃及之间所处的战略地位，并没有什么不同。正如这场大战已经表明的那样，苏伊士运河会把印度群岛和欧洲之间的繁忙贸易，推进到一支以巴勒斯坦为基地的军队的打击范围之内，而一条穿越雅法沿海平原的铁路干线也正在修建当中，这条铁路又将把"南中心地带"和"北中心地带"连接起来。此外，占领了大马士革的人，也将可以迂回到达另一条通道上，在两大海洋之间顺幼发拉底河河谷而下。同一个地区既是历史的起点，又是现代诸条交通干线最重要的交叉点，这是不可能纯属巧合的。

我们知道，在有史之初，是闪[1]的子孙——即闪米特人——征服了阿拉伯沙漠上的那些边缘开垦带；他们环绕着沙海而居，这与希腊人环绕着爱琴海而居是极为相似的。以色列的后裔贝尼-以色列人[2]从约旦之外对"应许之地"[3]的入侵，很可能只是贝都因人多次类似进袭中的一次罢了。迦勒底人就是闪族人，亚伯拉罕[4]正是从他们那座位于

---

[1] Shem：闪。基督教《圣经》中诺亚的长子，被认为是闪米特人（Semite，亦即犹太人）的祖先。

[2] Beni-Israel：贝尼-以色列人。游牧部落塞姆族（Semith）里的一个部落。注意，这里的"以色列"（Israel）即指《圣经》中的雅各以及雅各的后代，又被认为是"上帝的选民"。

[3] Promised Land：应许之地。《圣经》中上帝许给亚伯拉罕及其后裔居住的地方，即Canaan（迦南），位于死海和地中海之间，以耶路撒冷为中心。后多用于喻指"乐土，极乐世界"。

[4] Abraham：亚伯拉罕。《圣经》中的人物，相传为希伯来人的始祖，故亦称"众人之父"。

古巴比伦空中花园

beyond the Jordan by the Beni−Israel, the Children of Israel, was probably but one of many like descents of the Bedouin. The Chaldees, from whose city of Ur on the desert border Abraham migrated along the beaten track into Palestine, were Semites who supplanted the non−Semitic Accadians in the land which became Babylonia; and the Dynasty of the Shepherd Kings in Egypt was also apparently of Semitic origin. So it came about that all the peoples of Arabia — Arabs, Babylonians, Assyrians, Syrians, Phoenicians, and Hebrews — spoke dialects of the same Semitic family of speech. Today Arabic is the universal tongue from the Taurus to the Gulf of Aden, and from the Persian Mountains to the oases in the Sahara west of the Nile.

沙漠边缘的乌尔城[1]出发，沿着一条老路迁进巴勒斯坦的，他们赶走了不属于闪米特族的阿卡德人，在这片土地上建立了巴比伦王国；而埃及希克索斯王朝[2]的历任君主，显然也是闪米特人的后裔。因此，阿拉伯半岛上的所有民族——即阿拉伯人、巴比伦人、亚述人、叙利亚人、腓尼基人和希伯来人——所说的，便都是同属于闪米特语系的方言。如今，阿拉伯语已是从托罗斯山脉到亚丁湾、从波斯山脉到尼罗河以西撒哈拉沙漠中各处绿洲这一广大区域里的一种通用语言了。

　　除了一个方向，阿拉伯高原的四周都陡峭地下落到了沿海地区；在东北方向上，阿

---

[1] Ur：乌尔城。古代美索不达米亚平原南部苏美尔人的一个重要城市，位于今伊拉克南部。

[2] Shepherd Kings：希克索斯（Hyksos）王朝。古埃及的一个王朝。希克索斯人是古代亚洲西部的一个混合民族，他们于公元前17世纪侵入埃及东部，并在那里建立起了第十五王朝和第十六王朝（约公元前1674年～公元前1548年）。

The Arabian tableland drops steeply to the sea shores around in all directions save one; northeastward it shelves gradually down to the depression occupied by the Euphrates and the Persian Gulf. That depression is 1800 miles long, from the gorge by which the Euphrates issues from its source valley in the Armenian Plateau to the Strait of Ormuz at the mouth of the Persian Gulf; throughout its length it is overlooked by the range of the Persian Mountains, the high Iranian brink of the Heartland. One of the great events of Classical History was when the Persian Highlanders came down on to the Euphrates plain under their King Cyrus, and, after conquering Babylon, passed on by the Syrian road through Damascus to the conquest of Egypt.

The gorge by which the Euphrates escapes from the Armenian upland is more than 800 miles in a direct line from the river mouth and only a little more than 100 miles from the northeastern corner of the Mediterranean Sea near Aleppo, Immediately west of this gorge the High Upland of Armenia, some one and a half miles in average elevation, drops to the much lower peninsular tableland of Asia Minor. A second great event in Classical History was when the Macedonians, under King Alexander, having crossed the Dardanelles and traversed the open center of Asia Minor, descended by the Taurus passes into Cilicia, and struck through Syria into Egypt, and then from Egypt back through Syria to the Euphrates, and down the Euphrates to Babylon. It is true that Alexander thus led his Macedonians overland into Arabia, but their attack was really based on sea-power, as is evident from the rapid rise which ensued of the great Greek-speaking ports of Alexandria and Antioch, the coastal capitals, that is to say, of seamen going inland.

拉伯高原是和缓而逐渐地下降到了幼发拉底河与波斯湾所在的那片低地上。这片低地长达1800英里，从幼发拉底河在亚美尼亚高原上发源的那个峡谷起，直抵波斯湾入口处的霍尔木兹海峡；波斯山脉则一路耸立，俯瞰着这片低地，而波斯山脉正是"中心地带"伊朗一侧那座高耸的山脉。这里曾经发生过古罗马历史上的一次重大事件，那就是高地上的波斯人在国王居鲁士[1]的率领下，袭击了幼发拉底河平原，并在征服了巴比伦之后，又沿着叙利亚那条道路，经由大马士革征服了埃及。

幼发拉底河在亚美尼亚高原上发源的那个峡谷，与幼发拉底河河口之间的直线距离长达800多英里，但距阿勒颇附近的地中海东北角却只有100多英里。在紧挨着这个峡谷以西的地方，平均海拔约为1.5英里的亚美尼亚高原，下落到了平均海拔低得多的小亚细亚半岛高原上。古罗马历史上的第二桩重大事件，就是马其顿人在国王亚历山大大帝的统率下，越过达达尼尔海峡，横穿小亚细亚开阔的中央地带，经由托罗斯山脉的各个隘口而下并进入西里西亚，然后穿过叙利亚攻入埃及，接下来又从埃及回师，再通过叙利亚到达幼发拉底河，最后沿着幼发拉底河而下，攻入了巴比伦。亚历山大大帝的确是如此率领着手下的马其顿人横越大陆并攻入了阿拉伯半岛的，不过马其顿人的进击倚赖的实际上是海上力量；这一点是很明显的，因为随后就迅速崛起了说希腊语的亚历山大和安塔基亚两大海港——这两大海港，也可以说是海洋民族赖以进入内陆的沿海首府。

假如从地理的角度来研究这些事实，我们就可以看到，有一片肥沃地带从幼发拉底

[1] Cyrus：居鲁士。此处指居鲁士大帝（Cyrus the Great，公元前590~529年），古代波斯帝国的缔造者（公元前550~529年在位）。他以伊朗西南部的一个小首领起家，经过一系列的胜利，打败了3个帝国，即米底、吕底亚和巴比伦，统一了大部分的古中东，建立了从印度到地中海的大帝国。今天，伊朗人将居鲁士尊称为"国父"。亦译赛勒斯。

波斯国王居鲁士

波斯国王居鲁士

If these facts be considered with a geographical eye, a belt of fertility will be seen extending northwestward up the Euphrates, then curving to southward along the rain-gathering mountains of Syria, and ending westward in Egypt. It is a populous belt, for it is inhabited by the settled plowmen. Except for two intervals of sterility, the trunk road of antiquity ran through its cornfields from Babylon to Memphis. The key to some of the greater events of Ancient History is to be found in the subjection of the peoples of this agricultural strip now to this and now to that neighboring race of superior mobility. From the south, with all the depth of Arabia behind them, the camel-men advanced northeastward against Mesopotamia, northwestward against Syria, and westward against Egypt; from the northeast, with all the vast depth of the Heartland behind them, the Horsemen came down from the Iranian upland into Mesopotamia; and from

河向西北延伸而上，然后转而向南，沿着叙利亚那些雨水汇集的山脉，再向西而去，直到埃及境内为止。这是一个人口稠密的地带，因为这一带居住的都是农民。除了中间隔着两处不毛之地外，这条古老的大道经过的都是良田沃土，从巴比伦直抵孟斐斯[1]。这条农业带上的各个民族，经常被机动性更强的邻近种族所征服；从这一事实中，我们便可以看出古代历史中一些较重大事件的关键来。由于骑骆驼的民族有着广袤的阿拉伯半岛为后盾，所以他们能够从南面向东北进犯美索不达米亚、向西北进犯叙利亚、向西进犯埃及；由于骑马民族有整个广袤无垠的"中心地带"为后盾，所以他们能够从东北方向冲下伊朗高原，入侵美索不达米亚平原；而从西北方向，由于乘船民族有整个欧洲的水路为后盾，所以无论是越过小亚细亚半岛还是直接到达黎凡特[2]沿海，他们都能进犯

---

[1] Memphis：孟斐斯。古埃及的一座城市，其废墟在今开罗以南。据说它由统一埃及的第一位国王美尼斯（Menes）所建，在亚历山大大帝占领埃及之前一直都保持着原样。

[2] Levantine shore：黎凡特沿海。Levant（黎凡特）指的是地中海东部自土耳其至埃及地区的诸国。

the northwest, whether across the peninsula of Asia Minor or directly to the Levantine shore, came the shipmen against Syria and Egypt, having behind them all the water ways of Europe.

In Asia the Romans did but take over the western portion of the Macedonian conquests. As the Rhine and Danube, defended by the Legions, marked the extent of Roman penetration northward from the Mediterranean, so the Upper Euphrates, where it flows from north to south before bending southeastward, marked the limit, defended by other Legions, of their eastward penetration from the Mediterranean. The Roman Empire was, in fact, in the large sense, a local Empire; it belonged wholly to the Atlantic Coastland. The further provinces which had been under the Macedonian sway fell in Roman times to the Parthians, successors of the Persians, who in their turn descended from Iran upon Mesopotamia.

Once more came the opportunity of the camel-men. Inspired by the preaching of Mohammed, the Arabs of the central oasis of Nejd, and of its western extension in the Hedjaz of Mecca and Medina, sent forth the Saracen armies, who drove the Parthians from Mesopotamia, and the Romans from Syria and Egypt, and established a chain of inland Capitals — Cairo, Damascus, and Bagdad — in the ancient trackway of fertility. From this fertile base the Saracen power was carried into all the regions around in such manner as to make a bid for a truly World-Empire. Northeastward the Mohammedans ascended from Bagdad into Iran by the same passway which had guided the Parthians and Persians downward, and they spread even into Northern India. Southward they crossed from the Yemen headland of Arabia to the African coast south of the Sahara, and penetrated on their camels and horses through the whole breadth of the Sudan. Thus, like a vast eagle, their Empire of Land-power spread its wings from the

叙利亚和埃及。〔作者注：参见图20。〕

在亚洲，罗马人并没有接管马其顿人征服地区的西部。正如罗马军团防守的莱茵河与多瑙河标志着罗马人从地中海北进的最远之处那样，幼发拉底河上游自北向南流去、还未折向东南、且由其他军团所防守的那一段，也标志着他们从地中海东进的最远距离。事实上，从广义上来看，罗马帝国只是一个局部帝国；因为整个帝国都处于大西洋沿海地区。在罗马时代，过去由马其顿统治的那些偏远省份都落入了帕提亚人[1]手中；后者继波斯人之后，也从伊朗高原下来，占领了美索不达米亚。

骑骆驼的民族再一次抓住了机会。在穆罕默德教义的激励之下，内志[2]中部绿洲上以及这处绿洲位于麦加和麦地那的汉志境内的西延部分上的阿拉伯人派遣撒拉逊军队，把帕提亚人赶出了美索不达米亚，把罗马人赶出了叙利亚和埃及，并在这条富庶的古道之上，建立起了一连串的内陆首府，即开罗、大马士革和巴格达。从这个富饶的基地出发，撒拉逊人将势力渗透了周围所有的地区，企图建立起一个真正的世界帝国来。信奉穆罕默德的伊斯兰教徒们从巴格达向东北进击，沿着引领帕提亚人和波斯人从高原南下的那条原路攻进了伊朗，甚至渗透到了印度北部。他们还从阿拉伯半岛上的也门海岬渡海向南，抵达了撒哈拉沙漠以南的非洲海岸，并且骑着马和骆驼深入到了苏丹全境。这样一来，他们的陆权帝国就像一只巨大的雄鹰，从阿拉伯半岛中央地带展开了两翼，一翼盖住了"北中心地带"并深入到亚洲腹地，另一翼则覆盖了"南中心地带"，并且同

---

[1] Parthians：帕提亚人。帕提亚（Parthia）是里海东南部的一个古国，我国史书曾称之为"安息"。

[2] Nejd：内志。阿拉伯半岛中部广阔高原地区的统称，原为独立王国，后与Hejaz（即后文中的Hedjaz，汉志）合并，称为沙特阿拉伯（Saudi Arabia）。

撒拉逊战士

Arabian Centerland, on the one hand over the Northern Heartland, far into the depths of Asia, and on the other hand over the Southern Heartland equally far into the depths of Africa.

　　But the Saracens were not content with a dominion based only on the means of mobility proper to their steppes and deserts; like their predecessors, the Phoenicians and Shebans, they took to the sea. Westward they traveled along the north coast of Africa, both on sea and land, until they came to two countries, Barbary and Spain, whose broad tablelands, neither utterly sterile like the Sahara, nor yet forested like most of the European Peninsula, repeated in some degree the conditions of their own homeland. On the other hand, eastward from Yemen, at the mouth of the Red Sea, and from Oman, at the mouth of the Persian Gulf, they sailed on the

样深入到了非洲腹地。

　　不过，撒拉逊人并不满足于这些只是倚赖适合于其草原和沙漠的机动手段而攫取的领土；跟他们的先人腓尼基人和舍班人[1]一样，他们也开始向海洋进军了。他们沿着非洲北部海岸西行，海陆并进，直达巴巴里[2]和西班牙两国；这两个国家都有着广阔的高原地带，它们既不像撒哈拉沙漠那样荒芜贫瘠，也不像欧洲半岛上大多数地方那样森林密布，而是在某种程度上就像撒拉逊人的又一个故乡。另一方面，他们又从位于红海海口的也门和位于波斯湾入口的阿曼向东，利用夏季风航行到了印度沿海的马拉巴尔，甚至还到达了遥远的马来群岛，然后再利用冬季风返航回国。这样一来，阿拉伯人的单桅帆船便勾勒出了一个海洋帝国，这个帝国的轮廓从直布罗陀海峡延伸到了马六甲海峡，

---

　　[1] Sheban：舍班人。Sheba（舍班）是阿拉伯半岛南部的一个古国，其范围包括如今的也门。舍班人从公元前10世纪开始在埃塞俄比亚殖民，并以富庶和商业繁荣而著称。

　　[2] Barbary：巴巴里。现指埃及和大西洋之间的北非伊斯兰教地区。

summer Monsoon to the Malabar coast of India, and even to the far Malay Islands, and returned home on the winter Monsoon. Thus the Arab dhows sketched out a Sea-Empire, extending from the Straits of Gibraltar to the Straits of Malacca, from the Atlantic gate to the Pacific gate.

This vast Saracen design of a northward and southward Dominion of camel-men crossed by a westward and eastward Dominion of shipmen was vitiated by one fatal defect; it lacked in its Arabian base the necessary man-power to make it good. But no student of the realities about which must turn the strategical thought of any government aspiring to world-power can afford to lose sight of the warning thus given by History.

※　　　　※　　　　※　　　　※　　　　※　　　　※　　　　※　　　　※　　　　※

也从大西洋的门户延伸到了太平洋的门户。

撒拉逊人由骑骆驼的民族统治向北和向南的领土、由乘船民族统治向西和向东的领土并且让二者相互交叉的这一宏伟计划，因为具有一个致命的缺陷而宣告破产了；这个缺陷，就是他们的阿拉伯半岛基地上缺乏必要的人力来实现这一宏图大业。不过，凡是研究这些现实情况——它们必定会让任何政府的战略思想，都转变成致力于建立起一个世界性的强国来——的人，都不能无视历史因此而给予我们的警告。

※　　　　※　　　　※　　　　※　　　　※　　　　※　　　　※　　　　※　　　　※

后来撒拉逊帝国被推翻了；可推翻它的并不是欧洲或印度群岛的国家，而是来自北方"中心地带"的国家——这是一个意义重大的事实。除了朝着"中心地带"的那一面，

伊凡三世率军队取得俄罗斯的独立

The Saracen Empire was overthrown, not from Europe or the Indies, but from the Heartland in the north — a significant fact. Arabia is sea-girt or desert-girt in every other direction but towards the Heartland. The western sea-power of the Arabs was no doubt countered from Venice and Genoa, and their eastern sea-power was subdued by the Portuguese after they had rounded the Cape of Good Hope, but the downfall of the Saracens in Arabia itself was due to Turkish land-power. We must give some further consideration to the characteristics of the great Northern Heartland, and in the first place to those of the long Grassy Zone which, south of the Forest Zone, extends across its whole breadth, overlapping westward and eastward some distance into the adjoining parts of the two Coastlands.

The steppes begin in the center of Europe, where the Hungarian Plain is completely surrounded by a ring of forested mountains, the Eastern Alps and the Carpathians. Today fields of wheat and maize have in large part replaced the native grass, but a hundred years ago, before the railways had brought markets within reach, the sea-like levels of Hungary east of the Danube were a prairie land, and the wealth of the Hungarians was almost exclusively in horses and cattle. Beyond the forested barrier of the Carpathians begin the steppes of the main belt, spreading eastward, with the shore of the Black Sea to the south and the edge of the Russian Forest to the north. The forest edge crosses the Russian Plain sinuously, but in a generally oblique direction, from the northern end of the Carpathians in the fiftieth parallel of latitude to the foot of the Ural Range in the fifty-sixth parallel. Moscow stands a short way within the forest, where are the broad clearings which constituted all of inhabited Russia until the recent colonization of the steppe southward. As far as the Volga and the Don the wheat fields have now in large measure replaced the steppe grass, but until a hundred years ago the Cossack outposts of Russia were still based on the Dnieper and Don Rivers, the trees along whose banks alone

阿拉伯半岛的其他方向上要么环海，要么就是被沙漠包围着。虽说阿拉伯人在西方的海上力量无疑受到了威尼斯和热那亚的抵抗，而阿拉伯人在东方的海上力量也在葡萄牙人绕航好望角之后，被葡萄牙人压制住了，但撒拉逊人在阿拉伯半岛本土上衰亡下去，却是由于土耳其的陆军力量所致。我们必须进一步研究广袤的"北中心地带"的诸多特点，并且首先应当研究那片漫长草原区的诸多特点才行；这片草原区位于森林区以南，横贯整个"北中心地带"，其西段和东段都与各自接壤的沿海地区都有部分重叠的地区。

大草原始于欧洲中部；匈牙利平原在此被一圈森林密布的山脉，即东阿尔卑斯山脉和喀尔巴阡山脉完全包围着。［作者注：请参见图18。］如今，原先草地的大部分都已开垦成了麦田和玉米地，可100年之前，在铁路还没有让市场近便可及的时候，多瑙河以东那片大海一般的匈牙利平原却还是一片草原，而匈牙利人的财产也几乎全部都是牛羊马匹。大草原的主体带始于喀尔巴阡山脉那道森林屏障，然后向东延伸，南边是黑海沿岸地区，北面则是俄罗斯森林的边界。这道森林边界蜿蜒曲折，横亘整个俄罗斯平原，不过方向总体上是从位于北纬50°的喀尔巴阡山脉北端开始斜斜向北，直到位于北纬56°的乌拉尔山脉脚下。莫斯科位于森林之内，离森林边界不远；那里是一片片开阔的空地，直到最近南边的大草原得到开垦之前，所有的俄罗斯人都居住在那里。从莫斯科到遥远的伏尔加河和顿河，以前的草原如今大都已经为麦田所取代，不过直到100年之前，哥萨克人的前哨还是建立在第聂伯河和顿河两岸；只有河流两岸的树木，让这片牧草起伏或者雪花飞舞的平原不再单调。

覆盖着乌拉尔山脉末端的那片森林形成了一个犄角，向南楔入了这片开阔的大草

broke the vast levels of waving grass or of snow. The forests which clothe the end of the Ural Mountains form a promontory southward into the open steppes, but the grass is continuous through the gateway of plain which leads from Europe into Asia between the Ural Range and the northern end of the Caspian Sea. Beyond this gateway the steppes expand again to even greater breadth than in Europe. To the north of them are still the forests, but to the south are now the deserts and sub-arid steppes of Turkestan. The Transiberian railway traverses the Grassy Zone from Chelyabinsk, the station at the eastern foot of the Ural Mountains where the lines from Petrograd and Moscow unite, to Irkutsk on the Angara River just below its exit from Lake Baikal. Wheat fields are beginning in large measure to replace the grass along the line of the railway, but the thread of settled population is still a narrow one, and the Tartar and Khirghiz horsemen are still nomad over wide areas.

The edge of the forest bends southward along the boundary between Western and Eastern Siberia, for Eastern Siberia is filled with forested mountains and hills, which fall in elevation gradually from the Transbaikalian Plateau into the northeastern promontory of Asia towards Bering Strait. The Grassy Zone bends south with the forest and continues eastward over the lower level of the Mongolian uplands. The slope upward from the Great Lowland into Mongolia is through the "Dry Strait" of Zungaria, between the Tianshan Mountains on the south and Altai Mountains on the north. Beyond Zungaria the steppes, now at upland level, continue round the southern edge of the forested Altai and Transbaikalian Mountains, with the Gobi Desert to the south of them, until they reach the upper tributaries of the Amur River. There is a forest belt along the eastern, outward face of the Kingan Range, by which the Mongolian upland drops to the lowland of Manchuria, but there is a last detached grassland in Manchuria, to be compared with the similarly detached grassland of Hungary five thousand miles away at the west end of

原，但在乌拉尔山脉和里海北端之间、从欧洲一直延伸到亚洲的那条通道上，草地却仍然连绵不绝。过了这个通道，大草原再次延伸，宽度甚至比它在欧洲的范围更广阔了。其北面依然是森林，可南面如今却是土耳其斯坦的沙漠和半干旱草原了。西伯利亚铁路从车里雅宾斯克出发横贯草原区，直达伊尔库茨克；车里雅宾斯克是位于乌拉尔山脉东麓的一个车站，从彼得格勒和莫斯科来的铁路在此交汇，而伊尔库茨克则位于安加拉河上，离安加拉河在贝加尔湖的发源地不远。铁路沿线的草地，如今大多正在为麦田所取代，不过一路上定居人口带还是很狭窄，而鞑靼人[1]和吉尔吉斯人也仍然骑着马儿在广阔的地域内游牧生活着。

森林的边缘沿着西西伯利亚和东西伯利亚之间的分界线折而向南了，因为东西伯利亚到处都是森林茂密的山脉和丘陵，这些山脉和丘陵的高度从外贝加尔高原开始逐渐下降，直到面朝白令海峡的那个亚洲的东北大海角。草原区也随着森林折而向南，并且继续向东延伸，越过了海拔较低的蒙古高原。从"大低地"向上进入蒙古的那个斜坡，便是穿过准噶尔盆地这处"旱峡"；它夹在两座山脉之间，南边是天山山脉，北边则是阿尔泰山脉。出了准噶尔盆地，如今已来到高原之上的大草原便继续绕过阿尔泰和外贝加尔这两条森林茂密的山脉的南界延伸，随着南面的戈壁大漠，直达阿穆尔河上游的各条支流。兴安岭的外侧东坡有一条森林带，蒙古高原即由此下降到满洲里的低地之上；但在满洲里，还有最后一片与世隔绝的草地，可与位于草原带西端、距此远达5000英里的那处同样孤立的匈牙利草原相媲美。然而，满洲里的草原并没有延伸到太平洋沿岸，因

---

[1] Tartar：鞑靼人。指在中世纪入侵西亚和东欧并居住于中亚的突厥和蒙古部落的成员。

the steppe belt. Grassy Manchuria does not, however, extend through to the Pacific shore, for there a coast range of mountains, thickly forested, enframes the open country and deflects the eastward flowing Amur to a northward mouth.

Let us clear this long ribbon of steppes of its modern railways and corn fields, and people it again in imagination with horse-riding Tartars, who are none other than Turks; it is said that the Turkish language of Constantinople can to this day be understood by the Arctic tribe at the mouth of the Lena River. For some recurrent reason — it may have been owing to spells of droughty years — these Tartar mobile hordes have from time to time in the course of history

为那里有一条森林茂密的沿海山脉围住了开阔的原野，并让本向东流的阿穆尔河转而向北入海了。

我们不妨想象一下，在这条漫长的草原带上把现代的铁路线和玉米地都清除掉，并再次让骑马的鞑靼人——他们不是别人，正是土耳其人——繁衍其间；据说，位于勒拿河口的北极部落，时至今日也还听得懂君士坦丁堡时期的土耳其语呢。由于某种反复出现的原因——或许是因为干旱年份作祟——在整个历史上，这些鞑靼人的游牧民族会时不时地集中起全部力量，并像摧毁一切的雷霆那样，进击中国或欧洲那些定居的农耕民族。在西方，我们最初听说他们的时候，是把他们叫做匈奴人；公元五世纪中叶，他们在一位伟大而又令人生畏的首领阿提拉[1]率领下，骑马侵入了匈牙利。从匈牙利出发，他们又兵分3路，继续向西北、西面和西南3个方向四处劫掠。在西北方向，他们令日耳曼人陷入了恐慌之中，以至于离海最近的那两个日耳曼民族，即盎格鲁人和撒克逊人，

---

[1] Attila：阿提拉（约公元406年～公元453年）。匈奴帝国国王（约公元433年～公元453年在位），亦被称作 the Scourge of God（上帝之鞭，喻其执政严酷）。

罗马大主教利奥和阿提拉的会面

图22　东欧的森林和大草原。（根据1904年我在《地理学杂志》上发表的《历史的地理学枢要》一文中的一幅图表所绘制。）

gathered their whole strength together and fallen like a devastating avalanche upon the settled agricultural peoples either of China or Europe. In the West we hear of them first as the Huns, who in the middle of the fifth century after Christ rode into Hungary under a great but terrible leader, Attila. From Hungary they raided in three directions — northwestward, westward, and southwestward. Northwestward they caused so much commotion among the Germans, that those tribes nearest the sea, the Angles and Saxons, were in part driven over the water to a new home in the island of Britain. Westward they penetrated far into Gaul, but were defeated in the great battle of Chalons, where the Frank, the Goth, and the Roman Provincial, standing shoulder to shoulder against the common enemy from the East, began that fusion from which has sprung

有一部分不得不漂洋过海，到不列颠岛上去另寻新的家园。向西，他们虽说深入到了高卢地区内部，却在查隆大战[1]中战败了；那里的法兰克人、哥特人以及罗马帝国的外省人，都肩并肩地抵抗来自东方的共同敌人，并因此开始融合，从而诞生出了现代的法兰西民族。在西南方向，阿提拉远征到了米兰，一路上摧毁了罗马的阿奎莱亚[2]和帕多

---

[1] the Battle of Chalons：查隆大战。公元451年，匈奴军队与西罗马帝国军队在马恩河畔查隆附近的卡太隆尼平原进行的一次会战。会战中双方损失惨重，最终匈奴人被赶到莱茵河以东，随后阿提拉率余部转入北意大利。

[2] Aquileia：阿奎莱亚。意大利东北部位于亚得里亚海附近的一座城市，公元前181年由罗马人作为前哨基地建立，阿提拉在公元452年将其摧毁。

the modern French people. South-westward Attila advanced as far as Milan, destroying on the way the important Roman cities of Aquileia and Padua, whose inhabitants fled to the lagoons by the sea and there founded Venice. At Milan Attila was met by Bishop Leo of Rome, and, for whatever reason, went no farther, with the result that the Roman See won a great prestige. Thus can it be said with much truth that from the reaction of the coast-men against this hammer blow from the Heartland, there arose the English and French nationalities, the sea-power of Venice, and the supreme mediaeval institution of the Papacy. Who shall say what great and, let us hope, beneficent things may not grow out of the reaction which has been compelled by the hammer blow of our modern Huns?

The Hunnish raids ceased after a few years, for it is probable that the man-power behind them was not very considerable; the force of a blow may be due as much to its speed as to its

weight. But some Hunnish remnants probably lingered in the grassy vacancy of the Hungarian Plain, to be absorbed by new tribes of horsemen advancing westward, the Avars, against whom Charlemagne made war, and presently the Magyars. In the year 1000 these Magyar Turks, who had done much ravaging in Germany during the previous century, were converted to Christianity from Rome, and became thenceforth some sort of a bulwark to Latin

查理曼大帝（742～814）。法兰克王国加洛林王朝的国王（公元768年～814年在位），也是神圣罗马帝国的皇帝（公元800年～814年在位）。

瓦[1]这两座重镇，其中的居民纷纷逃到了海边的一些环礁湖上，从而在那里建立了威尼斯。在米兰，罗马大主教利奥接见了阿提拉，不知什么原因，阿提拉自此不再征战，结果这事让罗马主教获得了巨大的声望。这样，我们便可以相当有把握地说，英格兰和法兰西这两个民族，还有威尼斯那个海上强国，以及成为中世纪最高政治制度的教皇统治，都是在沿海民族对从"中心地带"而来的这种猛击进行抵抗的过程中产生的。谁又能说，在被迫对我们现代那些匈奴人的猛击进行抵抗的过程中，不会产生出一些伟大的事物，不会产生出一些我们所希望的有利事物来呢？

数年之后，匈奴人的进袭便停止了，原因很可能在于他们没有大量的人力做后盾；而一种打击的力量，可能既取决于打击的速度，也取决于打击的气势。但是，一些匈奴的残余力量很可能仍然游荡在草地茂密、空旷广袤的匈牙利平原上，后来则被一些新的、向西进军的游牧部落同化了；那些新的游牧部落，就是查理曼大帝曾经对其发动过

---

[1] Padua：帕多瓦。意大利东北部位于威尼斯西部的一个城市，中世纪时曾是一个重要的文化中心。

Christendom, so that no more Tartars were admitted into Hungary. But the economic life of the Magyars continued in the main to be that of the steppes until less than a hundred years ago.

When we reflect that through several centuries of the Dark Ages the Norse pagans in their ships were at piracy on the northern seas, and the Saracen and Moorish infidels in their ships at piracy on the Mediterranean, and that the horse-riding Turks from Asia raided thus into the very heart of the Christian Peninsula when it was clasped by hostile sea-power, we have some idea of the pounding, as between pestle and mortar, which went to the making of modern Europe. The pestle was land-power from the Heartland.

　　※　　　　※　　　　※　　　　※　　　　※　　　　※　　　　※　　　　※　　　　※

If these historical events be followed on the map, the strategical fact of decisive meaning which emerges is that the continuous plains of the Great Lowland overlap from the Continental and Arctic drainage of the Heartland into the East of the European peninsula. There was no impediment to prevent the horsemen from riding westward into regions drained by such wholly European rivers as the Dnieper and Danube. In sharp contrast to this open passage from the Heartland into Europe is the system of mighty barriers which separate the Heartland along its eastern and southeastern border from the Indies. The populous lands of China proper and India lie round the eastern and southern slopes of the most massive uplands on the Globe; the southern face of the Himalaya Range, curving for 1500 miles along the north of India, rises from levels at most only 1000 feet above the sea to peaks of 28,000 and 29,000 feet. But the Himalaya is only the edge of the Tibetan Plateau, which is as large as France, Germany, and Austria-Hungary put together, and of an average elevation of 15,000 feet, or the peak height

征战的阿瓦尔人，也就是如今的马扎尔人[1]。公元1000年，在前一个世纪中曾经大肆劫掠过德意志的这些马扎尔族土耳其人，皈依了从罗马传来的基督教，并从此成为了拉丁基督教国家某种意义上的防卫力量，所以再也没有鞑靼人进入匈牙利了。不过，直到几十年前，马扎尔人的经济活动基本上依然是大草原上的那种经济活动。

假如我们细细思考，在黑暗时代那数个世纪当中，古挪威的异教徒乘着战船，在北方海域干着海盗行径，撒拉逊人和摩尔人[2]这些异教徒也乘着战船，在地中海上四处劫掠，而来自亚洲的骑马的土耳其人，又如此一路奔袭到当时为敌对的海上力量所包围的这个基督教半岛的中心地带，那么我们便能大致领会到，现代欧洲是锤炼出来的，就像是放在一个研钵子里，用杵捣击成一样。而这根杵，就是来自"中心地带"的陆上力量。

　　※　　　　※　　　　※　　　　※　　　　※　　　　※　　　　※　　　　※　　　　※

如果我们在地图上来理解这些历史事件，那我们就会发现下述这个具有决定意义的战略事实：从"中心地带"的大陆和北极地区的流域起，"大低地"上绵延不断的平原一直交迭延伸到了欧洲半岛的东部。这里没有屏障，无法阻挡骑马民族长驱直入，阻挡他们西进到像第聂伯河与多瑙河这样完全属于欧洲的河流流域。与这条从"中心地带"畅通无阻地进入欧洲的通道形成鲜明对照的是，沿着"中心地带"的东面和东南边界，有着一连串雄伟的屏障，将"中心地带"与印度群岛隔了开来。人口稠密的中国本土和印度，分处于地球上最雄伟的那座高原的东坡和南坡之上；喜马拉雅山脉的南面沿

---

[1] Magyar：马扎尔人。匈牙利一个主要的少数民族，为蒙古族的后裔。

[2] Moor：摩尔人。公元8世纪入侵西班牙的穆斯林民族之一，直到15世纪晚期才在安达卢西亚建立起文明社会。

印度莫卧儿王朝时期

of Mont Blanc in the Alps. As compared with such facts as these, the distinction between the lower uplands and the lowlands, between the Iranian Upland, let us say, and the Great Lowland, becomes altogether subordinate. Tibet, with its attendant Himalaya, Pamirs, Karakoram, Hindu Rush, and Tianshan — call them together the Tibetan Heights — has no parallel on earth for combined height and area, or, in a single word, for massiveness. When the Sahara shall be crossed and recrossed daily by the traffic of civilization, it is probable that Tibet, the "roof of the world," will still deflect round its flanks and widely separate the overland routes into China and India, thus giving a special significance to the Northwest Frontiers of those two countries.

North of Tibet, a considerable part of which has a continental drainage, and is, therefore, included within the Heartland, spreads the Mongolian Upland, also largely of the Heartland. This Mongolian Upland is of a much lower elevation than Tibet, and is in fact comparable in point of level with the Iranian Upland. Two natural ways come over the arid surface of Mongolia to drop down into the fertile lowland of China; the one through the Province of Kansu, round the northeastern corner of Tibet, to the great city of Sinan, of a million inhabitants; the other directly southeastward from Lake Baikal to Pekin, which city also has about a million inhabitants. Sinan and Pekin, thus just within the Chinese Lowland, are capitals founded by conquerors from the Heartland.

Across the Iranian Upland into India there are also two natural ways, the one over the lofty but narrow spine of the Hindu Kush, down the Cabul Valley, and over the terminal Kaibar Pass to the crossing of the Indus River at Attack; the other through Herat and Kandahar, round the ends of the Afghan ridges, and by the Bolan Gorge down to the Indus. Immediately east of the Indus River is the Indian Desert, extending from the ocean to within a short distance of the Himalaya, and the Bolan and Kaibar ways converge, therefore, through the ante-chamber of the Punjab to the inner entry of India, which is the passage left between the desert and the

着印度北部蜿蜒长达1500英里，并从顶多只有1000英尺的海拔上升到了高达28000英尺到29000英尺的顶峰。不过，喜马拉雅山脉只是西藏高原的边缘，而西藏高原的面积，相当于法、德和奥匈帝国这三国面积的总和，平均拔海则达15000英尺，与阿尔卑斯山脉上勃朗峰的高度相当。与这些情况相比，低海拔高原和低地之间的区别、我们姑且所称的伊朗高原与"大低地"之间的差异，完全就是次要的了。西藏，以及与之相随的喜马拉雅山脉、帕米尔高原、喀喇昆仑山脉、兴都库什山脉和天山山脉——不妨将它们总称为西藏高原——其总高度和总面积都举世无双，或者用一个词来概括的话，就是"硕大"。等到将来，就算是每天都有人凭借着现代的交通工具在撒哈拉沙漠上来去，可西藏这个"世界屋脊"也很可能仍然会让人们不得不绕道而行，并且仍然会把进入中国和印度的陆路全面隔离开来，从而会给这两个国家的西北边界赋予一种特殊的重要性。

西藏的大部分地区都属于大陆流域，故也包括在"中心地带"内；而西藏的北面，又绵亘着大部分区域亦属于"中心地带"的蒙古高原。这个蒙古高原的海拔比西藏高原要低得多，实际上，它的海拔跟伊朗高原差不多。其间有两条天然的途径，越过蒙古的干旱地区，南下通往中国富庶的低海拔地区：一条是经由甘肃省，绕过西藏的东北角，到达有着100万居民的重镇西安；另一条是直接从贝加尔湖出发，往东南而去，到达也有大约100万人口的北京城。西安和北京正好处在中国低地区域内，都是来自"中心地带"的征服者建立起来的都城。

横跨伊朗高原进入印度，也有两条天然的道路：一条是翻过兴都库什山脉那条高耸而狭窄的山脊，沿着迦步勒峡谷而下，越过峡谷尽头的开伯尔山口，前往阿托克的印度

印度莫卧儿王朝时期

mountains. Here stands Delhi, at the head of the navigation of the Jumna–Ganges, and Delhi is a capital founded, like Sinan and Pekin in China, by conquerors from the Heartland. By these narrow and difficult ways both China and India have repeatedly been invaded from the Heartland, but the Empires thus founded have usually soon become detached from the rule of the steppemen. So was it, for instance, with the Moguls of India, who were derived from the Mongols of the Interior.

　　　　※　　　※　　　※　　　※　　　※　　　※　　　※　　　※　　　※

The conclusion to which this discussion leads is that the connection between the Heartland,

河渡口；另一条是经由赫拉特和坎大哈[1]，绕过阿富汗诸岭的末端，并沿着波伦峡谷[2]而下，前往印度河。印度沙漠就在印度河的东面，它从海边延伸到了距喜马拉雅山脉不远的地方，所以经由波伦和开伯尔的那两条路线便会合一处，穿过旁遮普地区这个"前厅"，进入了印度的内部入口，即沙漠和山脉之间留下的那条通道。朱木拿河与恒河航道的起点，便是德里；而德里与中国的西安和北京一样，也是由来自"中心地带"的征

[1] Kandahar：坎大哈。阿富汗东南部的一座城市，毗邻巴基斯坦边界，一直是通往中亚的贸易线路上的战略要地。

[2] Bolan Gorge：波伦峡谷。位于巴基斯坦西部的一条具有战略意义的山脉通道，其山口一直都是通往印度的门户。

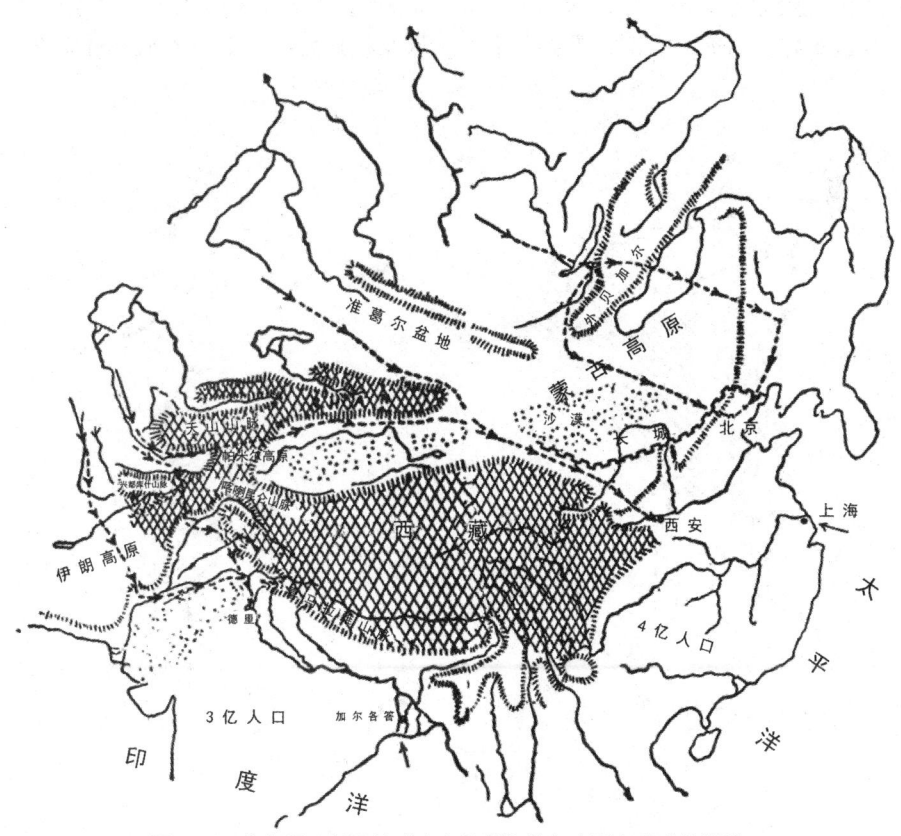

图23　西藏高原，以及从"中心地带"进入中国和印度的通道。

and especially its more open western regions of Iran, Turkestan, and Siberia, is much more intimate with Europe and Arabia than it is with China and India, or yet with the Southern Heartland of Africa. The strong natural frontiers of the Sahara Desert and the Tibetan Heights have no equivalent where the Northern Heartland merges with Arabia and Europe. The close connection of these three regions is well typified by that geographical formula into which it was attempted to crystallize just now certain essential aspects of Mesopotamian and Syrian history; the plowmen of Mesopotamia and Syria have always been exposed to descents of the horsemen from the Heartland, of the camel–men from Arabia, and of the shipmen from Europe. None the less — and indeed just because of its more transitional character — the boundary between the Heartland on the one hand, and Arabia and Europe on the other, is worth following with some care.

服者建造起来的一座都城。来自"中心地带"的民族曾经取道这些狭窄难行的路线，一再入侵过中国和印度，但由此而建立起来的各个帝国，往往很快便摆脱了草原民族的统治。比如说，印度的莫卧儿王朝便是这样；而莫卧儿人，则是内陆蒙古族人的后裔。

※　　　※　　　※　　　※　　　※　　　※　　　※　　　※　　　※

　　我们从上面这种讨论可以得出一个结论："中心地带"，尤其是其中较为空旷开阔的伊朗、土耳其斯坦和西伯利亚等西部地区，它们与欧洲和阿拉伯半岛的关系，比它们跟中国和印度的关系更加密切，甚至比它们跟非洲这个"南中心地带"的关系也更为密切。在"北中心地带"与阿拉伯半岛和欧洲接壤的地方，并没有撒哈拉沙漠和西藏高原那样强大的天然边界。用一条地理规则，便可以很好地说明这3个地区的紧密关系，而我们如今也正好利用这一规则，来将美索不达米亚和叙利亚历史中的某些重要方面加以

图24　"中心地带"，加上黑海和波罗的海分场，以及中国和印度诸河最重要的（高原）河谷。

君士坦丁堡

图25　图中表明了当地中海的海上强国进入黑海后"中心地带"的疆界（＋＋＋＋＋），以及陆上强国从大草原进入托罗斯山脉和迪纳拉阿尔卑斯山脉后"中心地带"的疆界（－－－－－）。

The long range of the Persian Mountains bends westward round the upper end of Mesopotamia and becomes the Taurus Range, which is the high southern brink of the peninsular upland of Asia Minor. The surface of Asia Minor is a patch of steppes, verging on desert in the center, where salt lakes receive some of the streams from the Taurus; but the larger rivers flow northward to the Black Sea. Beyond the break made by the Aegean Sea, we have the great basin of the Danube, also draining into the Black Sea; the head-streams of the Danube tributaries rise almost within sight of the Adriatic, but high on those Illyrian Uplands whose steep outer brink forms the mountain wall above the beautiful Dalmatian coast. That wall we name the Dinaric Alps.

Thus the Taurus and the Dinaric Alps present steep fronts to the Mediterranean and Adriatic, but send long rivers down to the Black Sea. But for the Aegean Sea, breaking through

具体化；美索不达米亚和叙利亚的农耕民族，一直都很容易受到来自"中心地带"的骑马民族、来自阿拉伯半岛的骑驼民族以及来自欧洲的乘船民族的进袭。尽管如此——事实上，也正是由于它具有此种过渡性的特征——一边是"中心地带"、一边是阿拉伯半岛和欧洲的这条界线，还是值得我们来慎重地加以关注的。

绵延不断的波斯山脉绕过美索不达米亚平原北端并在此折而向西，变成了托罗斯山脉，成了小亚细亚半岛高原南部高耸的边缘。小亚细亚是一片草原，而其中心地区差不多属于沙漠，从托罗斯山脉流下来的一些小河则注入了沙漠中的座座盐湖；但是，其间较大的河流都是向北而流，注入了黑海。在爱琴海所形成的断裂带以外，有一个了不起的多瑙河流域，其中的河流也都注入了黑海；多瑙河各条支流的上游，虽说几乎都发源

the uplands towards the Black Sea, and but for the Dardanelles, whose current races southward with the water of all the Black Sea rivers, these high, outward fronts of the Taurus and Dinaric Alps would be a single curving range, the edge of a continuous bar of land dividing the inner Black Sea from the outer Mediterranean and Adriatic. Were it not for the Dardanelles that edge would form the border of the Heartland, and the Black Sea and all its rivers would be added to the "Continental" systems of drainage. When the Dardanelles are closed by land-power to the sea-power of the Mediterranean, as they have been in the Great War, that condition of things is in effect realized so far as human movements are concerned.

The Roman Emperors put their Eastern capital at Constantinople, midway between the Danube and Euphrates frontiers, but Constantinople was to them more than the bridge-town from Europe into Asia. Rome, the Mediterranean Power, did not annex the northern shore of the Black Sea, and that sea, therefore, was itself a part of the frontier of the Empire. The steppes were left to the Scythians, as the Turks were then called, and at most a few trading stations were dotted by the seamen along the coast of the Crimea. Thus Constantinople was the point from which Mediterranean sea-power held the middle sea-frontier, as the land-power of the Legions held the western and eastern frontiers along the rivers. Under Rome, sea-power thus advanced into the Heartland, if that term be understood, in a large, a strategical sense, as including Asia Minor and the Balkan Peninsula.

Later history is no less transparent to the underlying facts of geography, but in the inverse direction. Some of the Turks from Central Asia turned aside from the way down into Arabia, and rode over the Median and Armenian uplands into the open steppe of Asia Minor, and there

于看得见亚得里亚海的地方，但都是从伊利里亚那些耸立的高地奔腾而下的；那些高地的外缘都非常陡峭，形成了一道山峦重叠的屏障，俯瞰着美丽的达尔马提亚海岸。我们称这道屏障为迪纳拉阿尔卑斯山脉。

这样一来，托罗斯山脉和迪纳拉阿尔卑斯山脉虽说陡峭地屹立于地中海和亚得里亚海面前，却使得条条长河奔腾而下，注入了黑海。倘若没有爱琴海将那些向黑海延伸的高地切断，倘若没有达达尼尔海峡中的洋流挟着所有注入黑海的河水奔腾南下，那么托罗斯山脉和迪纳拉阿尔卑斯山脉这些高耸而向外突出的前沿，就会变成一道单一的弧形山脉，就会变成一道连绵不断的陆上屏障的边缘，将里面的黑海与外面的地中海和亚得里亚海隔离开来。倘若没有达达尼尔海峡，这道边缘就会成为"中心地带"的边界，而黑海以及黑海流域的所有河流，就会加入到整个"大陆"水系中去。倘若像此次大战中业已做到的那样，陆上强国将达达尼尔海峡封锁起来，不让地中海地区的海上强国通行，那么从人类的迁徙角度来看，实际上就是实现了上面所说的那种情况。

罗马帝国的历任皇帝，虽然都把他们的东方首都建在位于多瑙河和幼发拉底河边缘区域之间的君士坦丁堡，但对他们而言，君士坦丁堡并非只是他们从欧洲进入亚洲的桥头堡。罗马这个地中海强国并未吞并黑海北岸，因此黑海本身就成了罗马帝国边疆的一个部分。大草原留给了时称斯基泰人[1]的土耳其人，而克里米亚沿海也顶多只是点缀着由海洋民族所建立的为数不多的贸易站点。这样，君士坦丁堡就成了地中海地区的海上力量赖以据守中部海疆的据点，就像罗马军团的陆上力量沿着诸条河流据守罗马的西部和东部边疆那样。倘若从广义和战略的角度来理解，"中心地带"这个术语包括了小亚

---

[1] Scythians：斯基泰人。南俄草原上的一个游牧民族，即后来的土耳其人。又译西古提人、西徐亚人或赛西亚人。

奥斯曼帝国骑兵

made their home, just as the Magyar Turks only a century or two earlier rode round the north of the Black Sea into the Hungarian Steppe. Under great leaders of cavalry of the Ottoman dynasty, these Turks crossed the Dardanelles, and, following the "Corridor" of the Maritza and Morava valleys through the Balkan Mountains, achieved the conquest of Magyar Hungary itself. From the moment that the city of Constantinople fell into Turkish hands in 1453, the Black Sea was closed to the Venetian and Genoese seamen. Under Rome, the realm of the seamen had been advanced to the northern shore of the Black Sea; under the Ottoman Turks the Heartland, the realm of the horsemen, was advanced to the Dinaric Alps and the Taurus. This essential fact has been masked by the extension of Turkish dominion into Arabia outside the Heartland; but it is evident again today when Britain has reconquered Arabia for the Arabs. Within the Heartland, the Black Sea has of late been the path of strategical design eastward for our German enemy.

We defined the Heartland originally in accordance with river drainage; but does not

细亚和巴尔干半岛在内的话，那么可以说，在罗马帝国的统治之下，海上力量正是如此这般地渗入了"中心地带"的内部。

在这些根本性的地理事实面前，后来的历史虽然还是一目了然，但历史发展的方向却正好相反。中亚细亚的一些土耳其人，避开南下进入阿拉伯半岛的那条道路，骑马越过中央高原和亚美尼亚高原，进入了小亚细亚的开阔草原，并在那里定居下来，就像只有一两个世纪以前马扎尔族土耳其人骑马绕过黑海北端进入匈牙利大草原那样。在奥斯曼帝国那些伟大的骑兵领袖们的统率下，这些土耳其人越过达达尼尔海峡，顺着马里乍与摩拉瓦两河河谷这条"走廊"，穿过巴尔干山脉，征服了马扎尔匈牙利本土。自君士坦丁堡于1453年落入土耳其人手中的那一刻起，威尼斯和热那亚的海洋民族就无法再在黑海上通行了。在罗马帝国的统治之下，海洋民族的活动范围已经深入到了黑海北岸；

第一次世界大战时期的德国舰队

第一次世界大战时期的德国潜艇

第一次世界大战时期的协约国军队

history, as thus recounted, show that for the purposes of strategical thought it should be given a somewhat wider extension? Regarded from the point of view of human mobility, and of the different modes of mobility, it is evident that since land-power can today close the Black Sea, the whole basin of that sea must be regarded as of the Heartland. Only the Bavarian Danube, of very little value for navigation, may be treated as lying outside.

One more circumstance remains to be added, and we shall have before us the whole conception of the Heartland as it emerges from the facts of geography and history. The Baltic is a sea which can now be "closed" by land-power. The fact that the German Fleet at Kiel was responsible for the mines and submarines which kept the Allied squadrons from entering the Baltic does not, of course, in any way vitiate the statement that the closing was by land-power; the Allied Armies in France were there by virtue of sea-power, and the German sea defenses of the Baltic were there as a result of land-power. It is of prime importance in regard to any terms of peace which are to guarantee us against future war that we should recognize that under the conditions of today, as was admitted by responsible Ministers in the House of Commons, the Fleets of the Islanders could no more penetrate into the Baltic than they could into the Black Sea.

The Heartland, for the purposes of strategical thinking, includes the Baltic Sea, the navigable Middle and Lower Danube, the Black Sea, Asia Minor, Armenia, Persia, Tibet, and Mongolia. Within it, therefore, were Brandenburg-Prussia and Austria-Hungary, as well as Russia — a vast triple base of man-power, which was lacking to the horse-riders of history. The Heartland is the region to which, under modern conditions, sea-power can be refused access, though the western part of it lies without the region of Arctic and Continental drainage.

而在奥斯曼土耳其帝国的统治下，作为骑马民族活动范围的"中心地带"，则推进到了迪纳拉阿尔卑斯山脉和托罗斯山脉。这个重要的事实，因土耳其帝国的疆域扩张到了"中心地带"以外的阿拉伯半岛而被掩盖起来了；但是，如今英国替阿拉伯人重新征服了阿拉伯半岛，这个事实便再次变得清晰起来了。不久之前，我们的德意志敌人已经做出战略部署，打算把位于"中心地带"内部的黑海当成东进的通道。

我们最初是按照河流流域来划定"中心地带"的；但经过上述这样的说明之后，历史难道没有表明，为了实现某些战略思想，"中心地带"的范围应该稍加扩大呢？从人类迁徙以及迁徙方式不同的角度来看，既然陆上力量如今能够将黑海封锁起来，那么我们必须将整个黑海盆地看作是"中心地带"的一部分，这一点就是显而易见的了。只有巴伐利亚境内的多瑙河流域因为航运价值不大，故可看作是位于"中心地带"之外。

还要加上另外一种情况，才能让"中心地带"这个整体概念从地理和历史的诸多事实中逐渐浮现出来，呈现在我们的面前。波罗的海如今已经是一个可以被陆上力量"封锁"的大海了。虽说驻扎在基尔港的德国舰队曾经布下水雷、派出潜艇，阻止协约国舰队进入波罗的海，但这个事实无论从哪方面来看，与"封锁是由陆上力量执行的"这个说法当然并不相悖；驻扎在法国的协约国军队倚赖于海上力量，而德国在波罗的海拥有海上防御力量，却是因为该国拥有强大的陆上力量。我们应该认识到，在如今的形势下，各个岛国的舰队既无法再深入到波罗的海，也无法再深入到黑海，而下议院中一些负有责任的大臣也已经承认了这种情况；要想制定出能够确保我们未来不再受战争之害的和平条约，我们认识到这一事实就是极其重要的。

从实现战略思想的目的来看，"中心地带"包括了波罗的海、可通航的多瑙河中

德国派军队占领中国胶州

There is one striking physical circumstance which knits it graphically together; the whole of it, even to the brink of the Persian Mountains overlooking torrid Mesopotamia, lies under snow in the winter time. The line indicative of an average freezing temperature for the whole month of January passes from the North Cape of Norway southward, just within the "Guard" of islands along the Norwegian shore, past Denmark, across Mid–Germany to the Alps, and from the Alps eastward along the Balkan range. The Bay of Odessa and the Sea of Azof are frozen over annually, and also the greater part of the Baltic Sea. At mid–winter, as seen from the moon, a vast white shield would reveal the Heartland in its largest meaning.

游和下游地区、黑海、小亚细亚、亚美尼亚、波斯、西藏和蒙古。因此，勃兰登堡-普鲁士、奥匈帝国以及俄罗斯都位于"中心地带"内部——它们形成了一个广袤的、三者合一的人力基地，而历史上的骑马民族却从来都没有过这样的基地。尽管"中心地带"西部位于北极地区和大陆流域之外，但在现代条件下，"中心地带"却仍是海上力量无法进入的一个区域。有一个显著的自然条件，把"中心地带"的各个区域清晰地连成了一体；这个自然条件就是，整个"中心地带"，甚至是远至俯瞰着气候炎热的美索不达米亚平原的波斯山脉边缘，冬季都覆盖着皑皑白雪。表示一月份平均气温为冰点的那条

When the Russian Cossacks first policed the steppes at the close of the Middle Ages, a great revolution was effected, for the Tartars, like the Arabs, had lacked the necessary man-power upon which to found a lasting Empire, but behind the Cossacks were the Russian ploughmen, who have today grown to be a people of a hundred millions on the fertile plains between the Black and Baltic Seas. During the nineteenth century, the Russian Czardom loomed large within the great Heartland, and seemed to threaten all the marginal lands of Asia and Europe. Towards the end of the century, however, the Germans of Prussia and Austria determined to subdue the

线，从挪威的北角[1]向南，沿着挪威海岸，正好位于沿海岛屿的"护卫"之内，经过丹麦，横跨德国中部到达阿尔卑斯山脉，再从阿尔卑斯山脉沿着巴尔干山脉向东。敖德萨湾[2]和亚速海[3]每年都会封冻，波罗的海的大部分海域也是这样。隆冬时节，要是从月球上俯瞰地球，我们就会看到一片广袤的白色大地，从而清晰地揭示出"中心地带"最重要的意义。

俄罗斯的哥萨克人在中世纪末第一次统治了大草原之后，引发出了一场伟大的革命，原因在于鞑靼人和阿拉伯人一样，没有建立一个永久性帝国所必须的人力资源，而

[1] North Cape：北角。挪威北部北角县马格尔岛北端的一个海岬，常被认为是欧洲的最北方。

[2] The Bay of Odessa：敖德萨湾。敖德萨是俄罗斯欧洲部分西南部濒临黑海的一个港口城市，是鞑靼人在14世纪作为要塞而建立的。

[3] The Sea of Azof：亚速海。指黑海北部、位于俄罗斯欧洲部分南部的海域，其浅海有重要的渔场。Azof亦拼成Azov。

图26　由部分并行的铁路和航空线路连为一体的"世界岛"，这种情况不久之后即会实现。

第一次世界大战时期的德军飞机

Slavs and to exploit them for the occupation of the Heartland, through which run the land–ways into China, India, Arabia, and the African Heartland. The German military colonies of Kiauchau and East Africa were established as termini of the projected overland routes.

Today armies have at their disposal not only the Trans–Continental Railway but also the Motor–Car. They have, too, the Aeroplane, which is of a boomerang nature, a weapon of land–power as against sea–power. Modern artillery, moreover, is very formidable against ships. In short, a great military power in possession of the Heartland and of Arabia could take easy possession of the cross–ways of the world at Suez. Sea–power would have found it very difficult to hold the Canal if a fleet of submarines had been based from the beginning of the war on the Black Sea. We have defeated the danger on this occasion, but the facts of geography remain, and offer ever–increasing strategical opportunities to land–power as against sea–power.

哥萨克人身后却有俄罗斯农民的支持——这些农民如今已经发展成了一个人口上亿的民族，繁衍生息在黑海和波罗的海之间一些富饶的平原上。整个19世纪，沙皇俄国在广袤的"中心地带"内部都势力日盛，并且似乎已经威胁到了欧、亚两洲所有的边缘地区。然而，到了19世纪末，普鲁士和奥地利的日耳曼人决心征服斯拉夫人，并且利用斯拉夫人来占领"中心地带"，然后再通过"中心地带"，由陆路渗入中国、印度、阿拉伯半岛和非洲的"中心地带"。德国在胶州和东非地区的各个军事殖民地，都是当作这一计划中的陆路终点而建立起来的。

如今，陆军部队不但可以随意使用横贯大陆的铁路，还可以随意使用汽车了。他们也拥有飞机，而飞机可以像回旋镖那样飞来飞去，是陆上力量对付海上力量的一种武器。而且，现代火炮对付起舰船来，也是威力无比。总而言之，倘若一个军事大国占据

It is evident that the Heartland is as real a physical fact within the World–Island as is the World–Island itself within the Ocean, although its boundaries are not quite so clearly defined. Not until about a hundred years ago, however, was there available a base of man-power sufficient to begin to threaten the liberty of the world from within this citadel of the World–Island. No mere scraps of paper, even though they be the written constitution of a League of Nations, are under the conditions of today a sufficient guarantee that the Heartland will not again become the center of a World–War. Now is the time, when the Nations are fluid, to consider what guarantees, based on Geographical and Economic Realities, can be made available for the future security of Mankind. With this in view, it will be worth our while to see how the storm gathered in the Heartland on the present occasion.

了"中心地带"和阿拉伯半岛,便可以轻而易举地占领这个位于苏伊士的世界通衢交叉点。如果在战争伊始的时候,敌方便将一队潜艇部署在黑海之上,那么海上力量就会发现,要想牢牢据守苏伊士运河,是很困难的。虽说这一次我们已经消除了危险,但那些地理现实却依然存在,并且与给陆上力量提供了越来越多对抗海上力量的战略机遇。

显然,处于"世界岛"内部的"中心地带",与为海洋环抱的"世界岛"本身一样,都是切切实实存在的自然现实,只是"中心地带"的边界划定并不像"世界岛"那样清晰罢了。然而,直到大约100年前,才有了一个足以从"世界岛"这座大本营内部开始威胁到世界自由的人力基地。在如今的形势之下,纯粹的几张纸——就算这几张纸是一个国际联盟的成文宪法,也并不足以确保"中心地带"将来不会再次成为一场世界大战的中心。现在这个国际联盟还没有定型,所以正是考虑我们以地理现实和经济现实为基础,能够做出什么样的保证来确保人类未来的安全这个问题的时候了。带着这一观点,我们再来看一看这场世界大战的风暴如何在"中心地带"聚积起来,就是很有意义的了。

V   THE RIVALRY OF EMPIRES

A most interesting parallel might be drawn between the advance of the sailors over the ocean from Western Europe and the contemporary advance of the Russian Cossacks across the steppes of the Heartland. Yermak, the Cossack, rode over the Ural Mountains into Siberia in 1533, within a dozen years, that is to say, after Magellan's voyage round the world. The parallel might be repeated in regard to our own days. It was an unprecedented thing in the year 1900 that Britain should maintain a quarter of a million men in her war with the Boers at a distance of 6000 miles over the ocean; but it was as remarkable a feat for Russia to place an army of more than a quarter of a million men against the Japanese in Manchuria in 1904 at a distance of 4000 miles by rail. We have been in the habit of thinking that mobility by sea far outran mobility upon the land, and so for a time it did, but it is well to remember that fifty years ago 90 per cent, of the world's shipping was still moved by sails, and that already the first railway had been opened across North America.

One of the reasons why we commonly fail to appreciate the significance of the policing of the steppes by the Cossacks is that we think vaguely of Russia as extending, with a gradually diminishing density of settlement, from the German and Austrian frontiers for thousands of miles eastward, over all the area colored on the map with one tint and labeled as one country, as far as Bering Strait. In truth Russia — the real Russia which supplied more than 80 per cent, of the recruits for the Russian armies during the first three years of the War — is a very much smaller fact than the simplicity of the map would seem to indicate. The Russia which is the homeland of

第五章   帝国之间的竞争

我们可以在航海者从西欧出发、漂洋过海的推进和同时代俄罗斯哥萨克人横跨"中心地带"上的大草原的进击之间，做一个极其有意思的比较。1533年，哥萨克人雅尔马克纵马越过乌拉尔山脉，进入了西伯利亚，也就是说，此时距麦哲伦完成环球航行不过十多年。就我们目前所处的这个时代而言，也可以进行这样的对比。1900年，英国在与本土相距6000英里的海外与布尔人作战时能够维持25万人的给养，还是一件史无前例的事情；不过，1904年俄国派了一支25万多人的军队，坐火车走上4000英里到满洲去跟日本人作战，也是一桩非同寻常的壮举。我们都已经习以为常，认为经由海上进行机动的速度要远远超过在陆上进行机动；虽说过去有一个时期确实如此，但我们应当还记得，50年前全世界90%的航运量还是由帆船来进行的，而当时也已开通横贯北美洲的第一条铁路了。

我们之所以通常认识不到哥萨克人统治大草原的重要性，原因之一就在于我们都模糊地认为，俄国从德国和奥地利两国边境起向东延伸达数千英里，定居人口的密度也逐渐下降，覆盖了在地图上用同一种颜色标注为一个国家的那片地区，远至白令海峡。实际上，俄罗斯——在这次大战的前3年中为俄国军队提供了80%以上新兵的、名副其实的俄国——比在地图上似乎简单地显示出来的范围要小得多。属于俄罗斯民族故土的那个俄罗斯全部位于欧洲，所占的面积也只有我们通常所称的俄国欧洲部分的一半左

集结的俄军哥萨克骑兵

日俄战争期间俄军坐火车在奉天集结的德军飞机

the Russian people, lies wholly in Europe, and occupies only about half of what we commonly call Russia in Europe. The land boundaries of Russia in this sense are in many places almost as definite as are the coasts of France or Spain. Trace a line on the map from Petrograd eastward along the Upper ; Volga to the great bend of the river at Kazan, and thence southward along the Middle Volga to the second great bend at Czaritzin, and finally southwestward along the lower river Don to Rostof and the Sea of Azof. Within this line, to south and west of it, are more than a hundred million Russian people. They, the main stock of Russia, inhabit the plain between the Volga and the Carpathians and between the Baltic and Black Seas, with an average density of perhaps 150 to the square mile, and this continuous sheet of population ends more or less abruptly along the line which has been indicated.

Northward of Petrograd and Kazan is North Russia, a vast somber forest land with occasional marshes, more than half as large as all the region just defined as the Russian Homeland. North Russia has a population of less than two millions, or not three to the square mile. East of the Volga and Don, as far as the Ural Mountains and the Caspian Sea, lies East Russia, about as large as North Russia, and with a population also of about two millions. But in the Kama Valley, between North and East Russia, is a belt of settled country, extending eastward from Kazan and Samara to the Ural Range, and over that range, past the mines of Ekaterinburg, into Siberia, and right across Western Siberia to Irkutsk, just short of Lake Baikal. This belt of population beyond the Volga numbers perhaps twenty millions. The whole of it, from Kazan and Samara to Irkutsk, in so far as it is occupied by plowmen and not by wandering horsemen, is of recent settlement.

右。从这个意义上来说，俄罗斯的陆地边界在许多地方就跟法国或西班牙的海岸线一样明确。在地图上顺着一条线，从彼得格勒往东沿伏尔加河上游到该河位于喀山的大拐弯处，再从那里沿着伏尔加河中游南下，来到这条河位于察里津的第二个大拐弯处，最后沿着顿河下游往西南而去，就到了洛斯托夫和亚速海。在这条线以内，即这条线的南边和西边，居住着1亿多俄罗斯人民。他们是俄罗斯民族的主体，在伏尔加河和喀尔巴阡山脉之间、波罗的海和黑海之间的平原上繁衍生息，平均人口密度大约为每平方英里150人，可这条绵延不断的人口带，挨到前面所述的那条线便差不多马上终止了。

从彼得格勒和喀山往北是北俄罗斯，那是一片广袤而幽暗的林地，其中间或有些沼泽，面积占我们刚刚确定的那个俄罗斯族故土总面积的一半多。北俄罗斯的人口少于200万，就是说每平方英里还不到3人。东俄罗斯位于伏尔加河和顿河以东，远至乌拉尔山脉和里海，它的面积与北俄罗斯差不多，人口也是差不多200万。不过，位于北俄罗斯和东俄罗斯之间的卡马[1]河谷，却是一片有人居住的狭长乡村；它从喀山和萨马拉[2]往东延伸到乌拉尔山脉，然后越过这条山脉，经过叶卡捷琳堡[3]的矿区，进入西伯利亚，并完全横过西西伯利亚到达伊尔库茨克，只是没有抵达贝加尔湖罢了。伏尔加河以东这条人口带的人口数量大约达2000万。整个人口带从喀山和萨马拉到伊尔库茨克，由于居住的都是农民而非到处漂泊的游牧民族，所以人们在此定居应该还没有多久。

[1] Kama：卡马河。俄罗斯欧洲部分以东的一条河流，发源于乌拉尔山脉中部，是伏尔加河的一条主要支流。

[2] Samara：萨马拉。伏尔加河中游的重工业城市，1935年更名为古比雪夫，1991年苏联解体后恢复旧称。

[3] Ekaterinburg：叶卡捷琳堡。乌拉尔山脚下的著名工业城市，现名斯维尔德洛夫斯克。

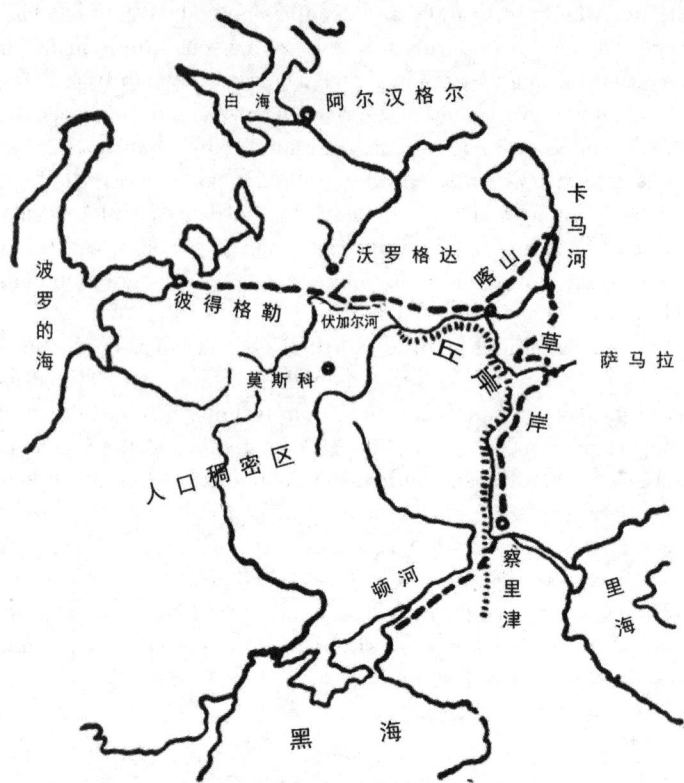

图27 图中所示为俄罗斯人口密度较大的区域之界线（－－－－－）。

The Middle Volga, flowing southward from Kazan to Czaritzin, is a remarkable moat not only to Russia but to Europe. The west shore, known as the Hill Bank, in opposition to the Meadow Bank on the other side, is a hill face, some hundred feet high, which overlooks the river for 700 miles; it is the brink of the inhabited plain, here a little raised above the sea level. Stand on the top of this brink, looking eastward across the broad river below you, and you will realize that you have populous Europe at your back, and in front, where the low meadows fade away into the half sterility of the drier steppes eastward, you have the beginning of the vacancies of Central Asia.

A striking practical commentary on these great physical and social contrasts has been supplied in the last few months by the Civil War in Russia. In all North Russia there are

　　从喀山向南流到察里津的伏尔加河中段不仅是俄罗斯一条了不起的护城河，也是欧洲一条了不起的一条护城河。人称"丘岸"且同对面"草岸"隔水相望的西岸，是一片海拔大约100英尺且沿河壁立、长达700英里的丘陵；这片丘陵，正是那片有人居住的平原的边界，其地势则稍高于海平面。站在这条边界的最高处放眼东望，远眺脚下那条大河的对岸，你就会看到，你的身后是人口稠密的欧洲，而你的前面，随着低矮的草地逐渐东延变成水草稀少的半干旱草原，正是中亚细亚无人地带的起点。

　　最近数月间发生的俄国内战，显著而切实地说明了这些巨大的自然差别与社会差别。在北俄罗斯全境，只有两三个城镇的规模比村子大，而由于布尔什维克以城镇居民为根

俄国内战时期白军的宣传画。

俄国内战时期白军的宣传画

英国远征军

but two or three towns larger than a village, and, since the Bolsheviks are based on the town populations, Bolshevism has had little hold north of the Volga. Moreover the sparse rural settlements, chiefly of foresters, have, in their simple, colonial conditions, no grounds for agrarian political feeling, and there is thus no peasant sympathy for the Bolsheviks. As a result, the railway from Archangel to Vologda on the Upper Dwina long remained open for communication with the ocean and the West. The Transiberian line runs from Petrograd through Vologda, and there is a direct line from Moscow to Vologda which may be considered as leaving Russia proper and entering North Russia at the bridge over the Volga at Jaroslav. For these reasons it was that the Allied Embassies established themselves at Vologda when they retired from Petrograd and Moscow: apart from the convenience of alternative communications with Archangel and Vladivostok, they were outside Bolshevik Russia.

基，所以布尔什维克主义在伏尔加河以北的那些地区并没有什么势力。此外，由于乡村地区人烟稀少，并且主要都是林中居民，生活条件简单得很，没有产生"平均地权"这种政治觉悟的土壤，因此那里的农民与布尔什维克并没有同感。结果就是，沿德维纳河上游从阿尔汉格尔到沃罗格达的那条铁路在很长时间内一直都畅通无阻，并未中断海洋和西部地区之间的交通。西伯利亚大铁路从彼得格勒出发，穿过了沃罗格达，并且此处还有一条铁路从莫斯科直达沃罗格达；我们可以把它看成一条离开俄罗斯本土、在雅罗斯拉夫跨越伏尔加河上的大桥进入北俄罗斯的铁路。正是由于这些原因，撤出彼得格勒和莫斯科后，协约国的大使们才在沃罗格达住了下来：除了这里与阿尔汉格尔和符拉迪沃斯托克有着便利

Even more significant was the action of the Czecho–Slovaks on the Moscow branch of the Transiberian line. Advancing from the Ural Mountains, with the support of the Ural Cossacks, they took Samara at the point where the railway reaches the Meadow Bank, and they seized the great bridge over the river at Syzran. They even penetrated a short way along the line to Penza within the real Russia, but through a rather sparsely–populated neighborhood. Also, they struck up the river to Kazan. In truth they were thus hovering round the edge of the real Russia and threatening it from outside. The British expedition from Archangel by boat up the Dwina River to Kotlas, and thence by railway to Vyatka on the Transiberian line, appears a less foolhardy enterprise when seen in the light of these realities.

This definition of the real Russia gives a new meaning not only to the Russia but also to the Europe of the nineteenth century. Let us consider that Europe, with the help of the map. All the more northern regions of Scandinavia, Finland, and Russia, and also East Russia southward to the Caucasus, are excluded as being mere vacancies, and with them the Turkish dominion in the Balkan Peninsula. It will be remembered that Kinglake in Eöthen, writing in 1844, considered that he was entering the East when he was ferried across the river Save to Belgrade. The boundary between the Austrian and Turkish Empires as settled by the Treaty of Belgrade in 1739, was not varied until 1878. Thus the real Europe, the Europe of the European peoples, the Europe which, with its overseas Colonies, is Christendom, was a perfectly definite social conception; its landward boundary ran straight from Petrograd to Kazan, and then along a curved line from Kazan by the Volga and Don Rivers to the Black Sea, and by the Turkish

可选的交通，他们所处的地方也已不在俄罗斯苏维埃联邦社会主义共和国之内了。

更为重要的是，捷克斯洛伐克人在西伯利亚大铁路的莫斯科支线上采取了行动。在乌拉尔哥萨克人的支持下，他们从乌拉尔山脉进军，攻取了西伯利亚铁路与"草岸"相接处的萨马拉，并且占领了塞兹兰的伏尔加河大桥。他们甚至还沿着通往奔薛的那段铁路线深入了一段不长的距离，挺进到了真正的俄罗斯，但他们经过的都是铁路线附近人烟相当稀少的地区。此外，他们还溯河而上，打到了喀山。因此，实际上他们是围着真正俄罗斯的边缘左奔右突，从外部对它构成威慑。英国远征军从阿尔汉格尔乘船溯德维纳河而上，到达了柯特拉斯，之后又从那里乘坐火车到达了西伯利亚大铁路上的维亚特卡[1]；根据这些现实情况来看，英军的行动似乎还不是那么有勇无谋。

"真正的俄罗斯"这个定义，不但为俄罗斯赋予了新的含义，也为19世纪的欧洲赋予了新的含义。我们不妨借助地图，来仔细研究一下那个19世纪的欧洲。斯堪的纳维亚、芬兰和俄罗斯所有位置较北的地区，还有南至高加索地区的东俄罗斯，因为纯属无人区而被排除在欧洲之外，而跟这些地区一起被排除的，还有土耳其在巴尔干半岛上的领土。我们应当记得，金莱克[2]在1844年写的《艾奥森》一书中曾说，当他渡过萨瓦河到达贝尔格莱德时，他还以为自己来到了东方。1739年《贝尔格莱德条约》划定的奥地利帝国和土耳其帝国之间的边界，直到1878年都没有变动过。这样一来，真正的欧洲，即欧洲各民族的欧洲、有着诸多海外殖民地并信奉基督教的欧洲，就是一个相当明确的社会学概念了：它的陆上疆界，是从彼得格勒直到喀山，然后顺着一条弧线，从喀山沿伏尔加河和顿河直到黑海，再沿着土耳其边界到达亚得里亚海北端附近。这个欧洲，一

---

[1] Vyatka：维亚特卡。俄罗斯西部的一个城市，现名基洛夫（Kirov）。

[2] Kinglake：金莱克（Alexander William Kinglake，1809～1891）。英国历史学家和旅行家。

frontier to near the head of the Adriatic. At the one end of this Europe is Cape St. Vincent standing out to sea; at the other end is the land cape formed by the Volga elbow at Kazan. Berlin is almost exactly midway between St. Vincent and Kazan. Had Prussia won this War it was her intention that Continental Europe from St. Vincent to Kazan, with the addition of the Asiatic Heartland, should have become the naval base from which she would have fought Britain and America in the next war.

Let us now divide our Europe into East and West by a line so drawn from the Adriatic to the North Sea that Venice and the Netherlands may lie to the west, and also that part of Germany which has been German from the beginning of European history, but so that Berlin and Vienna are to the east, for Prussia and Austria are countries which the German has conquered and more or less forcibly Teutonized. On the map thus divided let us "think through" the history of the last four generations; it will assume a new coherency.

端是向海洋中突出的圣文森特角；另一端则是伏尔加河在喀山拐弯所形成的那个陆上岬角。柏林差不多正好处在圣文森特角和喀山的中间。倘若普鲁士赢得了这场大战，它就会把从圣文森特角到喀山的这个欧洲大陆，再加上亚洲的"中心地带"，变成一个海上基地，从而在下一场战争中用来对付英、美两国。

现在，我们不妨划出一条从亚得里亚海到北海的界线，把欧洲分成东西两个部分：威尼斯、荷兰以及自欧洲有史以来就属于日耳曼人的那一部分德意志，都可以划在线的西边；但柏林和维也纳应当划在此线以东，因为普鲁士和奥地利是被日耳曼人征服且多少被迫德国化了的两个国家。在如此划分的地图上，我们不妨再来"彻底回顾"过去四个世代的历史；如此一来，这段历史就会呈现出一种新的相关性。

图28　真正的欧洲：东欧和西欧，再加上巴巴里、巴尔干半岛和小亚细亚。

※　　　　※　　　　※　　　　※　　　　※　　　　※　　　　※　　　　※　　　　※

The English Revolution limited the powers of Monarchy, and the French Revolution asserted the rights of the people. Owing to disorder in France, and her invasion from abroad, the organizer Napoleon was thrown up. Napoleon conquered Belgium and Switzerland, surrounded himself with subsidiary kings in Spain, Italy, and Holland, and made an alliance with the subordinate Federation of the Rhine, or, in other words, with the old Germany. Thus Napoleon had united the whole of West Europe, saving only insular Britain. Then he advanced against East Europe, and defeated Austria and Prussia, but did not annex them, though he compelled them to act as his allies when he afterwards went forward against Russia. We often hear of the vast spaces for Russian retreat which lay behind Moscow; but, in fact, Napoleon at Moscow had very nearly marched right across the inhabited Russia of his time.[1] Napoleon was brought down partly by the exhaustion of his French man-power, but mainly because his realm of West Europe was enveloped by British sea-power, for Britain was able to bring to herself supplies from outside Europe and to cut West Europe off from similar supplies. Naturally she allied herself with the Powers of East Europe, but there was only one way by which she could effectively communicate with them, and that was through the Baltic. This explains her naval action twice at Copenhagen. Owing to her command of the sea, Britain was, however, able to land her armies in Holland, Spain, and Italy, and to sap the Napoleonic strength in rear. It is interesting to note that the culminating victory of Trafalgar and the turning-point of Moscow lay very nearly at the two extremes of our real Europe. The Napoleonic War was a duel between West and East Europe, whose areas and populations were about evenly balanced, but the superiority due to the higher civilization of West Europe was neutralized by British sea-power.

[1] And therefore across the territory which could afford supplies to the contending armies.

※　　　　※　　　　※　　　　※　　　　※　　　　※　　　　※　　　　※　　　　※

英国革命限制了君主的权力，而法国革命则维护了人民的权利。由于法国发生内乱并遭到了外部侵略，所以造就了拿破仑这个组织者。拿破仑征服了比利时和瑞士，让周围的西班牙、意大利和荷兰等国的君主都成了他身边的附庸，并且跟俯首帖耳的莱茵联邦——换言之，即过去的德意志——结成了联盟。这样一来，除了不列颠这个岛国，拿破仑便统一了整个西欧。然后他开始进击东欧，打败了奥地利和普鲁士；虽然后来出兵进击俄罗斯的时候他强迫这两个国家同法国协同作战，但他没有吞并这两个国家。我们常常听人说起，莫斯科后方幅员辽阔，可供俄罗斯人撤退；可实际上，拿破仑在莫斯科战役中就已经差不多横扫了当时俄国有人居住的地区。〔作者注：因此也就横扫了能为俄罗斯作战部队提供给养的那片领土。〕后来拿破仑之所以被赶下台去，部分原因在于他的人力资源业已枯竭，但主要原因还是在于，他在西欧的势力范围被英国的海上力量包围了；因为英国不但能够从欧洲以外的地区获取给养，还能切断西欧获得相同给养的渠道。自然，英国也与东欧一些强国结成了同盟，但只有一条路线可以让它有效地跟这些东欧国家进行联系，那就是经由波罗的海的水路。这就解释了英国海军在哥本哈根进行了两次作战的原因。然而，正是因为掌握了制海权，所以英国才能够让陆军在荷兰、西班牙和意大利登陆，才能蚕食掉拿破仑的后方实力。有意思的是，在取得最终胜利的特拉法尔加海战和标志着战争转折点的莫斯科战役中，两处战场离我们这个真正的欧洲的东西两端都很近。拿破仑战争是西欧和东欧之间的决斗，虽说双方的面积和人口差不多不相上下，但西欧由于文明程度较高而具有的那种优势，却被英国的海上力量抵消掉了。

英国革命

法国革命中人民攻占巴士底狱

拿破仑和他的军队

莫斯科战役

After Waterloo, East Europe was united by the Holy League of the three Powers — Russia, Austria and Prussia. Each of the three advanced westward a stage, as though drawn by a magnet in that direction. Russia obtained most of Poland, and thus extended a political peninsula into the heart of the physical peninsula of Europe. Austria took the Dalmatian coast, and also Venice and Milan in the mainland of Northern Italy. Prussia obtained a detached territory in the old Germany of the West, which territory was divided into the two provinces of the Rhineland and Westphalia. This annexation of Germans to Prussia proved to be a much more significant thing than the addition of Poles to Russia and of Italians to Austria. The Rhineland is an anciently civilized country, and so far Western that it accepted the Code Napoleon for its law, which it still retains. From the moment that the Prussians thus forced their way into West Europe a struggle became inevitable between the Liberal Rhineland and the Conservative Brandenburg of Berlin. But that struggle was postponed for a time owing to the exhaustion of Europe.

British naval power continued the while to envelop West Europe from Heligoland, Portsmouth, Plymouth, Gibraltar, and Malta. By changes precipitated in the years 1830 to

滑铁卢之战后，东欧被俄罗斯、奥地利和普鲁士这3个强国所组成的"神圣同盟"统一起来了。这3个国家仿佛都受到了西面的磁铁吸引一样，都向西进击了一段距离。俄罗斯攫取了波兰的大部分领土，从而把一个政治意义上的半岛楔入了地理上的欧洲半岛的中心。奥地利占领了达尔马提亚沿海，以及位于北意大利本土的威尼斯和米兰两地。普鲁士得到了原属西欧老德意志的一处"飞地"，并把这处领土分割成了莱茵兰和威斯特伐利亚两个省。结果表明，与俄国兼并波兰人、奥地利兼并意大利人相比，普鲁士此次兼并日耳曼人的意义更为重大。莱茵兰是一个文明古邦，因为与西欧相距极近，所以它接受了《拿破仑法典》并将其当作自己的法律，一直保留到如今。自普鲁士人气势汹汹地攻进西欧的那个时候起，自由的莱茵兰省与柏林守旧的勃兰登堡之间，就必定会爆发出一场斗争。不过，由于当时整个欧洲都已筋疲力尽，所以这场斗争便推迟了一个时期才爆发。

在此期间，英国的海军力量继续从赫里戈兰、朴次茅斯、普利茅斯、直布罗陀和马

1832 the temporary reaction in the West was brought to an end, and the middle classes came into power in Britain, France and Belgium. In the years from 1848 to 1850 the democratic movement spread eastward of the Rhine, and Central Europe was ablaze with the ideas of freedom and nationality, but from our point of view two events, and two only, were decisive. In 1849 the Russian Armies advanced into Hungary and put the Magyars back into their subjection to Vienna, thereby enabling the Austrians to reassert their supremacy over the Italians and Bohemians. In 1850 took place that fatal conference at Olm ü tz when Russia and Austria refused to allow the King of Prussia to accept the All-German Crown which had been offered to him from Frankfurt in the West. Thus the continuing unity of East Europe was asserted, and the Liberal movement from the Rhineland was definitely balked.

In 1860 Bismarck, who had been at Frankfurt, and who had also been Ambassador in Paris and Petrograd, was called to power at Berlin, and resolved to base German unity not on the idealism of Frankfurt and the West, but on the organization of Berlin and the East. In 1864 and 1866 Berlin overran West Germany, annexing Hanover and thereby opening the way into the

奥托·冯·俾斯麦

耳他出发，以包围整个西欧。经过1830年到1832年间突发的剧变[1]，西欧结束了短暂的反动统治，而中产阶级则在英、法和比利时等国开始掌权。从1848年到1850年，民主运动蔓延到了莱茵河以东，中欧开始闪耀着自由和民族主义思想的光芒；但在我们看来，有两个事件，也只有这两个事件才具有决定性的意义。1849年，俄国军队攻入了匈牙利，使得马扎尔人重新臣服于维也纳，从而让奥地利人得以再次凌驾于意大利人和波希米亚人之上。1850年，在奥尔姆茨[2]举行了一次命运攸关的会议；在此次会议上，俄国和奥地利都不同意让普鲁士国王接受"一统全德"的皇冠，而这顶皇冠，又是西欧的法兰克福献给普鲁士国王的。这样，东欧的统一得以维持下去，而从莱茵兰地区开始传播的自由主义远动，却无疑受到了阻碍。

1860年，曾经到过法兰克福并担任过驻巴黎和驻彼得格勒大使的俾斯麦，奉召在柏林上台掌权了；他决定不以法兰克福和西欧的理想主义为基础，而是以柏林和东欧的组织为基础来统一德国。1864年和1866年，柏林击溃了西德意志，吞并了汉诺威，从而

---

[1] 指1830年革命，即19世纪30年代初欧洲各国革命力量与贵族之间爆发的对抗。革命从法国开始，席卷了波兰、比利时、意大利、德意志、希腊等国家和地区，被誉为"自由主义的突破"。

[2] Olm ü tz：奥尔姆茨。捷克摩拉维亚中部的一个州，首府为奥洛姆克（Olomouc）。Olm ü tz是Olomouc的德语形式。

三帝同盟之一 俄国皇帝亚历山大二世　　三帝同盟之二 德国皇帝威廉一世　　三帝同盟之三 奥匈皇帝约瑟夫

Rhine–land for Junker militarism. At the same time Berlin weakened her competitor Austria by helping the Magyar to establish the dual government of Austria–Hungary, and by depriving Austria of Venice. France had previously recovered Milan for the West. The War of 1866 between Prussia and Austria was, however, in essence merely a Civil War; this became evident in 1872 when Prussia, having shown that her power was irresistible in the War against France, formed the League of the Three Emperors, and thus reconstituted for a time the East Europe of the Holy Alliance. The center of power in East Europe was now, however, Prussia, and no longer Russia, and East Europe had established a considerable Rhenish "Glacis" against West Europe.

For some fifteen years after the Franco–Prussian War Bismarck ruled both East and West Europe. He ruled the West by dividing the three Romance Powers of France, Italy and Spain.

为容克[1]军国主义进入莱茵兰地区打通了道路。与此同时，通过帮助马扎尔人建立起了一个奥–匈联合政府并从奥地利手中夺取了威尼斯，柏林削弱了其对手奥地利的实力。在此之前，法国已经让米兰重新回到了西欧的怀抱。然而，1866年的普奥战争本质上只是一场内战；1872年，当普鲁士在对法战争中显示了自己的力量不可抗拒，继而建立起"三帝同盟"[2]，并因此而短暂地重建了东欧的"神圣同盟"之后，这一点就变得很明显了。但是，此时东欧的权力中心已是普鲁士而不再是俄罗斯，并且东欧也已在莱茵河两岸建立起一条巨大的"缓冲带"来跟西欧对抗了。

普法战争之后的差不多15年里，东欧和西欧都在俾斯麦的统治之下。他是用离间法国、意大利和西班牙这3个日耳曼强国的方法来统治西欧的。他之所以能够做到这一

[1] Junker：容克。本义指"地主之子"，原为普鲁士的贵族地主阶级，19世纪后开始资本主义化并成为半封建的贵族地主。后多用于指年轻的德国贵族。

[2] the League of the Three Emperors：三帝同盟。又称"湟同盟"。指俾斯麦上台后，想要恢复神圣同盟、防止俄国与法国联手而撮合俄皇亚历山大二世、德皇威廉一世以及奥皇约瑟夫，于1873年签署的、以孤立法国为目标的同盟。

This he accomplished in regard to their relations to Barbary, the "Island of the West" of the Arabs. France had taken the central portion of Barbary, known as Algeria, and by encouraging her to extend her dominion eastward into Tunis and westward into Morocco, Bismarck brought her interests into conflict with those of Italy and Spain. In East Europe there was a somewhat similar rivalry between Russia and Austria in respect of the Balkan Peninsula, but here the effort of Bismarck was to hold his two allies together. Therefore, after making the Dual Alliance with Austria in 1878, Bismarck negotiated his secret Reinsurance Treaty with Russia. He desired a solid East Europe under Prussian control, but a divided West Europe.

※　　　　※　　　　※　　　　※　　　　※　　　　※　　　　※　　　　※　　　　※

The events which we have thus briefly called to mind are no mere past and dead history. They show the fundamental opposition between East and West Europe, an opposition which becomes of world-significance when we remember that the line through Germany which History indicates as the frontier between East and West is the very line which we have on other grounds taken as demarking the Heartland in the strategical sense from the Coastland.

In West Europe there are two principal elements, the Romance and the Teutonic. As far as the two chief nations, Britain and France, are concerned, there is and can be in modern times no question of conquest of the one by the other. The Channel lies between them. Away back in the Middle Ages it is true that for three centuries French Knights ruled England, and that for

点，是利用了这3个国家同巴巴里那个阿拉伯人的"西方之岛"的关系。法国已经占领了巴巴里的中部地区，即人们所知的阿尔及利亚，而通过怂恿法国扩张领土、向东侵入突尼斯且向西侵入摩洛哥，俾斯麦又令法国和意大利、西班牙两国产生了利益冲突。在东欧，俄、奥两国对巴尔干半岛也存在着差不多相似的竞争；不过在这里，俾斯麦的意图却是让他的这两个盟国团结起来。因此，在1878年和奥地利缔结两国同盟之后，俾斯麦又同俄国进行秘密谈判，签订了一份《再保险条约》[1]。他所期望的，是一个由普鲁士人掌控的、团结一致的东欧和一个分裂的西欧。

※　　　　※　　　　※　　　　※　　　　※　　　　※　　　　※　　　　※　　　　※

我们如此简短地回忆起来的这些事件，都并非只是过眼云烟和冷冰冰的历史。因为它们表明了东、西欧之间那种根本性的对立；倘若我们还记得，贯穿德国境内且历史业已表明属于东、西欧之间分界的那条线也正是我们出于别的理由而从战略意义上来划分"中心地带"和沿海地区的那条线，那么这种对立便更具全球性的重大意义了。

西欧有两个主要的组成部分，即罗曼语系国家和日耳曼语系国家。就英、法这两个主要国家来说，在现代并不存在、也不可能存在一国征服另一国的问题。因为两国之间，横亘着英吉利海峡。回望遥远的中世纪，法兰西骑士曾经统治英国达三个世纪，这是事实；而英国也曾有一个世纪想要统治法国，这也是事实。但是，在女王玛丽丢掉加来港之后，这种关系便永远结束了。两国在18世纪发生了数场大战，目的主要都是为了阻止法兰西的君主独霸整个欧洲大陆。至于其他的，都是双方为争夺殖民地和贸易而进行的战争。而就莱茵河两岸的日耳曼语系国家来说，过去它们对法兰西人自然也并不存

---

[1] Reinsurance Treaty：《再保险条约》。指俾斯麦为孤立法国和讨好俄国，而在1887年6月同俄国签订的一项密约。由于1878年的德奥同盟已经保证奥地利在德、法战争中保持中立，而这一条约又保证俄国的中立，德国因而获得了双重保险，故有此名。

another century the English tried to rule France. But those relations ended for good when Queen Mary lost Calais. The great wars between the two countries in the eighteenth century were waged primarily to prevent the French Monarchy from dominating the Continent of Europe. For the rest, they were wars of colonial and commercial rivalry. So far, also, as the Teutonic element along the Rhine is concerned, there was certainly in the past no very deep-seated hostility to the French. The Alsatians, though German by speech, became — it is one of the great facts of history operative to this day — French in heart. Even what is now the Rhine province of Prussia accepted, as we have seen, the Code Napoleon.

In East Europe there are also two principal elements, the Teutonic and the Slavonic, but no equilibrium has been established between them as between the Romance and Teutonic elements of West Europe. The key to the whole situation in East Europe — and it is a fact which cannot be too clearly laid to heart at the present moment — is the German claim to dominance over the

玛丽女王。英国历史上第一位女王（1553年～1558年在位）。她在国内推行暴政，人称"血腥玛丽"。她让英国参加了反法战争，战败后让英国丧失了在欧洲大陆的据点加来港。

Slav. Vienna and Berlin, just beyond the boundary of West Europe, stand already within territory that was Slav in the earlier Middle Ages; they represent the first step of the German out of his native country as a conqueror eastward. In the time of Charlemagne the rivers Saale and Elbe divided the Slavs from the Germans, and to this day, only a short distance south of Berlin, is the Circle of Kottbus, where the peasantry still speak Wendish, or the Slav tongue of all the region a few centuries ago. Outside this little Wendish remnant, the Slav peasantry have accepted

在什么根深蒂固的敌意。阿尔萨斯人虽然说的是日耳曼语——这是迄今为止仍然具有影响力的伟大历史事实之一——但他们的内心深处，却是法兰西人。正如我们所看到的那样，即便是如今属于普鲁士莱茵省的那个地区，也接受了《拿破仑法典》。

东欧也有两个主要的组成部分，即日耳曼语系国家和斯拉夫语系国家，但这两个组成部分之间，却并不像西欧的罗曼语系国家和日耳曼语系国家之间那样势均力敌。东欧整体形势的关键——这也是目前我们还无法清楚地理解的一个事实——就是日耳曼人要求统治斯拉夫人。恰好处在西欧边界之外的维也纳和柏林，都已处在中世纪早期属于斯拉夫人的地盘之内；它们代表了日耳曼人作为征服者迈出故土、向东扩张的第一步。在查理曼大帝时代，萨勒河[1]与易北河将斯拉夫人和日耳曼人隔离开来了；而迄今为止，柏林以南不远的地方就是"科特布斯圈"，那里的农民仍然说着温德语，或者数个世纪前这一整个地区都说的那种斯拉夫语。除了为数极少的那些文德语残余势力，斯拉夫族的农民都已经接受了日耳曼贵族的语言；这些日耳曼贵

---

[1] Saale：萨勒河。发源于德国中部卡塞尔以东的一条河流，流程大约426公里，向北注入易北河（Elbe）。

the language of the German Barons who rule them in their large estates. In South Germany, where the peasantry is truly German, the land is held by small proprietors.

No doubt there is a difference of impression made on foreigners by the Austrians and by the Prussians of noble birth; that difference comes, no doubt, from the fact that the Austrians advanced eastward from South German homes, whereas the Prussians came from the harsher North. But in Prussia and Austria alike, the great landowners were autocrats before the War, though we commonly think of the Junker as Prussian only. The peasantry of both countries was in a state of serfdom until a comparatively short time ago.

The two long limbs of territory thrust out by Prussia in northeasterly and southeasterly directions have a deep historical meaning for those who read history on the map, and it is

族都拥有自己的大庄园，在庄园里统治着斯拉夫农民。而在德国南部，由于当地农民都是纯正的日耳曼人，所以土地都分由小地主所有。

毫无疑问，奥地利贵族给外国人的印象并不同于普鲁士贵族给外国人的印象；而那种不同，毫无疑问就是源自下述这一事实：奥地利人是从南方日耳曼人的大本营向东进击，而普鲁士人却是来自较为荒芜的北方。但是，尽管我们通常认为只是普鲁士才有容克贵族，可在普鲁士和奥地利两国，此次大战前的大地主却同样都是那些专横霸道的君主。直到不久之前，两国的农民还都是农奴。

对于那些利用地图来研究历史的人来说，普鲁士向东北方向和东南方向伸出来的那两条长长的领土，有着深远的历史意义；正是地图所表述的历史，构成了我们在重建过

图29　科特布斯仍然残存的各个温德语（即斯拉夫语）孤岛，为四周说日耳曼语的地区所包围。

history on the map which constitutes one of the great realities with which we must deal in our Reconstruction. The map showing the distribution of languages tells in this instance even more than the political map, for it shows three tongues of German speech and not merely two. The first lies northeastward along the Baltic Shore; it represents a German conquest and forced Teutonization of the later Middle Ages. By the coastwise water way the Hanseatic Merchants of L ü beck and the Teutonic Knights, no longer occupied in Crusading, conquered all the shorelands to where now stands Petrograd. By subsequent history half of this strip of "Deutschthum" was incorporated with the Berlin Monarchy, and the other half became the Baltic Provinces of the Russian Czardom. But the Baltic Provinces retained, to our days, their German merchant community of Riga, their German University of Dorpat, and their German Barons as landlords. Under the Treaty of Brest–Litovsk the German element was again to have ruled in these lands of Courland and Livonia.

The second pathway of the Germans was up the Oder River to its source in the Moravian Gate the deep valley leading from Poland towards Vienna between the mountains of Bohemia on

程中必须应对的一个伟大的现实。在这个例子当中，语言分布图甚至比政治性的地图更能说明问题，因为语言分布图上表明有三种日耳曼语，而并非只有两种日耳曼语。第一种日耳曼语位于东北方向的波罗的海沿岸地区；它象征着中世纪晚期日耳曼人征服了这个地区并强迫当地的人日耳曼化。吕贝克[1]汉萨同盟[2]的商人和日耳曼族的勇士们不再进行十字军东征之后，便通过那条沿岸水道征服了所有的沿海地带，直到如今的彼得格勒。在随后的历史时期，这条"德国文化精华"地带的一半都并入到了柏林的君主统治之下，而另一半则变成了沙皇俄国治下的波罗的海各省。但直到今天，在波罗的海这些省份中，仍然保留着里加[3]的日耳曼商人社团、多帕特[4]日耳曼大学以及属于地主阶层的日耳曼贵族。根据《布勒斯特–里托夫斯克条约》[5]的规定，这个日耳曼人的组成部分将再次统治库尔兰[6]和利福尼亚[7]这些地区了。

日耳曼人的第二条通道便是溯奥德河而上，到达其位于摩尔维亚山路[8]的源头；摩

---

[1] L ü beck：吕贝克。德国北部港口城市，濒临波罗的海，现为著名的旅游城市。

[2] Hanseatic：汉萨同盟的。汉萨同盟（Hanseatic League）是中世纪德意志北部各城市之间形成的政治和商业联盟，13世纪时逐渐形成，14世纪达到兴盛，加盟城市最多达到160个。1367年成立以吕贝克城为首的领导机构，有汉堡、科隆、不莱梅等大城市的富商、贵族参加。

[3] Riga：里加。今拉脱维亚共和国的首府。最初由波罗的海商旅居住而成为商贸中心，后于1282年加入汉萨同盟，并先后被划归波兰（1481年）、瑞典（1621年）和沙俄（1710年）。

[4] Dorpat：多帕特。Tartu（塔尔图）的德语名称。

[5] Treaty of Brest–Litovsk：《布勒斯特–里托夫斯克条约》。第一次世界大战中苏俄政府与德国及其同盟在布勒斯特–里托夫斯克（即如今的布勒斯特）签订的和约，规定苏俄割让上百万平方公里领土、赔款60亿马克给德国，使苏俄成功地退出了第一次世界大战。德国战败后，苏俄政府于1918年11月12日宣布废除此条约。一般认为，这是苏俄政府以空间换时间的成功外交。

[6] Courland：库尔兰。历史上的一个地区，位于波罗的海和西德维纳河之间，1795年转给俄国，1918年大部分并入了拉脱维亚。

[7] Livonia：利福尼亚。苏联欧洲部分西部的一个地区，由拉脱维亚南部及爱沙尼亚北部组成，历史上曾是波兰、俄国和瑞典争夺的焦点，最后于1721年交给了俄国。

[8] Moravian Gate：摩尔维亚山路。欧洲中部的一条山路，位于苏台德山脉与西喀尔巴阡山脉之间，过去一直是一条战略贸易和交通要道。亦作Moravian Gap。

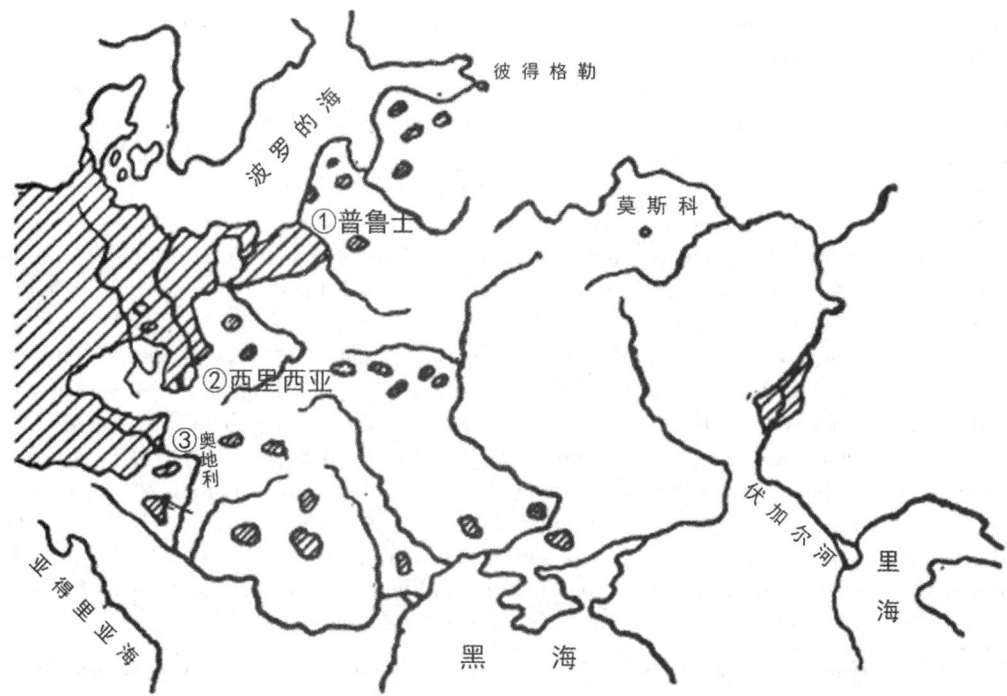

图30　图中所示为3个向东的日耳曼语言带，以及远至伏尔加河的日耳曼人零星殖民地。

the one hand, and the Carpathian Mountains on the other hand. The German settlements along the Upper Oder became Silesia, of which the greater part was taken from Austria by Prussia under Frederick the Great. The salience of these northeastward and southeastward limbs of German-speaking country is still further accentuated by the Polish-speaking Prussian province of Posen in the reentering angle between them.

　　The third eastward path of the Germans was down the Danube, and by southward passes also into the Eastern Alps. This has become the Austrian Archduchy about Vienna, and the Carinthian Duchy — German-speaking — in the Austrian Alps. Between the Silesian and Austrian Germans projects westward the province of Bohemia, mainly of Slav speech. Let us not

尔维亚山路是个深谷，从波兰通向维也纳，一边是波希米亚山脉，另一边则是喀尔巴阡山脉。奥德河上游沿岸的那些日耳曼人殖民地变成了西里西亚，其中的大部分地区都是腓特烈大帝统治时期的普鲁士从奥地利手中夺取过来的。这两条说日耳曼语并向东北和东南方向凸出去的乡村地带，因为普鲁士那个说波兰话的波森省[1]从相反的角度楔入其间而显得更加明显了。

　　日耳曼人第三条东进的路径便是顺多瑙河而下，并且通过那些向南的隘口，也进入了东阿尔卑斯山地区。这一支日耳曼人变成了维也纳附近的奥地利大公国，以及奥属阿尔卑斯山地区说日耳曼语的卡林西亚公国。在西里西亚和奥属日耳曼地区之间，是朝西突伸且主要是说斯拉夫语的波希米亚省。我们不要忘记，波森省和波希米亚省都保存了

---

　　[1] Posen：波森。即波兹南（Poznan），今波兰的一个城市。

forget that Posen and Bohemia have retained their native tongues, and that the three salients of German speech represent three streams of conquest.

Beyond even the utmost points of these three principal invasions of Deutschthum, there are many scattered German colonies of farmers and miners, some of them of very recent origin. They occur at many points in Hungary, although for political purposes the Germans have there now very much identified themselves with the Magyar tyranny. The Saxons in Transylvania share with the Magyars of that region a privileged position amid a subject population of Rumanian peasants.[1] In Russia a chain of German settlements lies eastward through the north of the Ukraine almost to Kieff. Only on the Middle Volga, about the city of Saratof, do we come to the last patch of these German colonists.

We must not, however, think of German influence among the Slavs as being limited to these extensions of the German tongue, though they are a very powerful factor — since German Kultur has gone wherever the German language has given it entry. The Slav kingdom of Bohemia was completely incorporated into the German Imperial System; the King of Bohemia was one of the Electors of the Emperor under the constitution which came to an end only in 1806, after the battle of Austerlitz. The Poles, the Czechs, the South Slavs of Croatia, and the Magyars are Roman Catholic — that is to say, of the Latin or Western branch of the Church, and this has certainly meant an extension of German influence as against the Greek Church of

---

[1] The statements here made are left in the form that held before the War, for the memory of them is more potent than the as yet vague regrouping of the future.

本民族的语言，而那3条凸出的日耳曼语地带则代表了3次征服的趋势。

甚至在"德国文化精华"这3次主要入侵所占的最远之处以外，也还有着许多零星分布的日耳曼殖民地，其间居住的主要是农民和矿工，当中有一些还是最近才拓殖的。在匈牙利，这样的殖民地有很多，但出于政治目的，此处的日耳曼人如今已经认同马扎尔人的暴政了。特兰西瓦尼亚[1]的撒克逊人则与那一地区的马扎尔人一起，在被压迫的罗马尼亚农民当中同处于一种特权地位。〔作者注：这里仍然是按照战前的情况来说明的，因为记住这些情况，比迄今仍然模糊的、将来进行的重新分组更有效果。〕俄国境内也有许多的日耳曼人殖民地，它们穿过乌克兰北部向东延伸，差不多到达了基辅。只有到了伏尔加河中游的萨拉托夫市附近，我们才到达了这些日耳曼殖民者聚居区的尽头。

然而，我们绝不能认为日耳曼人在斯拉夫人中的影响力，只限于说日耳曼语的这些地区之内，虽然这些地区是一个极为有力的影响因素——因为凡是说日耳曼语的地区，也都渗入了日耳曼文化。斯拉夫人的波希米亚王国，已经完全兼并进了德意志帝国体系；宪法规定，波希米亚国王是德意志帝国的选帝侯之一，而这部宪法直到1806年奥斯特里茨战役[2]之后才被废除。波兰人、捷克人、克罗地亚的南斯拉夫人以及马扎尔人都

---

[1] Transylvania：特兰西瓦尼亚。历史上罗马尼亚西部的一个地区，以特兰西瓦尼亚阿尔卑斯山脉和喀尔巴阡山脉为界。曾是古罗马达西亚省的一部分，后来被日耳曼民族所占领，还曾被各种政权所控制。二次世界大战以后，该地区最终成为了今罗马尼亚的一部分。

[2] the battle of Austerlitz：奥斯特里茨战役。奥斯特里茨是捷克的一个城镇，1805年拿破仑在此击败了俄、奥联军。

the Russians. After the siege of Vienna in 1683, the Austrian Germans advanced step by step in the eighteenth century, driving the Turks before them from Hungary, until by the Treaty of Belgrade in 1739 they fixed the line which, for more than a hundred years, afterwards delimited Turkish power towards Christendom. Undoubtedly the Austrians thus rendered a great service to Europe, but the incidental effect, so far as the Croatians, Magyars, Slovaks, and Rumanians of Transylvania were concerned, was merely to substitute the mastery of the German for that of the Turk. When Peter the Great of Russia moved his capital at the beginning of the eighteenth century from Moscow to Petrograd, he went from a Slavonic to a German environment, a fact recorded in the German name St. Petersburg. As a consequence, throughout the eighteenth and nineteenth centuries, German influence was great in Russian Government. The Russian bureaucracy, on which the Czardom depended, was, in large measure, recruited from among the cadets of the German baronial families of the Baltic provinces.

Thus East Europe has not consisted, like West Europe, of a group of peoples independent of one another,

彼得大帝

是罗马天主教教徒——也就是说，他们都属于罗马天主教的拉丁分支或者西方分支；这自然意味着日耳曼人扩张了自己的影响力，以对抗俄罗斯人所信奉的希腊正教。经过了1683年的维也纳之围后，奥地利的日耳曼人便在18世纪开始逐步进击，将先于他们居下来的土耳其人赶出了匈牙利，直到1739年，他们才根据《贝尔格莱德条约》[1]的规定确定了一条界线；此后的100多年中，这条线都是土耳其势力和基督教国家之间的分界线。奥地利人此举无疑是为欧洲做了一件大好事，但就克罗地亚人、马扎尔人、斯洛伐克人和特兰西瓦尼亚的罗马尼亚人而言，此举的影响，不过是把土耳其统治者换成了日耳曼统治者罢了。当俄国的彼得大帝在18世纪初把首都从莫斯科迁往彼得格勒时，他其实是从一个斯拉夫语社会迁到了一个日耳曼语社会；这个事实，显然被"圣彼得堡"这个日耳曼名称记录下来了。结果便是，日耳曼势力在18世纪和19世纪对俄国政府的影响力始终都很强大。沙皇俄国所依赖的俄罗斯官僚，大部分都来自波罗的海地区的省份，都是从日耳曼贵族家庭的子弟中招募来的。

---

[1] Treaty of Belgrade：《贝尔格莱德条约》。1739年9月，奥地利哈布斯堡君主国与奥斯曼帝国签署的条约。

and — until Alsace was taken by Prussia — without serious frontier questions between them; East Europe has been a great triple organization of German domination over a mainly Slavonic population, though the extent of the German power, no doubt, varied in different parts. In this fact we have the key to the meaning of the volte–face of 1895, when was concluded the incongruous Franco–Russian alliance between Democracy and Despotism. When Russia allied herself with France against the Germans, much more was implied than merely a reshuffling of the cards on the play–table of Europe. Something fundamental had happened in East Europe from the point of view of Berlin. Prior to that great and significant event there had been long bickerings between the Russian and Austrian Governments as the result of their rivalry in the Balkans, but these were in the nature of family quarrels, no less than was the short war between Prussia and Austria in 1866. When Russia advanced to the Danube against Turkey in 1853 and Austria massed forces to threaten her from the Carpathians, the friendship of the Holy Alliance, which had subsisted since 1815, was, no doubt, suspended until Bismarck brought the three despotisms together again in his Three–Kaiser Alliance of 1872. But it so happened that, during the interval, Russia was not in a position to advance afresh against the Turks, owing to the losses which she had experienced in the Crimean War, and therefore no irremediable breach ensued between her and Austria. But the Three–Kaiser Alliance could not last long after Austria had given notice of her Balkan ambitions by occupying the Slav Provinces of Bosnia and Herzegovina in 1878. Some uncomfortable years followed, during which German strength was mounting up, before Russia was convinced that the alternative before her was either an alliance with the French Republicans or the acceptance of a position of subordination to Germany, like that to which Austria had been reduced.

※　　　※　　　※　　　※　　　※　　　※　　　※　　　※

　　因此，东欧与西欧不同，并非由许多各自独立的民族组成，并且在阿尔萨斯被普鲁士占领之前，各民族之间也没有什么严重的边界问题；而东欧则一直是一个巨大的三重组织：其主要人口斯拉夫人由日耳曼人统治着，但日耳曼人的掌控程度无疑又是因地而异的。从这一事实当中，我们获得了理解1895年"大转变"的意义的钥匙；民主和专制之间，竟然在那一年缔结了一个不相调和的法俄同盟。俄国与法国结盟来对抗日耳曼人这一史实所隐含的，并非仅仅是欧洲这个牌桌上重新洗牌，而是含有丰富得多的意义。在柏林看来，东欧已经发生了某些根本性的变化。在这个重大事件发生之前，俄、奥两国政府由于争夺巴尔干半岛而一直龃龉不断；不过，这在性质上跟家人间的吵嘴一样，而1866年那场短暂的普奥战争也是如此。当俄国在1853年进至多瑙河去攻打土耳其，而奥地利结集兵力从喀尔巴阡山脉威慑俄国之后，自1815年起就一直存续下来的"神圣同盟"之友谊无疑就此中止了，直到1872年俾斯麦通过"三帝同盟"才重新把这3个专制国家团结起来。不过，巧的是在这段时间内，由于在克里米亚战争[1]中遭受重创，俄国无力再次去进击土耳其人，所以后来俄、奥两国之间的关系并没有无可挽回地破裂。但奥地利在1878年占领了波斯尼亚和黑塞哥维那这两个斯拉夫省份，使得该国在巴尔干半岛的野心昭然若揭之后，"三帝同盟"就不可能再长久维持下去了。接下来的数年形势令人不安，期间德意志的实力日益增强，而俄国也是后来才确信自己的面前只有两种选择，即

---

　　[1] Crimean War: 克里米亚战争。指1853年~1856年俄国为争夺巴尔干半岛的控制权而同英、法、土耳其以及撒丁王国进行的一场战争。1853年7月，俄国入侵土耳其，拉开了战争序幕；1854年3月，英、法对俄宣战，战争全面爆发。1856年，战争以俄国失败而告终，从而引发了俄国国内的革命斗争。

So much in regard to the history of West and East Europe during the Victorian Age. There was, however, a contemporary history of the Not-Europe which we must now bring into our reckoning. The Naval warfare which culminated in the battle of Trafalgar had the effect of dividing the stream of the world's history into two separate currents for nearly a century. Britain enveloped Europe with her sea-power, but save in so far as it was necessary at times for her to intervene around the Eastern Mediterranean because of her stake in the Indies, she took no serious part in the politics of the European Peninsula. British sea-power, however, also enveloped the great world promontory which ends in the Cape of Good Hope, and, operating from the sea-front of the Indies, came into rivalry with the Russian-Cossack Power, then gradually completing its hold on the Heartland. In the far north the Russians descended the great Amur River to the Pacific Coast before the Crimean War. It is usual to attribute the opening of Japan to the action of the American Commodore Perry in 1853, but the presence of the Russians in the island of Sakhalin, and even as far south as Hakodate in Yesso, had done something to prepare the way. In regard to Britain, the most immediate Russian menace was, of course, beyond the Northwest Frontier of India.

In the nineteenth century Britain did what she liked upon the Ocean, for the United States were not yet

美国海军准将佩里（Matthew C. Perry，1794～1858）。1853年6月3日，他率领美国东印度舰队的4艘军舰擅自在日本浦贺港停靠，史称黑船事件。之后，两国签订了《日美亲善条约》（即《日美神奈川条约》），日本被迫开放下田、箱馆（今函馆）两港口。不久，英、俄、荷等国援例而至，也和日本政府签订了类似条约。

要么和法兰西共和国联盟，要么承认臣服于德国，就像已经臣服于德国的奥地利那样。

　　※　　　　※　　　　※　　　　※　　　　※
　※　　　　※　　　　※　　　　※

　　关于西欧和东欧在整个维多利亚时代的历史，我们就说这么多。然而，同期还有一段"非欧洲"的历史，我们如今也必须加以考虑。以特拉法尔加之战而宣告结束的海上战争所带来的影响，就是将世界历史之潮流分成了两支，时间长达大约一个世纪。英国用其海上力量包围了整个欧洲，但除了为保护英国在印度群岛的利益而必须偶尔出面对东地中海地区加以干预，该国并没有郑重其事地参与欧洲半岛的政治。然而，英国的海上力量还包围了止于好望角的那个"世界大海角"，并且还从印度群岛的濒海地区出动，开始与俄罗斯的哥萨克势力争雄，之后便逐渐掌控了"中心地带"。在遥远的北方，俄国人在克里米亚战争之前就已沿着伟大的阿穆尔河南下，进击到了太平洋沿岸。人们通常都将日本门户的打开归因于1853年美国海军准将佩里采取的军事行动，不过俄国军队抵达库页岛、甚至南下远至虾夷[1]的函馆，也为打开

[1] Yesso：虾夷。日本北海道的古称，为Ezo的另一英语拼写。Hakodate（函馆）是北海道西南部的一个港口城市。

powerful, and Europe was fully occupied with its wars. Shipping and markets were the objective of the Nation of Shopkeepers under the ré gime of the Manchester School of political thought. The principal new markets offering were among the vast populations of the Indies, for Africa was unexplored, and for the most part went naked, and the Americas were not yet populous. Therefore, while Britain might have annexed almost every coast outside Europe except the Atlantic coast of the United States, she limited herself to calling ports for her shipping on the ocean road to the Indies, and to such colonial developments in unoccupied regions as were forced on her by her own adventurers, whom she tried in vain to check. But she was compelled to make a steady advance in India, of that kind which old Rome had known so well, when one new province after another was annexed for the purpose of depriving invaders of their bases against the territory already possessed.

The map reveals at once the essential strategic aspects of the rivalry between Russia and

日本门户铺平了道路。至于英国，当时俄国对它最直接的威胁，自然是在印度的西北边疆之外。

在19世纪内，英国在海洋上为所欲为，因为那时美国尚不够强大，而欧洲各国又在一心作战。在崇尚曼彻斯特学派政治思想的那种政权的统治下，这个小店主之国[1]的目标是航运和市场。当时可供英国利用的最主要的新兴市场，就是印度群岛的广大人口，因为非洲尚未开发，因为绝大多数地区都是一穷二白，而整个美洲的人口也还不多。因此，虽说英国本来可以把欧洲之外、除美国大西洋沿岸之外几乎每一个沿海地区都吞并掉，但该国却只是占领了通往印度群岛那条海路上的一些停泊港以供航运，而在那些无人占领的地区，该国也只是进行了一些本国冒险者强行要求的殖民开发工作；英国虽想约束这些冒险家，却是徒劳无用。不过，在一个接一个地吞并掉新的省份之后，英国在

---

[1] the Nation of Shopkeepers：小店主之国。语出经济学家亚当·斯密（Adam Smith）写于1776年的《国家财富》（Wealth of Nations）一书，指英国或者英国人善于做生意。

19世纪的英国东印度公司

Britain during the nineteenth century. Russia, in command of nearly the whole of the Heartland, was knocking at the landward gates of the Indies. Britain, on the other hand, was knocking at the sea gates of China, and advancing inland from the sea gates of India to meet the menace from the northwest. Russian rule in the Heartland was based on her man-power in East Europe, and was carried to the gates of the Indies by the mobility of the Cossack cavalry. British power along the sea frontage of the Indies was based on the man-power of the distant islands in West Europe, and was made available in the East by the mobility of British ships. Obviously there were two critical points in the alternative voyages round from West to East; those points

we know today as the "Cape" and the "Canal." The Cape lay far removed from all overland threat throughout the nineteenth century; practically South Africa was an island. The Canal was not opened until 1869, but its construction was an event which cast its shadow before. It was the Frenchman, Napoleon, who gave to Egypt, and therefore also to Palestine, its modern importance, just as it was the Frenchman Dupleix, who, in the eighteenth century, showed that it was possible to build an empire in India from the coast inward, on the ruins of the Mogul Empire which had

杜普雷（Joseph Fran ois Dupleix, 1697～1763），
法国在印度的殖民地总督（1742年～1754年在任）。

印度也不得不用古罗马人所熟悉的那种方式持续推进了；而吞并这些新的省份，则是为了拔掉入侵者赖以进击英国业已获得之领土的那些基地。

在地图上，我们马上就能看出俄、英两国在19世纪相互争雄时的主要战略特点。俄国几乎掌控了整个"中心地带"，正在进击印度群岛朝着内陆的各个大门。而另一方面，英国则在进击中国的海上门户，并且从印度的海上门户向内陆进击，去应对来自西北的威胁。俄国对"中心地带"的统治，是以该国在东欧的人力为基础，并且通过哥萨克骑兵的机动，把该国的统治扩张到了印度群岛的门户。英国在印度群岛沿海地区的实力，是以遥远的西欧诸岛上的人力为基础，并且通过英国舰船的机动，在东方扩张自己的势力。很显然，从西方绕道到达东方的那两条不同的航道上，有两个关键之处；这两个关键点，便是我们今天所知的一"角"一"运河"。好望角所处之地，在整个19世纪都远离来自陆上的所有威胁；实际上，南部非洲相当于一个岛屿。虽说苏伊士运河直到1869年才开通，但人们早就有了建造这条运河的计划。是拿破仑这个法国人，使得埃及、并因而也使得巴勒斯坦在现代具有了重要性，正像是杜普雷这个法国人在18世纪就已表明，可以从印度沿海向内陆推进，在原本从德里向外扩张而建立起来的莫卧儿帝国的废墟之上，建起一个帝国来那样。从本质上来说，拿破仑

been built from Delhi outward. Both ideas, that of Napoleon and that of Dupleix, were essentially ideas of sea-power, and sprang not unnaturally from France in the Peninsula of West Europe. By his expedition to Egypt Napoleon drew the British Fleet to the battle of the Nile in the Mediterranean, and also drew the British Army from India, for the first time, overseas to the Nile Valley. When, therefore, Russian power in the Heartland increased, the eyes both of Britain and France were necessarily directed towards Suez, those of Britain for obvious practical reasons, and those of France partly for the sentimental reason of the great Napoleonic tradition, but also because the freedom of the Mediterranean was essential to her comfort in the Western Peninsula.

But Russian land-power did not reach, in the eyes of people of that time, as far as to threaten Arabia. The natural European exit from the Heartland was by the sea-way through the Straits of Constantinople. We have seen how Rome drew her frontier through the Black Sea, and made Constantinople a local base of her Mediterranean sea-power against the Scythians of the steppes. Russia, under Czar Nicholas, sought to invert this policy, and, by commanding the Black Sea and its southward exit, aimed at extending her land-power to the Dardanelles. The effect was inevitably to unite West Europe against her. So it happened that when Russian intrigue had involved Britain in the First Afghan War in 1839, Britain could not view with equanimity the encampment of a Russian Army on the Bosporus in order to defend the Sultan from the attack, through Syria, of Mehemet Ali, the insurgent Khedive of Egypt. Therefore Britain and France dealt with Mehemet themselves, by attacking him in Syria in 1840.

In 1854 Britain and France were again involved in action against Russia. France had assumed the protectorate of the Christians in the Near East, and her prestige in that respect was being damaged by Russian intrigue in regard to the Holy Places at Jerusalem. So France and

和杜普雷两人的观点都属于海上强国的观点，所以它们源自西欧半岛上的法国就是顺理成章的事情了。通过远征埃及，拿破仑非但引得英国舰队引入地中海，进行了尼罗河河口之战，也引得英国陆军第一次从印度漂洋过海进入了尼罗河流域。因此，当"中心地带"内的俄国势力日益强大起来之后，英、法两国的目光必然就投向了苏伊士运河；英国关注苏伊士运河，是出于明显的实利原因，而法国之所以关注苏伊士运河，虽说部分是出于拿破仑时代那种感情用事的伟大传统，但也是因为在地中海上自由来去是法国在西欧半岛坐享安逸不可或缺的一个条件。

但是在当时的人看来，俄罗斯的陆军力量还没有强大到足以威胁阿拉伯半岛的程度。从"中心地带"通往欧洲的天然出口，就是穿过君士坦丁堡海峡的那条海路。我们已经看到，罗马是怎样让自己的疆界穿过黑海，从而把君士坦丁堡变成该国地中海海上力量抗击来自大草原的斯基泰人的一个本地基地的。沙皇尼古拉一世统治之下的俄罗斯试图反用这一政策，通过控制黑海及其南部出口，来将本国的陆上力量扩张到达达尼尔海峡。这样做的结果，便是西欧各国必然会团结起来对付它。当俄国玩弄计谋，令英国卷入了1839年的第一次阿富汗战争之后，情况正是这样：对于俄国为了保卫苏丹、使苏丹不致遭受埃及叛乱总督穆罕默德·阿里[1]经由叙利亚发动的进攻而陈兵博斯普鲁斯海峡的做法，英国是无法等闲视之的。因此，英、法两国便在1840年亲自动手，通过在叙利亚发动进攻来对付穆罕默德。

---

[1] Mehemet Ali：穆罕默德·阿里（1769~1849）。埃及总督，土耳其苏丹的潘王，曾两次对土耳其发动旨在夺取叙利亚的战争，都因英、法干涉而未果。

沙皇尼古拉一世

索尔兹伯里侯爵（Robert Arthur Talbot Gascoyne-Cecil, 1830～1903）。英国政治家，维多利亚时期曾经三次任英国首相，并且在此期间使不列颠殖民帝国广为扩张。

Britain found themselves involved in support of the Turks when the Russian armies came against them on the Danube. Lord Salisbury, shortly before his death, declared that in supporting Turkey we had backed the wrong horse. Is that so certain in regard to the middle of last century? Time is of the essence of International Policy; there is an opportunism which is the tact of politics. In regard to things which are not fundamental, is it not recognized that in ordinary social intercourse it is possible to say the right thing at the wrong time? In 1854 it was Russian power, and not yet German power, which was the center of organization in East Europe, and Russia was pressing through the Heartland against the Indies, and by the Straits of Constantinople was seeking to issue from the Heartland into the west, and Prussia was supporting Russia.

In 1876 Turkey was again in trouble and was again backed by Britain, though necessarily without the support of France. The result was to head off Russian power from Constantinople,

　　1854年，英、法两国又卷入了联手对抗俄国的军事行动。法国在近东地区承担着保护基督教徒的责任，但俄国对圣地耶路撒冷的阴谋活动却损害了法国在这个方面的声望。于是，当俄国陆军在多瑙河开始进击土耳其人时，法、英两国便都加入战争去支援土耳其人。索尔兹伯里勋爵在逝世前不久曾经宣称，我们支援土耳其是下错了赌注。就上世纪中叶的形势而言，此种结论有这样可靠吗？时间是制定国际政策的一大要素；有一种机会主义，属于政治上的老练。难道我们不承认，对于一些并不重要的事情，我们在日常社交中有可能在错误的时间说出正确的话语吗？在1854年那个时候，东欧的组织核心是俄国势力，还不是日耳曼势力；俄国当时正穿过"中心地带"向印度群岛逼近，

but at the cost of giving to the Germans then—first step towards the Balkan Corridor by handing over to Austrian keeping the Slav Provinces, hitherto Turkish, of Bosnia and Herzegovina. On that occasion the British Fleet, by Turkish sufferance, steamed through the Dardanelles to within sight of the minarets of Constantinople. The great change in the orientation of Russian policy had not yet occurred, and neither Russia nor Britain yet foresaw the economic methods of amassing man—power to which Berlin was about to resort.

When we look back on the course of events during the hundred years after the French Revolution, and consider East Europe as the basis of what was on the whole a single force in the world's affairs, do we not realize that separate as people of the Victorian Age often thought the politics of Europe from those of the Not—Europe outside, there was, in fact, no such separation. East Europe was in command of the Heartland, and was opposed by the sea—power of Britain round more than three—quarters of the margin of the Heartland, from China through India to Constantinople. France and Britain were commonly allied in action in regard to Constantinople. When, in 1840, there was danger of war in Europe because of the quarrel between the Khedive and the Sultan, instinctively all eyes were turned to the Rhine, where Prussia had established her outpost provinces. Then it was that the German song, the "Wacht am Rhein", was written! But the war threatened against France was not in respect of Alsace and Lorraine, but in support of Russia; in other words, the quarrel was between East and West Europe.

In 1870 Britain did not support France against Prussia. With the after wisdom of events should we not, perhaps, be justified in asking whether we did not in this instance fail to back the right horse? But the eyes of the islanders were still blinded by the victory of Trafalgar. They knew what it was to enjoy sea—power, the freedom of the ocean, but they forgot that sea—power is, in large measure, dependent on the productivity of the bases on which it rests, and

并且试图经由君士坦丁堡海峡从"中心地带"进入西欧，而普鲁士也在支持着俄罗斯。

1876年，土耳其又碰到了麻烦，并且再次得到了英国的支援，而法国却必定不会再支持土耳其了。结果是，英、土两国虽然挡住了来自君士坦丁堡的俄国兵力，却付出了代价，把一向属于土耳其的斯拉夫族波斯尼亚和黑塞哥维那两省交由奥地利掌控，从而让日耳曼人迈出了向"巴尔干走廊"扩张的第一步。就在那一次，英国舰队在土耳其的默许下穿过达达尼尔海峡，抵达了看得见君士坦丁堡宣礼塔[1]的海域。当时俄国政策走向方面的剧变还没有发生，而俄、英两国也都没有预见到柏林将会利用各种积聚人力资源的有效方法。

当我们回顾法国大革命后那100年间的历史进程，并将东欧整体上看成是世界事务中一股单独力量的基础时，我们难道没有认识到，虽然维多利亚时代的人经常以为欧洲的政治与其他"非欧洲"地区的政治是各自独立的，可事实上却并没有这种独立性？虽说东欧制约着"中心地带"，但与之抗衡的英国海上力量，却从中国经过印度再到君士坦丁堡，包围了"中心地带"3/4以上的边缘地区。在与君士坦丁堡相关的问题上，法、英两国通常都是联合采取行动。1840年，当欧洲因埃及总督和苏丹之间不和而有爆发战争的危险之时，各国便都本能地把目光投向了莱茵河地区，当时普鲁士已经在那儿设立起了前哨省份。《保卫莱茵河》这首日耳曼歌曲，正是那个时候写的！但是，法国所面临的战争威胁，与阿尔萨斯和洛林并不相干，而在于它支持了俄国；换言之，这场

---

[1] minaret：宣礼塔。指清真寺周围高耸的尖塔。

that East Europe and the Heartland would make a mighty sea-base. In the Bismarckian period, moreover, when the center of gravity in East Europe was being shifted from Petrograd to Berlin, it was perhaps not unnatural that contemporaries should fail to realize the subordinate character of the quarrels between the three autocracies, and the fundamental character of the war between Prussia and France.

The recent Great War arose in Europe from the revolt of the Slavs against the Germans. The events which led up to it began with the Austrian occupation of the Slav provinces of Bosnia and Herzegovina in 1878, and the alliance of Russia with France in 1895. The Entente of 1904 between Britain and France was not an event of the same significance; our two countries had cooperated more often than not in the nineteenth century, but France had been the quicker to perceive that Berlin had supplanted Petrograd as the center of danger in East Europe, and our two policies had, in consequence, been shaped from different angles for a few years. West Europe, both insular and peninsular, must necessarily be opposed to whatever Power attempts to organize the resources of East Europe and the Heartland. Viewed in the light of that conception, both British and French policy for a hundred years past takes on a large consistency. We were opposed to the half-German Russian Czardom because Russia was the dominating, threatening force both in East Europe and the Heartland for half a century. We were opposed to the wholly German Kaiserdom, because Germany took the lead in East Europe from the Czardom, and would then have crushed the revolting Slavs, and dominated East Europe and the Heartland. German Kultur, and all that it means in the way of organization, would have made that German domination a chastisement of scorpions as compared with the whips of Russia.

※　　　※　　　※　　　※　　　※　　　※　　　※　　　※　　　※

Thus far we have been thinking of the rivalry of Empires from the point of view of

纷争实际上是东欧与西欧之间的纷争。

1870年，英国并没有支持法国去对抗普鲁士。我们都有着事后诸葛亮般的智慧，那么难道我们就不该问一问，在这件事上我们是不是也没有下对赌注呢？可岛国人的目光，却仍被特拉法尔加战役的胜利蒙蔽了。虽然他们明白拥有海上力量、拥有海上自由的意义，可他们却忘了，海上力量在很大程度上倚赖的是它所依托的那些基地的生产能力，并且东欧和"中心地带"可以成为一个强大的海上基地。何况，在俾斯麦时代，东欧的重心正从彼得格勒转移到柏林，所以当时的人并没有认识到这三个专制国家之间纷争的次要性质以及普、法战争的重大意义，就在情理之中了。

最近的这次大战，是由于斯拉夫人反抗日耳曼人而在欧洲爆发的。引发战争的那些事件，始于1878年奥地利占领波斯尼亚和黑塞哥维这两个斯拉夫省份以及1895年形成的俄法联盟。1904年缔结的英法协约，并不是一桩具有相同重要性的事件；虽然两国在19世纪经常合作，但法国却比英国先认识到，柏林已经取代彼得格勒，成为了东欧的危险中心，因此数年来我们两国的政策都是从不同角度来制定的。既是岛屿、又是半岛的西欧，必定会反抗任何企图把东欧和"中心地带"的资源组织起来的势力。按照那种观点来看，过去100年间英、法两国的政策都在很大程度上都是一致的。我们反对半日耳曼性质的沙皇俄国，因为俄国在半个世纪内都是主宰东欧和"中心地带"的威胁力量。我们反对全日耳曼性质的德意志帝国，因为德国从沙俄手中夺取了东欧的主导权，并且接下来会镇压起来革命的斯拉夫人，从而主宰东欧和"中心地带"。德国文化及其在组织方式上所意味着的一切，都会使德国人的统治与俄罗斯的统治比起来更加有如蛇蝎般残酷。

strategical opportunities, and we have come to the conclusion that the World-Island and the Heartland are the final Geographical Realities in regard to sea-power and land-power, and that East Europe is essentially a part of the Heartland. But there remains to be considered the Economic Reality of man-power. We have seen that the question of base, not only secure but also productive, is vital to sea-power; the productive base is needed for the support of men not only for the manning of ships, but for all the land services in connection with shipping, a fact today more clearly realized in Britain than ever before. In regard to land-power we have seen that the camel-men and horsemen of past history failed to maintain lasting empires from lack of adequate man-power, and that Russia was the first tenant of the Heartland with a really menacing man-power.

But man-power does not imply a counting only of heads, though, other things being equal, numbers are decisive. Nor does it depend merely on the number of efficient human beings, though health and skill are of the first importance. Manpower — the power of men — is also, and in these modern days very greatly, dependent on organization, or, in other words, on the "Going Concern", the social organism. German Kultur, the "ways and means" philosophy, has been dangerous to the outer world because it recognizes both Realities, Geographical and Economic, and thinks only in terms of them.

The "Political" Economy of Britain and the "National" Economy of Germany have come from the same fountain, the book of Adam Smith. Both accept as their bases the division of labor and competition to fix the prices at which the products of labor shall be exchanged. Both, therefore, can claim to be in harmony with the dominant tendency of thought in the nineteenth century as expressed by Darwin. They differ only in the unit of competition. In Political Economy that unit is the individual or firm; in National Economy it tends to become the State

※　　　※　　　※　　　※　　　※　　　※　　　※　　　※　　　※

到目前为止，我们都是从战略机会的角度来研究帝国间的竞争的，并且我们已经得出了这样一个结论：对于海上力量和陆上力量而言，"世界岛"和"中心地带"都是两个无可更改的地理现实，而从本质上来说，东欧又是"中心地带"的一部分。不过，我们还需研究一下人力这个经济现实。我们已经看到，拥有一个安全而物产丰富的基地这个问题，对于海上力量来说至关重要；它需要一个物产丰富的基地来提供人力，不单是给舰船配备人员，还要提供与航运相关的所有陆上服务——这个事实，英国如今已经认识得比过去任何时候都要清楚了。至于陆上力量，我们已经看到历史上骑骆驼的民族和骑马的民族由于没有充足的人力，所以都没能将他们的帝国长久维持下去，故俄国才是第一个占据了"中心地带"且拥有真正可怕之人力的国家。

但是人力并不仅仅意味着点一点人头就行了，尽管在其他条件平等的情况下，数量起着决定性的作用。人力也并非仅仅依赖于高效能干的人员数量，但人力的健康状况和技能水平也是极其重要的。在现代社会，人力——即人的力量——在很大程度上也是依赖于组织，或者换句话说，依赖于"进行中的事业"，亦即整个社会机体的。德国文化这种讲求"手段和方法"的哲学对外部世界来说一直都很危险，因为它不但认识到了地理上的和经济上的两种现实，而且只根据这两种现实来考虑问题。

英国的"政治"经济学和德国的"国家"经济学，二者都起源于亚当·斯密的观点。它们都接纳了"劳动分工"和"竞争确定用于交换的劳动产品的价格"的观念，并将这两种观念当成它们的基础。因此，这两种经济学可以说都是与19世纪达尔文所表述的

亚当·斯密

李斯特（Friedrich List, 1789~1846）。德国政治经济学家。他是古典经济学的怀疑者和批判者，是德国历史学派的先驱。他的国家经济学与亚当·斯密的自由主义经济学相左，认为国家应该在经济生活中起到重要作用。这一思想对后世德国的统一产生了重要影响。

布莱特（John M. Bright, 1811~1889）。英国自由党政治家、经济学家和演说家，他与科布登一起领导了1838年到1846年的反谷物法联盟。

among States. This was the fact appreciated by List, the founder of German National Economy, under whose impulse the Prussian Zollverein or Customs Union was broadened until it included most of Germany. The British Political Economists welcomed the Zollverein, regarding it as an installment of their own Free Trade. In truth, by removing competition in greater or less degree to the outside, National Economy aimed at substituting for the competition of mere men that of great national organizations. In a word, the National Economists thought dynamically, but the Political Economists in the main statically.

　　This contrast of thing between Kultur and Democracy was not at first of great practical

主流思潮相一致的。它们之间的差别，仅在于各自选取的竞争单位不同。在政治经济学中，竞争单位是个人或者公司；而在国家经济学中，竞争单位则倾向于联邦中的邦国。德意志国家经济学的奠基人李斯特充分理解了这一事实，所以在他的推动下，普鲁士的"德意志商业同盟"即"关税同盟"[1]不断扩大，直到后来德意志的大部分邦国全都加入进来了。英国的政治经济学家们对"关税同盟"持欢迎态度，认为"关税同盟"是他们自己所崇尚的"自由贸易"的一部分。实际上，国家经济学会或多或少地把竞争排除在外，它的目的是想以大规模的国家机构间的竞争，来取代纯属个人之间的竞争。简而言之，

---

　　[1] Zollverein：（德意志）商业同盟。Zollverein是Customs Union的德语，故又译"关税同盟"。德意志关税同盟于1834年由38个德意志邦联的邦国组成。在当时工业革命的浪潮下，同盟的成立有助于贸易往来和减少内部竞争。同盟成立的主要功臣就是李斯特。

significance. In the fifties and sixties of last century the Germans were at their wars. The British Manufacturer was top dog, and, as Bismarck once said, Free Trade is the policy of the strong. It was not until 1878, the date of the first scientific tariff, that the economic sword of Germany was unsheathed. That date marks approximately a very great change in the arts of transport to which due weight is not always attached. It was then that British-built railways in America and British steel-built ships on the Atlantic began to carry bulk-cargoes.

What this new fact of the carriage of bulk — wheat, coal, iron ore, petroleum — means will be realized if we reflect that in Western Canada today a community of a million people raise the cereal food of twenty millions, and that the other nineteen millions are at a distance — in Eastern Canada, the Eastern United States, and Europe. Prior to 1878 relatively light cargoes of such commodities as cotton, timber, and coal had been transported over the ocean by sailing ship, but the whole bulk of the cargoes of the world was insignificant as measured by the standards of today. Germany grasped the idea that under the new conditions it was possible to grow man-power where you would, on imported food and raw material, and therefore in Germany itself, for strategical use.

Up to this time the Germans, like the British, had freely emigrated, but the German no less than the British populations in the new countries made an increased demand for British manufactures. So the British people grew in number at home as well as in the Colonies and the United States. Cobden and Bright had foreseen this; they meant to have cheap food and cheap raw materials wherewith to make cheap exports. But the rest of the world looked upon our Free Trade as a method of Empire rather than of Freedom; the reverse of the medal was presented to them; they were to be hewers and drawers for Great Britain. The British Islanders unfortunately made the mistake of attributing their prosperity mainly to their free imports, whereas it was

国家经济学家是动态地考虑问题，而政治经济学家基本上都是静态地考虑问题。

德国文化与民主思想之间的此种差别，起初并没有太大的实际意义。上个世纪五六十年代，德国人正在打仗。当时"不列颠制造商"是老板，并且正如俾斯麦曾经说过的那样，"自由贸易"是强者的政策。直到1878年第一种科学性的关税诞生之后，德意志的经济利刃才算是出了鞘。那一年差不多也是运输技术发生巨变的一年，可人们通常都并不重视运输技术。正是那个时候，英国在美洲建造的铁路和在大西洋上航行的英国铁船才开始运载大宗散货。

假如我们想象一下，在加拿大的西部，如今有一个拥有100万人口的社区种植了足够2000万人吃的谷物，而其余那1900万人都处在相距遥远的地方——加拿大的东部、美国的东部和欧洲，那么我们就会认识到散货运输——即运载小麦、煤、铁矿砂、石油——这一新事实的意义了。1878年以前，较轻的货物，比如棉花、木材和煤等商品，一直都是由帆船在海上运输的，但以如今的标准来衡量，当时整个世界的帆船载货量只能算是微不足道的。德国明白，在新的形势下，可以在自己愿意的地方凭借进口的食物和原材料来发展人力，因此在德国本土发展人力以备战略之用也是可能做到的。

直到此时，德国人还跟英国人一样自由地移民国外，不过移居国外的德国人和英国人都使得对英制商品的需求日益增加了。因此，不列颠民族的人口在本国、各个殖民地和美国都增长起来了。科布登和布莱特都已经预见到了这一点；他们想要用廉价的食品和廉价的原材料制成廉价的出口商品。不过，世界上其他各国都将我们的"自由贸易"当成是一种走向帝国而非走向自由的途径；他们只是看到了这个问题的反面；他们

19世纪后期德国商业

chiefly due to their great "Going Concern", and the fact that it had been set going before it had competitors. It was because they were "the strong" in 1846, that they could adopt Free Trade with immediate advantage and without serious immediate disadvantage.

From 1878 Germany began to build up her man-power by stimulating employment at home. One of her methods was the scientific tariff, a sieve through which imports were "screened", so that they should contain a minimum of labor and especially of skilled labor. But every other means was resorted to for the purpose of raising a Going Concern which should yield a great production at home. The Railways were bought by the State, and preferential rates granted. The Banks were brought under the control of the State by a system of interlocked shareholding, and credit was organized for industry. Cartels and Combines reduced the cost of production and distribution. The result was that about the year 1900 German emigration, which

以为，那样一来，自己就会变成大不列颠的苦力。可惜的是，不列颠的岛民犯了一个错误，把英国的繁荣主要归因于他们的自由进口行为；而实际上，英国的繁荣却主要源于他们那种伟大的"进行中的事业"，在于英国不待竞争对手出现就已着手进行这一事业的事实。正是由于当时他们是"强者"，所以1846年英国才能采取能够带来直接利益却没有直接损失的自由贸易政策。

从1878年起，德国开始通过刺激国内就业来逐步积蓄人力。该国所用的方法之一就是科学性关税，而科学性关税就像是一面筛子，用于"过滤"进口货物，从而确保它们都是含最低劳动力的货物，尤其是确保它们都是含有最低熟练劳动力的货物。但是，为了发展"进行中的事业"，从而大幅提高国内生产，德国还采用了各种各样的方法。

had been steadily falling, ceased altogether, except in so far as balanced by immigration.

The economic offensive was increased by methods of penetration abroad. Shipping lines were subsidized, and banks were used as trade outposts in foreign cities. International Combines were organized under German control, very largely with the help of the Jews of Frankfurt. Finally, in 1905, Germany imposed such a system of commercial treaties on seven adjoining nations as meant their economic subjection. One of these nations was Russia, then weak from war and revolution. Those treaties are said to have taken ten years to think out — a characteristic efflorescence of Kultur!

The rapid German growth was a triumph of organization, or, in other words, of the strategical, the "ways and means" mentality. The fundamental scientific ideas were, most of them, imported, and the vaunted German Technical Education was merely a form of organization. The whole system was based on a clear understanding of the Reality of the Going Concern — Organized Man-power.

But the Going Concern is a relentless fact, for the first political attribute of the animal Man is hunger. In the ten years before the War Germany was growing at the rate of a million souls a year — the difference between deaths and births. That meant that the productive Going Concern must not only be maintained, but that its "going" must be constantly accelerated. In the course of forty years the hunger of Germany for markets had become one of the most terrible realities of the world. The fact that the commercial treaty with Russia would come up for renewal in 1916 was probably not unconnected with the forcing of the War; Germany required, at all costs, a subject Slavdom to grow food for her and to buy her wares.

铁路为国家所收购，并且规定了优惠价格。银行通过关联持股制度被纳入了国家的掌控之中，而且还为产业组建了信贷体系。同业联盟和企业联合都降低了生产成本和流通成本。结果是，到了1900年左右，除了与移入人口相抵的那一部分，德国本在稳步下降的对外移民就完全停止了。

通过向海外渗透的方式，德国的经济攻势也加强了。航运公司获得了补贴，而银行则被当成了在外国城市中进行贸易的前哨。在德国的掌控之下组建起了国际联合企业，并且它们主要都是在法兰克福犹太人的协助之下建立起来的。最后，到了1905年，德国又把一整套商务条约强加给了7个邻国，旨在让这7个国家在经济上臣服于德国。俄国便是其中之一，因为当时战争和革命已经导致俄国的国力很衰弱了。据说那些条约是费了10年心血才想出来的——这正是德国文化一个典型的全盛时期！

德国的迅速崛起，是组织的一大成功，或者换句话说，是战略性的、"手段和方法"式思想的成功。德国绝大多数最基本的科学观念，都是从国外引入的，而德国人为之自负的那种日耳曼实业教育，不过是组织的一种形式罢了。德国的整个体制，都是在清楚地理解"进行中的事业"这一现实——即有组织的人力——的基础上建立起来的。

但"进行中的事业"是一种残酷的现实，因为拥有动物性的人类的第一种政治特征就是饥饿。此次大战之前的10年间，德国的人口年均增长了100万——即死亡人口与新生人口之间的差数。这就意味着，德国非但必须维持有生产价值的"进行中的事业"，还必须不断地加速其"进行"才可以。在40年的时间里，德国对市场的渴望已经变成世界上最可怕的现实之一了。德、俄之间的贸易条约在1916年需要重新续签这一事实，很可能与促成这次大战不无关系；德国需要不惜一切代价地去征服斯拉夫民族，使之为德国种植粮食作物并购买德国的商品。

The men who, at Berlin, pulled the lever in 1914, and set free the dammed—up flood of German man—power, have a responsibility which has been analyzed and fixed, so far as our information yet goes, with keen research by the unfortunate generation which has had to fight the fearful duel. But before History their guilt will be shared by those who, in years past, set the Concern Going. In this matter British Statesmen and the British People will not be held wholly blameless.

It is the theory of Free Trade that the different parts of the world should develop on the basis of their natural facilities, and that different communities should specialize and render service to one another by exchanging their products freely. It was firmly believed that Free Trade thus made for peace and the brotherhood of men. That may have been a tenable theme in the time of Adam Smith and for a generation or two afterwards. But under modern conditions the Going Concern, or, in other words, accumulating Financial and Industrial strength, is capable of outweighing most natural facilities. The Going Concern of the Lancashire Cotton Industry is an instance of this on a great scale. A very small difference of price in cheap lines of export will hold or lose a market, and the great Going Concern can best afford to cut prices. Hence Lancashire has maintained her cotton industry for a century against all competitors, though the sources of the raw material and the principal markets for the finished goods are in distant parts of the world. Coal and a moist climate are her only natural facilities, and they can be paralleled elsewhere. The Lancashire cotton industry continues by virtue of momentum.

The result, however, of all specialization is to make growth lopsided. When the stress began after 1878, British agriculture waned, though British industry continued to grow. But presently lopsidedness developed even within British industry; the cotton and shipbuilding branches still

1914年，在柏林拉下闸门并让受到掌控的德国人力宛如洪水般奔涌而出的那些人，是负有责任的；根据我们目前所了解的情况来看，那一代被迫进行这场险恶的决斗的不幸者已经进行了深入的研究，分析并确定了这些人应负的责任。但在历史面前，他们的罪责将由过去那些年间使得这一"事业"得以"进行"的人来一起分担。在这个问题上，英国的政治家和英国人民并不是全无责任的。

"自由贸易"理论认为，世界各地应当以各地的自然条件为基础来发展，而不同社会的人应当术有专攻，并且通过自由交换产品来为彼此服务。一些人坚定不移地认为，"自由贸易"因此而有益于和平、有益于人类的团结友爱。在亚当·斯密那个时代及其之后的一两个世代，这可能是一种站得住脚的主题。但在现代条件下，"进行中的事业"，或者换句话说，不断积累经济实力和产业实力，却能够胜过大多数天然的便利条件。兰开夏[1]的棉花产业协会这种"进行中的事业"，在很大程度上正是这一点的一个例证。廉价出口商品价格上的微小差异，会让你保住或者失去一个市场，而一种大规模的"进行中的事业"，却最能承受减价所带来的压力。因此，尽管原材料产地和成品的主要市场都位于世界上与之相距遥远的地区，但兰开夏还是在长达一个世纪的时间里，击败了所有的竞争对手，维持住了该地的棉花产业。兰开夏在自然上的便利条件，只有煤炭和湿润的气候；而在其他地方，可能也有与此类似的条件。兰开夏的棉花产业得以持续下去，凭借的是动力。

然而一切的专业化，结果就是使得发展出现不均衡。1878年局势开始紧张起来之

---

[1] Lancashire：兰开夏。英国英格兰西北部的一个郡，曾是英国最大的纺织工业区，也是英国工业革命的发源地。

英国工业革命

grew, but the chemical and electrical branches did not increase proportionately. It was not only that German penetration designedly robbed us of our Key industries, for the ordinary operation of specialization in a world which was becoming industrially active outside Britain was bound to produce some such contrasts. Britain developed vastly those industries into which she gradually concentrated her efforts. Therefore she, no less than Germany, became "market–hungry", for nothing smaller than the whole world was market enough for her in her own special lines.

Britain had no tariff available as a basis for bargaining; in that respect she stood naked before the world. Therefore, when threatened in some vital market, she could but return threats of sea–power. Cobden probably foresaw this in his later days when he declared the need for a strong British Navy, but the rank and file of the Manchester School were so persuaded that Free Trade made for peace that they gave , little thought to the special industrial requirements of sea–power; in their view any trade was equally good provided it were profitable. Yet Britain was fighting for

后，尽管英国的工业在继续增长，但英国的农业却衰落下去了。可是不久之后，即便是英国工业内部也出现了不均衡；棉纺织业和造船工业仍在增长，但化工和电气工业却没有同比增长起来。这并非仅仅是因为德国的蓄意渗入夺走了我们的支柱产业，还是因为在英国之外，在任何一个积极发展工业的国家，正常的专业化都必定会导致出现这样一些反差。英国大规模地发展了一些产业，并且逐渐把精力全都集中于这些产业之上了。于是，英国便跟德国一样产生了"市场饥饿"感，因为从英国的专业化范围来看，只有整个世界才能满足它的市场需求。

此时英国并没有关税，所以无法将关税当成谈判的基础；从这个方面来看，英国就是手无寸铁地站在世界各国的面前。因此，当某些极其重要的市场受到威胁时，该国就只能凭海上力量来进行威慑了。科布登在暮年时期很可能已经预见到了这一点，当时他宣称英国必须拥有一支强大的海军，但是曼彻斯特学派的大多数成员都对这种学说深信

her South American markets when her fleet maintained the Monroe doctrine against Germany in the Manila incident, and for her Indian market when her fleet kept Germany at bay during the South African War, and for the open door to her China market when her fleet supported Japan in the Russian War. Did Lancashire realize that it was by force that the free import of cottons was imposed on India? Undoubtedly India has profited vastly on a balance by the British Raj, and no great weight of guilt need rest on the Lancashire conscience in this matter; but the fact remains that repeatedly, both within and without the Empire, free-trading, peace-loving Lancashire has been supported by the force of the Empire. Germany took note of the fact and built her fleet, and that fleet in being, and still in being to the end of the War, neutralized a mighty British effort which would have been available otherwise in support of our army in France.

The momentum of the Going Concern is very difficult to change in a democracy. The one hope of the future is that, as a result of the lesson of this War, even democracy may learn to take longer views. In an economically lopsided community the majority is on the overdeveloped side, and it is the majority which chooses the rulers in a democracy. The vested interests as a consequence tend to vest ever deeper, both the interest of labor in earning and buying in particular ways, and of capital in making profit in those same ways; on the average there is nothing to choose between labor and capital in these regards; they both take short views.

But there is the same difficulty of changing the Going Concern in an autocracy, although that difficulty is felt in a different way. The majority in a democracy will not change its economic routine, but autocracy often does not dare to do so. Germany under the Kaiserdom aimed at a World Empire, and to achieve it resorted to appropriate economic expedients for

不疑，以为"自由贸易"有利于和平，所以他们几乎都没有考虑过发展海上力量所需的那些特殊产业；在他们看来，只要有利可图，任何贸易都是一样的好。但是，当英国舰队在马尼拉事件中对抗德国来支持门罗主义之时，英国实际上是为其南美市场而战；当英国舰队在南非战争中牵制住德军时，英国实际上是在为其印度市场而战；而当英国舰队在日俄战争中支援日本时，英国实际上也是为了打开通往中国市场的门户而战。兰开夏是否认识到，英国是通过武力把自由进口棉花的条款强加给了印度的呢？毋庸置疑，在英国的统治之下，印度总的说来是获得了巨大的好处，所以兰开夏在这个问题上没必要太过负疚于心；不过事实仍然是，在大英帝国内外，进行自由贸易和爱好和平的兰开夏，一再受到了帝国武力的支持。德国注意到了这一事实，所以才建立了自己的舰队；那支舰队一直保存下来了，并且一直存续到了本次战争结束，压制了英国很大一部分力量，而英国的这部分力量本来是可以用在别的地方，支援法国境内的英国陆军的。

在一个民主国家中，"进行中的事业"的动力是很难改变的。我们对于未来的希望，就是汲取此次大战的教训，使得即便是民主国家，也可以变得目光远大起来。在一个经济发展不平衡的社会里，大多数人都会站在过度发展的那一边；而在民主国家里选举出统治者的，也正是这大多数人。因此，那些特权阶层往往便会获取更多的利益，既在通过特定途径赚取和购买的过程中获得劳动力上的利益，又在通过同样的途径获利的过程中得到资本上的利益；一般说来，劳动力和资本在这些方面并没什么区别：因为它们所关注的，都是眼前利益。

但在专制国家里，改变"进行中的事业"也存在着同样的困难，只是人们对这种困难的看法并不相同。民主国家中的大多数人，都是不肯改变本国经济上的常规做法，而

building up her man-power; presently she dared not change her only too successful policy even when it was forcing her to war, for the alternative was revolution. Like Frankenstein she had constructed an unmanageable monster.

In my belief, both Free Trade of the laissez-faire type and Protection of the predatory type are policies of Empire, and both make for War. The British and the Germans took seats in express trains on the same line, but in opposite directions. Probably from about 1908 a collision was inevitable; there comes a moment when the brakes have no longer time to act. The difference in British and German responsibility may perhaps be stated thus: the British driver started first, and ran carelessly, neglecting the signals, whereas the German driver deliberately strengthened and armored his train to stand the shock, put it on the wrong line, and at the last moment opened his throttle valves.

The Going Concern is, in these days, the great Economic Reality; it was used criminally by the Germans, and blindly by the British. The Bolsheviks must have forgotten that it existed.

在专制国家里，大多数人往往却是不敢去改变。皇权统治之下的德国想要建立起一个世界帝国，而为了实现这一目标，德国采用了一些正确的经济对策来增强该国的人力；不久之后，就算是这种政策令该国不得不发动战争，德国也不敢去改变此种极其成功的政策了，因为改变此种政策的后果就是革命。与弗兰肯斯坦[1]一样，德国也造就了一只无法掌控的怪兽。

我相信，放任式的"自由贸易"和掠夺式的"保护贸易"都是帝国的政策，都会促成战争的爆发。英国人和德国人乘坐的是同一条铁路线上的两列快车，可方向却正好相反。十有八九，从1908年左右起，这两列快车撞车就已经是不可避免的了；而到了后来，甚至连刹车都来不及了。英、德两国所应承担的不同责任，也许可以这样来进行说明：英国这位司机率先出发，却开得漫不经心，毫不理会信号；而德国那位司机却故意加固了自己的火车，并给火车配上装甲以便经得起撞击，然后把火车开上错误的路线，并且还在最后一刻打开了节流阀。

"进行中的事业"在如今这个时代已是一种伟大的经济现实；德国人罪恶地利用了它，而英国人则是盲目地利用了它。布尔什维克党人一定是早已不记得"进行中的事业"是一种实际存在的现实了。

---

[1] Frankenstein：弗兰肯斯坦。英国女作家Mary Wollstonecraft Shelley于1818年所著小说《弗兰肯斯坦》中的主人公。他是一个年轻的医学研究者，创造了一个毁灭了他自己的怪物。这部小说曾经改编成电影《科学怪人》。

VI THE FREEDOM OF NATIONS

The Allies have won the War. But how have we won? The process is full of warning. We were saved, in the first place, by the readiness of the British Fleet, and by the decision which sent it to sea; so British communications with France were secured. That readiness and decision were the outcome of the British habit of looking to the one thing essential in the midst of many things that we leave slipshod; it is the way of the capable amateur. We were saved, in the second place, by the wonderful victory of French genius on the Marne, prepared for by many years of deep thought in the great French École Militaire; in other respects the French Army was not as ready as it might have been, except in courage. We were saved in the third place by the sacrifice — it was no less — of the old British professional army at Ypres, a name that will stand in history beside Thermopylae. We were saved, in short, by exceptional genius and exceptional heroism from the results of an average refusal to foresee and prepare: eloquent testimony both to the strength and the weakness of democracy.

Then for two years the fighting was stabilized, and became a war of trenches on land and of submarines at sea, a war of attrition in which time told in favor of Britain but against Russia. In 1917 Russia cracked and then broke. Germany had conquered in the East, but postponed

第六章　国家自由

协约国赢得了这次世界大战。可是，我们是怎样获胜的呢？我们获胜的过程中，教训比比皆是。首先，挽救我们的是英国舰队准备充分，以及英国政府做出的、派遣这支舰队出海的决定；这样，英、法两国之间的交通就确保安全了。而此种充分的准备和英明的决定，则是英国人有着在许多我们所不经心的事物当中抓住最主要的一件加以关注这种习惯的结果；这是能干的外行者的做法。其次，挽救我们的是法国那些天才人物在马恩河战役中取得的辉煌胜利，此战是伟大的法国军事学院经过多年深思熟虑和精心准备而取得的一次大捷；在其他方面，可以说法国军队并没有做好应有的准备，只是勇气可嘉罢了。第三，挽救我们的是原英国职业陆军在伊珀尔[1]所做出的牺牲；这个地名将会跟塞莫皮莱[2]并驾齐驱并永留青史。总而言之，是我们通常都不愿有先见之明和做好准备而导致涌现出来的非凡天才和非凡的英雄主义挽救了我们：这一点，雄辩有力地证明民主的长处和短处。

接下来，战况稳定了两年，变成了陆上的堑壕战和海上的潜艇战，变成了一场在时间上来说有利于英国却不利于俄国的消耗战。1917年俄国战败，接着就放弃了抵抗。德国已经在东线获得了胜利，却为了先打败西线的敌人而没有马上去彻底征服斯拉夫人。

---

[1] Ypres：伊珀尔。比利时西部靠近法国边境的一个城市，中世纪时是著名的服装业中心，而在第一次世界大战期间则是三次大规模战斗的所在地。亦拼作Ieper。

[2] Thermopylae：塞莫皮莱。古希腊东部的一个山隘，现为岩石平原。公元前480年，斯巴达人在此英勇抵抗波斯人。亦译"温泉关"或"汤泉关"。

the utter subjection of the Slavs in order first to strike down her Western foes. West Europe had to call in the help of America, for West Europe alone would not have been able to reverse the decision in the East. Again time was needed, because America, the third of the greater democracies to go to war, was even less prepared than the other two. And time was bought by the heroism of British seamen, the sacrifice of British merchant shipping, and the endurance of the French and British soldiers against an offensive in France which all but overwhelmed them. In short, we once more pitted character and a right insight into essentials against German organization, and we just managed to win. At the eleventh hour Britain accepted the principle of the single strategical command, giving scope once more to the École Militaire.

But this whole record of Western and Oceanic fighting, so splendid and yet so humiliating, has very little direct bearing on the International Resettlement. There was no immediate quarrel between East Europe and West Europe; the time was past when France would have attacked Germany to recover Alsace and Lorraine. The War, let us never forget, began as a German effort to subdue the Slavs who were in revolt against Berlin. We all know that the murder of the Austrian (German) Archduke in Slav Bosnia was the pretext, and that the Austrian (German) ultimatum to Slav Serbia was the method of forcing the War. But it cannot be too often repeated that these events were the result of a fundamental antagonism between the Germans, who wished to be Masters in East Europe, and the Slavs, who refused to submit to them. Had Germany elected to stand on the defensive on her short frontier towards France, and had she thrown her main strength against Russia, it is not improbable that the world would be nominally at peace today, but overshadowed by a German East Europe in command of all the Heartland. The British

西欧不得不向美国求援，因为单凭西欧是无力扭转东线全面溃败之局势的。而这一点又需要时间才能做到，因为美国是第三个参战的民主大国，它的准备工作比其他两国做得更不充分。英国水兵所表现出来的英雄主义、英国商船运输业所做出的牺牲以及英、法陆军在法国境内不屈不挠地抵挡住了一场差点儿将其击溃的攻势，为他们争取到了时间。总而言之，是我们又一次以骨气和对本质的正确洞察来对抗德国的组织，并且没法获得了胜利。英国直到危急关头才接受战略上统一指挥的这条原则，从而让法国军事学院再次获得了发挥自身长处的机会。

但是，西线战事和海上战争的整个过程虽说如此辉煌却又极其屈辱，但它对重置国际关系却没有产生什么直接的影响。西欧和东欧之间并未发生什么直接的纷争；而法国为了收复阿尔萨斯和洛林两地而去进攻德国的那个时代，也已经一去不复返了。我们绝对不要忘记，此次大战是因为德国人试图征服那些反抗柏林的斯拉夫人而引发的。我们都知道，奥地利（德意志）大公[1]在斯拉夫的波斯尼亚被暗杀是一个借口，而奥地利（德意志）向斯拉夫的塞尔维亚发出最后通牒，则是促成大战爆发的一种方法。不过，这些事件都是因为德国人跟斯拉夫人之间存在着根本性的敌对——德国人想要主宰东欧，可斯拉夫人却不肯臣服——而导致的，这一点怎样反复强调都不过分。倘若当初德国选择在短短对法边境上采取守势，倘若德国把主要兵力都用去对付俄国，那么，如今的世界名义上处在和平状态、实际上却由掌控着整个"中心地带"的德属东欧所统治这

---

[1] Austrian Archduke：奥地利大公。指奥地利王储弗朗茨·斐迪南，他于1914年6月28日在波斯尼亚的萨拉热窝被刺杀，此次事件成了第一次世界大战的导火索。"大公"是当时奥匈帝国王位继承人的称呼。

第一次世界大战中的美军

and American insular peoples would not have realized the strategical danger until too late.

Unless you would lay up trouble for the future, you cannot now accept any outcome of the War which does not finally dispose of the issue between German and Slav in East Europe. You must have a balance as between German and Slav, and true independence of each. You cannot afford to leave such a condition of affairs in East Europe and the Heartland, as would offer scope for ambition in the future, for you have escaped too narrowly from the recent danger.

A victorious Roman general, when he entered the City, amid all head-turning splendor of a "Triumph", had behind him on the chariot a slave who whispered into his ear that he was mortal. When our Statesmen are in conversation with the defeated enemy, some airy cherub should whisper to them from time to time this saying:

Who rules East Europe commands the Heartland;

Who rules the Heartland commands the World-Island;

Who rules the World-Island commands the World.

※ ※ ※ ※ ※

※ ※ ※ ※

Viscount Grey once attributed the whole tragic course of recent events to the breach of

格雷子爵。原名爱德华·格雷（Edward Grey，1862～1933），英国政治家，曾任外交大臣长达11年。

样的情况，就并不是不可能出现的。英、美两个岛国民族可能是不到为时已晚就认识不到这种战略危险的。

倘若没有最终解决东欧的日耳曼人和斯拉夫人之间的争端，你们现在就不能承认这次大战的任何结果，除非你们是准备给将来留下后患。你们必须让日耳曼人和斯拉夫人之间保持平衡，并且让双方保持真正的独立。你们不能把这样一种局面留给东欧和"中心地带"，以免让将来的野心家有机可乘，因为你们是九死一生才逃过了这次危险的。

一位得胜的罗马将军在驾着战车班师进入罗马城的时候，虽然身处万众瞩目、无比辉煌的"凯旋仪式"[1]之中，战车后面却有一个奴隶在他耳边低语，提醒说他只是一个凡人。当我们的政治家与战败之敌进行谈判的时候，也应当有某个想象中的天使，时时在他们耳边低语，如此叮嘱他们：

谁统治东欧，谁便控制了"中心地带"；

谁统治"中心地带"，谁便控制了"世界岛"；

谁统治"世界岛"，谁便控制了全世界。

※ ※ ※ ※ ※ ※ ※ ※ ※

格雷子爵曾经把最近诸多事件所导致的整个悲剧，归因于1908年奥地利撕毁《柏

---

[1] Triumph：凯旋仪式。古罗马时代为欢迎凯旋归来的将领及其军队而举行的公共庆祝活动。

the public law of Europe when Austria tore up the Treaty of Berlin by annexing Bosnia and Herzegovina in 1908. Undoubtedly that was a milestone in history, but the original occupation of these two Slav provinces of Turkey by Austria in 1878, under that very Berlin Treaty, was perhaps nearer to the source. It meant to the Slav mind notice that the Prussian German stood behind the Austrian German in his advance over the country for which the Slav had fought with the Turk, for the War of 1876, it must be remembered, which led up to the Congress of Berlin, began with a rising of the Slavs of Bosnia and Herzegovina against Turkey, and became European because of the sympathy of the neighboring Slavs of Serbia and Montenegro, which impelled them also to fight against the Turk. After 1878 there followed a few years of Russian hesitancy while Germany was beginning to build up her man-power. Then, in 1895, came the Alliance between the Czardom and the French Republic. France needed an Ally because of the still open Alsatian wound in her side; Russia needed an Ally because of the German bully by her side. Russia and France were not immediate neighbors, so that the incompatibility of Democracy and Autocracy was not under the circumstances an impediment sufficient to forbid the marriage. But it was none the less some measure of the need in which Russia stood.

In 1905, when Russia was weak after the Japanese War and her first revolution, Germany imposed upon her a punishing Tariff. In 1907 Russia went so far, in consequence, as to accept an understanding even with Britain, her rival of two generations and the ally of her late enemy, Japan. Again we have evidence of the stress that was on her, especially if we remember the German .influences in her Court and Bureaucracy.

When, therefore, in 1908, Austria took that further action in regard to Bosnia and Herzegovina

林条约》、吞并波斯尼亚和黑塞哥维那两地这种违反欧洲公法的做法。毋庸置疑，那次事件的确是历史上的一处里程碑，可起初奥地利正是根据这份《柏林条约》才在1878年占领了土耳其的这两个斯拉夫省份的，这一点或许更加接近于战争的源头。在斯拉夫人看来，注意到普鲁士的日耳曼人支持奥地利的日耳曼人向这片土地进击，而斯拉夫人在1876年战争中曾经为了这片土地跟土耳其人打过仗的时候，我们必须记住，导致后来召开柏林会议的这场战争，始于波斯尼亚和黑塞哥维那两地的斯拉夫人起而反抗土耳其，又因邻近的塞尔维亚和黑山[1]两地的斯拉夫人在同情之心的驱使下也开始抗击土耳其人，而演变成了一场席卷欧洲的战争。1878年之后的数年间，俄国一直犹豫不决，而德国却开始增强自己的人力。接下来，便是沙皇俄国和法兰西共和国在1895年结成了同盟。法国之所以需要一个盟国，是因为在该国一侧的阿尔萨斯这个伤口还没有愈合；俄国之所以需要一个盟国，则是因为在该国的一侧有个日耳曼恶棍。俄、法两国并非直接毗邻，因此在当时的形势下，民主和专制之间的势不两立并非是一个足以阻碍两国结盟的障碍。但尽管如此，结盟仍是俄国出于需要才采取的一种措施。

1905年，当俄国国力在经历了日俄战争和第一次国内革命而衰弱下去之后，德国便将一种惩罚性的关税强加给了俄国。结果，俄国在1907年政策大变，甚至与英国达成了谅解——英、俄两国本是两代世仇，并且英国还是日本这个俄国新仇的盟友。因此，我们再次有了表明当时俄国所受压力之大的证据；如果我们还记得日耳曼势力对于俄国朝廷和官吏的影响，就尤其明白俄国承受的压力了。

因此，奥地利在1908年对波斯尼亚和黑塞哥维那采取进一步行动，就是在往这两

---

[1] Montenegro：门的内哥罗。南斯拉夫西南部的一个地区，旧译"黑山"。此处从旧译。

1914年，奥匈帝国皇储斐迪南大公（中）和德国皇帝威廉二世（前左一）在英国某地狩猎。

to which Viscount Grey attached such importance, she dealt a blow where there were already bruises. The little neighbor Serbia protested, and the big sister Russia supported her, for it meant the definite closing of the door to the historic aspirations of Serbian nationality, proudly held ever since the great defeat of Kossovo in the fourteenth century. But the Kaiser of Berlin put on his "shining armor" at Vienna, and shook his "mailed fist" in the face of the Czar at Petrograd. A few more uncomfortable years, and then, in 1912, came the First Balkan War, when the united Balkan Slavs overthrew the German-trained Turkish Army. In 1913 the Bulgarian Slavs, instead of submitting the dispute in

个地区的伤口上撒盐；格雷子爵认为这次行动具有极其重大的意义。小邻居塞尔维亚一抗议，大姐俄罗斯便来进行支援，因为奥地利的行动意味着塞尔维亚这个民族一直抱有的那扇希望之门真的关上了，而自14世纪科索沃那次大败[1]以来，塞尔维亚民族始终都自豪地保持着这种希望。可是，柏林的德国皇帝还是在维也纳披上了他那袭"闪亮的盔甲"，并在彼得格勒的沙皇面前晃动着他那"铁拳"。后来又过了令人不安的几年，接着便在1912年爆发了第一次巴尔干战争，当时巴尔干的斯拉夫人团结起来，打垮了由德国训练的土耳其军队。1913年，保加利亚的斯拉夫人在瓜分从土耳其手中夺取的领土时，非但没有按照《巴尔干同盟条约》[2]的规定把这一纠纷交由沙皇仲裁，反而中了德

---

[1] The great defeat of Kossovo：科索沃大败。指1389年奥斯曼帝国与塞尔维亚在科索沃平原进行的一次战役。在此役中，塞尔维亚大败，之后为奥斯曼帝国统治达5个世纪之久。

[2] Treaty of the Balkan Alliance：《巴尔干同盟条约》。巴尔干同盟是指巴尔干半岛各民族为反抗奥斯曼土耳其封建贵族的统治和压迫而成立的一个政治和军事同盟。这些民族和国家间相互签订了一系列同盟条约，总称《巴尔干同盟条约》。

regard to the division of the territory taken from Turkey to the arbitration of the Czar, as had been provided by the Treaty of the Balkan Alliance, were persuaded by German intrigue to attack the Serbian Slavs. The Second Balkan War ensued, in which the Bulgarians were defeated owing to the intervention of the Rumanians, and the Treaty of Bukharest registered a severe check to German ambition, and gave new hope to the subject Slavs of Austria.

The very remarkable report sent from Berlin to Paris, three months after the Treaty of Bukharest, by M. Jules Cambon, the French Ambassador, makes it clear that Germany had then decided to obtain by her own sword, whenever an opportunity could be made, the position which she had failed to win vicariously. Accumulating evidence goes to show that within a week of the murder of the Archduke Franz Ferdinand, Germany had decided to seize that pretext in order to force the issue. Austria sought to impose such terms of punishment on Serbia for her assumed complicity in the murder as no free nation could accept, and when Serbia had gone to the utmost limit of concession, and even Austria hesitated, Germany hastened to fasten her quarrel on Russia, the ultimate reserve of ail Slavdom. Had Russia submitted, as in 1908, she would have gone into the question of the renewal of the Tariff Treaty with Germany in 1916 with no option but a surrender into economic slavery. All this is a familiar story, but it is necessary to keep it clearly in mind, if we are to appreciate the fact that the key to the resettlement is in the East, though the decisive fighting has been in the West.

How came it that Germany made the double mistake of invading France and of invading her through Belgium? Germany knew the weakness of Russia; there was no illusion of the "steam roller" for her. Her choice of the more difficult offensive must have been on the assumption that the British democracy probably, and the American democracy certainly, were, from her point of view, asleep. She meant the German superman to rule the world, and she thought she saw a short

国的阴谋，去进攻塞尔维亚的斯拉夫人。之后第二次巴尔干战争接踵而至，在这次战争中保加利亚人因为罗马尼亚人的干涉而战败了，而之后签订的《布加勒斯特条约》则极大地遏制了德国的野心，并给臣服于奥地利的斯拉夫人带来了新的希望。

《布加勒斯特条约》签订3个月之后，法国大使朱尔斯·康邦先生从柏林向巴黎发出了一份非同寻常的报告；这份报告表明，德国当时已经下定了决心，该国一有机会便将亲舞刀剑，来获取假手别国所未能获得的地位。越来越多的证据表明，距弗朗茨·斐迪南大公被刺还不到一周，德国便已经决定抓住这一借口，以武力来解决问题。奥地利想当然地说塞尔维亚共谋实施了这次暗杀，试图把任何一个自由国家都无法接受的惩处条件强加给塞尔维亚，而在塞尔维亚做了最大限度的让步，甚至连奥地利也犹豫起来的时候，德国却加速与俄国纠缠不休，因为俄国是所有斯拉夫国家最后的靠山。倘若此时又像1908年那样对德屈服，俄国就必须在1916年与德国续签《关税条约》，并且除了投降、除了成为德国的经济奴隶，俄国并没有别的道路可选。这一切对我们来说都很熟悉，不过倘若我们想要理解虽然具有决定意义的战争发生在西欧、但重置国际关系的关键却是在东欧这一事实，那么我们就必须清楚明白地记住这一切。

德国犯下了侵略法国并经由比利时去侵略法国这样的双重错误，是怎么回事呢？德国很清楚俄国有着什么样的弱点；德国没有受到蒙蔽，并不认为俄国有什么"高压手段"能够来对付它。德国之所以选择难度较大的进攻方式，一定是想当然地认为英国这个民主国家十有八九是睡熟了，而美国这个民主国家也肯定是睡熟了，因为在德国看来，当时的形势就是如此。德国打算让日耳曼超人来统治整个世界，并且觉得自己看到

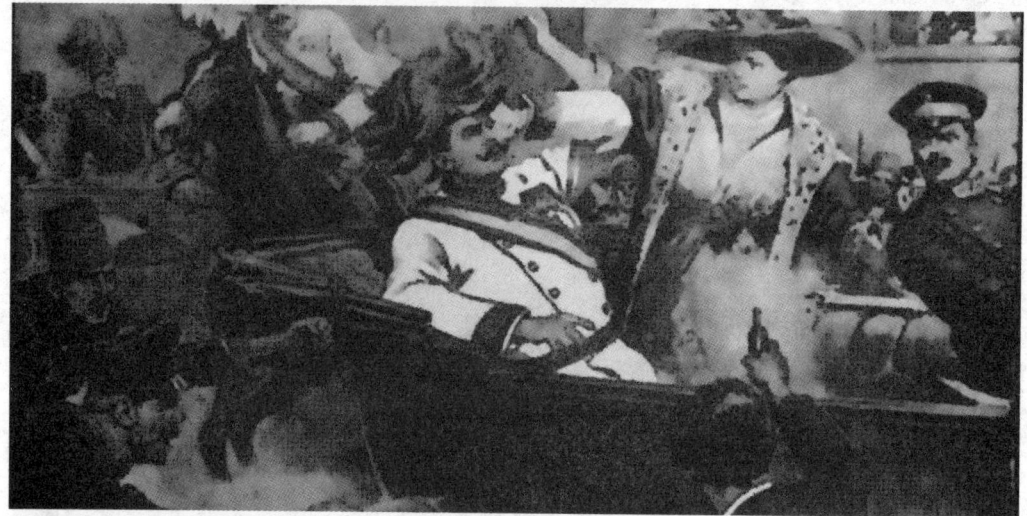

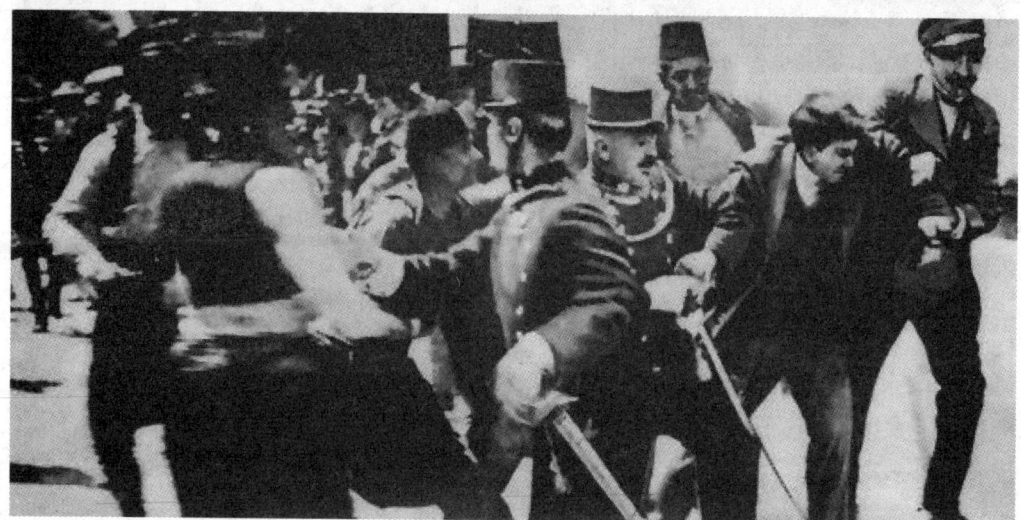

奥地利斐迪南大公遇刺

cut to her end, in the place of the longer path through the Heartland, the command of which would fall to her inevitably, could she but deprive the Islanders of their "bridge-head" in France. But there was another and even stronger reason for what she did; she was in the grip of economic fate. She was out against the Slavs for markets, for raw materials, and for wider fields to till; a million people were being added annually to her stay-at-home, kept-at-home family. But to develop that mighty Going Concern of her man-power, so strong for conquest if she could keep it going, but so insatiably hungry, she had built up Hamburg, and all that Hamburg stood for in the way of overseas adventure and home industries. Hamburg had her own momentum, and it was not eastward. Thus German strategy was biased by political necessity.

The result was that Berlin committed a fundamental mistake; she fought on two fronts without fully making up her mind on which front she meant to win. You may strike at the two flanks of your enemy, the right and the left, but unless your force is sufficient to annihilate you must decide beforehand which stroke is to be the feint and which the real attack. Berlin had not decided between her political objectives — Hamburg and overseas dominion or Bagdad and the Heartland — and therefore her strategical aim also was uncertain.

※　　　※　　　※　　　※　　　※　　　※　　　※　　　※　　　※

The German blunder, under compelling destiny, having given us Victory, it is essential that we should focus our thought on the stable resettlement of the affairs of East Europe and the Heartland. If we accept anything less than a complete solution of the Eastern Question in its largest sense we shall merely have gained a respite, and our descendants will find themselves under the necessity of marshalling their power afresh for the siege of the Heartland. The essence of the resettlement must

了实现这一目标的一条捷径，不用穿越"中心地带"那条遥远的道路，而是只要夺取岛国人在法国境内的"桥头堡"，那么"中心地带"的控制权便必然会落入德国手中。但德国这样做，还有一个更加有力的原因，那就是德国任由经济命运摆布自己。德国进击斯拉夫人，是为了市场、原材料以及更广阔的耕地，因为德国国内那个大家庭里每年都会增长100万人口。不过，为了要发展德国人力这种强大的"进行中的事业"——假如能够让这一事业进行下去，那么这一事业虽说可以强大到去征服别国，但同时又会贪得无厌、永不知足——德国建起了汉堡，而整个汉堡又代表了德国的海外扩张和国内工业这两个方面。汉堡具有自己的发展动力，可这种动力的发展方向，却并不是往东。这样一来，德国的战略便因为政治需要而产生了偏差。

结果便是，柏林犯下了一个根本性的错误；德国虽然同时在东、西两线作战，却又没有彻底下定决心，没有打算好究竟打赢哪条线。虽然可以同时进击敌人的左、右两翼，但除非兵力足以全歼敌人，否则事先就得决定好哪一边是佯攻、哪一边是实击。在德国的两大政治目标间，柏林并没有决定好是要汉堡与海外霸权呢，还是要巴格达和"中心地带"，因此德国的战略目标也是变化无常的了。

※　　　※　　　※　　　※　　　※　　　※　　　※　　　※　　　※

在无可抗拒的天命之下德国人犯下的大错让我们取得了胜利，而如今我们则必须集中精力，考虑如何平稳地重新安排东欧和"中心地带"的事务。假如我们接受任何不能彻底解决最为广义的东欧问题的方案，那我们不过是得到了喘息之机罢了，而我们的后代就必须重新组织力量去包围"中心地带"才行。重建问题的本质必定是领土问题，因为在东欧，并且更大程度上是在"中心地带"的其他地区，我们都必须安排好经济刚刚

冯·比洛（Bernhard Heinrich Karl
Martin von Bülow, 1849～1929）。德国政治
家，1900年至1909年任德意志帝国总理。

莎士比亚

be territorial, for in East Europe, and in still greater measure in the remainder of the Heartland, we have to deal with regions whose economic development has only commenced. Unless you look forward, the growth of the peoples will by and by unbalance your settlement.

No doubt it may be urged that German mentality will be altered by the German defeat. He would be a sanguine man, however, who would trust the future peace of the world to a change in the mentality of any nation. Look back to old Froissard or to Shakespeare, and you will find your Englishman, Scotsman, Welshman, and Frenchman with all their essential characteristics already fixed. The Prussian is a definite type of humanity with his good and his bad points, and we shall be wise if we act on the assumption that his kind will breed true to its type. However great the defeat which in the end we may have inflicted on our chief enemy, we should only be

开始起步的那些区域。除非向前看，否则各个民族的发展就会逐步让我们的重建变得不再平衡。

毫无疑问，有的人可能会竭力认为，德国的心态会因战败而发生改变。然而，一个把整个世界将来的和平希望全都寄托在任何民族的心态发生改变的人，只能说是一个乐天派。回顾一下老弗鲁瓦沙尔[1]或者莎士比亚的作品就会发现，英格兰人、苏格兰人、威尔士人或者法兰西人所有基本的民族特征，都是早已定型、无可改变的了。普鲁士人是一个类型明确的民族，既有优点也有缺点，而倘若假定这个民族的后代会跟其祖先一

[1] Froissard：弗鲁瓦沙尔（1337～1410）。法国历史学家和诗人。多拼作Froissart。

cheapening our own achievement if we did not recognize in the North German one of the three or four most virile races of mankind.

Even with revolution in Germany let us not be too sure in regard to its ultimate effect. The German revolutions of 1848 were almost comic in their futility. Since Bismarck there has only been one German Chancellor with political insight, and he — Von Billow — has declared in his book on Imperial Germany that "the German has always accomplished his greatest works under strong, steady, and firm guidance." The end of the present disorder may only be a new ruthless organization, and ruthless organizers do not stop when they have attained the objects which they at first set before them.

It will be replied, of course, that though Prussian mentality remain unchanged, and though a really stable Prussian Democracy be slow in its development, yet that Germany will, in any case, be so impoverished that she cannot do harm for the better part of a century to come. Is there not, however, in that idea a misreading of the real nature of riches and poverty under modern conditions? Is it not productive power which now counts rather than dead wealth? Shall we not all of us — and now in some degree even the Americans also — have spent our dead capital, and shall we not all of us, the Germans included, be starting again in the productive race practically from scratch? The world was astonished at the rapidity with which France recovered from her disaster of 1870, but the power of industrial production was as nothing then to what it is now. Sober calculation in regard to Britain leads to the conclusion that her increased productive power, owing to reorganization and new methods compelled by the War, should far exceed the interest and sinking fund even of her vast War debts. No doubt you have the Paris Resolutions, and can deny to a refractory Germany the raw materials wherewith to compete with you. If you resort to that method, however, you postpone your League of Nations,

模一样，并且按照这一假定来行事，那么我们就应当谨慎才是。无论最终能让我们这个主要的敌人遭受多么巨大的失败，倘若没有认清德国北部属于人类最强大的三四个民族之一的这个普鲁士民族的真正面目，那么我们就只是在糟蹋自己的成功而已。

即便是德国发生了革命，我们对革命的最终影响无需抱有太大的把握。1848年的德国革命白费力气，几乎就是一出闹剧。自俾斯麦之后，德国只出现过一位具有政治远见的总理，就是冯·比洛；他在所著的《德意志帝国》一书中曾说："德国一直都是在其有力、扎实而坚定不移的引导之下完成其最伟大的事业的。"目前这种混乱局面，结果可能只是出现一个残酷无情的新组织罢了，而残酷无情的组织者在实现他们起初为自己定下的那些目标之后，也是不会停下脚步的。

当然，可能有人会回应说，尽管普鲁士人的心态并未改变，尽管一个真正稳定的民主普鲁士发展起来会很缓慢，但无论如何德国都已经贫困不堪，所以在未来的大半个世纪中德国是不可能为害的。然而，这种观点难道不是曲解了现代条件下财富和贫穷的真正性质吗？如今重要的难道不是生产力而非闲置的财富吗？我们大家——如今在某种程度上来说连美国人也算——不是都已经耗尽了我们的闲置资本，而我们大家，包括德国人在内，不是几乎都要再次白手起家并展开生产力的竞赛吗？法国从1870年的那场灾难中迅速恢复过来，世界都为之震惊，但那时的工业生产能力与如今比起来，可以说是微不足道的。假如冷静地估量一下英国，我们就可以得出这样一个结论：因为英国在战争的压力下进行了重新组织并采用了新的方法，所以该国增长的生产力甚至应该远远超出了其巨额战争债务所带来的利息和偿债基金。毋庸置疑，你们有了《巴黎决议》，可以

and you remain a League of Allies. Are you certain, moreover, that you would win in an economic war? You might undoubtedly handicap Germany, but a handicap may only lead to greater effort. Did not Napoleon limit the Prussian Army after Jena to 42,000 men with the colors, and was not the Prussian effort to circumvent his prohibition the origin of the whole modern system of short-service national armies? Economic war, with Germany exploiting the Slavs, and presently the Heartland, would in the long run merely serve to emphasize the distinction between the Continent and the Islands, and between land-power and sea-power, and no one who contemplates the unity of the Great Continent under modern railway conditions can view unconcernedly either the preparation for the World-War which would be inevitable, or the ultimate result of that War.

We, the Western nations, have incurred such tremendous sacrifices in this conflict that we cannot afford to trust to anything that may happen at Berlin; we must be secure in any case. In other words, we must settle this question between the Germans and Slavs, and we must see to it that East Europe, like West Europe, is divided into self-contained nations. If we do that, we shall not only reduce the German people to its proper position in the world, a great enough position for any single people, but we shall also have created the conditions precedent to a League of Nations.

You plead that if we inflict a decisive peace we shall leave such bitter feelings that no workable League of Nations can ensue. You have in mind, of course, the results of the annexation of Alsace in 1871. But the lessons of History are not to be learned from a single instance. The great American Civil War was fought to a finish, and today the Southerners are as loyal to the Union as are the Northerners; the two questions of Negro slavery and of the right of particular States to secede from the Federation were finally decided, and ceased to be the

不向桀骜不驯的德国出售原材料，使之无法与你们来竞争。然而，如果采用此种方法，你们便会推迟国际联盟的成立，你们就仍旧不过是一个协约国联盟罢了。何况，你们是否有把握打赢一场经济战争呢？你们无疑可以遏制住德国，但此种遏制，只会令德国更加发奋图强。耶拿战役之后，拿破仑不是也把普鲁士的现役陆军限定为42000人，而普鲁士不是也尽力避开了这道禁令，从而开创了全国陆军短期服役这一整套现代化的制度吗？假如任由德国剥削斯拉夫人，并且不久之后又去剥削“中心地带”，那么从长远来看，经济战争只会让大陆与岛屿之间、陆上力量与海上力量之间的差别变得更加突出，而凡是深思过现代铁路条件下“大大陆”的统一这个问题的人，都是不可能对准备好打一场必将爆发的世界大战，或者对这场大战的最终结果漠然视之的。

我们这些西欧国家在此次大战中已经遭受了巨大的损失，因此再也不能相信柏林可能做出的任何承诺了；我们在任何情况下都必须确保自身安全才行。换句话来说就是，我们必须解决日耳曼人和斯拉夫人之间的问题，并且必须确保东欧和西欧一样分成为若干个独立自主的国家。如果做到了这一点，那么我们不但会把日耳曼民族约束在其应处的位置——这个位置对任何一个民族来说都是相当重要的——上，还将为国际联盟创造出先决条件。

你们反驳说，倘若把一份坚定果断的和约强加于人，我们就会让别的国家产生出怨恨之情，从而不可能形成一个切实可行的国际联盟。当然，你们都还记得1871年吞并阿尔萨斯的后果。不过，从单个事例中并不能汲取到历史所赋予的全部教训。伟大的美国内战打得很彻底，所以如今的南方人跟北方人一样，对美利坚合众国都忠心耿耿；黑奴制度和个别州有权退出联邦这两个问题最终也得到了解决，不再是各州间纷争的根

普奥战争

causes of quarrel. The Boer War was fought to a finish, and today General Smuts is an honored member of the British Cabinet. The War of 1866, between Prussia and Austria, was fought to a finish, and within a dozen years Austria had formed the Dual Alliance with Prussia. If you do not now secure the full results of your victory and close this issue between the German and the Slav, you will leave ill-feeling which will not be based on the fading memory of a defeat, but on the daily irritation of millions of proud people.

※　　　※　　　※　　　※　　　※　　　※　　　※　　　※　　　※

The condition of stability in the territorial rearrangement of East Europe is that the division should be into three and not into two State-systems. It is a vital necessity that there should be a tier of independent States between Germany and Russia.[1] The Russians are, and for one, if

[1] The details of the discussion of the territorial resettlement which here follow will, of course, become in large measure obsolete with the announcement of the decisions of the Peace Congress. My object is not, however, so much to debate certain solutions of the problems immediately confronting us, as to give a concrete aspect to the general idea which I am endeavoring to build up. My purpose will still be served if it is borne in mind that what I have written on these particulars represents the outlook at Christmas 1918.

源了。布尔战争[1]打得很彻底，所以史沫兹将军如今成了英国内阁中的一位荣誉阁员。1866年的普奥战争打得很彻底，所以十多年后奥地利便与普鲁士结成了两国同盟。假如你们如今不保护好自己的全部胜利并解决日耳曼人和斯拉夫人之间的这一问题，你们就会让别的国家产生敌意；这种敌意，并不是以日渐淡忘的战败记忆为基础，而是源自数百万自负国民日复一日的愤怒之情。

※　　　※　　　※　　　※　　　※　　　※　　　※　　　※　　　※

在对东欧领土进行重新安排时，保持稳定的条件就是把东欧分成3类而非2类国家体制。在德、俄两国之间，必须有一个由独立国家所组成的中间层。〔作者注：自然，下文所要讨论的关于重新安排领土的具体内容，大部分都随着和平会议诸决议的宣

[1] the Boer War: 布尔战争。英国和布尔人为了争夺南非殖民地而进行的战争，一共有两次，第一次发生于1880年至1881年，第二次发生在1899年至1902年。

not two, generations must remain, hopelessly incapable of resisting German penetration on any basis but that of a military autocracy, unless they be shielded from direct attack. The Russian peasantry cannot read; they have obtained the only reward they looked for when they sided with the revolutionaries of the towns, and now as small proprietors they hardly know how to manage their own country–sides. The middle class have so suffered that they were ready to accept order even from the hated Germans. As for the workmen of the towns, only a small minority of the Russian population, but because of their relative education and of their command of the centers of communication the rulers today of the country, Kultur knows well how to "influence" them. In the opinion of those who know Russia best, autocratic rule of some sort is almost inevitable if she is to depend on her own strength to cope with the Germans.

The Slav and kindred nations which inhabit the borderland between the Germans and the Russians are, however, of a very different caliber. Consider the Czechs: have they not stood proof against Bolshevism and asserted their capacity of nationhood under amazing conditions in Russia? Have they not shown the most extraordinary political capacity in creating anew and maintaining Slav Bohemia, though beset on three sides by Germany and on the fourth side by Hungary? Have they not also made Bohemia a hive of modern industry and a seat of modern learning? They, at any rate, will not lack the will to order and to independence.

Between the Baltic and the Mediterranean you have these seven non–German peoples, each on the scale of a European State of the second rank — the Poles, the Bohemians (Czechs and Slovaks), the Hungarians (Magyars), the South Slavs (Serbians, Croatians, and Slovenes), the Rumanians, the Bulgarians, and the Greeks. Of these, two are among our present enemies — the Magyars and the Bulgarians. But the Magyars and Bulgarians are engirt by the other five peoples, and neither of them will be powerful for harm without Prussian support.

布而变成废话一堆了。然而，我的主要目的并不是辩论我们直接面临的问题的某些解决办法，而是对我正在努力形成的整体概念加以具体说明。假如大家记住，我关于这些具体问题所写下的主张代表着我在1918年圣诞节时的看法，那么还是达到了我的目的。］俄国除非受到保护、不会受到直接攻击，否则的话，在一个世代——就算不是两个世代——的时间里，俄国根本就不可能抵抗德国的渗入，除非该国变成一个军事独裁国家。俄国的农民都不识字；他们支持城市里的革命者之后，已经获得了他们曾经寄望的唯一回报，可如今变成自耕农之后，他们却不知道如何才能管理好他们的乡村。中产阶级遭受了如此沉重的苦难，以至于都乐于听从可恶的德国人的吩咐了。至于城镇里的工人阶级，虽说只占俄国人口中的极小一部分，但由于他们的文化水平相对较高并且掌控了各大交通中心，所以如今他们成了俄国的统治者；对于这一部分人，德国文化明白怎样去"影响"他们。在最熟悉俄国情况的那些人看来，倘若俄国想靠自己的力量来对付德国人，就必然会采取某种形式的专制统治。

然而，住居在德、俄两国边境地区的斯拉夫民族及其兄弟民族，却有着极其不同的本领。仔细想一想捷克人吧：他们不是抵挡住了布尔什维克主义，并且表明他们就算是在俄国种种令人惊讶的条件之下也有建国的能力了吗？他们不是在重新建立并维护斯拉夫波希米亚——尽管斯拉夫波希米亚三面受德国包围，而另一面又为匈牙利包围——的过程中，表明自己具有非凡的政治才能了吗？他们不是也让波希米亚发展成了一个现代工业密集之所和现代知识的渊薮了吗？不管怎样，他们都并不缺乏让社会秩序井然并保持国家独立的愿望。

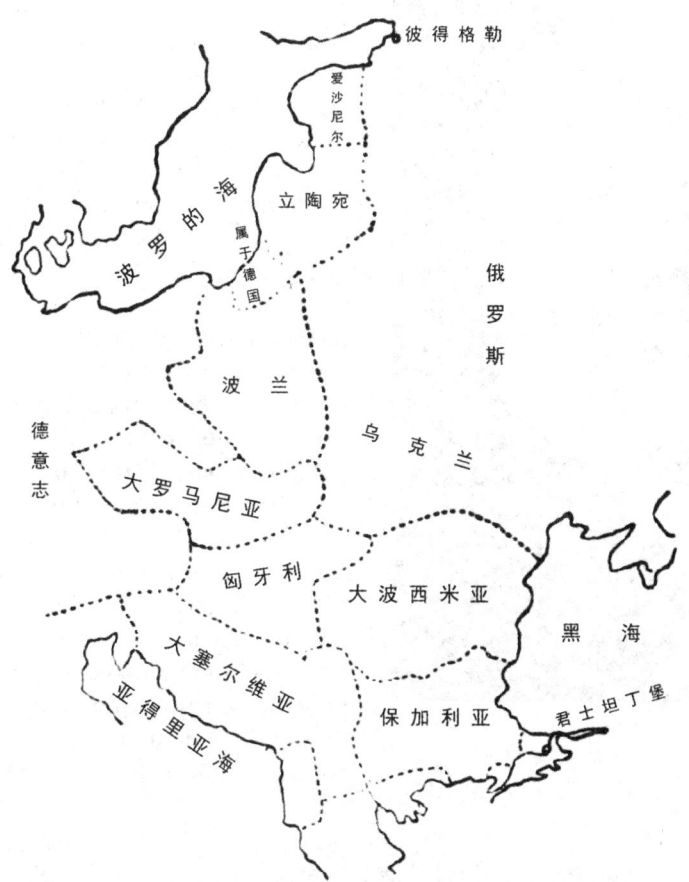

图31　德、俄两国之间的中间层国家。还有许多边界问题需要解决。

Let us count over these seven peoples. First we have the Poles, some 20 million of them, with the river Vistula for their arterial waterway, and the historic cities of Cracow and Warsaw. The Poles are a more generally civilized people than the Russians, even in that part of Poland

　　在波罗的海和地中海之间，有着7个非日耳曼民族，并且每个民族的规模都相当于欧洲一个二流国家的规模——波兰人、波希米亚人（包括捷克人和斯洛伐克人）、匈牙利人（马扎尔人）、南斯拉夫人（包括塞尔维亚人、克罗地亚人和斯洛文尼亚人）、罗马尼亚人、保加利亚人和希腊人。其中有两个民族，站在我们目前的敌对阵营之中——即马扎尔人和保加利亚人。不过，马扎尔人和保加利亚人都被其他5个民族包围着；倘若没有普鲁士支持，这两个民族都是无力作恶的。

　　我们不妨重新来看一看这7个民族。首先是人口大约为2000万的波兰人，他们有维斯瓦河这条水上大动脉，以及克拉科夫[1]和华沙这两座历史名城。波兰人是一个文化程

────────────

　　[1] Cracow：克拉科夫。波兰南部维斯瓦河上的一个城市，始建于公元8世纪，在1305年到1595年期间曾为波兰首都。

凡尼济洛斯（Eleftherios Venizelos,
1864～1936）。希腊政治家，曾数任希腊总理，
并在第一次世界大战期间使希腊与协约国结盟。

which has been tied to Russia; in the Prussian province of Posen they have enjoyed the advantages of Kultur, without some of the debasement which Kultur brought to the master German. Undoubtedly there are strong currents of party among the Poles, but now that the Polish aristocracy of Galicia is no longer bribed to the support of the Haps-burg throne by leave to oppress the Ruthenians of East Galicia, at least one motive of party, one vested interest, should have disappeared.

By some means the new Poland must be given access to the Baltic Sea, not only because that is essential to her economic independence, but also because it is desirable to have Polish ships on the Baltic, which strategically is a closed sea of the Heartland, and, further, there must be a complete territorial buffer between Germany and Russia. Unfortunately the province of East Prussia, mainly German by speech and Junker by sentiment, would be detached from Germany by any strip of Poland going down to the sea. Why should we not contemplate an exchange of peoples as

度普遍高于俄罗斯人的民族，就算是在波兰已被俄国控制的那部分地区，也是如此；在普鲁士的波森省，波兰人虽说吸收了德国文化的优点，却并没有染上德国文化给它的主子日耳曼人所带来的某些低劣品质。毋庸置疑，波兰人当中党争激烈，但由于如今加利西亚[1]的波兰贵族已经不再受到收买去支持哈布斯堡王朝并任由哈布斯堡王朝压迫东加利西亚的鲁塞尼亚人了，所以他们的党争动机中至少有一个动机已经不复存在，即至少会有一个既得利益群体已经不复存在了。

我们必须通过某种途径，让新的波兰拥有一个通往波罗的海的出海口才行，原因不仅在于出海口对波兰的经济独立来说必不可少，还在于让波兰船只在波罗的海上航行符合我们的利益——从战略上看，波罗的海就是"中心地带"的一个内海；此外，在德、俄两国之间，也必须有一条完整的缓冲地带。可惜的是，无论波兰从哪个地带出海，这个地带都会将主要是说日耳曼语而又有着容克贵族情绪的东普鲁士与德国割裂开来。我们为什么就不能考虑考虑，把维斯瓦河以东的普鲁士人与波森省的波兰人对调过来呢？［作者注：我写下这段文字之后，凡尼济洛斯先生曾于1919年1月14日在巴黎接受《泰晤士报》记者的采访时如此说道："这样做，仍然会让小亚细亚中心地区成千上万的希腊人处在土耳其的统治之下。这个问题只有一种解决办法，那就是鼓励进行一次大规模的人口互换。"］在这次大战中，我们曾经从事过许多规模更大的

---

[1] Galicia: 加利西亚。包括波兰东南部和乌克兰西北部的地区，曾经是奥地利王室领地。

between Prussia east of the Vistula, and Polish Posen?[1] During this War we have undertaken much vaster things, both in the way of mere transport and also of organization. In the past, in order to deal with such difficulties, diplomatists have resorted to all manner of "servitudes" as the land lawyers would say. But rights-of-way over other people's property usually become inconvenient and lead to disputes. Would it not pay Humanity to bear the cost of a radical remedy in this case, a remedy made just and even generous towards individuals in every respect? Each proprietor should be given the option of exchanging his property and retaining his nationality or of retaining his property and changing his nationality. But if he selects the latter alternative there must be no reservation of special rights in respect of schools and other social privileges. The United States in her schools sternly imposes the English language on all her immigrants. Because the conquerors of old time did their work ruthlessly, countries like France and England are today homogeneous and free from that mixture of races which has made the Near East a plague to humanity. Why should we not use our modern powers of transport and organization to achieve the same happy condition of affairs — justly and generously? The reasons for doing so in this particular instance are far reaching; a Polish Posen would bite a very threatening bay into the Eastern frontier of Germany, and a German East Prussia would be a stepping-stone for German penetration into Russia.[2]

---

[1] Since I wrote this paragraph, M. Venizelos, in an interview with a Times correspondent, dated Paris, January 14, 1919, has used these words: "This would still leave some hundreds of thousands of Greeks under Turkish rule in the centre of Asia Minor. For this there is only one cure, and that is to encourage a wholesale and mutual transfer of population."

[2] To meet the obvious argumentum ad hominem, let me say that I see no really comparable strategical

事情，既有纯粹通过运输系统来进行的，也有通过组织来进行的。过去为了解决此种难题，外交家们曾经利用了地产律师所称的各种各样的"役劝权"[1]。但对他人的财产行使役劝权，通常很不方便，还会引起纠纷。在此种情况下，人类是否值得付出代价来采取一种激进的补救措施，采取一种在各个方面都公平、甚至是慷慨地对待每一个人的补救措施呢？应当允许每一个地主都能够选择，要么是交换财产、保留国籍，要么就是保留财产、改变国籍。不过，倘若地主选择了后面这种方式，就不能再给他保留教育方面的特权以及其他的社会特权了。美国的学校强制所有移民都学英语。正是因为旧时的征服者都冷酷无情地这样干，像法国和英国这样的国家如今才会同族同宗，才不至于民族混杂——近东地区就是由于民族混杂而变成了人类的一大祸患。为什么我们就不能利用现代的运输力量和组织力量，公平而慷慨地实现一种同样的幸福局面呢？在这个具体的例子当中，这样做的理由更有着深远的意义；波兰人的波森省会让一个威慑力极大的海湾深深地楔入德国的东部边疆，而日耳曼人的东普鲁士则是日耳曼人势力深入俄罗斯的一块垫脚石。〔作者注：为了驳斥那种明显的"仅从个人感情出发的论证"，请让我说，在爱尔兰的情形中我并没有看到什么真正能够与此相比的战略必要！〕

我们的"边疆"民族中，接下来便是捷克人和斯洛伐克人；直到近来，这两个民族都被将奥地利和匈牙利分隔开来的那道界线隔开了，就像波兰人被俄国、普鲁士和奥地利的边境分隔开来了那样。捷克人和斯洛伐克人的总人口可能有900万；他们会成为欧洲最强有力的少数民族之一，并且他们拥有一片非同寻常的国土，有煤、金属、木材、

---

[1] Servitude：役劝（权）。法律上指动用他人财产的权利。

Next among our "Border" peoples are the Czechs and Slovaks, until recently severed by the line dividing Austria from Hungary, as the Poles were severed by the frontiers between Russia, Prussia, and Austria. The Czechs and Slovaks together number perhaps nine millions; they will make one of the most virile little peoples in Europe, and they are equipped with a remarkable country, offering coal, metals, timber, water—power, corn, and wine, and centered on the main line of railway from the Baltic and Warsaw to Vienna and the Adriatic.

Then we come to the South Slavs — Jugo means South — in their three tribes of Slovenes, Croatians, and Serbs. They number about twelve millions. They also have been sundered by the line between Austria and Hungary; moreover, they are of the rival Latin and Greek Churches. For any one who knows the Balkans, it is eloquent testimony indeed to the effect of Austro—Hungarian tyranny that the Roman Catholic Slovenes and Croatians should have made the pact of Corfu with the Greek Orthodox Serbs. The South Slavs will have access to Dalmatian ports on the Adriatic, and one of the trunk railways of the world will run down the Save Valley to Belgrade, and then through the Morava and Maritza "Corridor" to Constantinople.

Rumania is the next State of this middle east of Europe. The natural focus of Rumania is the great Transylvanian bastion of the Carpathians, with fruitful valleys, metalliferous mountains, oil wells, and splendid forests. The Transylvanian peasantry is Rumanian, but a "privileged" minority of Magyars and "Saxons" have been the rulers. Here again it should be no quite impossible feat of statesmanship to arrange for an equitable exchange of homes, or a full acceptance of Rumanian Nationality, though it must be admitted that the hostility between Saxon and Ruman is not so acute as that between Prussian and Pole.

---

necessities in the case of Ireland!

水力、谷物和葡萄酒，人们则集中居住在从波罗的海和华沙到维也纳和亚得里亚海的铁路干线沿线。

其次便是南斯拉夫人——"优戈"[1]就是"南方"的意思——他们分成了3个部族，即斯洛文尼亚人、克罗地亚人和塞尔维亚人。他们的人口总数约为1200万。他们也被奥、匈两国间的那条界线分隔开来了；此外，他们分别信奉罗马天主教和希腊正教这两种相互对立的宗教。对于任何一个熟悉巴尔干半岛情况的人来说，信奉罗马天主教的斯洛文尼亚人和克罗地亚人居然跟信奉希腊正教的塞尔维亚人签订了《科孚协定》[2]，事实上就是奥匈帝国暴政的有力证据。南斯拉夫人将会拥有一条到达亚得里亚海的达尔马提亚沿岸诸港的通道，而世界的铁路干线中，也有一条将经过萨瓦河谷南下通往贝尔格莱德，然后再穿过摩拉瓦和马里乍"走廊"，到达君士坦丁堡。

东欧这个中部地区的下一个国家，就是罗马尼亚。喀尔巴阡山脉中特兰西瓦尼亚这个伟大的要塞，是罗马尼亚的天然中心，那里有物产丰富的山谷、蕴藏金属的山脉、油田以及壮丽神奇的森林。特兰西瓦尼亚地区的农民都是罗马尼亚人，但统治者却一直都是一小撮享有特权的马扎尔人和"撒克逊人"。在这里又可以说，尽管我们必须承认撒克逊人和罗马尼亚人之间的敌意并不像普鲁士人和波兰人之间那样尖锐，但利用政治能力做出安排，让人们公平地互换家园或者完全加入罗马尼亚国籍，这一点也并不是完全做不到的。

---

[1] Jugo：现在拼作Yugo，"南斯拉夫"即Yugoslavia。此处从音译。

[2] Corfu：科孚。位于爱奥尼亚群岛中的一个希腊岛屿。

The rest of Rumania, the present kingdom, is the glacis, eastward and southward, of Transylvania, watered by the Transylvanian rivers. This fertile glacis is one of the chief sources in Europe of oil, wheat, and maize; the twelve million Rumanians will be a rich people. At Galatz, Braila, and Constanza they have ports on the Black Sea, and it will be a prime interest of all free peoples that there should be Rumanian ships on that sea, for it is naturally a closed water of the Heartland. The time will never come when the League of Nations will be able to regard the Baltic and Black Seas without concern, for the Heartland offers the basis of an all-powerful militarism. Civilization consists in the control of nature and of ourselves, and the League of Nations, as the supreme organ of united humanity, must closely watch the Heartland and its possible organizers, for the same reason that the control of the police in London and Paris is regarded as a national and not merely a municipal concern.

The Greeks were the first of our seven peoples of the Middle Tier to achieve their emancipation from German control in this War for the simple reason that they are outside the Heartland and therefore accessible to sea-power. But in these days of submarines and aeroplanes, the possession of Greece by a great Heartland power would probably carry with it the control of the World-Island; the Macedonian history would be re-enacted. Now as to the Magyars and Bulgarians. The truth is that both of them were exploited by, although not subject to, the Prussians. Every one who knows Budapest is aware of the deeply alien feeling of the Magyars toward the Germans; the recent alliance was strictly one of convenience and not of hearts. The ruling Magyar caste of about a million people has been oppressive of the other nine millions of its own race no less than of the subject races. The alliance with Prussia — for it has in reality been an alliance with Prussia rather than with Austria — has been strictly in return for support of the Magyar oligarchy. No doubt the Magyars have begotten deep feelings

罗马尼亚的其他地区，即目前的罗马尼亚王国，位于特兰西瓦尼亚向东和向南延伸且由特兰西瓦尼亚诸河灌溉的一片缓坡。这处肥沃的缓坡是欧洲石油、小麦和玉米的主产区之一； 1200万罗马尼亚人将会是一个富有的民族。他们在黑海上有加拉茨、布勒伊拉和康斯坦萨等港口；罗马尼亚的船只在黑海上航行对于所有的自由民族来说都是极为有利的，因为黑海天生就是"中心地带"的一个内海。国际联盟永远都不应有漠视波罗的海和黑海的时候，因为"中心地带"可以孕育出一个无比强大的军国主义国家来。文明在于掌控大自然和我们人类自身，而国联作为人类的最高共同机构，则必须密切关注"中心地带"及其可能出现的组织者；这样做的原因，与掌控伦敦、巴黎的警察是英、法两国全国上下都很关注而非仅仅是这两个城市关注的事情并无两样。

处于中间层的那7个民族当中，希腊人是此次大战中第一个摆脱德国的控制并获得解放的民族，原因很简单，就是因为他们处在"中心地带"之外，可以获得海上力量的支援。但在如今这个有了潜艇和飞机的时代，倘若"中心地带"的一个强国占领了希腊，那么这个强国很可能随之便会控制"世界岛"；这样一来，就会重新上演马其顿的历史。接下来，就是马扎尔人和保加利亚人。事实上，这两个民族虽然没有臣服于普鲁士人，但都受到了普鲁士人的剥削。熟悉布达佩斯的人都知道，马扎尔人完全将日耳曼人视为异族；严格说来，最近双方结盟只是权宜之计，而非出自真心。马扎尔人中大约100万统治阶层压迫起本民族其余的900万人来，一直都不亚于他们对臣服民族的压迫。严格地说，他们和普鲁士结成同盟——事实上，此种同盟一直是与普鲁士而非与奥地利的结盟国——就是为了换取普鲁士对马扎尔寡头政府的支持。毫无疑问，马扎尔人在斯

第二次巴尔干战争

of hostility among the Slavs and Rumanians, but if there be no more profit to be made from farming Slavs in the German behalf, a democratic Hungary will sooner or later adapt herself to the new environment. The Bulgarians fought, let us remember, as allies of the Serbs against the Turks, and the difference between Serb and Bulgar, though bitter for the time being, is a family difference. It is a difference of recent growth, and based largely on rival ecclesiastical organizations of recent foundation. The Bulgarians must not be allowed to exploit their treachery in the Second Balkan War, but if an equitable settlement be dictated by the Allies, both nations, the Bulgarians and the Serbs, deeply war-weary, will probably accept it joyfully. For twenty years only one will, that of the German Czar Ferdinand, has counted in Bulgaria.

The most important point of strategical significance in regard to these Middle States of East Europe is that the most civilized of them, Poland and Bohemia, lie in the North, in the position

拉夫人和罗马尼亚人中引起了深深的敌意，不过，要是不能再代表日耳曼人从以农耕为业的斯拉夫人那里获得更多利益的话，那么一个民主的匈牙利迟早也会适应这种新的环境。我们不要忘记，保加利亚人曾经是塞尔维亚人的盟友，曾经与土耳其人打过仗，而塞尔维亚人和保加利亚人之间的分歧尽管目前很尖锐，却还是属于家庭内部分歧。此种分歧最近才形成，而且主要是因为那些成立不久的宗教组织之间的纷争引起的。我们绝不能允许保加利亚人再利用他们在第二次巴尔干战争当中背信弃义的做法来获得好处，不过如果协约国能够定下一种公平的解决办法，那么，对战争已经深感厌倦的保加利亚人和塞尔维亚人这两个民族，十有八九都会欣然接受这个解决办法的。20年来，保加利亚国内只有一种意志在发挥着作用，那就是日耳曼沙皇斐迪南的意志。

东欧这些中间层国家最重要的战略意义，就是其中文明程度最高的波兰和波希米亚都位于北方，且都最易受到普鲁士人的进犯。除非从亚得里亚海和黑海一直延伸到波

most exposed to Prussian aggression. Securely independent the Polish and Bohemian nations cannot be unless as the apex of a broad wedge of independence, extending from the Adriatic and Black Seas to the Baltic; but seven independent States, with a total of more than sixty million people, traversed by railways linking them securely with one another, and having access through the Adriatic, Black, and Baltic Seas with the Ocean, will together effectively balance the Germans of Prussia and Austria, and nothing less will suffice for that purpose. None the less the League of Nations should have the right under International Law of sending War fleets into the Black and Baltic Seas.

※　　　　※　　　　※　　　　※　　　　※　　　　※　　　　※　　　　※　　　　※

This great deed of International Statesmanship accomplished, and there would appear to

罗的海有一大批独立的国家楔入，并且波兰人和波希米亚人处在这个楔形的顶端，否则这两个民族便无法确保独立；不过，这7个独立国家的总人口达6000多万，其间铁路纵横，牢固地将它们联结起来，还能经由亚得里亚海、黑海、波罗的海通往海洋，所以它们齐起心来就会有效地与普鲁士和奥地利的日耳曼人抗衡，少了一国便不足以达到那一目标。尽管如此，国际联盟也应当拥有根据《国际法》派遣军舰舰队进驻黑海和波罗的海的权利。

※　　　　※　　　　※　　　　※　　　　※　　　　※　　　　※　　　　※　　　　※

待国际政治家们完成这一大业之后，实现国际联盟这个民主的理想似乎就并非不可

国际联盟会场

be no impossibility of realizing the democratic ideal, the League of Nations, whose mirage has haunted our Western peoples from afar over the desert of War. What are the essential conditions which must be fulfilled if you are to have a real and potent League of Nations? Viscount Grey, in his recent pamphlet, laid down two such conditions. The first was that "the Idea must be adopted with earnestness and conviction by the Executive Heads of States". The second was that "the Governments and Peoples of the States willing to found it understand clearly that it will impose some limitation upon the national action of each, and may entail some inconvenient obligation. The stronger nations must forego the right to make their interests prevail against the weaker by force."

These are excellent and very necessary theses, but do they carry us far enough? Before you undertake any general obligation, is it not well to consider what it is likely to mean in concrete terms? Your League will have to reckon with certain realities. There was before the War an incipient League of Nations; its members were the States party to the system of International Law. Have we not had to fight the War just because two of the greater States broke the International Law, first in regard to one and then another of the smaller States, and have not those two greater States very nearly succeeded in defeating a very powerful League of Nations which intervened in behalf of the Law? In the face of such a fact, is it quite adequate to say that stronger nations must "forego" the right to make their interests prevail by force against the weaker? In a word, do not our ideals involve us in a circle unless we reckon with realities?

Is it not plain that if your League is to last there must be no nation strong enough to have any chance against the general will of Humanity? Or, to put the matter in another way; there must be no predominant partner or even group of partners in your League. Is there any case

能了，而国际联盟这个海市蜃楼般的幻景，一直都在战争沙漠遥远的上空萦绕在我们西方的各个民族的心头。如果你们打算拥有一个真正而有力的国际联盟，那么必须满足哪些必要条件呢？格雷子爵在他不久前才发表的那篇短论中提出了两个这样的条件。第一个条件是，"各国的执政首脑必须真心实意且坚定不移地接受此种理想"。第二个条件是，"愿意成立国际联盟的各国政府和人民应当明白，国联会对各个国家的行为施加某种约束，并且可能会让各国承担某种令人为难的义务。较强大的国家必须放弃通过武力让本国利益凌驾于较弱小国家之上的权利。"

这两个方面都是非常优秀和很有必要的观点，但它们会不会让我们取得长足的进步呢？你们在承担任何普遍义务之前是不是最好考虑一下，在具体的谈判中这两个条件又意味着什么呢？你们的国联必须考虑到某些现实情况才行。此次大战前就出现了一个国际联盟的雏形；其成员都是《国际法》体系中的各方。我们被迫打这场大战，难道不就是因为有两个较强的国家先是对一个小国、后来又对另一个小国违反了《国际法》，而那两个较强的国家，不是差点儿就打败了一个代表《国际法》出面干预的、强大得很的国际联盟吗？面对着这样一个事实，你们说强国必须"放弃"通过武力让本国利益凌驾于弱国之上的权利，是不是十分恰当呢？总而言之就是，假如不考虑现实，我们的种种理想会不会让我们陷入一个怪圈呢？

倘若你们的国联想要长久存在，便绝不能允许哪个国家强大到足以有机会去违背人类的最高意志，这一点不是很明显的吗？或者说，我们不妨换种方式来说明这个问题；这就是在你们国联的内部，绝不能有一个占据支配地位的会员国，绝不能有一个占据支配地位的会员国集团。世间有没有一个会员占据了支配地位、而联盟仍然运作得很成功

of a successful federation with a predominant partner? In the United States you have the great States of New York, Pennsylvania, and Illinois, but no one of them counts for more than a small fraction of the whole Union. In Canada you have Quebec and Ontario balancing one another, so that the smaller provinces of the Dominion are never likely to be bullied by either. In the Commonwealth of Australia you have the approximately equal States of New South Wales and Victoria. In Switzerland not even the large Canton of Berne is anything like predominant. Has not German Federation been a pretense because of the dominance of Prussia? Is not the chief difficulty in the way of devolution within the British Isles, even if Irishmen would agree among themselves, the predominance of England? Did not this War originate from the fact that you allowed an almost dominant Germany to arise in Europe? Have not the great Wars of the past in Europe come from the fact that one State in the European System, under Napoleon, Louis XIV., or Philip II., had become too powerful? Is it not necessary, if your League of Nations is to have any chance of success, to face this cumulative evidence and not to gloss it over?

Is there not also another Reality with which you must reckon; the Reality of the Going Concern? If the nations of your League are to settle down to a quiet life, there are two different ways, it seems to me, in which you will have to face the Reality of the Going Concern; in respect of the Present and of the Future. What is meant by this Reality in the Present will best be conveyed by concrete consideration of the States available as the units to be leagued together.

The British Empire is a Going Concern. You will not persuade a majority of Britons to risk the coherence of the Empire, which has so triumphantly stood the test of this War, for any paper scheme of a Universal League. It follows, therefore, that the governing units of the British Empire can only grow by gradual process into their place as units of your League. Yet

的例子呢？在美利坚合众国，虽然有纽约、宾夕法尼亚、伊利诺伊这样的大州，但它们的重要性在整个联邦中都只占一小部分。在加拿大，有魁北克和安大略这两个相互制衡的省份，从而使得该国那些较小的省份绝不可能遭到这两个大省的欺凌。在澳大利亚联邦，也有实力大致相当的新南威尔士州和维多利亚州。在瑞士，甚至连伯尔尼那样的大州也不占有支配地位。德意志联邦不是正因为其中的普鲁士占据了支配地位，才变成了一个有名无实的联邦吗？不列颠诸岛权力下放之路上的主要困难——就算爱尔兰人的内部意见保持着一致——不就是因为英格兰占据了支配地位吗？这次大战之所以爆发，原因不就是在于你们允许在欧洲崛起一个几乎占据了支配地位的德国这一事实吗？欧洲以前爆发过多次大战，不都是因为欧洲系统中有一个国家，在拿破仑、路易十四或者菲利普二世的统治下，变得太过强大的这个事实吗？假如你们的国联想要成功，那么正视这些积累起来的证据而不加以掩饰，难道不是必须的吗？

另外，你们不是还有一个现实情况必须考虑，即必须考虑"进行中的事业"这个现实吗？如果你们国联中的各个国家想要安定下来过平静日子的话，那么在我看来，就必须用两种不同的方式来面对"进行中的事业"这个现实；其中，一种是关于"现在"的，另一种是关于"将来"的。对可以联合起来成为国联一员的那些国家进行具体研究，将会最好地表达出"现在"这个现实的含义。

大英帝国是一个"进行中的事业"。我们不可能说服大多数不列颠人，让他们为了什么"全球联盟"这样有名无实的计划，而拿在此次大战中成功地经受住了考验的、整个帝国的凝聚力去冒险。由此就可得出结论说，大英帝国中的各个行政单元，都只能一步一步地发展成为你们的国联成员。不过，大英帝国中实际上已经有六个国家之间的关

the relations of six of them are already, in fact, the relations of equality and, under their British League, of independency. Only last year was the last word said in that matter. The Prime Ministers of the Dominions are henceforth to communicate directly with the Prime Minister of the United Kingdom, and no longer through the subordinate Colonial Secretary; the Parliament at Westminster is no longer to be called the Imperial Parliament but only the Parliament of the United Kingdom. It only remains that the King should no longer be called King of the United Kingdom and of the Dominions beyond the Seas, but that the equality of all the Dominions should be recognized by some such title as King of all the Britains. Even in respect of realities — though in such matters names become realities — have we not now the certainty that the United Kingdom, Canada, and Australia will each have its own fleet and army, to be put under a single strategical command only on the outbreak of War? As regards population, too, is it not now a question of only a few years before Canada and Australia will equal the Motherland in power? We shall then have the three minor Dominions — New Zealand, South Africa, and Newfoundland — counting the more because of the balance between the three major Dominions.

France and Italy are Going Concerns. Are they going to enter a League in which the British Empire is a unit? Fortunately we have achieved the single strategical command in the later stages of the War, so that the name Versailles has now an added historic meaning. No longer merely through their Ambassadors, but in the persons of their Prime Ministers, the United Kingdom, France, and Italy have acquired the habit of taking counsel together. These three countries of West Europe are not unfitted by any decisive inequality of size to be fellow members of a League. Is it not probable that occasions will occur when the Prime Ministers of Canada and Australia may be called into conference with the Prime Ministers of the United Kingdom, France, and Italy? They will be occasions of all the more value if you recognize the

系是平等的，并且在英联邦治下它们实际上也已是彼此独立的关系了。这个问题还是去年才尘埃落定的。自此以后，各个自治领的总理就是直接联系联合王国的首相，而不用再通过殖民大臣这个下属；位于威斯敏斯特的国会也不再称为"帝国国会"，而是只称为"联合王国国会"了。唯一尚待解决的问题便是，国王不应该再称为"联合王国以及海外各自治领的国王"，而是应当用诸如"大英帝国全体成员国国王"之类的称号，以承认所有自治领的地位一律平等。就算从现实来看——尽管在这些问题上，名号也已变成了现实——如今我们是不是能够肯定地说，联合王国、加拿大和澳大利亚都会拥有本国的舰队和陆军，只有在爆发战争的时候，才会置于统一的战略指挥之下呢？从人口方面来看，如今不也是只需要数年的时间，加拿大和澳大利亚的实力就会与其母国相当了吗？到了那时，我们就会让那3个较小的自治领——即新西兰、南非和纽芬兰——因为三个主要的自治领相互抗衡而发挥更多的作用。

法国和意大利也是两种"进行中的事业"。这两个国家会不会加入一个大英帝国也在其中的联盟呢？可喜的是，我们在此次大战后期已经实现了统一的战略指挥，因此凡尔赛这个名称如今又增添了一层历史含义。联合王国、法国和意大利之间已经不再只是通过各国大使传话，而是形成了各国首相亲自进行共同协商的习惯。这三个西欧国家并没有因为国家大小方面有着什么关键性的不平等而不适合一起加入某个联盟。把加拿大和澳大利亚两国的总理请来，让他们与联合王国、法国以及意大利三国的首相一起举行会议，难道完全没有这样的时机吗？如果你们承认如今各个"进行中的事业"、不想只获得有名无实的进步的话，那么此种时机就会具有更大的意义。不要忘了，1918年德国

Going Concerns of today and do not attempt to make merely paper progress. Remember that it required the peril of the German offensive of 1918 to secure the unity of strategical command.[1]

Then what of the United States? There is no good in pretending, that the separate American States can be units in your League; the Republic fought the greatest War in History, before this War, in order to weld them together. Yet the United States form something very like a predominant partner as against the separate allied countries of West Europe. The United States must be in your League; and that means that, for healthy working, the six Britains must be held together as a counterbalance. Fortunately 3000 miles of undefended frontier in North America constitute a fact of good omen, though, to be quite frank, it would signify more if the countries which that frontier has separated had been less unequal; the test would have been more severe.

But the need of a reasonable equality of power as between a considerable number of the members of the League, so that in future crises — and they will occur — it may not be exposed to danger from predominance in any quarter, is less urgent in respect of the insular than of the continental members. There are the obvious limitations of sea-power; there are also natural boundaries which define the spread of any one insular, or even peninsular, base of power. The test of the League will be in the Heartland of the Continent. Nature there offers all the prerequisites of ultimate dominance in the world; it must be for man by his foresight and by the taking of solid guarantees to prevent its attainment. Notwithstanding their revolutions the German and Russian peoples are Going Concerns, each with a powerful historical momentum.

Therefore let the idealists who, now that the nations are locked into a single world system,

---

[1] Since this was written the Paris Conference has treated the British Empire as a hybrid — a unit for some purposes.

发动进攻所带来的危险局势，正是促成统一的战略指挥所必备的条件。〔作者注：写下这段文字之后，巴黎和会已经把大英帝国视作一个混合体——即在某些场合下的一个单元了。〕

那么，美国又如何呢？伪称美国各个州都可以自成一体地加入你们的国际联盟，这种做法并无好处；此次大战之前，这个共和国曾经为了把各个州结成一体而打了一场历史上规模最大的战争。不过，与西欧各个单独的盟国相比，美利坚合众国在某些方面却很像是一个占据了支配地位的伙伴。合众国必须加入你们的国联；这意味着，为了正常运作，大英帝国中的六个国家必须联成一体来跟合众国抗衡。幸运的是，北美洲那道长达3000英里的不设防边界，是一种实实在在的好兆头，尽管相当坦率地说，要是被这道边界分隔开来的那两个国家[1]相差没那么悬殊的话，这道边界就更加重要了；而此种形势所带来的考验，也会更加严峻。

但是，在国际联盟众多的会员国之间需要保持一种合理的力量平衡，以便在将来出现危机——危机肯定会出现——的时候，国联不会有被任何地区支配的危险；只是对于岛国来说，这种需要并不像大陆国家那样紧迫。海上力量具有一些明显的弱点；任何一个岛国的实力基地，甚至是任何一个半岛的实力基地，其扩张范围也都受到了天然边界的限定。国际联盟所要经受的考验，在于大陆的"中心地带"。那里的大自然提供了

---

[1] 此处的"两个国家"指美国和加拿大。前文中的"3000英里不设防的边界"则是指美、加之间的边界。

rightly see in the League of Nations the only alternative to Hell on Earth, concentrate their attention on the adequate subdivision of East Europe. With a Middle Tier of really independent States between Germany and Russia they will achieve their end, and without it they will not. Any mere trench-line between the German Powers and Russia, such as was contemplated by Naumann in his Central Europe, would have left German and Slav still in dual rivalry, and no lasting stability could have ensued. But the "Middle Tier", supported by the outer nations of the World League, will accomplish the end of breaking-up East Europe into more than two State-systems. Moreover, the States of that Tier, of approximate equality of power, will themselves be a very acceptable group for the recruitment of the League.

Once thus remove the temptation and opening to World-Empire, and who can say what will occur among the German and Russian peoples themselves? There are already indications that Prussia, which, unlike England or France, is a purely artificial structure, will be broken into several Federal States. In one region the Prussians belong by history to East Europe and in another to West Europe.

诺曼（Friedrich Naumann, 1860～1919）。德国自由主义政治家，19世纪"国家社会主义"的创始人。

最终统治全世界的所有先决条件；因此，必须有人凭借自己的远见卓识并采取可靠的保障措施，防止出现一国称霸世界的局面才行。尽管德、俄两国都爆发了革命，但两国人民都是"进行中的事业"，并且每一个民族都有着强大的历史动力。

所以，既然各国如今都被纳入了一个统一的世界体系当中，就不妨让那些正确地认识到国际联盟是不让人间变成地狱的唯一选择的理想主义者们，把他们的注意力都集中在对东欧恰当地进行重新划分的问题上。倘若德、俄之间具有真正独立的中间层国家，这些理想主义者们就会实现自己的目标，否则的话，他们就不会成功。德意志列强和俄罗斯之间，倘若只是有一条堑壕为界，就像诺曼在其《中欧》一书中所期待的那样，那么日耳曼人和斯拉夫人就会仍然处在双重的敌对状态之中，也就不可能形成持久的稳定局面。不过，假如这个"中间层"得到"世界联盟"中其他外层国家的支持，这个"中间层"就能实现将东欧分成不止两种国家体制的目标。而且，那个"中间层"里各个国家的实力都大致相当，本身就是国际联盟完全可以接收为会员国的一个群体。

谁能说得清，一旦如此消除导致出现"世界帝国"的诱因和机会，德、俄两个民族内部会出现一种什么样的局面呢？已经有迹象表明，不同于英、法两国且纯属于一个二次结构的普鲁士，将会分裂成数个联邦国家。从历史来看，普鲁士人在一个地区属于东欧，而在另一个地区可能又属于西欧。俄罗斯难道没有可能分裂成具有某种松散的联

Is it not probable that the Russians will fall into a number of States in some sort of loose federation? Germany and Russia have grown into great Empires out of opposition to one another; but the peoples of the Middle Tier — Poles, Bohemians, Hungarians, Rumanians, Serbs, Bulgarians, and Greeks — are much too unlike to federate for any purpose except defense, yet they are all so different both from Germans and Russians that they may be trusted to resist any new organization of either great neighbor making towards the Empire of East Europe.

There are certain strategical positions in the Heartland and Arabia which must be treated as of world importance, for their possession may facilitate or prevent a world domination. It does not, however, follow that it would be wise to commit them forthwith to an untried international administration; here, too, it is very necessary to bear in mind the truth of the Going Concern. Condominium has not, as a rule, been a success, for the reason that the agents of the joint protecting Powers almost inevitably take sides with the local nationalities or parties. The most effective method of international control would seem to be that of commissioning some one Power as trustee for humanity — a different Power, of course, in the case of different positions. That was the method experimentally tried when Austria–Hungary was entrusted with the 'administration of Bosnia and Herzegovina at the Congress of Berlin, and it succeeded so far as the material advancement of the protected provinces was concerned. There is no reason why the new principle and the facts of the Going Concern should not be reconciled in the cases of Panama, Gibraltar, Malta, Suez, Aden, and Singapore, by regarding the American Republic and the British Empire as World Trustees for the peace of the Ocean and of the straits connecting the basins of the Ocean. This, however, would amount merely to a regularization of existing facts. The test of the principle, as of most other World principles, is in connection with the Heartland and Arabia. The Islanders of the world cannot be indifferent to the fate either of

邦关系的数个国家吗？德、俄两国在彼此对抗的过程中，都已发展成了大帝国；但处于中间层的各个民族——即波兰人、波希米亚人、匈牙利人、罗马尼亚人、塞尔维亚人、保加利亚人和希腊人——除非是为了自卫，否则就是不太可能为了其他目的而结成联邦的，而因为他们与德国人、俄国人都大不相同，故可以确信，不管这两个大邻国中的哪一个为了建立一个东欧帝国而形成什么新的组织，这些民族都是会进行抵抗的。

"中心地带"和阿拉伯半岛上都存在着某些战略位置，我们必须认为它们具有全球性的重要性而对其加以郑重对待才行，因为占领这些要地，可以促成或者阻止世界霸权的出现。然而，我们不能因此就得出结论，说把这些要地交给一个未经过考验的国际机构来管理的做法是明智的；在此，我们也极有必要牢牢记住"进行中的事业"的真正面目。通常来说，共管之所以一直都没有成功实施过，原因即在于实施共同保护的各个列强的政府代表，几乎都必定会偏袒当地的某些民族或者政党。国际共管最有效的办法，似乎就是委托某一个强国对人类来进行托管——当然，在不同的情况下应当委托不同的强国才行。柏林会议委托奥匈帝国来管理波斯尼亚和黑塞哥维那两地，尝试的就是这种办法，而从受到保护的那两个省份在物质方面的进步来看，这种方法是获得了成功的。通过让美利坚合众国和大英帝国作为"全球托管国"来维护海上和平、维护连接诸海洋盆地的各个海峡的和平，"进行中的事业"的新原则和诸多客观事实，是没有理由不能与巴拿马、直布罗陀、马耳他、苏伊士、亚丁和新加坡等地的情况保持一致的。然而，这样做不过是把现存的事实加以调整罢了。考验这一原则，跟考验其他大多数全球性的原则一样，涉及"中心地带"和阿拉伯半岛。全世界的岛国人对哥本哈根、君士坦丁堡

Copenhagen or of Constantinople, or yet of the Kiel Canal, for a great Power in the Heartland and East Europe could prepare, within the Baltic and Black Seas, for War on the Ocean. During the present War it has taken the whole naval strength of the Allies to hold the North Sea and the Eastern Mediterranean. An adequate submarine campaign, based on the Black Sea from the beginning of the War, would probably have given security to an army operating overland against the Suez Canal. It follows, therefore, that Palestine, Syria, and Mesopotamia, the Bosporus and the Dardanelles, and the outlets from the Baltic must be internationalized in some manner. In the case of Palestine, Syria, and Mesopotamia, it has been understood that Britain and France would undertake international trusts. Why should we not solve the problem of Constantinople by making that historic city the Washington of the League of Nations? When the network of railways has covered the World-Island, Constantinople will be one of the most accessible places on the globe by Railway, Steamer, and Aeroplane. From Constantinople the leading nations of the West might radiate light through precisely those regions, oppressed during many past centuries, in which light is most to be desired from the point of view of humanity at large; from Constantinople we might weld together the West and the East, and permanently penetrate the Heartland with oceanic freedom.

The Jewish National seat in Palestine will be one of the most important outcomes of the War. That is a subject on which we can now afford to speak the truth. The Jew, for many centuries shut up in the Ghetto, and shut out of most honorable positions in Society, developed in an unbalanced manner and became hateful to the average Christian by reason of his excellent, no less than his deficient, qualities. German penetration has been conducted in the great commercial centers of the world in no small measure by Jewish agency, just as German domination in Southeastern Europe was achieved through Magyar and Turk, with Jewish assistance. Jews are among the

或者基尔运河的命运都不可能漠然视之，因为一个地处"中心地带"和东欧的强国可以在波罗的海和黑海地区内部做好准备，来发动海上战争。在目前这场大战中，协约国为了守住北海和东地中海，动用了全部的海军力量。倘若从大战伊始就以黑海为基地发起一场恰当的潜艇战，十有八九就能保证一支从陆上进击苏伊士运河的陆军的安全。因此，我们可以说巴勒斯坦、叙利亚、美索不达米亚、博斯普鲁斯海峡、达达尼尔海峡以及波罗的海的各个出海口，都必须用某种方式置于国际共管之下才行。至于巴勒斯坦、叙利亚和美索不达米亚，我们已经得知，英、法两国将会承担起对这些地方进行国际托管的义务。为什么我们不能通过把君士坦丁堡变成国际联盟的华盛顿来解决这座历史名城的问题呢？倘若铁路网络覆盖了整个"世界岛"，那么君士坦丁堡就会成为全球经由铁路、汽轮和飞机最容易到达的地点之一了。各个主要的西方国家，也都可以从君士坦丁堡向四周辐射出光明，正好照亮过去许多个世纪以来都受到压迫的那些地区，而从整个人类的角度来看，那些地区都极其渴望着此种光明；我们也可以从君士坦丁堡出发，把西方和东方融为一体，并将无限的自由永远渗透整个"中心地带"。

犹太民族在巴勒斯坦建国，将是此次大战最重大的成果之一。这是我们如今能够实话实说的一个问题。犹太人数百年来都被封锁在聚居区内，且被拒之于大多数受人敬重的社会地位门外；由于在一种不平衡的状态中发展起来，并且既具有杰出的才能也具有并不完善的品质，他们还受到了普通基督徒的嫌恶。日耳曼势力的渗透，在很大程度上是通过犹太人在世界上一些大型的商业中心实施的，就像德国通过马扎尔人和土耳其人、并在犹太人的协助下控制了东南欧地区那样。犹太人也是俄国布尔什维克党人中的

chief of the Bolsheviks of Russia. The homeless, brainful Jew lent himself to such internationalist work, and Christendom has no great right to be surprised by the fact. But you will have no room for these activities in your League of independent, friendly nations. Therefore a National Home, at the physical and historical center of the world, should make the Jew "range" himself. Standards of judgment, brought to bear on Jews by Jews, should result, even among those large Jewish communities which will remain as Going Concerns outside Palestine. This, however, will imply the frank acceptance of the position of a Nationality, which some Jews seek to forget. There are those who try to distinguish between the Jewish religion and the Hebrew race, but surely the popular view of their broad identity is not far wrong.

In the vast and populous regions of Asia and Africa which lie beyond the girdle of the great deserts and plateaux there are Going Concerns, such as the British Raj in India, which it would be folly indeed to shake down in your hurry to realize a world-symmetry for your League of Nations. But it is essential that neither Kiauchau nor East Africa should go back to the Power which took them with a keen strategical eye to the day when armies marching overland should find in each of them a citadel already prepared; which took them, moreover, with the clear intention that the Chinese and the Negroes should be utilized as subsidiary manpower to help in the conquest of the World-Island. What part may ultimately be played by that half of the Human Race which lives in "The Indies" no man can yet foresee, but it is the plain duty of the Insular peoples to protect the Indians and Chinese from Heartland conquest.

German Southwest Africa and the German Australasian Colonies must not be returned; the principle of independence within the League implies that, subject to an International Trust in the case of a few critically important positions, each Nation must be mistress in her own house, and that principle holds in regard to South Africa and Australia. Any other principle would

主要成分之一。无家可归却又头脑精明的犹太人从事此种国际主义者的工作,基督教徒们对此并不应感到惊讶才是。不过,在你们那个由独立、友好的国家所组成的国际联盟里,并不会有从事这些活动的空间。因此,在世界的自然和历史中心成立一个"民族家园",就应该能让犹太人"安置"他们自己了。然后,应当由犹太人制定出针对犹太人的评判标准,即便是那些不在巴勒斯坦地区之内、仍然属于"进行中的事业"的大型犹太人社区,也应当如此。然而,这样做就意味着要毫无保留地承认一个民族的地位,可有些犹太人却想要忘记这一点。有些人想要把犹太教和希伯来种族区分开来,但人们通常认为两者总体来说是一回事,这种观点自然也并没有错得离谱。

亚、非两洲中,在那些处于大沙漠和大高原之外、广袤而人口众多的地区,也有"进行中的事业",比如英国在印度的殖民统治,而在仓促地为你们那个国际联盟实现一种世界性的平衡格局的过程中,不顾及这一点确实是很愚蠢的。不过,胶州湾和东非都不绝应当重新回到德国手中,因为当初德国是带着一种敏锐的战略眼光占领了这些地方,并且看到了有朝一日,对于从陆路推进的军队而言,这些地方就是早已准备妥当的大本营;此外,在占领这些地方的时候德国就有了明确的意图,要把中国人和黑人当作协助德国征服"世界岛"的辅助性人力。现在还没人能够预计,居住在"印度群岛"的那一半人类最终会起到什么样的作用,但保护印度人和中国人免遭来自"中心地带"的征服,却是岛国民族显而易见的责任。

德国占领的西南非洲及其在澳大拉西亚[1]的各个殖民地,都绝不能归还给该国;

[1] Australasian:澳大拉西亚的。澳大拉西亚(Australasia)是澳大利亚、新西兰其及附近南太平洋诸岛的总称,即如今所称的"澳洲"。

英国殖民统治下的印度

leave the seeds of future quarrels and would impede disarmament.

※   ※   ※   ※   ※   ※   ※   ※   ※

So much in respect of the starting of the League and of the Going Concern in the Present. It remains for us to speak of the Going Concern in the Future. Viscount Grey has described the state of mind which will be required when we approach this great International enterprise: is there not something more precise to be said in that matter also?

I have expressed my belief that both Free Trade of the Laissez–faire type and Predatory Protection of the German type are principles of Empire, and that both make for War. Fortunately the younger Britains refused to accept the Free Trade of Manchester; they used the fiscal independence granted to them by the Motherland to pursue that economic ideal which was foreshadowed by the great American statesman, Alexander Hamilton — the ideal of the truly in dependent nation, balanced in all its development. This does not in the least imply that a great international trade should not be done, but it should be a trade so controlled that the effect of it is always tending towards the balance aimed at, and is not accumulating, beyond hope of recovery, economic one–sidedness.

No stable League of Nations appears to me possible if any nation is allowed to practice commercial "penetration", for the object of that penetration is to deprive other nations of their fair share of the more skilled forms of employment, and it is inevitable that a general soreness should ensue in so far as it succeeds. Nor, to speak quite plainly, is there any great difference in result if some nations feel that they are

国际联盟内部的独立原则是指，除去一些极其重要的地区由国际托管国进行管辖外，每个国家都必须自己当家作主，而这一原则对于南非和澳大利亚也同样适用。其他的任何原则，都会埋下将来产生纷争的种子，都会妨碍军备裁减。

※   ※   ※   ※   ※

※   ※   ※   ※

亚历山大·汉密尔顿（1757～1804）。美国的开国元勋和美国宪法的起草人之一，财经专家，美国第一任财政部长。他是美国政党制度的创建者，在美国金融、财政和工业发展史上都占有重要的地位。

关于国际联盟的始创和当前的"进行中的事业"，我们就说到这里吧。我们还需说一说未来的"进行中的事业"。格雷子爵已经描述过我们开始进行这项伟大的国际事业时所必须具备的那种心态：但在这个问题上，我们还有没有更加明确的东西要说呢？

我已经说明过自己的观点，那就是放任式的自由贸易和日耳曼式的掠夺性保护贸易都是帝国的原则，并且两种原则都会导致战争。幸亏，英国那些新兴的自治领都不愿接受曼彻斯特学派的自由贸易观念；这些自治领都利用母国所赋予的财政独立权，以追随伟大的美国政治家亚历山大·汉密尔顿曾经预示过的那种经济理想——即国家真正独立自主、各个方面发展都很均衡的理想。但这绝不是指我们不该进行大规模的国际贸易，而是指此种贸易应当加以管控，使得其结果始终都有助于实现我们所期待的那种平衡，

reduced to the position of hewers and drawers owing to the industrial specialization of another country under the r é gime of unrestricted Cobdenism; wherever an industry is so developed in one country that it can be content with no less than a world-market for its particular products, the economic balance of other countries tends to be upset. No important country, after this War, is going to allow itself to be deprived either of any "key" or of any "essential" industry.[1] By the time you have exhausted these two categories, you will find that you might just as well have adopted the attractive positive ideal of general economic independence instead of being driven from one expedient to another in mere defensive-ness. If you attempt to maintain a negative Cobdenism with exceptions, you will, under the conditions of the world that are opening before us, very soon build up a large and clumsy body of merely ad hoc machineries. A general system of low duties and bounties would enable you to deal quickly and lightly with each difficulty as it develops, because you would have the appropriate machinery of control at your hand. But I am not here going into the detail of these questions of machinery; I am dealing with the question of ideal and aim. The Cobdenite believes that international trade is good in itself, and that specialization as between country and country, provided that it arises blindly under the guidance of natural

---

[1] The distinction between these two terms is not always observed. Key industries are those which, although themselves relatively small, are necessary to other and much greater industries. Thus, for instance, aniline dye-stuffs to the value of two million pounds a year were utilised in Great Britain before the War in textile and paper manufactures of the annual worth of 200 millions. The proportion was something like that of a key to the door which it unlocks. Essential industries there are which have not this character of a small key; such, for instance, in this twentieth century is the steel industry. It is well to preserve the distinction, because different defensive measures may perhaps be needed in the two cases.

并且不会令经济发展的不均衡性日积月累到无望恢复的地步。

在我看来，倘若容许任何国家进行贸易"渗透"的勾当，就不可能有一个稳定可靠的国际联盟，因为那种渗透的目的，是为了剥夺其他国家在较需技能的就业形式方面的份额；假如渗透成功，随之而来的必然就是普遍的愤慨之情。非常坦率地来说，倘若有些国家觉得，它们由于别的国家在践行自由的科布登主义的政权领导下进行产业专业化而沦落成了苦役，那就不会出现什么大不相同的结果；凡是某一产业在一国之内发展到了非得以全世界为市场才能满足销售其特定产品之需要的程度，往往都是会扰乱其他国家的经济平衡的。此次大战之后，没有哪个重要的国家是会任由自己被他国夺走任何"关键"产业或者任何"基础"工业的。〔作者注：人们往往注意不到这两个术语之间的区别。"关键产业"是指本身规模虽然较小、却是其他产业和较大规模产业所必须的那些产业。因此，比如在这次大战前的英国，每年有价值200万英镑的苯胺染料用于年产值达2亿英镑的纺织工业和造纸业。这种关系，跟一把钥匙和它所开之门的关系有点儿类似。"基础工业"并不具有小钥匙的特点；比如在如今的20世纪，基础工业就是钢铁工业。保留这种差别是有道理的，因为在两种情形下可能需要采取不同的防御措施。〕到这两类产业都已经消耗殆尽的时候你就会发现，最好还是选择全面经济独立这种有魅力的积极理想，而不要只是为了防御而被迫去选择一个接一个的权宜之计。倘若你试图带有例外情况地去坚持那种消极的科布登主义，那么在世界展现于我们面前的这些条件下，你很快就会建立起一套庞大、笨重且纯属特设的机构来。一套全面的低关税和低补贴的制度，能让你迅速而又轻松地应对每一个逐步发展的

causes, should not be thwarted. The Berliner, on the other hand, has also encouraged economic specialization among the nations, but he operates scientifically, accumulating in his own country those industries which give most, and most highly-skilled, employment. The result is the same in each case; a Going Concern of Industry grips the nation and deprives it, as well as other nations, of true independence. The resulting differences accumulate to the point of quarrel and collision.

There are three attitudes of mind in regard to the Going Concern which spell tragedy. There is Laissez-faire, which is surrender and fatalism. This attitude produces a condition comparable with that of a disease brought on by self-neglect; the human body is a going concern which, becoming unbalanced in its functions, is organically affected, so that in the end no doctor's advice or even surgeon's scalpel can avail, since to stop the disease means the stoppage of life itself. No doubt it seemed, in the warm sunshine of Britain in the middle of the last century, that the wiser political philosophy was to live for the day and to trust in Providence. Fortunately disease had not progressed to a fatal stage when we came to the surgeon's table in August, 1914. But a million men of military age classified as unfit for military service constitute a symptom which almost makes one thank God that the War came when it did.

The second attitude of mind in relation to the Going Concern is that of Panic. This has been the attitude of Prussia, though it was hidden by the flattering philosophy of the Superman, not less pleasant, while it was credible, than the comforting religion of Laissez-faire. Nakedly stated, however, Kultur meant that, being obsessed with the idea of competition and natural selection, as finally expressed in Darwinism, and being frightened, the Prussians decided that if, in the end, men must come to man-eating in order to survive, they, at any rate, would be the cannibals! So they assiduously cultivated the strength and efficiency of the prize-fighter. But the monster Going Concern into which they developed their country grew hungrier and hungrier,

难题，因为你随时可以使用那种恰当的掌控机制。但是，我在此并不打算详细讨论这些机制的问题；我要阐述的，是理想和目标的问题。科布登主义者认为，国际贸易本身是好的，至于国家与国家之间的专业化，如果是在自然原因的引导下盲目地出现的，就不应当加以阻碍。另一方面，柏林当局也已经鼓励各个邦国进行经济专业化，不过是按照科学的方法来进行的，所以在国内积累起了可以为绝大多数人、可以为技术最熟练的工人提供就业机会的许多产业。这两种情形的结果都相同；产业上的"进行中的事业"控制了国家，并且剥夺了该国和其他国家的真正独立。由此导致的分歧会一步步聚积，直到产生出纷争和冲突的地步。

对于"进行中的事业"，人们有3种态度会招来灾难。首先是自由主义，它相当于投降主义和宿命论。这种态度所导致的情况，可以比作是由于自身疏忽而染上疾病；人体就是一种"进行中的事业"，当人体的各项机能失去平衡之后，器官便会受到感染，以至于到了最后，医嘱甚至是外科医生的手术刀也没什么用处了，因为阻断疾病就意味着终结本身的生命。毋庸置疑，在上个世纪中期不列颠和煦的阳光普照之下，较为明智的政治哲学似乎打算过一天算一天，并且打算听天由命。幸好，当1914年8月我们躺上外科医生的手术台时，我们的疾病还没有发展到无可救药的程度。但是，有100万适龄男子被划定为不适于服兵役，这实际上就是一种病症，几乎让人们在战争爆发的时候还谢天谢地呢。

关于"进行中的事业"的第二种态度，就是惊慌失措。普鲁士一直都持这样一种态度，尽管那种擅长吹捧的超人哲学掩盖了他们的惊慌失措；在这种超人哲学合理可信的时候，它与令人安逸的自由主义信仰一样讨人喜欢。然而实话实说，德国文化就是指：

and at last they had to let it feed. Half the cruel and selfish things which are done in this world are done for reasons of Panic.

The third attitude is that of the Anarchist and the Bolshevik — they would distinguish no doubt between themselves, but whether you break the Going Concern or take it to pieces makes little practical difference. This attitude means social suicide. It is vital that discipline should be maintained in the Western Democracies during the period of Reconstruction, whatever Bolshevism may happen in Central as well as East Europe. The Westerners are the Victors, and they alone are able to prevent the whole world from having to pass through the cycle so often repeated in the case of individual nations — Idealism, Disorder, Famine, Tyranny. Provided that we do not hasten to dismantle running social machinery, but accomplish our ideals by successive acts of social discipline, we shall maintain the steady output of production, the fundamental Reality, that is to say, on which now, more than ever before, Civilization rests. The disorder of a whole world, let us not forget, implies the absence of any remaining National base as a fulcrum for the restoration of order, and therefore the indefinite prolongation of Anarchy and Tyranny. It took several centuries to attain again to the stage of civilization which had been reached when the Roman World of Antiquity broke down.

But if drifting in the grip of the Going Concern leads to disease in a nation, and if we must not fall into panic because that results in crime, nor yet suffer revolt because that ends in suicide, what course remains open to us? Surely that of control, which in a democracy means self–control. If this War has proved anything, it has proved that these gigantic forces of modern production are capable of control. Beforehand it was assumed by many that a World–War would bring so general a financial crash that it would not — could not — be allowed to take place. Yet

由于沉迷于达尔文主义最终表述的那种弱肉强食、物竞天择的观念，同时内心又惊慌失措，所以普鲁士人决定，如果人类最终必须依靠相互残食才能生存下去，那么普鲁士人无论如何都会是食人者的角色！因此他们才孜孜不倦地培养出职业拳击手那样的实力和效率来。但是，他们让自己的国家逐渐变成了一头"进行中的事业"的怪兽，而这头怪兽又越来越饥饿，以至于普鲁士人最终不得不任由它去寻找猎物为食了。这个世界上发生的残暴之事与自私之事，半数都是因为内心惊慌失措而干出来的。

第三种态度，便是无政府主义者和布尔什维克的态度——他们无疑是认为彼此有别的，但无论是打碎"进行中的事业"还是把它拆成碎片，实际上并无差别。这种态度意味着群体性自杀。在重建期间，无论布尔什维克主义在东欧和中欧地区可能挑起什么样的事端，西方民主国家都应当保持克制，这一点是至关重要的。西欧各国是战胜国，只有它们才能让全世界不至于像个别国家一再出现的局面那样，不至于陷入理想主义、混乱、饥馑和暴政的恶性循环中去。倘若我们不去仓促地拆除运行中的社会机器，而是通过保持克制的一系列行动来实现我们的理想，就会维护好生产稳定这个根本现实——也就是说，维护好文明在如今比以往更需倚赖的那种现实。我们不要忘记，如果整个世界混乱不堪，那就意味着没有留下任何可作为恢复秩序的支点的国家基地，从而导致无休无止的无政府状态和暴政。古罗马解体之后，人类就用了好几个世纪才再次回复到过去已经达到的那种文明程度。

但是，假如任由"进行中的事业"摆布会导致一个国家产生弊端，假如我们绝不能惊慌（因为惊慌会导致错误行为）、也绝不能容忍叛乱（因为叛乱会以自杀告终），那我们还可以选择什么样的道路呢？我们无疑还可以选择控制之路，而在民主国家里，这

how easily, when it actually befell, were the British and German systems of credit disengaged by the simple device of using the national credits to carry the roots of individual credit which were pulled out of the enemy soil.

If you once admit control of the Going Concern to be your aim, then the ideal State-unit of your League must be the nation of balanced economic development. Raw materials are unequally distributed over the world, but the primary pursuits of men, other than the growing of the staples of food proper to each region, form in these days but a relatively small part of the total of Industry. Minerals must be won in the mines and tropical produce can only be grown within the tropics, but both minerals and tropical produce are now easy of transport, and the higher industries may, therefore, be located at the choice and will of mankind. We are what our occupations make us; every mature man is imprinted with the characteristics of his calling. So is it with the nations, and no self-respecting nation henceforth will allow itself to be deprived of its share of the higher industries. But these industries are so interlocked that they cannot be developed except in balance one with another. It follows, therefore, that each nation will strive for development in each great line of industrial activity, and should be allowed to attain to it.

This is the ideal, I am firmly persuaded, which will make for peace. In ordinary society it is notoriously difficult for people of very unequal fortune to be friends in the true sense; that beautiful relationship is not compatible with patronage and dependence. Civilization, no doubt, consists in the exchange of services, but it should be an equal exchange. Our economics of money have assessed as equal services of very unequal value from the point of view of the quality of the industrial employment which they give. For the contentment of nations we must contrive to secure some equality of opportunity for national development.

条道路就是指自我控制。假如说这次大战证明了什么的话，那就是证明了现代化生产的巨大力量是可以控制的。以前许多人都想当然地认为，一场世界大战会带来全面的经济崩溃，因此人们不会也不可能允许爆发这样的战争。但当战争真的爆发之后，英、德两国的信贷体系便多么轻而易举地分道扬镳了啊；它们所用的办法也很简单，那就是用国家信贷来容纳从敌国土壤里拔出来的个人信贷之根。

如果你们曾经承认你们的目标是控制"进行中的事业"，那你们的国际联盟中理想的成员国就必定是经济发展均衡的国家。世界各地的原材料分布并不均匀，但除了在每个地区种植相应的主要粮食作物，人类首要的那些事业如今在整个工业中都只占有相对较小的一部分。矿物须从矿山开采得来，而热带产品也只能在热带地区种植，但矿产和热带产品如今运输起来都很便利，因此高等产业可以按照人类的选择和意愿来分布了。我们是自己的职业造就的：每一个成年之人，都会留下各自职业特征的烙印。对于国家来说，也是如此：自此以后，没有哪个自尊自重的国家会容许他国来剥夺自己应有的那些高等产业。不过，这些高等产业交织得如此紧密，除非彼此之间保持平衡，否则它们都无法发展起来。因此我们可以得出结论说，每个国家在工业活动中的每一个大的领域中都会努力发展，而我们都应当容许它们实现这一目标才是。

我坚信，这就是能够带来和平局面的理想。在普通社会里，贫富极其悬殊的人很难成为真正意义上的朋友，这一点尽人皆知；此种美好的关系是与施舍和依赖格格不入的。文明无疑在于交换服务，但此种交换应为平等的交换才是。我们的货币经济学，就是把从服务业赋予产业就业率的质量这一角度来看那些价值极不相等的服务看作是同等的服务。为了让各国都感到满意，我们必须努力确保各国都获得某种平等发展的机会才是。

VII THE FREEDOM OF MEN

From the consideration of the Realities presented by the geography of our globe we have come to the conclusion that if the Freedom of Nations is to be secure, it must rest on a reasonable approach to equality of resources as between a certain number of the larger Nations. We have also seen that, given the imperious Reality of the Going Concern, it is necessary that the Nations should be so controlled in their economic growth that they do not tend to get out of hand and clash. But what have these principles to do with the Freedom of Men and Women? Will free Nations in a League be able to give more freedom to their citizens? Certainly the men who have been fighting, the men who have been sailing our ships through danger on the seas, and the mothers and wives who have been working, waiting, and mourning at home, are not looking for the mere defeat of a danger that threatened; they have positive visions of greater happiness in their own lives or in the lives of those dear to them.

第七章　人的自由

研究了地球的地形地貌呈现给我们的各种现实情况之后，我们已经得出了下述结论：要想确保各个国家的自由，那么一些大国之间必须采取一种平均分配资源的合理办法。我们也已看到，考虑到"进行中的事业"这种紧迫的现实，必须控制各国的经济增长速度，以免它们失控并发生冲突。不过，这些原则跟每一个男人和女人的自由又有什么样的关系呢？国际联盟中的那些自由国家，能够给予本国公民更多的自由吗？确实，对于那些一直在战斗的人，那些一直驾驶着舰船历经危险在海上航行的人，那些一直在家工作、等待并且悲伤的母亲和妻子们来说，他们所盼望的并非只是打败面临的某种危险；他们还有着积极乐观的梦想，要让自己或者亲人在生活中获得更大的幸福。

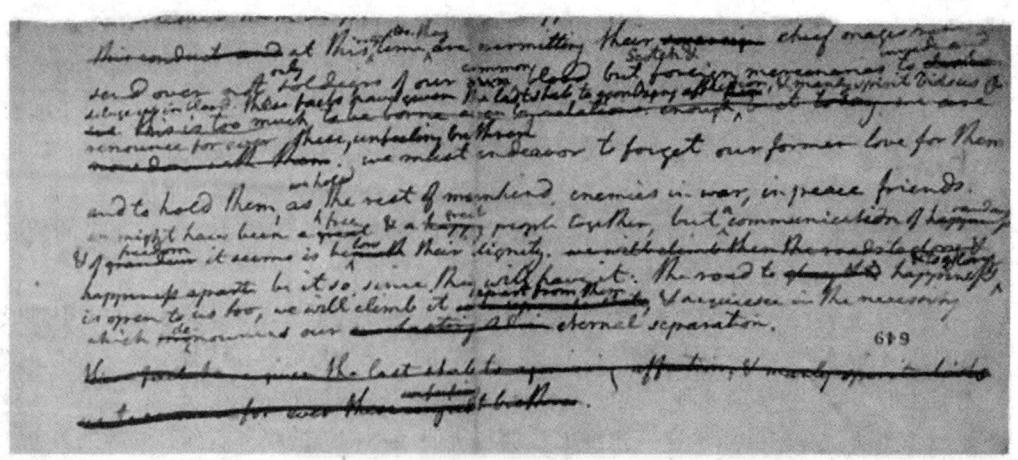

美国《独立宣言》手稿

Let us analyze from this point of view the successive stages of democratic idealism which were referred to in the opening pages of this book. The American Declaration of Independence claimed for all men the right to pursue happiness. The French Revolution crystallized this phrase into the single word Liberty, and added Equality, which implies control, and Fraternity, which implies self-control. Fraternity is of the essence of successful democracy, the highest but the most difficult of all modes of government, since it demands most of the average citizen. That is the first cycle of democratic thought; it pertains directly and obviously to the Freedom of Men.

In the middle of the nineteenth century began the second cycle, which has aimed at the Freedom of Nations. The claim of Nationality is to the right of a local group of men to pursue happiness together, with their own ways of control to secure equality among them. Fraternal feeling is not easy of attainment unless you have been brought up together; hence the part played by History in the National sentiment. But mere Nationalism claims only the right to pursue happiness together; it is not until we come to the League of Nations that we advance to an ideal which has been thought out to a stage equivalent to that of the great trilogy of the French Revolution. Some degree of control by the League is admittedly necessary to secure the equality of nations before the law, and I believe that in the ideal of the balanced development of each nation we have the self-control which is implied in fraternity. Without balanced development nations are sure to acquire special hungers, whether neglectfully or criminally, which can only be satisfied at the expense of other nations. In other words, we can only permanently secure equality among the nations by control from within as well as from without. But this involves the statement that home politics must be conducted with an eye to their effect on foreign politics, a truism in the superficial sense, but carrying deeper implications than are commonly admitted.

我们不妨从此种观点来分析一下民主理想主义相继经历过的各个阶段，这一点在本书开头部分曾经提到过。美国的《独立宣言》称，人人都有追求幸福的权利。法国大革命把这句话具体概括成了"自由"一词，并且加上了意指"控制"的"平等"一词，以及含有"自制"意义的"博爱"一词。"博爱"是成功的民主思想的精华，是所有政体形式中最高级、却也是最难实现的一种，因为它对普通公民的要求最高。这就是民主思想的第一个时代，它直接而明显地与人的自由相关联。

民主思想的第二个时代始于19世纪中叶，目标是获得民族自由。要求民族独立，就是要求局部群体拥有共同追求幸福、并用自己的控制方式确保群体之间平等的权利。除非人们是一起长大的，否则就很难拥有博爱感；因此，历史在民族情感中发挥了很大的作用。不过，纯粹的民族主义只是要求拥有共同追求幸福的权利；我们直到有了国际联盟，才进而想出了一个达到与法国大革命那三个伟大口号之境界相当的理想。人们一致认为，必须对国联进行某种程度的控制，才能确保各国在法律面前平等；而我认为，在各国平衡发展这一理想状况中，我们也拥有"博爱"一词所指的自制思想。倘若发展不均衡，那么无论是毫无顾忌还是应受谴责，各国必定都会产生种种特殊的欲望，只有通过牺牲别国利益才能满足这些欲望。换言之就是，我们只能既从外部、又从内部加以控制，才能确保各国之间永远平等相待。不过，这一点也包括了下述这种说法：在实施内政时，必须考虑到内政对国际政治的影响。虽然从表面来看道理是不言而喻的，但此种说法中，却还含有人们通常并未明白的一些深层意义。

It carries, I believe, this implication among others, that, since nations are local societies, their organization must, if they are to last, be based dominantly on local communities within them, and not on nation-wide "interests". That is the old English idea of the House of Commons. The word commons is, of course, identical with the French word "communes", signifying communities; the House of Communities — shires and burghs — would be the true modern translation. As a fact, the knights and the burgesses of the Middle Ages represented communities of far more complete and balanced life than the artificially equalized constituencies of today.

If the real organization of the Nation be by classes and interests — and that is the alternative to organization by localities[1] — it is quite inevitable that the corresponding classes in neighboring nations will get themselves together, and that what has been described as the horizontal cleavage of international society will ensue. Fortunately the Tower of Babel was the beginning of

[1] As has been pointed out by Mr. H. G. Wells, though he would — wrongly as I think — yield to current tendencies and accept organization by "interests".

赫伯特·乔治·威尔斯（Herbert George Wells, 1866～1946）。英国著名小说家，尤以科幻小说创作闻名于世，1895年出版《时间机器》一书而成名。他还是一位社会改革家和预言家，撰写过大量关注现实、思考未来的作品。

我觉得，这一说法当中还包含着下面这层意思：由于所有国家都是局部社会，所以要想长久存在下去，它们的组织就必须主要是以国内的局部社区为基础，而不能以全国性的"利益集团"为基础。这正是古代英国人对"下议院"一词的看法。当然，"平民"（commons）这个词等同于法语中的"大多数"（communes）一词，都是指社区；所以"下议院"真正的现代译名，应该是"社区（包括郡和自治市）议院"。实际上，中世纪的爵士议员和自治市议员代表了完整得多、生活也要均衡得多的社区，而如今社区中的选民则是人为地平衡过来的。

如果真正的国家是按照阶级和利益集团组织起来的——这是另一种按照地区来建立国家机构的组织办法［作者注：这是H·G·威尔斯先生所指出来的，虽然他也会屈从于当前的潮流并承认按照"利益集团"来建立的组织，不过我认为他这样做是错误的。］——那么各个邻国中对应的阶级就必定会团结起来，并且随之就会出现被称为国际社会横向分裂的局面。幸好，巴别塔[1]是某些大规模的"进行中的事业"的开端，而此种"进行中的事业"就是我们所知的语言，它们已经妨碍了国际间的友好合作。不过，现代

[1] Tower of Babel：巴别塔。据《圣经》创世记第11章记载，它是当时人类联合起来兴建、希望能够通往天堂的一座高塔。为了阻止人类这一计划，上帝便让人类说不同的语言，使之无法沟通，因此人类的这一计划失败了，而人类自此也各散东西。亦译作巴贝尔塔、巴比伦塔或通天塔。

certain great Going Concerns known as Languages, and these have impeded internationalism. But the development of the modern struggle between capital and labor has led to the use of some international phrases and words which have carried a few key ideas into common currency; they correspond unfortunately to certain social Realities which were rapidly gathering importance when this War came upon us. International Combines of Capital were obtaining such power as to overawe some of the smaller States of the world, and they were being used by Germany for purposes of penetration, or, in other words, to wreck the economic and social balance of rival nations. Labor could only follow suit, and also try to organize internationally. So came the idea of class warfare between the international proletariat and international capitalism. During the progress of the War we have gone to great trouble to break up the international organization of Capital. Is Labor now to reverse all that has been achieved in this respect by persisting with an international organization which sprang into existence for the very right purpose of fighting International Capital? No less than such a reversal is involved if the momentum of internationally organized labor becomes powerful, for a resuscitation of International Capitalism would then be inevitable. The economic war that would ensue could only end either in general Bolshevism or in the victory of one of the parties, and that party would then become the real Government of the World, a new Empire of organizers. If labor were to win, it would soon be found that Labor organizers would not differ from their Military and Capitalist predecessors in the essential respect that they would cling to power and continue blindly to organize until brought down by a new revolution. So the wheels of History would revolve again with the same recurrent phases of disorder and tyranny, and future students would be taught to recognize one more "Age", that of the Proletariat, following on the Ages of Ecclesiasticism, Militarism, and Capitalism. Become supreme, the Labor leaders of the future would no more hesitate to use machine-guns against the mob than any other panic-stricken riders of the whirlwind.

劳资之间斗争的发展已经导致人们开始使用一些国际性的短语和词汇，这些短语和词汇又把一些重要的观念变成了普遍流行的思想；不幸的是，它们与某些社会现实保持着一致，而在这次大战降临到我们头上的时候，这些现实也正在迅速变得日益重要起来。国际资本联合企业的势力正蒸蒸日上，以至于威慑到了世界上那些较小的国家；它们又被德国利用来进行渗透，或者换句话说，它们被德国利用去破坏敌对国家的经济和社会平衡。劳工们只能仿效这种做法，也试图形成国际性的组织。这样，就出现了国际无产阶级和资本主义之间进行阶级斗争的思想。在此次大战不断发展的过程中，我们费了九牛二虎之力才拆散这种国际间的资本组织。难道劳工阶层如今还要坚持成立那个只为对抗国际资本这一正确目标而形成的国际组织，让我们在这个方面所取得的一切成就都打回原形吗？倘若在国际范围内组织起来的劳工阶层的动力变得很强大，那么就会出现不亚于上述那种倒退的情况，因为到了那个时候，国际资本主义必然会复兴。随后可能会发生的那种经济战争的结果，只能是全面实现布尔什维克主义，或者是其中某一方取胜，而这一方接下来便会变成一个真正的世界政府，变成一个新的组织者的帝国。如果劳工阶层获胜，那么我们很快就会看出，劳工阶层的组织者们在本质上跟他们的前任——即军人和资本家——并没有什么区别，他们同样会紧抓权力并且继续盲目地组织，直到被一场新的革命推翻。这样，历史的车轮便会再一次转动，反复出现同样的混乱时期和暴政阶段，而将来的学生便得多去学习一个"时代"的知识——即在教会主义时代、军国主义时代和资本主义时代之后，还要加上一个无产阶级时代了。一旦大权在握，将来的劳工领袖可能就会与其他那些惊慌失措、叱咤风云的人物一样，毫不犹豫地用机枪来对付民众了。

But if it be held that organization based on local communities is essential to the stable and therefore peaceable life of Nations, then those local communities must have as complete and balanced a life of their own as is compatible with the life of the Nation itself. In no other way can you prevent a "class and interest" organization from crossing powerfully your locality organization. As long as you allow a great metropolis to drain most of the best young brains from the local communities, to cite only one aspect of what goes on, so long must organization center unduly in the metropolis and become inevitably an organization of nation-wide classes and interests. I believe that whether we look at the matter from the point of view of the freedom of men or of nations we shall come to the same conclusion; that the one thing essential is to displace class organization, with its battle-cries and merely palliative remedies, by substituting an organic ideal, that of the balanced life of provinces, and under the provinces of the lesser communities.

※　　　※　　　※　　　※　　　※　　　※　　　※　　　※　　　※

Let us approach the matter from the other end of the argument, that of the Freedom of Men. What does the ordinary man want? Mill says that after food and home he wants liberty, but the more modern democrat lays stress not merely on freedom to take Opportunity, but on the equality of Opportunity itself. It is for Opportunity to realize what is in him, to live a life of ideas and of action for the realization of those ideas, that the healthy man — in ever-increasing number — is asking. His ideas may be of love and of the noble upbringing of his children, or of his craft and delight in his dexterity, or of religion and the saving of souls, or of excellence in sport of some kind, or of the constitution of society and its improvement, or of the appreciation of beauty and of artistic expression; but in one way or another he wishes for the glow of intelligent life, and incidentally for a recognition of his human dignity.

但是，倘若我们认为各国要想过上稳定而太平的日子，必须在局部社区的基础上进行组织的话，那么这些局部社区就必定有着与国家本身一样完整而平衡的生活。除此之外，并没有别的办法能够阻止一个"阶级和利益"组织来有力地妨碍到你们的局部组织。只要你们允许一个大都市从各个局部社区中挖走大部分出类拔萃的年轻人才，组织就必然会过度持久地集中在这个大都市里，并且必然会变成一个全国性的阶级和利益集团的组织；这种情况，不过是目前形势的一个方面罢了。我认为，无论是从人的自由还是从国家自由的角度来看待这个问题，我们都会得出一个相同的结论：我们的第一要务，应当是用一种基本的理想——即各个省份生活均衡、而省以下各个较小社区也均衡发展的理想——来取代阶级组织，连同阶级组织的战斗口号及其那些纯属治标不治本的改良措施。

※　　　※　　　※　　　※　　　※　　　※　　　※　　　※　　　※

我们不妨从人的自由的这一观点的另一端来看一看这个问题。普通人需要的是什么呢？穆勒曾经说过，除了饮食和家庭，人类还需要自由；而更为现代化的民主主义者并非仅仅看重抓住机会的自由，还强调机会本身的均等性。健全之人——这种人的数量正与日俱增——要求的，是实现抱负的机会，是过上一种有着种种思想并用行动来实现这些思想之人生的机会。这种人的思想可能是关于爱、关于体面地将子女抚养成人的，可能是关于自己掌握的技艺以及对自己具有一己之长而感到快乐的，可能是关于宗教和拯救人类灵魂的，可能是关于擅长某种体育运动的，可能是关于社会体制以及社会改良的，也可能是关于美的欣赏和艺术表达的；但不管如何，这种人都渴望着获得智慧生活的光芒，并且同时也希望自己的人格尊严得到他人的认同。

穆勒（James Mill，1773～1836）。19世纪英国的
著名经济学家和哲学家，也是功利主义的创始人，著有
《精神分析》（Analysis of the Mind）等作品。

萧伯纳

By general elementary education we have begun to teach the art of manipulating ideas to those who in Ancient Society were slaves. The wholly unlettered man thinks only in concrete terms; therefore it was that the great religious teachers have spoken slowly in parables. The unlettered man is not open either to the pleasures or the dangers of idealism. Undoubtedly our Western communities are passing through a dangerous stage in this generation. Half-educated people are in a very susceptible condition, and the world today consists mainly of half-educated people. They are capable of seizing ideas, but they have not attained to the habit of testing them and of suspense of mind in the meantime. In other words, most people today are very open to "suggestion", a fact well known to the experienced in elections, who rarely stop to reason with their audiences. Suggestion is the method of the German propagandist.

Now the expression "Equality of Opportunity" involves two things. In the first place control, because, given average human nature, there cannot be equality without control; and in the second place it implies freedom to do and nott merely to think, or, in other words,

通过普及基础教育，我们已经开始把操纵别人思想的手段教给那些在古代社会里当奴隶的人了。完全没有受过教育的人，只会实打实地考虑问题；因此，宗教大师才会对他们慢慢地讲道。没有受过教育的人，既不会接纳理想主义所带来的种种欢乐，也不会承受理想主义所带来的各种危险。毋庸置疑，我们的西方社会在如今这个世代正经历着一个危险的阶段。没有完整地接受教育的人极其容易受到他人的影响，而如今这个世界却主要是由没有接受过完整教育的人所组成的。虽说他们能够理解各种思想，但他们却没有养成检验这些思想、并且同时不仓促地下结论的习惯。换言之就是，如今大多数人都很容易接受"暗示"；那些经验丰富的竞选者都很清楚这一事实，所以他们在竞选演说中很少停下来跟听众讲道理。"暗示"正是德国的宣传人员所利用的方法。

如今，"机会均等"这个表达涉及两个方面。首先是控制，因为考虑到普通的人性，不进行控制就不可能实现平等；其次，它意味着行动自由而不仅仅是思想自由，

opportunity to bring ideas to the test of action. Mr. Bernard Shaw says that "He who can, does; he who cannot, teaches." If you interpret the words "can" and "cannot" as implying opportunity and lack of opportunity, then this rather cynical epigram conveys a vital truth.[1] Those who are allowed opportunities of testing their ideas become responsible thinkers, but those who get no such opportunity may continue, for a time, to enjoy ideas, but irresponsibly and, as we say, academically. The latter condition is precisely that of a large part of our intelligent newspaper-reading working classes today, and some of them know it and regret it.

What is the bane of our modern industrial life? Surely monotony — monotony of work and of a petty social and communal life. No wonder our men took refuge before the War in betting on football. Most of the responsible decisions are reserved for a few, and those few are not even seen at their work, for they are away in the big centers.

What is it that in the last two or three generations has given such strength to the Nationality movement? Nationality had no great hold in the Middle Ages, or indeed in Modern Times until the nineteenth century. It has arisen as the modern States have not only increased in size, but have also grasped wider functions within the Community. Nationalist movements are based on the restlessness of intelligent young men who wish for scope to live the life of ideas and to be among those who "can" because they are allowed to do. In the old Greek and in the Mediaeval World, Society was so loosely knit that there was plenty of scope in any considerable town. Is it not that fact which makes town-history so interesting until we come to the eighteenth century and then so banal? Take up the history of one of our more significant British cities,

[1] Bernard Shaw, Man and Superman, 12th edition, p. 280.

或者换句话来说，就是包含了用行动检验思想的机会。萧伯纳先生曾经说过："有能者为，无能者教。"假如我们把"有能"和"无能"分别理解成"有机会"和"没有机会"，那么这句极为嘲讽的隽语则表达出了一种至关重要的真理。［作者注：参见萧伯纳所著的《人与超人》第12版，第230页。］那些拥有机会检验自己思想的人，都变成了可靠的思想家，而那些没有获得此种机会的人虽说暂时可能还会产生出一些想法，但它们都是不可靠的，并且像我们所说的那样，它们也都是一些脱离了实际的空想。后面这种情况，恰恰就是如今大部分能够阅读报纸的工人阶层的情况，其中有些人也明白这一点并为此感到遗憾。

我们现代的工业生活的致命祸根又是什么呢？无疑就是单调——比如工作上的单调，比如琐碎的社交和集体生活中的单调。所以在此次大战之前，我们的人都去赌足球以求逃避，这种做法就不足为奇了。绝大多数责任重大的决策，都是留给少数人去决定的，但人们甚至看不到这些人上班，因为他们都在一些遥远的大型中心城市里。

在最近两、三个世代的时间里，是什么赋予了民族运动如此巨大的力量呢？在中世纪，民族主义并没有多大的影响力，实际上民族主义在19世纪之前的近代都没有什么影响力。它是随着现代各国非但疆域扩大、而且在社会中发挥着更多作用而兴起的。民族主义运动是建立在有知识的年轻人不安于现状这一基础之上的，他们都希望能够发挥出自己的才干，过上一种有思想的生活，并且加入那些"有能者"之列，因为社会允许他们那样去做。在古希腊时代和中世纪，整个社会都松散得很，因此任何一个重要城镇中都有着大量的发展机会。使得18世纪以前的城镇史非常有意思、而此后的城镇史却乏味透顶的，不正是这一事实吗？我们不妨以英国一座较为重要的城市的历史为例，来看一

and see whether that be not true. When you come to the last few generations it becomes mere statistic of material growth; at the best the town becomes specialized in some important way, but it ceases to be a complete organism. All its institutions are second-rate, because its best people have gone away, unless it have some one establishment or industry of more than local fame, and that establishment or industry usually crushes rather than develops real local life.

Why were Athens and Florence the wonderful founts of Civilization which have made them the teachers of the world? They were small cities as we now count the size of cities, but they were sovereign cities both in the political and economic sense. The men who shook hands in their streets, and whose families intermarried, were not merely rival masters in the same industry or competing merchants on the same exchange; every principal category of supreme human activity was represented in one intimate circle. Think of the choice of activities open to the able young Florentine, to be practiced, remember, in and for his native town, and with no need to go away to some distant capital. Instead of Mayor he might be Prime Minister; instead of captain of Territorials he might be a general leading the town-force in actual battle — a small battle no doubt, but enough to give the fullest scope to the activity of his mind; if he were a painter, sculptor, or architect he would be employed on the monuments of his own place instead of seeing them designed by some visiting great man. Of course no one suggests that you should or could return to institutions on the Athenian or Florentine scale, but the fact remains that you have drained your local life of most of its value and interest by the development of nation-wide class organization.

Are you quite sure that the gist of the demand for Home Rule in Ireland, and in a less degree in Scotland, does not come mainly from young men who are agitating, though they do

看这种说法是不是正确。翻到该市最近数个世代的时候，该市历史便会变成纯属物质增长的统计数据；该市充其量也不过是以某种重要的方式实现了专业化，但已经不再是一个完整的有机体系了。所有的公共机构都不会是一流的，因为该市的精英都会离它而去了，除非此处拥有某一个远近闻名的企业或者拥有某一种名闻遐迩的产业；可此种企业或者产业往往也会毁掉当地的自然生活，而不会是让当地的自然生活变得更好。

雅典和佛罗伦萨为何会成为杰出的文明之源，并因此而变成了整个世界的导师呢？根据我们如今衡量城市大小的标准，这两处都是小城市，但在政治和经济意义上，它们却都是独立自主的城市。那些在大街上握手、家族间相互通婚的人，并非只是同一行业里的竞争对手或者只是在同一交易场所彼此竞争的商人；人类每一种主要的高级活动，都在一个关系亲密的圈子里得到了体现。想想一名年轻能干的佛罗伦萨人有多少机会可以选择自己的事业吧；我们还须记住，他是在生于斯长于斯的这个城市里从业，并且是为了这个城市而从业的，根本就无需到很远的某个首都去。他不会去当市长，却有可能当上首相；他不会去当一个地方长官，却有可能去当一个将军，率领着本城的武装力量，真正去与敌人作战——毋庸置疑，虽说这会是一种小规模的战斗，但也足以最为充分地发挥出他的聪明才智了；倘若他是一名画师、雕刻师或者建筑师，那么就会有人雇他去从事当地纪念物的建筑工作，而不是让他看着这些建筑由某个来访的大人物来设计。当然，我们并不是说你们应当或者可以回到雅典和佛罗伦萨时期的制度中去，不过事实仍然是，你们通过发展全国性的阶级组织，已经让本地生活中的绝大部分重要性和利益都流失掉了。

你们能否十分肯定地说，爱尔兰要求自治——苏格兰也是如此，只是程度没那么严

not fully realize it, for equality of opportunity rather than against the assumed wickedness of England? The Bohemians have achieved a very remarkable economic prosperity under the Austrian tyranny, and yet they fight for their Czecho-Slovak Nationality, Is there not something of the same human truth in the refractoriness of the shop stewards in our factories against the Union Executives away in London offices?

It is the principle of Laissez-faire which has played such havoc with our local life. For a hundred years we have bowed down before the Going Concern as though it were an irresistible God. Undoubtedly it is a Reality, but it can be bent to your service if you have a policy inspired by an ideal. Laissez-faire was no such policy; it was mere surrender to fate. You tell me that centralization is the "tendency" of the age: I reply to you that it is the blind tendency of every age — was it not said nineteen hundred years ago that "to him that hath shall be given"?

Consider the growth of London. A population of a million a century ago has risen to be more than seven millions today; or, to state the fact with more essential point, the London of a century ago contained a sixteenth of the population of England and now it has a fifth. How has it come about? When Parliament was originally set up, you had not only to pay the members to get them to attend, so busy were they with their absorbing local life, but before long you had also to find the communities which failed to elect their representatives. That was the right condition of things, a federalization against strong local magnetisms. When Macadamized roads were introduced a star of them was made, radiating from London; they brought the life of the country up to London, sapping it for the growth of London. When the railways were constructed the main lines formed a star from London, and the expresses run up and down, feeding London, milking

重罢了——的主要依据，并非主要源自年轻人呢？尽管并没有充分实现，但那些年轻人都是在鼓吹机会均等，而不是在反抗那种虚构的英格兰的穷凶极恶。在奥地利的暴政统治之下，波希米亚人虽然达到了一种非同寻常的经济繁荣局面，但也仍在为建立他们的捷克斯洛伐克这个国家而斗争着。这种情况，与我们的工会代表桀骜不驯地同远在伦敦办公室里的工会管理人员对着干的现象之间，难道没有相同的人性上的真理吗？

让我们的本地生活陷入巨大混乱当中的，正是自由主义的原则。100年来，我们都在"进行中的事业"面前卑躬屈膝，好像"进行中的事业"就是一个无可抗拒的上帝似的。毋庸置疑，"进行中的事业"是一种现实，不过，倘若你们在理想的启示之下制定出一种政策，那就可以让"进行中的事业"向你们屈服、为你们服务了。自由主义并不属于此种政策；它纯粹就是向命运举手投降。你们对我说，中央集权是如今这个时代的"大势所趋"；而我则要回答你们，不管是在哪个时代，这都是一种盲目的趋势——1900年前，不是就有人说过"已经拥有者，上天当给予更多"这句话吗？

我们不妨来细想一下伦敦的发展过程。伦敦的人口在一个世纪以前是100万，如今已经增长到了700多万；或者，不妨用更加关键的一点来说明这个事实：一个世纪以前，伦敦的人口才占整个英国人口的1/16，如今却已占到1/5了。这种情况，是怎样演变而来的呢？最初国会刚刚成立的时候，因为国会议员都忙于很有意思的当地生活，所以你们不但要花钱请他们来出席会议，而且不久之后又不得不去给那些没有推选出代表的社区提供资金。那是当时的正常状况，即联邦化与当地强大的吸引力相互对抗。而引入"碎石铺路法"之后，便开始从伦敦向四周辐射而形成了一种星状路网；它们把乡村的活力带到了伦敦，为了伦敦的发展而消耗乡村的活力。等铁路修建起来之后，各条干线又以伦敦为中心形成了一个星状铁路网，其间快车来来去去，用乡村之奶来哺育伦敦。不久之后，国家必

19世纪的伦敦

the country. Presently the State also must needs step in to accentuate the centralizing tendency by establishing such services as the parcel post. Thus it has come about that the market-towns for a hundred miles around are degraded in respect of the variety of their life.

Not in four out of five cases does the Londoner profit in any true sense from the change. He lives in a suburb; he is shot through a tube to an office-room in the City, and then shot back to his bedroom in the suburb; only on Saturdays and Sundays has he time for communal life, and then he amuses himself with neighbors who are tied to him by nothing essential. In the great majority of cases he never comes into living contact with a large and trained mind except through the printed page: for him, as for the industrial worker in the country, his life of ideas is detached from his responsible life, and both suffer infinitely in consequence.

Centralization, however, is only one form of a more general process which I would call the segregation of social and economic functions owing to the national fatalism in the presence of the Going Concern. You have allowed industrial life to crowd certain districts and to leave other districts poor. I grant that in the past that was inevitable to some extent owing to the need of generating power near the collieries, but not to the extent that has occurred. By proper control you could have substituted a "village region", with a community dependent on each factory or group of small factories, wherein rich and poor, masters and men, might have been held together in a neighborly responsible relationship; but you have allowed instead the East and West Ends to grow up in your great cities. Surely the essential characteristic of true statesmanship is foresight, the prevention of social disease; but our method for a century past has been to drift, and when

定需要介入进来，通过建立起诸如小包邮递之类的服务机构来加强此种集中化趋势。如此一来，就使得方圆100英里的那些商业城镇在生活的多样性方面都慢慢恶化下去了。

从这种变化中，伦敦人并非是十有八九都能够获得真正意义上的好处的。伦敦人都住在市郊；他们乘坐地铁飞速赶到城里的办公室，下班后又飞速返回市郊的家中；他们只是到了星期六和星期日才有社交生活的时间，那时他们会与邻居们一起自娱自乐，而这些邻居与他们之间的联系并无重要之处。在绝大多数情况下，除了通过书报，他们从来都不会与那些知识渊博而又训练有素的人发生真正的接触：对于他们来说，那种有着诸多想法的人生与他们那种可靠的生活脱了节，结果两种人生都会遭受无穷无尽的苦难；这种情况，对于乡间的产业工人而言也是如此。

然而，中央集权不过是某种更普遍之进程的一种形式罢了；我将此种进程称为因"进行中的事业"面前出现了国家宿命论而导致的社会和经济功能的隔离。你们已经容许工业产业聚集在某些地区，而让其他地区变得贫穷下去。我承认，在过去，由于需要在煤矿附近发电，所以这种情况在某种程度上是不可避免的，但也没有达到如今业已存在的这种程度。通过恰当的控制，你们本来是可以用依赖于每个工厂或者依赖于一批小工厂的社区，来代替"农村地区"的；在这种社区中，无论贫富、无论雇主还是员工，本来都可以团结在一起，形成一种睦邻友好的可靠关系的；可恰恰相反，你们却允许在你们的大都市里逐渐形成什么东区和西区[1]来。诚然，真正之政治才能的根本特征，就是深谋远虑、防止出现社会弊病；但在过去的一个世纪当中，我们的方法却是放任自流，而一旦事态严重，我

---

[1] East and West Ends：伦敦的东区和西区。东区指伦敦东部港口地区，是著名的贫民区，而西区基本上是豪华住宅区，也是与纽约百老汇齐名的戏剧表演中心。

things became bad we applied palliative remedies — factory legislation, housing legislation, and so forth. As things stand today, the only organic remedy is at any cost to loosen out the town.

These ideas apply not only to industry but also to our educational institutions and the learned professions. Our English system is to buy — we must use plain words, for the element of competition among the colleges exists — the best young brains by means of scholarships open to national competition. In the middle of last century we, in large measure, abolished the system of close scholarships, which tied particular schools to particular colleges; that was, in my opinion, by far the healthier system. By social custom you add to your scholars a number of other fortunate boys from well-to-do homes scattered over the country. So you recruit your public schools and your Oxford and Cambridge; from the beginning you lift your lads out of their local environment. From the Universities many of them pass into a centralized Civil Service, a centralized legal profession, and even a centralized, medical profession. In London they wait, eating out their hearts dining their best years. A few of them come through and shine in a great but unnaturally segregated competition of wits, and you complain of your Government by lawyers! The whole system results from historical momentum; when the Midlands, the East, and the South of England were all of England that counted, Oxford and Cambridge were local Universities, and London was the natural market center of a single countryside. But in the past century the roads and the railways have enabled the Metropolis to attract to itself the careers that were destined for the inspiration of other country-sides. The natural place of an exceptional man is to be leading his own people and helping them to bear their burdens. Your exceptional

们又会用治标不治本的办法来补救——比如工厂立法、住房立法，诸如此类。从如今的形势来看，唯一有组织的补救之法，便是不惜任何代价地解脱对城镇的束缚。

这些观点不仅适用于工业，也适用于我们的教育制度和学术性职业[1]。我们英国的制度，是通过面向全国性竞争的奖学金"收买"最有才能的年轻人——我们必须这样直截了当地来说，因为各个大学之间存在着竞争的因素。在上个世纪中期，我们基本上废除了封闭奖学金制度，因为此种制度把某些特定的中小学与某些特定的大学捆绑起来了；但在我看来，那其实是一种健全得多的制度。你们按照社会习俗，把散布在全国各地的富裕家庭中的其他许多幸运的孩子招来，充实到了你们的学生队伍中。于是，你们便充实了你们的公立中小学、充实了你们的牛津大学和剑桥大学；从一开始，你们便让青少年脱离了他们的当地环境。他们中的许多人，大学毕业后便进入了统一的公务员队伍，进入了统一的法律界，甚至进入了统一的医学界。他们在伦敦等待，忧心忡忡地度过他们人生当中最美好的年华。其中只有寥寥一些人会熬出头来，在激烈而残酷的不同智力竞争中显露出才华，可你们却还会发牢骚，说你们的政府被一群律师操纵着！整个制度都是历史的动力所导致的；在英格兰全境尚由中部、东部和南部地区组成的时候，牛津和剑桥都还是地方性大学，而伦敦也还是一个单一农村地区的天然之中心市场。但在上个世纪，诸多公路和铁路已经使得这个大都市能够把那些原本用于刺激其他农村地区发展的职业，全都吸引到它这儿来了。出类拔萃者的天赋大任，就是领导自己的人民并帮助人民承担重负。只有保持好自身特定土壤的活力，你们那种出类拔萃的才

---

[1] learned professionals：学术性职业，需要高深学问的职业。尤指牧师、律师、医生等职业。

brain is serving the nation best if it remains racy of its own particular soil.[1]

One of the most serious difficulties in the way of the realization of the balanced local community lies in the difference of dialect spoken by the common people and the upper classes. In England after the Norman Conquest our peas-lants talked English, but our knights French, and our priests Latin, with the result that a knight felt himself more at home with a knight from France than with his own people, and so was it also with the priests. Today there is a curious difference, it seems to me, in this respect, between the Scottish and English peoples. In England the upper professional classes go to the same schools and universities as the landed classes, and the merchants and captains of industry also send their sons to those schools. Therefore the line of social cleavage, as shown by speech and bearing, is between the upper and the lower middle classes. In Scotland, on the other hand, the people of the highest tier of society send their sons for the most part to the English Public Schools and the English Universities, whereas the

[1] As a loyal son of Oxford who gratefully recognizes what he owes to his Alma Mater, I would not have her flourish less but more in changing some of her lower functions for higher.

干才能最好地服务于整个国家。［作者注：作为牛津大学的忠实拥护者，我衷心感谢母校对我的栽培；我希望把该校的一些低等功能变成高等功能，这样做并不是要它由此衰落下去，而是要它变得更加兴旺。］

在实现局部社会发展均衡的过程中最严峻的困难之一，就在于普通百姓和上层阶级说的是不同的方言。在英格兰，因为自诺曼征服以后我们的农民说英语，可爵士们说的却是法语，而牧师们说的又是拉丁语，所以结果便是，一位爵士会觉得，与来自法国的另一位爵士待在一起会比跟他自己的人民待在一起更感自在，而牧师们的感觉也是这样。在我看来，如今在苏格兰人和英格兰人之间，这个方面还出现了一种很奇怪的差异。在英格兰，上流职业阶层和地主阶层的子女上同样的中小学和大学，而商人和实业巨头们也会把子女送进这些学校。因此，人们言谈举止所表现出来的那种社会分界线，便处在中产阶级的上层和下层之间。另一方面，在苏格兰，那些处于社会顶层的人，绝大多数都会把子女送到英格兰的公立中小学和英格兰的大学去就读，但苏格兰教会里的

诺曼征服。指1066年诺曼底威廉公爵对英格兰的军事征服，它加速了英国的封建化进程。

ministers of the Scottish Churches, the advocates in the Scottish Law Courts, and the doctors and schoolmasters are trained in the main in the local Universities, which are frequented by the sons of the shopkeepers and artisans to a greater extent than in England. The result, as I believe, is that the Scottish aristocracy has been, to a greater degree than in England, detached from the people. I do not blame them, for they have merely drifted in the grip of fate. It is said that a certain Scottish Baronet who had eight beautiful daughters approaching, some of them, to the age of marriage, put them all on a coach and drove them away from Edinburgh to London, because all the young Scotsmen of his acquaintance who had money, or the wits to make money, had already gone thither! In the end of the eighteenth century, and the beginning of the nineteenth, Edinburgh was one of the lamps of Europe, with its own particular tinge of flame. Today it is one more instance of the futility of trying to separate the economic from the other aspects of the life either of a nation or a province.

※　　　※　　　※　　　※　　　※　　　※　　　※　　　※　　　※

Whether we reason downward from the Freedom of Nations, or upward from the Freedom of Men, we come to the same conclusion. The nation which is to be fraternal towards other nations, must be independent in an economic as in every other sense; it must have and keep a complete and balanced life. But it cannot be independent if it is broken into classes and interests which are for ever seeking to range themselves for fighting purposes with the equivalent classes and interests of other nations. Therefore you must base national organization on provincial communities. But if your province is to have any sufficient power of satisfying local aspirations it must, except for the federal reservations, have its own complete and balanced life. That is precisely what the real Freedom of Men requires — scope for a full life in their own locality.

牧师、苏格兰法庭上的律师以及苏格兰的医生和教师，基本上却是在本地大学接受教育，而小店主和工匠们的子女往往也会就读于此种大学，且这种情形的普遍程度要甚于英格兰。我相信，这样做的结果就是，苏格兰的贵族阶层比英格兰的贵族阶层更加脱离了人民。我不会去指责他们，因为他们不过是任凭命运摆布罢了。据说有位苏格兰准男爵生了8个漂亮的女儿，其中有几个已经到了谈婚论嫁的年纪，他便用马车把这几个女儿从爱丁堡送到了伦敦，因为他认识的那些有钱或者有赚钱头脑的苏格兰小伙子，全都已经到伦敦去了！在18世纪末和19世纪初，爱丁堡还是欧洲的领头羊之一，有着自己的独特之处。而如今，此地却成了说明把经济与一个国家或省份活力中的其他方面拆分开来徒劳无益的又一个例证。

※　　　※　　　※　　　※　　　※　　　※　　　※　　　※　　　※

无论是从国家自由的角度向下推理，还是从人的自由角度向上推理，我们都会得出同样的结论。一个国家要想跟别的国家友好相处，那么它在经济和其他各个方面就必须独立自主；它必须拥有并维持一种完整而均衡的生活才行。但是，如果将一个国家分裂成不同的阶级和利益集团，那么这个国家就不可能做到独立自主；这些阶级和利益集团永远都会因为同样的战斗目标，而跟其他国家中同等的阶级和利益集团勾结起来。因此，你们必须以省级社区为基础来建立国家机构。不过，假如你们的省份想要拥有足够的权力来满足当地的发展愿望，那么除非联邦有着种种限制，否则省内就必须拥有自身完整而均衡的生活。拥有在本地过上充实生活的机会，这才是真正的人的自由所需要的。由全国性的阶级和利益集团所形成的那种组织是冲突导致的结果，但此种组织无法

The organization by nation-wide classes and interests is the outcome of conflict, but it cannot satisfy, for it removes the larger careers away to the metropolis. Moreover the slums, and most other material afflictions of the people, are the outcome of impotence of local life, for they all result from offenses against the principle of keeping that life complete and balanced.

Provinces of complete life, of course, imply a federal system. It is not a mere decentralization which is contemplated, but decentralization of the different social functions to the same local units. Undoubtedly that is the tendency at the present time, in the Anglo-Saxon world, in regard to the administration of Government. The United States, Canada, Australia, and South Africa are all, in greater or less degree, federal, and in Britain we seem to be not very far from becoming so. Only the Irish question blocks the way, but it is intrinsically a small question, and we ought not to allow the quarrels of four million people to impede permanently the organic remedy of the ills of more than forty millions. A division of England into Northern and Southern Provinces would probably be needed in order to remove the fact of the predominant partner, but from the point of view here taken that division would in itself be a good thing. To achieve the object in view it would not, however, be enough to give to your provinces merely "gas and water" powers; they must be so involved in the economic life of their regions that both masters and men will base their organizations on the Provincial Areas. If every unit of society — the Nation, the Province, the locality — were entitled, nay, were desired, to take appropriate steps to maintain the, completeness and balance of its life, the need for the wide-spreading organization of any class or interest, save for informative purposes, would gradually cease to be urgent.

Consider the life of trees. In the forests of nature competition is severe, and no tree attains to the full and balanced growth of which it is capable. The trees of the middle forest struggle

满足人的自由，因为此种组织把一些从事较重要职的人都转移到大都市里去了。此外，贫民窟以及人民其他大多数的物质上的困苦，都是源于当地生活的凋敝，因为这一切都是违反了保持当地生活完整和均衡这条原则而酿下的苦果。

各个省份都有着完整的生活，自然意味着我们必须采用联邦体制。这并非仅仅是指人们所期待的那种分权制，还是指把不同的社会功能分散到相同的本地单位中去。毫无疑问，这是盎格鲁-撒克逊人的世界中当前在政府行政方面的一种趋势。美利坚合众国、加拿大、澳大利亚以及南非或多或少都是采取联邦体制，而在英国，我们离采用联邦制的时间似乎也并不遥远了。只有爱尔兰问题挡住了路，不过从本质上来说，这还只是一个小问题，而我们也不该让400万人的怨言永久性地使得4000多万人无法系统地去根治他们的弊病。为了消除英格兰是占支配地位的伙伴这个事实，我们可能需要把英格兰分成南北两省，但从这里所表达的观点来看，将英格兰划分成南北两省本身可能就是一件好事。然而，为了实现这一目标，仅仅给予各省管理"煤气和自来水"的权力是不够的；各省必须全面地参与到本地的经济生活中去，从而让雇主和员工都在本省范围的基础上建立起他们的组织来。如果每一个社会单元——即国家、省份和地区——都有权采取恰当的措施，不，应该说是人们都希望它们采取恰当的措施，来维持这些社会单元内生活的完整性和均衡性，那么除非是为了互通消息，否则任何阶级或利益集团把各自的组织进行扩展的需要，就会慢慢变得不那么迫切了。

我们不妨细想一下树木的生活。在天然的森林中，竞争非常激烈，没有哪棵树木能够完全发挥出自身的潜力，充分而均衡地生长起来。森林中间的树木努力地往上生长，以争取阳光；森林边缘的树木，只有一面向外伸展；而在贫瘠、阴森的森林底部，则是

upward to the light; those of the border spread outward one-sidedly; and in the slum depths are all manner of rottenness and parasitism. If, as in Dante's dream, there were spirits imprisoned in the trees, one might imagine a forest league of the foliage against the roots for sending up too many trunks, and a forest league of the roots against the foliage for keeping away the sweet light and air. But they would be futile leagues, because each tree consists of roots and foliage. The Landscape Gardener of civilization, with his organic remedies, can alone achieve the perfect beauty of trees. He plants them apart, so that they may grow independently, each according to the ideal of its kind; he guides the sapling, prunes the young tree, and cuts away disease from the mature tree. So we enjoy one of the most inspiring sights on earth, a park of noble trees, each complete and balanced in its growth. Only the monkeys and squirrels, which leap from branch to branch, have suffered — the elusive international exploiters and profiteers of the forest.

This parable of the Gardener contains also the idea that the functions of growth and control are separate and should be kept separate. When officials of the State become socialistic, and try to initiate instead of merely assuring growth, they become less capable of their own proper function, which is criticism — understanding and sympathetic, but still criticism. The temper of criticism is incompatible with artistic and formative enthusiasm. We have had too little criticism based on steady watchfulness for the signs of imbalance in growth. The British Board of Trade under the régime of Laissez-faire was so penetrated with the advisability of doing nothing, that it had no appreciable machinery for even watching what the Going Concern was doing. Federal authorities of every description, whether of the League of Nations or of the Nations, should consist essentially of defensive and of outlook departments, and the watching or outlook departments should issue warnings, and repeat those warnings, until, thus enlightened,

各种各样的朽木腐叶和寄生生物。假如像但丁梦见的那样，树木当中都锁有精灵，那我们不妨设想一下，林中会有一个反对树根让太多树干往上生长的树叶联盟，还会有一个反对树叶遮挡了新鲜阳光和空气的树根联盟。但是，它们会是两个无效的联盟，因为每一棵树都既有树根又有树叶。那个美化文明的园丁掌握着系统性的纠正方法，只有他才能让树木的美充分呈现出来。他会将树木分散栽种，以便每一棵树木都按照各自的理想状态独立地生长；他会监管幼苗的生长方向，会修剪小树，并且会砍掉大树上的病枝。这样，我们就会欣赏到世间最令人鼓舞的景色之一了：满园树木葱郁壮观，其间每一棵都长得既充分又匀称。只有在树枝间跳来跳去的猴子和松鼠会不好过——可它们正是森林中狡猾的国际剥削者和投机商。

园丁这个比喻还隐含了这样一种观点：发展和控制是两种独立的功能，并且应当让这两种功能保持独立。当国家各级官吏变为社会主义者，并且试图创新而非只是确保国家发展之后，他们对于本职工作就会变得不那么称职了，因为他们的职责本来应该是批评——虽然带有谅解和同情，却仍属批评。批评的特点，与美妙而可塑的激情是格格不入的。针对发展过程中出现的种种不均衡的迹象，我们经过不懈和密切的关注而提出的批评意见实在是太少了。处于一个崇尚自由主义的政体之下的英国贸易委员会，因为沉迷在无为而治的明智当中，所以连监控"进行中的事业"之行为的机构也没有。联邦的各种权力机构，不管是属于国际联盟的还是属于各个国家的，都应当主要由防御和监管部门所组成，而担任监视或监管任务的部门则应当发出警告，并且应当反复发出那些警告，直到当地的开明舆论在还来得及的时候进行干预，防止"进行中的事业"出现某种畸形的产物而毁灭性地扰乱整个世界或者国家的平衡才行。我相信，美利坚合众国的

public opinion in the localities concerned intervenes while there is yet time to prevent some monstrous outgrowth of the Going Concern from fatally upsetting the equilibrium of the world or of the nation. In the United States the care of agriculture is, I believe, left to the separate States, but the Federal Bureau of Agriculture it is which issues warnings of the need of conserving the natural resources of the country. In Rome we already have an International Agricultural Institute which collects the statistics of the world harvests, and seeks to steady markets and prices by timely warnings; it has rendered considerable service to the Allies during this War.

I have no doubt that I shall be told by practical men that the ideal of complete and balanced economic growth in each locality is contrary to the whole tendency of the age, and is, in fact, archaic. I shall be told that you can only get a great and cheap production by the method of world-organization and local specialization. I admit that such is the present tendency, and that it may give you maximum material results for a while. But if you breed animals, does there not come a time when you have gone as far as you can with inbreeding, and must you not then resort again to cross-breeding?

Athens and Florence were great because they saw life whole. If you pursue relentlessly the idols of efficiency and cheapness, you will give us a world in which the young will never see life but only an aspect of life; national and international organizers will alone hold the keys admitting to the Observatory of the complete view. Is it in that way that you will get a continuous supply of fruitful brains, and happy, because intellectually active workers? All specialization contains the seeds of death; the most daring army must, at times, wait for the supply columns to come up. In the growth of brains and contentment something far more subtle is involved than any technical education or healthy housing. Is it quite certain that at the end of a century of

农业事务是由各州负责的，而联邦农业局则是一个负责发出警告、要求各州保护全国自然资源的机构。我们在罗马已经成立了一个国际农业研究所来收集整个世界农作物产量方面的统计数据，并且力求通过该机构发出及时的警告来稳定市场和价格；在此次大战中，这个机构已经为协约国做出了很大的贡献。

我敢肯定，有些务实的人会对我说，每个地区的经济都得到完整和均衡发展这一理想，与目前这个时代的整体趋势是背道而驰的，并且事实上也是过了时的。他们会对我说，只有通过世界性组织和地区专业化的办法，才能得到大规模的廉价产品。我承认目前的趋势确是如此，并且暂时可能让我们获得最大的物质成果。不过，就算你去饲养家畜，不是也会有对近亲繁殖问题束手无策的时候，到时不是也得再次去求助杂交繁殖的办法吗？

雅典和佛罗伦萨之所以伟大，是因为它们将生活当成一个整体来看待。倘若你们只是冷酷无情地把高效和廉价当成自己的目标，那么你们就会给我们带来一个这样的世界：在这个世界里，年轻人永远都看不到整个生活，而只能看到生活的一面；登上那个全景观测台的钥匙，只掌握在国家的组织者和国际组织者手里。用那种方式，你们是不是就会得到源源不断的有用人才，就会得到因为思想活跃而感到幸福的工人呢？所有的专业化，其实都孕育着消亡的种子；即便是最勇猛的军队，有时也必须等候后勤部队跟上来才行。培养人才和满足感的过程，涉及了比任何技术教育或健康居住之类的问题都要细微得多的一些方面。我们能不能十分肯定地说，在经历了不愿尽快变得富裕起来的一个世纪之后，我们不会比现在富有得多呢？

我知道，在这次大战中，你们已经定下了你们的管控人员，还设立了由管控人员所

refusal to get rich as quickly as possible, we should not have been far richer than we are?

I know that in this War you have set your controllers, and your international committees of controllers, to manage vast trades as single concerns, and that they have not let us starve. But in the crisis you have very rightly been using your capital of intellect and experience. Those men are the men that they are because they have built up private businesses with the fear of bankruptcy ever before them: they have grown up with their business lives always in their hands. Great organizations, whether of combines or Government services, in that they afford a sheltered life, will not give you unlimited crops of such men.

You urge that credit and insurance must have broad bases, and I agree: their function is to average away local deficiencies due to the varying seasons and the varying success of undertakings. But let us none the less recognize that they present the danger of a financial control of the world. Your League of Nations may have to take them in hand, lest we be ruled by one only of the "interests" of society. There are two courses open to us in regard to them: to control them federally, or to fight them and balance them by the international organization of other "interests". The federal authority, whether of the League or the Nation, is constituted of communities of complete growth, and cannot, from its nature, aspire to Empire, since it consists everywhere of balanced humanity. But great specialist organizations, guided by experts, will inevitably contend for the upper hand, and the contest must end in the rule of one or other type of expert. That is Empire, for it is unbalanced.

※　　　　※　　　　※　　　　※　　　　※　　　　※　　　　※　　　　※　　　　※

Do you realize that we have now made the circuit of the world, and that every system is now a closed system, and that you can now alter nothing without altering the balance of everything,

组成的各个国际委员会，以便像单个企业那样去管理大规模贸易，并且这些委员会也并没有让我们挨饿。但在这次危机中，你们一直都在恰当地运用自己的智力资本和经验资本。那些人之所以成为了他们那样的人，是因为他们是带着永远都得面对破产这种担忧而创立起自己的私人企业的：他们是掌握着自己企业的命运而成长起来的。对于大型组织来说，无论这种大型组织是联合企业还是政府部门，由于它们提供的都是一种没有风雨艰辛的生活，所以培养不出无穷无尽的此种人才来。

你们强调说，信贷业和保险业必须具有广泛的基础，我也同意这一点；它们的作用，都在于均摊因季节不同、企业成就不同而造成的局部亏损。但尽管如此，我们还是要承认，它们代表了金融控制世界的这种危险。你们的国际联盟必须紧紧将它们控制在手中才行，以免我们被社会的某一个"利益集团"所统治。对于这些利益集团，我们有两条路可以选择：在整个联邦范围内掌控它们，或者用其他"利益集团"的国际组织来与之对抗并抵消其影响。联邦的权力机构，不管是国际联盟的还是各个国家的，都是由全面发展的社区所组成，并且从其性质来看，此种联邦权力机构不可能有建立帝国的志向，因为它完全是由和谐稳定的人类所组成的。不过，大型的专业组织在专业人士的引导之下却必定会去争取优势地位，而这种竞争又必定会以此种或彼种专业人士的统治而告终。那样就成了帝国，因为它是不均衡的。

※　　　　※　　　　※　　　　※　　　　※　　　　※　　　　※　　　　※　　　　※

你有没有意识到，我们如今已经绕着整个世界兜了一圈，看到所有制度如今都成了封闭的制度，知道如今你要是不打破一切事物的平衡便改变不了任何东西，并且明白如今已经不再有荒凉的海滩可以安然容纳漂流过来的不完善的思想了呢？我们应当有条有

20世纪早期的伦敦

20世纪早期的伦敦

and that there are no more desert shores on which the jetsam of incomplete thought can rest undisturbed? Let us attempt logical, symmetrical thought, but practical, cautious action, because we have to do with a mighty Going Concern. If you stop it, or even slow down its running, it will punish you relentlessly. If you let it run without guidance, it will take you over the cataract again. You cannot guide it by setting up mere fences, and by mending those fences if it breaks them down, because this Going Concern consists of hundreds of millions of human beings who are "pursuing" happiness, and they will swarm over all your fences like an army of ants. You can only guide Humanity by the attraction of ideals. That is why Christianity wins on, after nineteen centuries, through all the impediments set up by criticism of its creeds and its miracles.

What we need, in my belief, to guide our Reconstruction is a presumption of statesmanship

理而又对称和谐地来思考问题，但要采取切合实际的、谨慎的行动，因为我们必须应对的是一种强大有力的"进行中的事业"。倘若你们挡住了它的去路，或者即便只是降低了其运转速度，它就会冷酷无情地惩罚你们。而倘若你们任由它盲目地运转，它就会再次把你们带到滔滔洪流之上。你们不能只是竖起些篱笆来引导它，也不能在它把篱笆撞破之后再去修修补补，因为这种"进行中的事业"是由千百万"追求"幸福的个人所组成，他们会像一大群蚂蚁那样一拥而上，爬过你们的所有篱笆。你们只能用理想的魅力来引导整个人类。这就是基督教在19个世纪之后，在经历了因世人责难其教义和奇迹而带来的重重阻碍后，仍然能够赢得世人追随的原因。

我认为，为了指导我们的重建工作，我们必须设想出某种政治手段才行；这种手段既有利于国家的均衡发展，也有利于各省的均衡发展，既不与自由贸易者同流，也不与

in favor of the balanced nation, and the balanced province, sinning neither with the Free Trader nor the Protectionist. If we persist for a generation or two, with such an ideal before us, we may gradually change the Going Concern, so that we shall have fraternal nations and fraternal provinces, instead of warring, organized interests ever striving to extend their limits to the international field in order to outflank opposing interests which still lag on the merely national scale. Remember how that curious negative ideal of Laissez-faire did through a couple of generations gradually assimilate the whole texture of British society, so that it has taken this World-War to overthrow the vested interests which grew up.

At present, it seems to me, we are thinking out our Reconstruction piecemeal, according to this and that detached ideal of the pre-War philanthropist — housing, temperance, industrial conciliation, and the rest of them. But if you build three hundred thousand new houses, and put them merely where they are "wanted", you may but be drifting again, though with heavier ballast.

In the War we have gradually risen to the conception of the single strategical command, and of the single economic control. Have you the courage for measures of like scope in regard to Peace, though more subtle and less executive because they will deal with growth and not with destruction?

"The fault, dear Brutus, is not in our stars
But in ourselves, that we are underlings."

贸易保护主义者合污。假如我们带着这样一种理想坚持一、两个世代的时间，我们或许就能逐步改变这种"进行中的事业"，从而使得我们拥有友好的国家和友好的省份，而不会再有敌对的、有组织的利益集团了；这种利益集团，一直都在努力把自己的势力范围扩张到国际领域，以便迂回包抄那些仍然落在后面、只是停留在国家规模上的敌对利益集团。我们要记住，那种古怪而消极的放任主义理想是怎样在两、三代人的时间里逐渐同化了英国社会的整个结构的，而其结果则是，它得借助这次世界大战，才能推翻那些发展起来的既得利益集团了。

在我看来，目前我们似乎正在根据战前那些博爱主义者们彼此并无关联的种种理想，零零碎碎地解决我们的重建问题——比如住房、禁酒、产业调停，以及其他一些问题。但是，如果你们盖了30万幢新房后，只是放置在人们"需要"它们的地方，那么尽管船上的压舱石更加沉重，你们这艘船可能也不过是再次在随波逐流罢了。

在这次大战中，我们已经逐渐接受了战略统一指挥和经济统一调控的观念。对于和平，你们敢不敢采取类似规模的措施，敢不敢采取因为要应对发展而非破坏、故更加微妙和更难执行的措施呢？

"亲爱的布鲁图斯，错不在吾辈之命运
而在吾辈之本身，因吾辈低人一等。"[1]

---

[1] The fault … that we are underlings：莎士比亚的悲剧《裘力斯·恺撒》第一幕第二场中的一处道白。Brutus（布鲁图斯）是剧中主角之一，对应的历史人物是Marcus Brutus（马库斯·布鲁图斯，公元前85年~公元前42年），他是古罗马的贵族政治家和将军，也是刺杀罗马独裁者恺撒的主谋。

VIII   POSTSCRIPT

Since the writing of this book I have fought a Parliamentary election in Scotland, with a Liberal and a Socialist for my opponents. Of Liberalism there is nothing just now to be usefully said; a sturdy individualism will always be one of the elements of character in our British race, whatever the fate of the political party which was its nineteenth-century expression. But the ever-recurrent propaganda of Socialism is at present in a very significant phase. Mere Bureaucratic Socialism has been criticised by events of late; the more we know of the working of dominant officialdom during the War, the less likely, I think, are we to desire it for a permanent master. My Socialist opponent was out to take away property in land and to abolish interest on capital; in other words, he would begin with a confiscatory revolution; but that was not of the essence of his position. His supporters — young men with a burning faith in their eyes, though often without the full power of expressing their argument — were, at almost every meeting, boldly defensive of the Russian Bolsheviks. There are two sides to Bolshevism; there is the mere violence and tyranny of the Jacobin, upthrown at a certain stage of most great revolutions; and there is the "Syndicalist" idealism. To do them justice, it is the latter aspect of Bolshevism which really attracts and holds my young Scottish antagonists. The Bolsheviks are in revolt against a Parliamentarism based on local communities or, as they would put it, on

第八章　后记

自开始写作本书之后，我在苏格兰地区参加了议员竞选；我的两个对手当中，一个是自由党人，一个是社会党人。对于自由主义，此刻我并无什么有用的东西要说；因为不论这个在19世纪信奉个人主义的政党命运如何，坚定的个人主义始终都会是我们不列颠民族性格特征中的一个构成要素。不过，一再出现的社会主义宣传活动，目前却正处在一个极其重要的阶段。纯粹的官僚社会主义已经因为最近发生的许多事件而遭到了世人的指责；而我认为，对主要的官场人物在此次大战期间的工作情况了解得越多，我们就越不可能想要这些人做我们永远的主人。我的那位社会党对手致力于没收土地和废除资本利润；换言之，他会发起一场把财产充公的革命，但这并不是他所站的立场不可或缺的一个方面。他的支持者——尽管常常没有充分表达自己主张的能力，但他们都是一些眼睛里燃烧着信念之火的年轻人——几乎在每一次集会上都大胆地为俄国的布尔什维克党人进行辩护。布尔什维克主义具有两面性；一面是雅各宾式的纯粹暴力和苛政，这种情况在绝大部分大规模革命的某个阶段都会出现；另一面就是"工团主义者"[1]式的理想主义。公正地来说，真正吸引并且让我那些年轻的苏格兰对手们入迷的，正是布

---

[1] Syndicalist：工团主义者。原文为法语，即英语中的工联主义。革命工团主义通常指法国劳工联合会书记费南德·佩卢蒂埃（1867~1901）的理论，以及该联合会在1902年并入法国总工会（CGT）后，由后者所制定的原则。工团主义强调的是行动而不是理论，其基调是要求会员发扬主动性，提倡战斗精神（包括怠工破坏活动），通过纯粹的工业组织和斗争来推翻资本主义和资本主义国家。

罗伯斯庇尔，雅各宾派政府的实际首脑之一。雅各宾派。法国大革命时期（1789～1794年）的激进民主主义者，因其俱乐部会址设在巴黎雅各宾修道院而得名。

so many social pyramids each with its Capitalist at the top. Their ideal is of a federation of vocational Soviets or unions — Soviets of workmen, of peasants, and, if you will, of professional men. Therefore the Bolsheviks, both in Petrograd and Berlin, have consistently opposed the meeting of national assemblies for the purpose of framing Parliamentary constitutions on the Western "bourgeois" model. Their revolt is towards an organization by interests rather than localities.[1] For the reasons stated in this book, such an organization would, in my belief, lead inevitably to the Marxian War of international classes, of Proletariat against Bourgeoisie, and finally of one section of the Proletariat against the other sections — already the Russian town-workers are at issue with the Russian peasants. The end could only be world-anarchy or aworld-tyranny.

Thus I come back to the quiet of my library with the conviction that what I have written is pertinent to the hot currents of real life in this great crisis of humanity. Our old English conception of the House of Commons or Communities, the American conception of the Federation of States and Provinces, and the new ideal of the League of Nations are all of them opposed to the

[1] The vocational soviet of the peasants is only incidentally local; it is not local in the fuller sense of combining various local interests into a community.

尔什维克主义的后一面。布尔什维克党人是在反抗一种建立在局部社区基础上的议会制度，或者用他们自己的话来说，这种制度是建立在许多的社会金字塔之上的，并且每座金字塔的塔顶都有一个资本家。他们的理想是成立一个由各种行业苏维埃或者行业工会所组成的联盟——比如工人苏维埃、农民苏维埃，并且你要是愿意的话，还可以有专业人员苏维埃。因此，彼得格勒和柏林两地的布尔什维克党人一直都在不屈不挠地反对国民会议，因为那种国民会议是为了按照西方的"资产阶级"模式来制定议会章程而召开的。他们反抗的目的，是要一个根据利益集团来进行的组织，而不是要一个按照地区来进行的组织。［作者注：农民这种行业苏维埃只是偶然带有地方性；从把局部的不同利益集团联合起来成为一个社区这种更全面的意义来看，它并不是地方性的。］出于本书中业已说明的理由，此种组织在我看来，必定会导致国际各阶级之间的马克思主义斗争，导致无产阶级反对资产阶级的斗争，并最终发展成为一部分无产阶级反对其他无产阶级的斗争——如今俄国的市镇工人已经在跟俄国农民唱反调了。而结果只能是出现一种世界范围的无政府状态，或者是出现一种世界范围的暴政。

于是，我回到自己那间安静的书房里，同时心中确信，我所写下的这些内容，与人类在此次巨大危机中的真实生活里那些热烈的潮流是密切相关的。我们英国人关于"下议院"或者"共同体"的古老观念，美国人关于"州、省联邦"的观念，以及国际联盟这

policies cast in the tyrannical molds of East Europe and the Heartland, whether Dynastic or Bolshevik. It may be the case that Bolshevik tyranny is an extreme reaction from Dynastic tyranny, but it is none the less true that the Russian, Prussian, and Hungarian plains, with their widespread uniformity of social conditions, are favorable alike to the march of militarism and to the propaganda of syndicalism. Against this two-headed Eagle of land-power the Westerners and the Islanders must struggle. Even in their own peninsulas and islands modern methods of communication are so leveling natural barriers that organization by interests constitutes a real threat. In the Heartland, where physical contrasts are few, it is only with the aid of a conscious ideal, shaping political life in the direction of nationalities, that we shall be able to entrench true freedom. If only as a basis for "penetrating" this dangerous Heartland, the Oceanic peoples must strive to root ever more firmly their own organization by localities, each locality with as complete and balanced a life of its own as circumstances may permit of. The effort must go downward through the provinces to the cities. East-ends and West-ends divide our cities into castes; at whatever sacrifice we must tone away such contrasts. The countryside, in which the successful leaders visibly serve the interests of their weaker brethren, must be our ideal.

There was a time when a man addressed his "friends and neighbors". We still have our friends, but too often they are scattered over the land and

伯里克利（时代）的。伯里克利（Pericles，约公元前495年～公元前429年）是古希腊的一位将领，也是奴隶主民主政治的杰出代表和古代世界最著名的政治家之一。他在执政时期进行了大刀阔斧的改革，使得雅典进入了黄金时代，史称这一时代为"伯里克利时代"（Periclean Age）。

个新的理想，都是与东欧和"中心地带"那种专制政体的磨子里铸就的那些政策——不是哪个王朝的政策，还是布尔什维克的政策——相对立的。情况或许是，布尔什维克的苛政是对王朝苛政的一种极端反应；但尽管如此，俄罗斯、普鲁士和匈牙利平原的社会条件具有广泛的一致性，它们既有利于军国主义的发展，同样有利于工团主义的传播，这一点也是事实。西欧民族和岛国人民必须奋起同这只陆上力量的双头鹰进行斗争才行。即便是在他们自己的半岛和岛屿上，现代化的交通方式也正在让天堑变成通途，以至于根据利益集团而形成的组织变成了一种真正的威胁。在"中心地带"，由于自然条件方面的差异不多，所以我们只有借助于自觉的理想，朝着民族性的方向来塑造政治生活，才能确立真正的自由。如果只是将其作为"渗入"这个危险的"中心地带"的基础，那么各个海洋民族就必须更加努力地巩固好他们自己根据地域所形成的组织，并且各个地区都应当在条件允许的情况下尽可能地保持自身生活的完整和均衡。这种努力必须自上而下，从各个省份到达各个城市。"东区"和"西区"把我们的城市分成了两种不同的社会等级；而无论做出多大的牺牲，我们也必须淡化这样的差别才行。一些成功的领导人显然正在乡间为弱小同胞的利益而服务，而这样的乡村，必须成为我们的理想。

人们曾经有一个时代，是用"朋友们和邻居们"来彼此称呼的。我们仍然有朋友，不过他们往往都天各一方，并且往往也与我们自己属于同一个社会阶层。或者，要是他

belong to our own caste in society. Or, if they happen to be near us, is it not because our caste has gathered apart into its own quarter of the town? So was it in the early Middle Ages, when we are told that three men might meet in the market-place the one obeying the Roman law, another the customs of the Franks, and a third those of the Goths. So is it today in India with Hindu, and Mohammedan, and Christian. So was it not either in fourteenth-century Florence, or Periclean Athens, or Elizabethan England.

With too many of us, in our urban and suburban civilization, that grand old word Neighbor has fallen almost into desuetude. It is for Neighborliness that the world today calls aloud, and for a refusal to gad ever about — merely because of modern opportunities for communication. Let us recover possession of ourselves, lest we become the mere slaves of the world's geography, exploited by materialistic organizers. Neighborliness or fraternal duty to those who are our fellow-dwellers, is the only sure foundation of a happy citizenship. Its consequences extend upward from the city through the province to the nation, and to the world league of nations. It is the cure alike of the slumdom of the poor and of the boredom of the rich, and of war between classes and war between nations.

们碰巧住在我们附近的话，不也是因为我们这个阶层脱离了其他阶层而集中居住在城市里的聚居区吗？中世纪早期正是这种情形，据闻那个时候要是有三个人在市场上邂逅的话，其中会有一人奉行罗马律法，另一人遵从法兰克人的习惯法，而第三个人则会信奉哥特人的习惯法。如今印度的印度教教徒、伊斯兰教徒和基督徒也是这个样子。但在14世纪的佛罗伦萨、伯里克利时代的雅典或者伊丽莎白时代的英格兰，却都并非如此。

如今，由于我们当中有太多的人住在城市和市郊开发区，所以"邻居"这个崇高而古老的名称差不多已经废弃不用了。当今这个世界所大声呼吁的，正是睦邻精神，并且拒绝仅仅因为有机会利用现代化的交通就永远都以四海为家的做法。我们不妨重新掌控好自己，以免变成纯粹的奴隶，受制于这个世界的地理状况，并被追求物质利益的组织者剥削。与那些比邻而居的人保持睦邻友好的关系，或者说对他们尽到兄弟般的友爱义务，是成为幸福公民的唯一可靠的基础。此种做法的影响会自下而上，从城市经由各省直到国家，并且还会到达整个世界的国家联盟这个层面。这是一副既可以消灭穷人的贫民窟、也可以让富人不觉得生活无聊，并且既可以消除阶级斗争、也可以消弭国家间战争的良药。

APPENDIX

NOTE ON AN INCIDENT AT THE QUAI DORSAY 25th JANUARY, 1919

The representatives of the Allied Nations were assembled in the second plenary session of their Conference at Paris. A resolution was before them to appoint committees for the purpose of reporting on the proposed League of Nations and other matters. The constitution of the committees, giving two members to each of the five Great Powers (U. S. A., British Empire, France, Italy, Japan), and five members to the Smaller Powers collectively, had been settled by the Council of Ten, representing only the Great Powers, and this constitution was now

附

1919年1月25日法国外交部一件小事备忘

协约国的代表在巴黎集会，准备召开大会的第二次全体会议。他们需要通过一项决议来委任若干个委员会，以就拟议中的国际联盟和其他问题向大会做出报告。各个委员会的构成方案已经由仅仅代表大国的那个"十人委员会"确定下来了，即5个大国（美利坚合众国、大英帝国、法国、意大利和日本）各派两名代表，而其他小国则合派5名

1919年在法国巴黎凡尔赛宫举行的巴黎和会。

克里孟梭（Georges Clemenceau, 1841～1929）。法国政治家、第三共和国总理，为第一次世界大战协约国的胜利和《凡尔赛和约》的签订做出了重要贡献，被当时的欧洲人称为"胜利之父"。

罗伯特·伯登爵士（Sir Robert Laird Borden, 1854～1937）。加拿大政治家，时任该国第九任总理。

劳合·乔治（David Lloyd George, 1863～1945）。英国自由党领袖，一战期间历任英国军需大臣、陆军大臣等职。1919年他出席并操纵巴黎和会，是巴黎和会上的"三巨头"之一。

威尔逊（Thomas Woodrow Wilson, 1856～1924）。美国第28任总统。

brought up at the plenary session for endorsement. There was not unnaturally discontentment among the Smaller Powers. Sir Robert Borden, on behalf of Canada, asked by whom and on what authority the constitution of the committees had been decided; the question should have been submitted to the Conference. The delegates of Belgium, Brazil, Serbia, Greece, Portugal, Czechoslovakia, Rumania, Siam, and China rose in turn to claim special representation for their several countries. Then M. Clemenceau interposed from his presidential chair, where he sat between Mr. Wilson and Mr. Lloyd George. He pointed out that at the cessation of hostilities, the Great Powers had twelve million men on the field of battle; that they might have decided the future of the World on their own initiative; but that, inspired by the new ideals, they had invited the Smaller Powers to cooperate with them. The resolution was passed, nemine contradicente, without alteration.

代表，此时是把这一构成方案提交给全会审议批准。各个小国有不满情绪，这是自然而然的。加拿大代表罗伯特·伯登爵士质问，各个委员会的构成方案是由谁、经谁授权决定的；他还说，这个问题应当提交给大会来决定才是。比利时、巴西、塞尔维亚、希腊、葡萄牙、捷克斯洛伐克、罗马尼亚、暹罗[1]和中国的代表也相继发言，要求本国在这些委员会中派驻特别代表。接着，担任主席的克里孟梭先生进行了干预，他当时坐在威尔逊先生和劳合·乔治先生之间。他指出，停战之时，五个大国总共有1200万人在战场上；这些大国本来是可以自己做主，定下世界未来之格局的；但是，由于受到了诸多新理想的启示，所以它们还是邀请了这些较小国家来与它们共同协作。于是，全会通过了这项决议案，既无反对意见，也没有对决议案做出修改。

[1] Siam：暹罗。泰国（Thailand）的旧称。

和会的"四人会议"：美国总统威尔逊、英国首相劳合·乔治、法国总理克里孟梭和意大利首相奥兰多。

Thus the rule of the world still rests upon force, notwithstanding the juridical assumption of equality between sovereign States, whether great or small. The theme of this book, that we must base our proposed League on Realities, if we would have it last, holds good. Let it be remarked, moreover, that the number of the Great Powers — five — is precisely the total of the pre-war Dual Alliance (Triple only with Italy) and Triple Entente, whose hostility caused the War. It follows that we shall be able to maintain our League as long as the five Powers, now allied, continue to agree. Their number is not sufficient to prevent a bid for predominance on the part of one or two of them. No doubt a new Germany and a new Russia will some day increase them to seven. Perhaps the Smaller Powers, taking note of the naked fact which was exposed by this incident, will set about federating among themselves. A Scandinavian group, a group of the Middle Tier of East Europe (Poland to Jugo-Slavia), and a Spanish South American group (if not also including Brazil) may all, perhaps, be attainable. In any case the League should do service in bringing the opinion of mankind to bear for the just revision of obsolescent treaties before they become unbearable misfits. But let us be rid of cant: Democracy must reckon with Reality.

所以，尽管法律认为各个主权国家不分大小一律平等，但统治世界所依赖的，却仍然是武力。不过，如果我们想让国际联盟永远存在下去，就必须让拟议中的国联建立在现实的基础之上，本书的这一主旨依然是适用的。此外我们还需留意，大国的数量是5个，正好是战前的"两国同盟"（只是意大利加入后，才成为"三国同盟"的）加上"三国协约"的总数；正是这两者之间的敌对，才引发了这次大战。因此我们可以得出结论说，只要如今结成了同盟的这五个大国继续保持意见一致，我们就能让国联存在下去。大国的数量，并不足以防止其中的一两个国家产生出争霸野心。毋庸置疑，终有一天，一个新的德国和一个新的俄国会加入进来，使大国的数量增加到七个。各个较小的国家或许会因为注意到了此次事件所暴露出来的那种赤裸裸的真相，从而开始抱成团联合起来。一个由斯堪的纳维亚国家所组成的集团、一个由东欧中间层国家（从波兰到南斯拉夫）所组成的集团，以及一个由西属南美洲的国家（要是不包括巴西在内的话）所组成的集团，说不定都有可能出现。无论在什么情况下，国联都应当发挥作用，都应当引领整个人类的信念来对各项即将废弃的条约进行公正合理的修订，以免它们变得令人无法容忍和不合时宜。但是，我们最好还是摒弃任何的伪善之言，因为民主必须考虑到现实才行。